DOMERS

Kevin Coyne

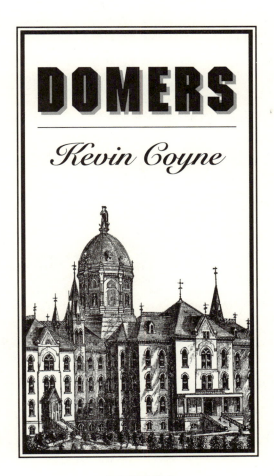

VIKING

VIKING
Published by the Penguin Group
Penguin Books USA Inc., 375 Hudson Street, New York, New York 10014, U.S.A.
Penguin Books Ltd, 27 Wrights Lane, London W8 5TZ, England
Penguin Books Australia Ltd, Ringwood, Victoria, Australia
Penguin Books Canada Ltd, 10 Alcorn Avenue,
Toronto, Ontario, Canada M4V 3B2
Penguin Books (N.Z.) Ltd, 182–190 Wairau Road,
Auckland 10, New Zealand

Penguin Books Ltd, Registered Offices:
Harmondsworth, Middlesex, England

First published in 1995 by Viking Penguin,
a division of Penguin Books USA Inc.

1 3 5 7 9 10 8 6 4 2

Grateful acknowledgment is made for permission to reprint excerpts from the following copyrighted works: "40," by Paul Hewson, Dave Evans, Larry Mullen, and Adam Clayton. © 1992 Polygram International Music Publishing B.V. "Notre Dame Victory March," lyrics by John F. Shea, music by Rev. Michael J. Shea. ©1928 (renewed) University of Notre Dame. All rights controlled by Edwin H. Morris & Company, a division of MPL Communications, Inc. All rights reserved.

Lithograph of campus and engraving of Main Building reproduced by permission of the archives of the University of Notre Dame.

A portion of this book first appeared in *Notre Dame* magazine.

LIBRARY OF CONGRESS CATALOGING-IN-PUBLICATION DATA
Coyne, Kevin.
Domers : a year at Notre Dame / Kevin Coyne.
p.   cm.
ISBN 0-670-85005-5
1. University of Notre Dame.   I. Title.
LD4114.C69   1995
378.772'89—dc20   95-7698

This book is printed on acid-free paper.
(∞)

Printed in the United States of America
Set in Minion
Designed by Katy Riegel

For my grandparents,
Henry S. Coyne (1906–1969)
and Johanna W. Coyne

FALL

1

The Dome that sits atop the Main Building at the University of Notre Dame rises 197 feet through the lush canopy of elms and oaks and maples that shades the campus, a height sufficient so that it can be seen, physically, all the way out to the Indiana Toll Road and, symbolically, clear to parts far beyond. From a distance it might easily be mistaken for a state capitol, sheathed in gold leaf and crowned by a draped female figure— Liberty, perhaps, or Democracy, or some similar secular icon. From nearer it is unmistakably a capitol with religious, not civic aspirations: It is the Virgin Mary who hovers over the school that takes its name from her—Notre Dame, "Our Lady." Crosses adorn many of the peaks on the building's ornate and craggy roof. The Dome itself is modeled after the pope's own, at St. Peter's in Rome. The Main Building is the hub around which the university turns, and its Dome is the center of a three-pronged skyline. Immediately west is the slender, reaching spire of the Basilica of the Sacred Heart, a church so gilded and grand it is often confused with a cathedral. To the east is the monstrous upended shoe box of the library, its façade wearing a giant mosaic of the risen Christ. In this architectural trinity, the church, naturally, is the Father, the library mural the Son, and the Dome, the locus of so much sentiment and desire, is something akin to the Holy Spirit—a form without a face, elusive, hard to define, but present everywhere and always.

The Dome was a directional landmark to early aviators, and it remains today an emotional landmark to another, wider constituency—those le-

gions of Americans, far greater in number than the ninety thousand ordained Domers who actually graduated from Notre Dame, whose hearts stir
and eyes mist over whenever they hear the "Victory March" ("Cheer, cheer
for old Notre Dame . . ."). The object of their devotion is not just the football team, nor is it God precisely, but, rather, some combination of the two.
Notre Dame has achieved a unique eminence among the nation's colleges
and universities, amassing a following that transcends boundaries of class
and geography, because it has managed to build in the unlikely spot of
South Bend, Indiana, a shrine that celebrates the glories not only of the
mind and body, but of the soul as well. Its ascent began fourscore years ago,
when Knute Rockne, first as a player and then as the coach, led the football
team from what was then a small and obscure Catholic school, buried deep
in the heartland of a Protestant nation, on a triumphant crusade against the
establishment powerhouses of the East. It continued four decades, and
seven national titles, later when Father Theodore Hesburgh opened his
thirty-five-year reign as president, determined to gain for Notre Dame an
intellectual ranking that would match its athletic and spiritual stature.
Catholicism is a religion rich with stories—a millennial tradition still thick
with parables and rituals, saints and martyrs, that have long since been
pruned away from most Protestant denominations—and Notre Dame gave
American Catholics some of the best stories they had yet been able to tell
about themselves. What Harvard was to New England Brahmins, what City
College was to New York Jews, what Howard was to black Americans, Notre
Dame became to American Catholics—the institution that, more perfectly
than any other, embodied their values and beliefs, that summed up the best
of who they were and what they might become.

Wearing a thin coat of twenty-three-karat gold, the Dome makes a bright
and tempting target for conquest. Generations of students have—illegally—
scaled it, or tried to, an act of both devotion and daring. In football seasons
they have veiled it with banners: "Beat Purdue" or "Hate State." (One
March 17 in the 1860s, a student with the wholly unsurprising name of Tim
O'Sullivan climbed onto the balcony that surrounded the dome of the previous Main Building—it was much smaller then, and only tin painted
white—and trumpeted "St. Patrick's Day in the Morning.") The current
president of the university, Father Edward Malloy, has climbed it four times,
which is four times more than Hesburgh—first as an undergraduate, most
recently as a theology professor leading an expedition of seventeen seminarians. Conquerors with larger motives have also set their sights on it. Because

Notre Dame is hallowed ground, the nearest thing Catholic America has to a capital city, it is also, like Jerusalem during the Crusades, contested ground, a Holy Land coveted by all factions. Liberals want it to be a pulpit for the causes of the Catholic left, for social justice and the ordination of women; conservatives want it to stand with tradition, to stay the course piloted by Rome. Both sides have established beachheads within the gaze of the Dome: Opus Dei, a voice from the right, has a house on Notre Dame Avenue, the entryway to campus; so, too, a few blocks south and far to the left, does the Catholic Worker movement.

The Dome is not designed for human occupation, and to ascend it now is an act that requires many of the traits Notre Dame has always prized in its students: faith, bravery, an acquaintance with local mythology and arcane lore, and a certain amount of athletic agility. It also requires an insider's knowledge of hidden passages and the capacity to pass through a pair of locked doors. The Main Building is an eccentric, turreted, yellow brick assemblage of Victorian Gothic flourishes, as gangly and sharp-elbowed as an adolescent; the Dome is an oversized Renaissance confection that looks as if it had been tacked on later, as it was; and to find the link between the two, you must first climb ten flights of age-scalloped steps. Once home to classrooms, dormitories, and dining halls, the first four floors have long since been carved up into administrative warrens, but the fifth floor hangs over it all like a memory. It is sealed off now, all rubble and tall shadows, a vast and vacant attic—its wide rooms empty, its floors suspect, its plaster crumbling. It offers a view out over the central rotunda beneath the Dome, and a door that leads up into the Dome itself.

A winding stairway is secreted between the walls, the last real steps on the journey up, and it opens onto a narrow balcony that encircles the rotunda's upper reaches. The walkway is precarious, the low balustrade small comfort against the fear of falling. The scabby, peeling paint is covered with the scrawls of earlier explorers. To continue higher still, you need all four limbs and the moves of a steeplejack. You get back into the wall and squeeze up through the support beams, climbing straight up on slats nailed at irregular intervals, higher and higher, wriggling through tight spots where the building constricts as if to swallow you, twenty feet, thirty feet, forty feet, saved from vertigo only by the competing impulses of claustrophobia, until you finally emerge in a dim, arching space like a cavernous hayloft. Nothing breaks the sepulchral darkness but a pair of naked light bulbs. A patina of dust covers everything, undisturbed by the faint, constant breeze. Despite

the great height, the feeling is oddly subterranean. You are now in the gap
between the inner dome and the outer: Above you is the gold, below is the
rotunda's concave ceiling.

On hands and knees now, like a pilgrim at a shrine, you crawl slowly up
and across the joists that support the shell of the inner dome, carefully
avoiding the spaces between, which are nothing but plaster and lath, not
meant to support a person's weight, the backside of Luigi Gregori's alle-
gorical mural *Religion Encircled by Philosophy, History, Science, Fame, Music and Poetry*. A single misplaced step might send your foot plunging
through, piercing one of the winged creatures beneath. At the apex of the
inner dome, you reach the foot of an ancient, rickety ladder that rises
straight up through the darkness, thirty feet toward heaven, like Jacob's
Old Testament dream. Its height is magnified by the yawning void that
surrounds it on all sides, and its top is obscured by the shadows that collect in the chamber's upper reaches like clouds. You climb it slowly, one
rung at a time, feet braced against the edges in case you hit a rotten one,
never looking down, a pure act of faith, always aware that you might fall,
tumble backward, crash through Religion or Philosophy or Fame, spin
down through space until you land, broken, on the rotunda floor, where is
emblazoned the seal of the Congregation of Holy Cross, the religious order that founded Notre Dame. "Crux Spes Unica," the seal reads: "The
cross is our only hope."

The ladder leads to a tenuous summit—an improvised crow's nest of
loose boards over cross beams, just a workmen's perch, not an observation
deck. You are at the peak of the Dome now, inside the pedestal that Mary—
all sixteen feet and forty-four hundred cast-iron pounds of her—stands
upon. The statue is hollow, with room enough to accommodate any guest
who wants to shimmy partway up inside, as Malloy once did. Names and
initials are carved into the wood and scratched into the old paint. Narrow
louvers open like gunsights on a broad and distant vista that is at once familiar and somehow inverted. You can see everything from up here, a pastoral, academic grove that unfolds like the Platonic ideal of a college
campus—out to the football stadium, back through the wide Gothic alley of
the South Quad, behind to the woods and the lakes, a rich panorama of the
place that came to symbolize the aspirations of generations of immigrant
Catholics, and that aided their climb through American society. You can see
everything, that is, except the one thing that shapes the view from every
other angle. You have traveled so deep inside the Dome that you have

achieved a strange kind of unity with Notre Dame's chief icon, an object seen so often for what it represents that it is rarely considered for what it is. You can no longer see the Dome, because you have, for a moment at least, become it.

2

They had been arriving for days, thousands of them, from all fifty states and many nations beyond, trundling across the Midwestern flatlands in a migration of almost Biblical proportions, streaming off I-80 and up Notre Dame Avenue. A flood of Plymouth Voyagers and Ford Tauruses (leave the Volvos to the Ivies; Notre Dame is a Detroit crowd) lapped around the feet of the Dome like the waters of a cresting river, depositing into the dorms their loads of stereos, color TVs, answering machines, beer refrigerators, battered rec-room couches, Apple Powerbooks, and Pearl Jam CDs, delivering unto the promised land all the Mikes and Megans, the Christophers and Jennifers, the class of 1996, whose great-grandfathers lived and died with the great Rockne, whose grandfathers watched Frank Leahy go four years without losing a single game, whose fathers cheered Ara Parseghian's resurrection act, whose grammar-school nuns said rosaries for that poor Gerry Faust when he was having such a hard time of it—and now that they had all finally made it here, they were sitting in the basketball arena listening to a story about a starker journey made to this same spot on the south bend of the St. Joseph River, 150 years earlier.

"When Father Sorin came here to found Notre Dame, he was twenty-eight years old, just ten years older than you are now," Patty O'Hara, the vice-president of student affairs, said in her welcoming address, the heart of which was an account of Notre Dame's origins—a creation myth that is, like the institution itself, equal parts Abraham Lincoln and God, Ellis Island and Genesis.

Father Edward Sorin was a new priest in a young French missionary order, the Congregation of Holy Cross, when he sailed from the port of Le Havre in August of 1841, bound for Indiana at a time when I-80 was not a travel option. He spent thirty-nine days crossing the Atlantic in steerage (he said eleven Masses and baptized a dying Protestant baby girl along the way), and twenty-four more days in steamboats, canal barges, and horse carts before finally reaching Vincennes in the southern part of the state. After a year there, the local bishop sent him north to build a college. Sorin and seven brothers, four of them Irish-born, traveled ten days and 250 miles through cold and snow in an oxcart and an old stagecoach, crossing the frozen St. Joseph River on November 26, 1842.

"The snow reminded them of the purity of the Mother of God," O'Hara told the freshmen and their parents, who had arrived at a balmier moment. "He vowed to build the greatest Catholic university in the world here."

The only thing on the site in 1842 was a log cabin that had served as a mission chapel. By spring, Sorin and his band were saying Mass in a new chapel. By summer, work had started on a school building. By 1844, the Indiana State Senate had granted a charter to the "University of Notre Dame du Lac," the first students were enrolled in what was more a trade school than a university, and Sorin's ambitions were growing more extravagant: "When this school, Our Lady's School, grows a bit more, I shall raise her aloft so that, without asking, all men shall know why we have succeeded here," he wrote that year, a declaration O'Hara recounted for the freshmen. "To that lovely Lady, raised high on a dome, a Golden Dome, men may look and find the answer."

The freshmen O'Hara was addressing, 1,882 of them, were a species apart from the twenty-five Sorin had first welcomed. They were still mostly Catholic (86 percent), and they were possessed of red hair and last names beginning with "Mc" in greater proportion than was the population at large, but they were no longer exclusively white and male: 44 percent were women, the largest number in any entering class in the twenty years since the sex barrier had fallen, and 14 percent were counted as minorities. They were smarter, with SAT scores up in the 1,200s and grades that put them in the top 10 percent of their high-school classes; in Sorin's era, the only requirement for admission was the ability to pay the tuition, whether in cash or corn or pigs. They were athletic (75 percent had earned at least one varsity letter in high school), conscientious (70 percent had done some kind of volunteer work), and more rich than not—no longer the children of pioneer farmers and immigrant laborers, but of Chicago lawyers and Cleveland doctors, hailing from all the parishes of upper-middle-class suburbia, their wealth a testament to Notre Dame's success in educating earlier generations of young Catholic men, their homogeneity a challenge to its future vitality as a university.

O'Hara's speech marched up into the present, her history lesson having built a platform from which she could better explain to the freshmen what Notre Dame would ask of them over the next four years, and why. She was perceived on campus as the chief disciplinarian, the architect of a social code that is at odds with most other colleges', and therefore also with the natural impulses of most college students—and she started with the policy most widely hated by students: parietals. Notre Dame has male dorms and female dorms, and fraternization between the sexes in them is not free and unlimited. Visiting hours, as she told the freshmen, end at midnight on weeknights, 2:00 a.m. on weekends. The alcohol policy was more complex—covering seven pages of *Du Lac*, the thick student rulebook, with a logical intricacy worthy of the medieval scholastics—but the drug policy was simple (get caught and you're in big, big trouble), as was the sexuality policy.

"We believe sexual intercourse is reserved for those who have a permanent and total commitment to each other in marriage, and we expect you to adhere to that," O'Hara said, reiterating what it says on page 27 of *Du Lac*. "Failure to do so will result in discipline."

The parents looked reassured, the freshmen uneasy, in the wake of such an unequivocal pronouncement—one that, as O'Hara acknowledged, they wouldn't likely hear elsewhere. "We don't apologize for being different. We proclaim it. We say it's part and parcel of being educated at Notre Dame. We are not Georgetown, or Boston College, or Duke, or Brown. We have our own unique traditions at Notre Dame. We believe a true education integrates both faith and reason."

They were still two days away from the start of classes, and two weeks away from the start of football season, but these freshmen had already been baptized as Domers.

"Four years from now, you will gather here for graduation," O'Hara said in closing. "Until that day, may Our Lady of Notre Dame keep you in her care, may her son Jesus Christ keep watch over you, and may God bless each and every one of you."

When the orientation program finally ended, the freshmen and their parents streamed out of the arena and past the football stadium across the street. Shrill whistles rose like birds from the practice that was under way on the field inside, and the curious bent futilely for a glimpse beneath the gate.

The big welcoming Mass wasn't until tomorrow, but it was clear that some kind of benediction had already been given.

"Sex is a gift from God, but not until marriage—what the hell?"

"They don't come knocking on your door and say, 'Hey, are you having sex?'—but if they catch you, you're dead."

"You go to a state school and go in a dorm and everybody's having sex."

Like the young of any species, the freshmen traveled in packs, wary of larger predators, and now sixteen of them were making their way to room 232 in Keenan Hall, trying to digest all they had learned so far. The mysteries of college are best confronted communally. Because student life at Notre Dame is so intensely dorm-centered, the one agent most responsible for shaping the social dynamics on campus is the computer in the housing office that randomly generates freshman room assignments—deciding who will live with whom in which dorm, and therefore who will be friends with whom for the next four years, and who will be ushers and bridesmaids at whose weddings five or ten years hence. In making its selections for the second floor of Keenan, it had also found a place for Steve Sabo to spend his fall break—in the suburban-Milwaukee home of his new friend, Patrick Lyons, who had already extended an invitation.

"We had them convinced that Steve was the second-string quarterback, behind Rick Mirer," Patrick said. Steve had played high-school lacrosse back in Colorado Springs, but he was not Rick Mirer's backup, despite what they had said at the mixer last night at St. Mary's, the neighboring women's college that is Notre Dame's sister school.

The second-floor freshmen had already established a habit of eating breakfast together in the dining hall, dubbing themselves the Cold Toast Club. Patrick produced their inaugural one-page newsletter, *The Cold Toast Worker*, on his Apple Powerbook, declaring himself the club's president-for-life. (Steve Sabo was prime minister.) He had achieved his position not because he was an athlete, a common coin of peer respect here, but because he was already a Domer: The campus and its customs were second nature to him, firmly imprinted on his consciousness by dozens of visits over the years in the company of his father, a lawyer who graduated with the class of 1967. Patrick did not need a map to find his way around. He knew where Fieldhouse Mall was—the area around the Stonehenge-like war memorial, once home to the cavernous, skylit, brick fieldhouse where his father had attended the raucous pep rallies in football season. He had known how to get to St. Mary's last night—the long walk between the lakes, through the woods, and across the highway—because his father had frequently made the same journey: Patrick's mother, a high-school teacher and administrator, graduated from St. Mary's with the class of 1968.

"I've pretty much been groomed since birth," he said. His parents had closed a large circle when they delivered him here to start his freshman year. "It was a major walk down memory lane for them."

The freshmen squeezed into room 232—a stark cell of painted cinder block and linoleum like every other room in Keenan, meant to endure the extraordinary havoc that young men are capable of wreaking. The chief element of the football-themed decor was a large blowup of the *Sports Illustrated* cover that had appeared when Notre Dame won its last national championship, back in 1988. The standard furnishings—bed, desk, dresser, sink—were augmented by a color TV, a recliner, and, since the occupant was an of-legal-age resident assistant, a refrigerator stocked with a twelve-pack of beer.

"Your room is your room," the RA, a senior, told them. "I'm not gonna come in and raid your room."

After enduring several big meetings full of theory, the freshmen were clearly relieved to be at a small meeting devoted to actual practice.

"They don't say openly that everybody can drink, but that's basically what they do," the RA continued, distilling the newly revised alcohol policy to its essence. The official party line was to acknowledge tacitly, but not encourage, the widespread fact of underage drinking—a strategy intended to keep students on campus, where the administration could exercise some measure of social control over their drinking behavior, rather than drive them out into South Bend, to bars and off-campus parties, where it could not. Drinking in public spaces was prohibited, as was the transportation of alcohol onto campus by anyone under the age of twenty-one, but if beer somehow wound up in your room, well, that was sovereign territory, and what you did with it there was mostly your own business. "I have pretty bad hearing, pretty bad eyesight, too. But don't ever ask me to buy for you—I can't."

The meeting moved on to other concerns. "The TV reception in this dorm sucks. . . . The dorm is the worst place to study. Two guys'll come in and three hours later you're still watching TV. . . . Girls' dorms are a great place to do your laundry. You meet a lot of girls that way." Mass in the dorm chapel was at eleven on weeknights, four-thirty on Sundays. "I usually attend Mass every week," the RA said, making it sound more like an optional dorm meeting than an obligatory religious ceremony. "I don't want to get too philosophical. It's kind of a social atmosphere to go to Mass. I don't want to pressure anybody to do it."

One important question remained. "Are we enemies of Zahm?" one freshman asked, referring to the dorm next door.

"Technically, we're enemies of Stanford," the RA clarified. Stanford was Keenan's Siamese twin, sharing with it a chapel and an entranceway, but the rigid protocol of dorm loyalty demanded that, no matter how thick the traffic at the two adjoining front doors, a Keenan man could use only the door on the Keenan side, and a Stanford man only the door on the Stanford side.

Notre Dame is an experience that, like a Mass, requires of its participants a series of ritual gestures, as large as singing the alma mater and as small as knowing which door to use, and these early days were a kind of crash catechism for the freshmen—immersing them quickly and deeply in tradition, exposing them to a concentrated dose of mythology, authority, and community, the three key principles animating the life of their new home. The campus that greeted them had been primped and polished to conform to all their postcard visions. It was verdant and bright, a seductive garden that, come November, would be remembered only as a cruel and broken promise. The older buildings were fringed with ivy—the oldest were built of yellow bricks the Holy Cross brothers had made from the marl of the lakes—but their faces were not as smugly Gothic as the old-money schools of the East. The chorus of the fight song hung in the air like a constant, ghostly soundtrack, floating up from band practice somewhere offstage. The sunny quads were as wide as football fields, and the freshmen who had been all-county quarterbacks back home, just fans now but still dreaming of the varsity, tested their arms against one another. The Knights of Columbus, on the South Quad, offered continuous showings of *Knute Rockne—All American*: "Take the train!" they shouted as Pat O'Brien boarded the fatal plane. The shade was deep beneath the tall elms, and their exposed roots reached out like a bony tangle of grasping fingers—leaving the impression that, though not planted long in this land, they had risen quickly above it.

Priests, nuns, and brothers had met the new arrivals in abundance, and the president—Father Malloy, better known to all by his childhood nickname, Monk—wandered widely among them, his ubiquity matched only by his informality. Like the Keenan freshmen, he made his home in a dorm, too. His tall, pale figure was easily and frequently spotted—crossing the quad in chinos and polo shirt; climbing the steps of the Main Building, headed to work in a Roman collar and black suit; standing and talking on the porch of Sorin Hall, where he lived in two small, book-lined rooms, sparser quarters than a graduate student might enjoy. When the freshmen and their parents gathered once again in the basketball arena, it was Malloy who led the dozens of priests concelebrating the opening liturgy.

"I confess to Almighty God," they prayed in unison, reciting the penitential rite that opens every Mass, "and to you, my brothers and sisters, that I have sinned through my own fault in my thoughts and in my words, in what I have done, and in what I have failed to do. . . ."

Yesterday the Keenan freshmen, like all their new classmates, had sat beside their parents in this arena; today all the freshmen were sitting together in seats on the floor, their parents arrayed above them in the stands, one step nearer to parting. Most students were in shorts, and some were already wearing Keenan T-shirts to distinguish themselves from classmates wearing shirts from Walsh or Morrissey or Pasquerilla West or any of the other dorms. Malloy wore a green chasuble over a white alb. The altar stood on a raised platform at about the same spot normally reserved for the basketball backboard. Just outside the arena doors, amid the old jerseys and Heisman trophies in the adjacent Sports Heritage Hall, was a relic from Malloy's earlier incarnation, when he was on the other side of the altar, wearing a different uniform. It was a blown-up, black-and-white 1962 photo of a jug-eared, wide-eyed, crew-cut varsity guard, poised to launch a bounce pass.

The day's readings were the same as the readings heard at every Catholic Mass around the world this Sunday, but they sounded as if they had been chosen specially for this place and this day. "I come to gather nations of every language; they shall come and see my glory," went the first reading, from the Book of Isaiah. "They shall bring all your brethren from all the nations as an offering to the Lord, on horses and in chariots, in carts, upon mules and dromedaries"—there was no mention of minivans—"to Jerusalem, my holy mountain, says the Lord. . . ."

". . . for whom the Lord loves, he disciplines; he scourges every son he acknowledges," went the second reading, from the Letter to the Hebrews, and also, implicitly at least, from the book of *Du Lac*. "At the time, all discipline seems a cause not for joy but for pain, yet later it brings the peaceful fruit of righteousness to those who are trained by it."

"For behold, some are last who will be first, and some are first who will be last," concluded the reading from the Gospel According to Luke, a prophecy that, at a school where the football team was a preseason favorite to win the national championship, sounded more like a warning.

At the consecration, when Malloy lifted up the host, ranks of cameras in the parents' section flashed like muzzle fire. "Take this, all of you, and eat it," he said, repeating Jesus' words from the Last Supper. "This is my body which will be given up for you."

The cameras started popping again after Mass, when the marching band paraded onto the floor playing the "Notre Dame Victory March," "the greatest of all fight songs," its volume raised now from a faint rumor into a roar. Those who knew the words already, Patrick Lyons among them, sang along:

> Cheer, cheer for old Notre Dame,
> Wake up the echoes cheering her name,
> Send a volley cheer on high,
> Shake down the thunder from the sky.
> What though the odds may be great or small
> Old Notre Dame will win over all,
> While her loyal sons are marching
> Onward to victory.

The leprechaun mascot, a red-bearded senior in a bright-green suit, led the clapping and singing and general noisemaking, as was his duty at all the pep rallies and games, but the purpose of this rally, coming as it did a full two weeks before the start of the football season, was to cheer for a different kind of victory. It was a pep rally not for a game, but for an idea. They were cheering for the victory of their idea of Notre Dame—an idea consisting, in various measure, of the school itself, God, the Virgin Mary, the team, and the ascent of Catholics into the varsity of American life.

When the Glee Club came out to sing the alma mater, the freshmen joined in, tentatively, arms draped over shoulders and swaying together slowly in a line. It is a plaintive tune, echoing like empty halls and tasting of ash, and it cast a brief, oddly funereal shadow over the proceedings, as if to remind them now, at the start of their journey, of its looming, inevitable end. The last line—"And our hearts forever love thee Notre . . ."—climbed to a final note—". . . Dame"—that escaped like a sob.

A procession of speakers followed—the student-body president, the athletic director, the women's basketball coach—but it was Lou Holtz, the football coach, who restored their sense of immortality. His appearance at the podium triggered more camera flashes than even the moment of transubstantiation.

"Notre Dame is about winning, and I don't mean just football games," Holtz told them. His accent was the standard coaches' twang, in which athlete is pronounced as a three-syllable word: "Ath-a-lete." His delivery, blurred at times by his slight lisp, was a breathless sprint, cutting and darting from one idea to the next like a swift tailback. His rhetoric was part locker-room exhortation ("This is your football team, not mine"), part corporate-speech sloganeering ("W-I-N, What's Important Now"), part sermon. The effect was of a pep talk, sending the freshmen out into Life's Big Game, reminding them to never lose sight of the Bigger Picture. "Our Lady on the Dome always has a way of putting things into proper perspective."

The Keenan crew convened back on the second floor in a room facing the Dome—a location that, according to campus lore, guaranteed its occupant, Patrick Lyons, an academically successful freshman year. The big orientation festivities were over; they belonged to Notre Dame now. It wasn't long before discussion turned to the weightiest of matters.

"You wanna get some pizza?" somebody asked.

They walked together through campus, past Zahm and St. Edward's and Cavanaugh, where one window already wore a "Beat Penn State" bedsheet, almost three months before the big game's kickoff. Parents were leaving in a flurry of choked farewells, empty cars streaming back to I-80. Upperclassmen were arriving amid a din of whining power saws, which cut four-by-fours and plywood sheets into lofts that subdivided their rooms more efficiently. Stereos waged cross-quad shouting matches, pitting U2's "Mysterious Ways" against Guns N' Roses' "Knockin' on Heaven's Door," and R.E.M. against New Order.

"They were Joy Division before their lead singer committed suicide, then they became New Order," Steve Sabo said. A Pearl Jam fan long before MTV made Pearl Jam fans of half his peers, he could trace the intricate genealogy of the Seattle grunge-rock scene—a skill he hoped would earn him a DJ slot at the campus radio station. " 'Love Will Tear Us Apart'—that was their big song when they were Joy Division."

Pepperoni was the pizza of choice in the Huddle, the food court in the student-center building. Hanging on the walls above their heads were a football-team photo and a poster for the Bengal Bouts, the annual student-boxing tournament that raises money for the Holy Cross missions in

Bangladesh: "Strong bodies fight, that weak bodies may be nourished," read the poster's legend.

"There were like a hundred girls and maybe twenty guys," Patrick Lyons said about the dance he and Steve had gone to at St. Mary's. This rare moment when the male-female ratio was tipped in favor of the males was made possible by the timing of their dorm meetings: Keenan's had started and ended earlier than the other dorms', giving them a head start on the competition. Back on campus later, at the Graffiti Dance on the South Quad, they had collected names and numbers on their white T-shirts. "I wrote a couple of numbers on a piece of paper so I'd remember who they were."

"I'm not ready for this," one of their floormates said. "This was the shortest summer of my life."

"It's eighteen grand a year—you better get ready," another suggested.

"The strings are cut now," said Steve Sabo, who had just watched his parents leave. He didn't expect to be home again until Christmas. "It's kinda sad when they turn their backs and start walking, and you think, 'Man, that's it.' "

"You just try to keep yourself busy and not think about it," Patrick said. There was some consolation, though: "It feels like we've been friends forever already."

The next day, the first Monday, the rains came, and the sky dimmed with the kind of gray Judgment Day clouds you can hear rumbling through the fight song. But as the Sacred Heart bells chimed through the thin drizzle at 6:00 p.m., the sun broke through again with a clumsy symbolic flourish, and a rainbow arched over the campus like an omen in a bad movie. From a distance it looked as if the rainbow were tracing the arc of the ultimate field goal, rising from the foot of the library's giant Jesus mosaic and landing in the south end zone of the stadium. The angle shifted as you got nearer, though, and it became clear that the rainbow's end was somewhere you couldn't see from here, somewhere far beyond the goalposts.

"My father was a blacksmith for the B&O Railroad who prized education," Brother Bonaventure Scully told the eighteen students in his Freshman Seminar class. "I resonate with people around here who come from simpler backgrounds. There's something to be said for that kind of background, but I'm sure yours have moved on from that now."

They had, as the introductions showed. They went around in a circle—name, hometown, intended major—and each one who said "Chicago," or any other city, soon qualified it by adding, "Well, just outside." Scully, a product of Depression-era Baltimore, was surrounded by the sons and daughters of the suburbs.

Scully's teaching style is as discursive as his appearance. He is bearish and rumpled, with an unruly fringe of graying hair, and when he is still in the middle of one idea it often steers him straight into a second and then a third, and he will chase them around through a series of interlocking stories, punctuating each chapter break with a short laugh, before finally looping back around to where he started. He has no shortage of stories to carry the ideas, having gathered them over four decades as a teacher and school administrator with the Xaverian brothers. His thick glasses have a habit of slipping down his nose, and his eyes often narrow into a squint that seems to see farther inside than you might always like.

"They all try to ferret out what faith is," he said about the authors the class would be reading: Willa Cather, Flannery O'Connor, and Thomas Merton. All freshmen—engineers and philosophy majors alike—are required to take a freshman seminar, and the shape of each seminar reflects the interests of its leader—who might be anybody from the president on down to a distracted graduate student. The idea is to force students to meet new books and new ideas, to puzzle over them with their peers, to learn how to read and think and write better. The instructors, not bound by any fixed reading list, are free to choose their own topics, and Scully's was "Americana and Catholicism."

"I know that sometimes this class will be low on your list of important things to do," he said. "You think chemistry is more important."

The building they were in was itself as recent an addition to campus as the freshmen—DeBartolo Hall, named for the wealthy donor whose family, as owners of the San Francisco '49ers, had also been the longtime employer of a fellow alumnus, Joe Montana. It was the first day of classes for building and students both, and the room smelled like a new car. DeBartolo was wired for speed, high-tech multimedia equipment snaking through it like a TV studio, but the monitor in room 344 stayed blank. As in every classroom, a crucifix hung on the wall. Scully went around the room again, asking the students their religion, trying to ferret out what their faith was.

"I'm a mediocre Catholic," one said. "I don't know how I feel about it."

"I'm Catholic," said another. "At least that's what I am now."

Though Scully taught just this one class, he was responsible for more students than most of his colleagues: His main job at Notre Dame was as the live-in rector of Keenan Hall, which made him both the pastor and mayor of a community of three hundred young men living in the closest of quarters. During orientation, he had welcomed Patrick Lyons and the other Keenan freshmen at a special meeting in the dorm chapel. Every dorm has a rector in residence, an adult who stays on duty when the daytime authorities desert the campus each evening. In the women's dorms, the rectors are mostly nuns; in all of the men's dorms except Keenan this year, they were Holy Cross priests or brothers.

"Sometimes I like to refer to myself as being on a mission here to convert the CSCs," he said, indulging in a little interorder rivalry and using the initials that identify the members of the Congregation of Holy Cross, "Congregatio a Sancta Cruce."

Scully surveyed the reading habits of his students, taking the measure of the field he would be tilling. A few had read some Willa Cather in high school. Some had heard of Thomas Merton, but none had read anything by him. No one had even heard of Flannery O'Connor.

"No one?" he asked, in disappointment and disbelief. "No one at all?"

The music was not a problem for Rachel Stehle. She had the fight song down cold already—since her high school, like hundreds of other Catholic high schools, had borrowed it as their own—and her trumpet audition had gone smoothly. It was the marching steps that were tripping her up. All the prospective trumpets were parading downfield, playing a brassy version of the fight song unanchored by any other instrument, and when they all turned crisply to the left, she turned to the right. She recovered quickly, and was back in stride within a second or two, but when she came off the field she was worried about how much the misstep would cost her. There were 350 people trying out for 280 slots in the marching band, and if she didn't make it, she would replay that wrong turn over and over again in her mind for many regretful months.

"When I first came, I was so intimidated, I thought, 'I can never do this,' " Rachel said. Band tryouts had brought her to campus earlier than her freshman classmates. "My whole high school is only as big as the whole band. But the first time we marched around the campus, and you could see all the people following the band—wow, it was so neat to think I could be part of this."

The drums beat a rhythm that bounced wildly through the indoor practice field at the Loftus Center—a full hundred yards of artificial green under a roof high enough to let a quarterback air his arm out. Twenty piccolo players were marching up the turf now, high-stepping like an aerobics class and trilling the fight song. "P-I-C-C-O-L-O," they shouted in unison when they finished, "that's how we spell 'piccolo.' " Older band members patrolled the field like assistant coaches, taking notes on clipboards.

"They say the director likes trumpets," Rachel said hopefully, still calculating her chances. If she did make it, she would be in a distinct minority among the trumpets: Of the fifty-four players in the section, maybe five would be women. "What's really intimidating is to come into a section that's so dominated by males."

Notre Dame became Rachel's college of choice the moment she arrived on her first visit and saw how closely it resembled the setting of *Dead Poets Society*, the movie that had most shaped her idea of what a campus should look like. Notre Dame was less decisive in its first look at her. Wait-listed initially, she made plans instead to attend Xavier University in Cincinnati, where, to her great disappointment, there was no marching band. Her late acceptance left her all the more wide-eyed and grateful. An uncle and a cousin had preceded her here, and another cousin had accompanied her as a freshman.

The band had no waiting list: By the time she went to sleep tonight, Rachel would know if she was in or not. When the tryout ended, the clipboards and the director would repair to a restaurant and discuss their choices over pizza, while Rachel went back to her dorm room and tried to concentrate on her first college writing assignment, a paper for English 109, Composition and Literature. The new roster would be posted in the band building sometime after 1:00 a.m. Just nine days later, the newest band members would march with the veterans out into the view of the national TV cameras at the season opener. Notre Dame football is an immense, complex piece of machinery, and cranking it up to full speed requires much effort by many people who will never wear gold helmets, who can't run the forty in anywhere near 4.4 seconds, who may be less interested in the game than in the spectacle that surrounds it.

"I hate football," Rachel said. "I didn't even know who Rick Mirer was."

The marching was tighter, and the odds of making it to opening day were longer, down at the other end of the practice field, where the final tryouts were under way for the Irish Guard, the solemn secret society of tall, kilted men who lead the band into the stadium on game days. A squadron of hopeful Guardsmen—including, for the first time anyone could remember, one hopeful Guardswoman—had been parading around campus for days like a renegade ROTC unit, knees up and arms pumping, and their ranks had thinned from forty-three to the twenty here tonight. Only five would be chosen.

Lou Blaum sat quietly on the sidelines, watching the close formation of grim-faced, short-haired marchers. "I wanted to be a Guardsman since I was seven years old and my father took me to a game," he said. "I thought it was the greatest thing I'd ever seen, so I drank my milk and ate my Wheaties and said my prayers and I got to be six two." The requirements for the Guard were strong legs, a minimum height of six feet two inches, and a willingness to endure boot-camp levels of abuse from veteran Guardsmen fond of acting like drill instructors. Lou had finally made it last year, as a junior. "You meet a guy who was a Guardsman and it's like you've known each other for a hundred years. They'll do anything for you."

The Irish Guard is the nearest thing to a fraternity on a campus that has none. They bond through a variety of rituals, both public and private, and they have a standing, annual date with the cheerleaders from the University of Southern California, who are popular figures in the lustful dreams of many male Domers. Their elaborate outfits make them look like a cross between Buckingham Palace guards and Irish step dancers—papal red doublets, traditional Irish kilts in a patented pattern known as "Notre Dame plaid," tall black bearskin shakos sporting orange plumes. Lou and the four other returning Guardsmen would decide who among the twenty would join them in the Guard, the "rooks," and they would then administer the customary initiation rites.

The drillmaster called a break, and the recruits' impassive masks dissolved into grimaces of pain and fatigue. Lou, as one of the veterans, was spared the worst of the marching, but he well remembered his own tryouts. "It felt like someone took a dagger to my legs," he said.

When the band lists finally went up, in the postmidnight quiet of the otherwise deserted band building, an anxious crowd collected to scan the names. Rachel Stehle stayed in her room. She wanted to confront the answer alone, later. But then the phone rang, a friend calling with some news about the lists. Rachel screamed, then made a call of her own to Sandusky, Ohio, where her mother didn't mind at all being awakened by one of the rookie trumpeters in the Notre Dame band.

The Irish Guard's final selections made no headlines: They stuck with tradition, choosing five new men, and passing on the chance to let a sister into what they often called their "brotherhood."

———

"Welcome to Philosophy 101," said Professor Tom Morris, Yale Ph.D., rock-and-roll guitarist, licensed real-estate broker, Southern Baptist believer from North Carolina, author of ten scholarly books, business speaker-for-hire, and television commercial spokesman for Disney's *Winnie the Pooh* home videos. His middle name is Victor, which allows him, to his great delight, to refer to himself as T.V. "I'm Tom Morris and I'm your host."

The 180 students Morris faced had come to the auditorium of the Hesburgh Library largely because they had to—two classes in philosophy and two more in theology are required of all Domers, and Philo 101 is where they all start—but his aim was to get them to stay because they wanted to. He confounded whatever musty expectations they might have had about a philosophy professor. Young and springy, just forty, he was natty in bow tie and blue blazer. His accent was guileless mid-South good-ole-boy, not clipped Oxbridge-don. As clean-shaven as an anchorman, with neatly combed black hair, he drove a white Cadillac Sedan de Ville, its front license plate a series of three nautical flags that read "WTP," for Winnie the Pooh, the animated bear who had helped him buy it. "My goal is to help get as many people as possible to philosophize about their lives," he often said, and his strategy was to be "serious without being somber."

Philosophy, Morris told his students, was something more than "unintelligible answers to unsolvable questions," and his teaching style was something more than a forced march through a dry country. "We're going to do stuff this semester that's so much fun it ought to be illegal." The undergraduate mind, as he well understood, is especially susceptible to the charms of philosophy—brazenly believing, as it does, in its own power to remake the world, to think things never thought before, to leave Plato in the dust—and he proceeded to seduce them by speaking a version of their own language. Though he cited some old and expected names in his lecture (Aristotle, Schopenhauer, Nietzsche, Wittgenstein), he also sprinkled among them some new and unexpected ones (Woody Allen, Pee-Wee Herman). He shared anecdotes from the lives of the great philosophers, and he told stories from his own life, which featured spring-break trips to Myrtle Beach, solemn testimonials to Tarheels basketball (the University of North Carolina was his undergraduate alma mater), and a wide cast of high-Faulkner comic-Gothic Southern characters.

"What is morality?" he asked rhetorically, running through a list of questions sufficient for a lifetime, let alone a single semester. "What is free will? Are we just physical organisms, or do we have souls? Is there a God? If there is a God, why is there evil in the world? Why is there so much human suffering? What is the meaning of life? Is there objective meaning to life or not? That's the question we'll answer by the end of the semester."

He piled onto his overhead projector an inventory of the heavy, big-ticket ideas they'd be covering—Knowledge, Ethics, the Mind-Body Problem, Death—but then he lightened the load with a line from Steve Martin, who had been, as he informed them, a philosophy major himself. "You remember just enough to mess you up the rest of your life," he quoted. The auditorium was an invitation to sleep—cushioned seats, lights dim as in a movie theater during previews—but all eyes looked open. Morris outlined his goals for the course with the kind of alliterative aphorism Lou Holtz would be proud of: the Three A's.

Analyze: "Philosophy improves your ability to analyze complex situations. We philosophers take apart what other people take for granted. We take apart some basic ideas that most of us are so unaware of, we don't even notice them anymore—they're like the air around us."

Assess: "Most people are either slaves to tradition or they're captivated by each new thing that comes along. They catch their beliefs like they catch the measles, from whoever happens to be around. That's not the best way to do it. Think of philosophy as kinda like a form of intellectual self-defense. You make yourself less vulnerable to specious ideas—ideas that look good on the surface but not down deep."

Argue: "If I ever happen to be watching *Donahue* or *Geraldo* or one of those shows like that, and these people are going on arguing about something, it's so depressing to me to see what they think of as an argument. It's like somebody'll say something and the other person'll say, 'Oh, yeah? Well, so's your mother.' In philosophy we learn to argue in such a way that we make intellectual progress and converge on the truth."

He paced quickly across the front of the room, slicing the air with his hands. Patrick Lyons sat in a row near the rear with a floormate from Keenan Hall, wearing a baseball cap, an accessory that male Domers wear to class as habitually as women once wore veils to church. "I think it'll be a pretty easy class," Patrick said. As a private-school graduate, he had waded into these waters before, and he did not share the fear of philosophy that some public-school graduates had.

"You'll be surprised, on your first trip back home, how you can irritate the heck out of your friends by asking annoying questions," Morris said. "I don't want to make you obnoxious persons. There's a fine line between being obnoxious and being gullible—I want you to find that midpoint. You'll be amazed at how sagacious you'll become."

The first assigned reading was Plato's *Apology*. "Don't let Plato pull anything on you. Just because Plato says it doesn't make it true. Don't let me pull anything on you either."

Most of the students spread out before him, so young and so convinced of their own immortality, had no appreciation yet of what a luxury they had been granted—the chance to mull the great issues for a full semester. Morris tried to pierce their cocoons with a voice from their future. " 'When I was in college,' " he said, quoting a woman he had met recently at one of his business-speaking engagements, " 'we used to sit up in the dorm late at night and talk about really important things, things that really mattered to us, deep important issues. Now I'm forty-five years old, I've lived these extra years, I've had some serious experiences, I've gained some wisdom—and nobody talks about important things anymore. All we talk about are the kids, and what's on sale at the mall, and who Notre Dame is playing next weekend.' I give you her words as a piece of advice."

The next class, according to the syllabus, would be devoted to "Belief, Truth and Knowledge." Next weekend, according to the schedule, Notre Dame would play Northwestern at Soldier Field in Chicago.

In the pantheon of dorm rooms prized for their party potential, the Quint in Sorin Hall—on the first-floor southwest corner, in one of the four graceful, rounded turrets that anchor the building—ranked at the very top, and on this first weekend it was loudly fulfilling its destiny. Five men lived in this two-room suite by day; its population tonight was more like 150. They packed themselves in like rush hour, sucking beer fumes and shouting themselves hoarse over the din. Women standing in the tall, stately windows danced while Madonna—the other one—sang "Express Yourself." The corner of the room was taken up by what the occupants called their "entertainment center"—a barlike structure that sheltered a TV, a stereo, and scores of CDs, which had taken a full three hours to maneuver inside on move-in day. Maybe a dozen people were perched on it now, like fans in the bleachers, watching the game unfold. The room's old floor was failing, and if too much spilled beer dripped through to the boiler room below, steam would rise and set off the smoke alarm. Diagonally across the first floor from the Quint, in the turret that faces the Dome and the church, was the two-room suite where Monk Malloy had lived for the last fourteen years. When he was in and free, he hung a welcome sign on his door and encouraged visitors.

Tonight his lights were off. It was not, in any case, a night when anybody wanted to see the president.

The students have evolved a distinct philosophy of interior design, shaped largely by the administration's distinct philosophy of social behavior. The guiding principle is the maximization of floor space: Dorm rooms, the only places where you can drink at least semilegally, are by default the chief party locales, and they have to be adapted accordingly, to accommodate several dozen of your closest friends at once. Elaborate lofts are one answer: In the Quint, which features the prized sixteen-foot ceilings of Sorin's first floor, all five residents slept in a loft that filled one entire room, in effect adding a second story. Neighboring double rooms often become *de facto* four-person quads, one room stacked high with all the beds, the other left clear to serve as what is euphemistically known as the "social room." Multiroom suites usually keep one room free for entertaining.

The clan of current Domers had convened for another year, and the campus thrummed with the full-throated cry of homecoming. In Zahm Hall—where, according to the rumor hotline, one party was stocked with sixty cases of beer—a red light flashed like an ambulance in one window, and a chorus of female voices accompanied a blaring stereo that was playing Billy Joel's unavoidable "Only the Good Die Young": "You Catholic girls start much too late," they sang. Bold freshmen tested the quality of their new fake IDs at Bridget McGuire's, the off-campus bar with the big "We ♡ Lou" sign. Seniors lined up to get into the squat, concrete-block Linebacker Lounge, where they drank Long Island Iced Teas and danced to more cheesy old songs—Neil Diamond's "Sweet Caroline," The Four Seasons' "December, 1963 (Oh, What a Night)"—than was probably healthy. Off-campus apartments readied for a round of 2-to-7s, so named because they start at 2:00 a.m., when parietals shut down the campus parties, and end when the last person falls asleep.

"If you see a guy named Eric, wish him happy birthday."

"Rico's gettin' laid—*not.*"

"She's drunk, but I'm OK."

"We're missing that party, we'll have to come back for them."

"It probably won't start till we get there—it never starts till we get there."

In Pasquerilla West, where two parties were brewing, young men arrived in clumps and walked the halls agape, uncertain how to act, like worshipers in the sanctuary of a faith not their own. Women's dorms, which host far fewer parties than men's, are foreign territory to many men, and are designed to stay that way. The doors are locked—you have to phone up to be admitted as a visitor—and security guards are posted at the front desks at night. The side doors trip an alarm if you try to sneak out after parietals: "virgin alarms," they are sometimes called. Pasquerilla West, PW to its friends, stands in the section of campus north of the library known as the Mod Quad—a generic, campus-Stalinist dormitory block where the two men's dorms, eleven-story towers, rise high above the four low-slung, pale brick fortresses of the women's dorms, the architectural equivalent of chastity belts.

"The one on the second floor is OK," one of the RAs, reporting back from her rounds, told Laurie Brink, PW's rector. "The one on the fourth, there's a parade of people arriving with cups."

Brink's room overlooked a busy internal intersection, and her chair was positioned at such an angle that you had to make an effort not to acknowledge her when you passed her open door. The room was a semipublic extension of the hallway, and a significant portion of the dorm's 238 citizens ventured inside as the evening progressed. A freshman stopped to introduce her boyfriend from home—a species better known here as an HTH, a hometown honey—who had driven all the way from Pennsylvania for the weekend.

"Where you staying?" Brink asked him right off. A motel out on 31, he answered, and she nodded with approval.

Brink had worked as a reporter in her native Tennessee before becoming a rector, and her personal style still reflected the sharp informality of a newsroom. At a reception for new rectors once at Corby Hall, the dignified old rectory adjacent to Sacred Heart, she donned a World War I helmet that was on display there. "This is what we'll wear if the dorms go coed," she said, and then picked up a saber and poked it playfully in the belly of a silverhaired priest. "Next time, bub, you better put the seat down." The crowd was too startled to laugh, because they knew, as she didn't, just whose belly that was: Father Hesburgh's. He was more amused than offended, and she left with an invitation to bring her Freshman Seminar class to visit his suite of offices atop the library.

"I'm not a Domer," she said. "I'm not into the mystique."

She leaned to the left, and her language largely followed the guidelines of the politically correct, but she was far from the radical feminist she was sometimes typecast as by some of the more traditional voices on campus. Her fondness for liberal liturgies, and for letting women, including herself, preach homilies, made it slightly harder to find priests who would celebrate

Mass in PW's chapel. She had worked as a lay missionary in Jamaica and had earned a master's degree in theology before coming to Notre Dame, where she was starting her third, and final, year as a rector. When her seniors graduated in the spring, she planned to leave, too—to start her novitiate year in the community of Dominican nuns she had joined.

"It's great when women live together, but when men live together it's like being in a zoo," she said. "Women can be more fully themselves when they're around other women, and guys can be their own raunchy, disgusting selves. Men could benefit by living with women, but women tend to lose when men come in."

Waiting to be graded on Brink's desk was the first batch of papers from her Freshman Seminar class. "Books of Color" was the seminar topic, and they were exploring "how culture and religion affect a people." In class this week she had described the hallmarks of indigenous people, enumerating a list of traits that seemed equally to fit the tribe of Domers she was living among: They have distinct cultural traditions, she said; they conceive of themselves as a nation; they have the right to decide who is a member and who isn't; they have a primal identification with the earth—perhaps even going so far as to build a stadium around a small patch of grass, and then to flock there on autumn Saturdays to worship.

"The fourth floor is kinda loud," the RA told Brink after making her rounds again, reporting on the progress of a distinct cultural tradition.

After the weekend parties had all finally ended, deep into Sunday morning, the Masses started, and the diocese of Notre Dame divided itself into more than a score of smaller parishes—one in every dorm, each with its own chapel, pastor, and style of celebration. Sacred Heart, as the campus's mother church, was host to the largest and most formal of the liturgies, the Solemn Opening Mass of the Academic Year, complete with incense, choir, and a colorful procession of faculty members draped with the peacock plumage of their academic hoods. Malloy was the presiding celebrant. He used a chalice that had once belonged to Sorin.

The day's Gospel was from Luke, a parable about humility that Jesus told the dinner guests at the home of a Pharisee: "For everyone who exalts himself will be humbled, but the one who humbles himself will be exalted." When you are invited to a banquet, Jesus said, do not seat yourself at the place of honor, and when you hold your own banquet, "invite the poor, the crippled, the lame, the blind; blessed indeed will you be because of their inability to repay you." Each of the day's homilists, preaching to their different congregations, found it in a different message.

"In the end, then, humility is knowing who we are," Tim O'Meara, the university's provost, said that morning from the pulpit in Sacred Heart. "This is important for all, but in a special way for those in positions of authority, since pride is an occupational hazard for those with power." The crowd listened intently, attuned to the homily's subtext, hearing in it an oblique commentary on the events of the previous spring—when the faculty senate had risen in revolt against what it perceived as an excessively authoritarian administration, stopping just short of a vote of no-confidence in the president. "Authority is not the problem, only its misuse. Authority must be just. Authority must not be arrogant, not arbitrary, not self-serving, not based on ignorance, not based on title. It must show no favoritism. Authority must be based on knowledge, on justice, on truth, on understanding, on compassion. . . . In exercising our authority, we must have an attentive ear; we must avoid confrontation; we must be wise, disarming of hostility, concerned with the good of the community."

Brother Bonaventure Scully heard in the Gospel a call to service. "The one man who came to mind when we read that was Jimmy Carter," he said, speaking that afternoon in Keenan Hall's chapel. Carter and his wife, Rosalynn, had been on campus last semester to accept the first Notre Dame Award, given in recognition of their humanitarian work—which ranged from mediating international conflicts through the Carter Center to swinging hammers for Habitat for Humanity, and which made him the kind of role model Scully hoped his students would try to emulate. "Now, there is a man who has proved his Christiantity time and time again." Scully would often ask the men of Keenan to prove themselves similarly: He was already helping to organize some student relief efforts for the victims of the big hurricane that had just hit South Florida, and he was still trying to recruit another student to live this year at Dismas House, a transitional home for ex-offenders in downtown South Bend. He reserved his greatest admiration not for students who got into the best law schools, but for those who instead devoted themselves to helping the people who most needed it, "the poor, the crippled, the lame, the blind" of Luke's Gospel.

"They told me the areas I needed to work on the most were my humility skills," Laurie Brink said that night in PW's chapel, recalling the evaluation she had received upon joining the Dominicans. Knowing laughter erupted from the barefoot women sitting cross-legged on the floor. Brink's own homily, laced with gentle humor, extracted from Luke's parable a more private message, a lesson about the proper posture to maintain as you walk through your days. "There are times in our lives when it's important to puff ourselves up, to be stronger on the outside than maybe we really are on the inside." The freshmen would know times like that, she said, as they faced the new world of college; and the seniors would know them, too, as they faced the new world of life. "But be mindful that, when you present yourself to God, the God who created us, God already knows what you are. We don't want to puff ourselves up before God. . . . To stand in the right relationship before God, you can only be humble."

The grand, tree-lined lawn of the South Quad sweeps far and clear into the distance like a vast football field, maybe ten times again as long as the one in the stadium, a gridiron of concrete crosswalks laid over it as if to mark off the yards. In the soft dusk on the Thursday before the Michigan game, a crowd was gathering at what would roughly be the thirty-yard line, right in front of Dillon Hall. The autumn's biggest weekend had already arrived—a visit by presidential candidate Bill Clinton tomorrow, the home-football opener against fifth-ranked Michigan on Saturday—and the men of Dillon Hall were kicking it off with their annual dorm pep rally, a high-volume, open-air preview of the main pep rally tomorrow night. A stage had been set up in front of the dorm, and a student band, XYZ Affair, was pounding out Van Halen's "Panama." A gang of Dillon freshmen, draped in togas and fortified with alcohol, slam-danced in front of the stage and loosed an unharmonized chorus of rebel yells.

"Your mothers would be proud of you guys," said Mike Somerville, a Dillon junior and the emcee of the Dillon Hall pep rally, when the band stopped. "Eighteen thousand dollars a year and you're wearing sheets and screaming."

The freshmen responded with a rendition of the Dillon fight song. The words are meant to be a dorm secret, and they have mostly remained so, even through repeat public performances like this, because of the un–Glee Club–like manner in which they are usually sung—unintelligibly, by an unruly choir with impaired diction and wavery pitch. "Assholes of the world" was one decipherable phrase. A knot of men in sweatshirts from Alumni

Hall, Dillon's neighbor and chief rival, stood together off to the side, smoking cigars and looking on disdainfully.

"I think you've all sobered up from the big weekend in Chicago—most of you anyway," Mike Somerville said. He was comfortable in front of the crowd—he had been there before, when he won a stand-up comedy contest on campus the previous year—and his stage presence was free of the self-conscious mannerisms that usually inflict college students who are put on public display. "In case you don't remember, we had a big victory over Northwestern."

Enough Domers had flocked to Soldier Field for the season opener last Saturday that it should have been counted as a home game. The outcome was rarely in doubt—Northwestern had last beaten Notre Dame in 1962—but the gab industry that feeds on the football program needed a story anyway: They decided that, despite the lopsided final score of 42–7, the defense looked suspect, and discussion thereof had occupied the sports pages, talk shows, and beer klatches all week.

"Now we've got Michigan coming in," Mike said.

"Michigan sucks dick!" somebody shouted.

"Hey, none of that," Mike warned.

Notre Dame and Michigan are the two winningest teams in college-football history—Michigan has the most wins, but Notre Dame has the highest winning percentage—and their rivalry is, unsurprisingly, long and sometimes bitter. Notre Dame was a small, obscure school, still referred to as "the Catholics" by sportswriters, when it upset a powerful Michigan team in 1909. Michigan raised questions about the eligibility of several Notre Dame players, and the next year, as the Notre Dame team was on its way to Ann Arbor, Michigan, canceled their scheduled game. Notre Dame was later denied admittance to the Western Conference, which Michigan played in, the precursor to the Big Ten. The public reason was that its teams were too mediocre; the private reason, many in South Bend believed, was really that they were too Catholic. "The dispute seems to have been fought on theological grounds rather than athletic," Father Thomas Crumley, the chairman of Notre Dame's athletic board, said at the time.

"I don't think the Notre Dame Fighting Irish can be stopped this year," Mike Somerville said, his voice rising. "We're too big, we're too strong. Can they stop us?"

"*Noooooo*," the crowd called.

"To my left I wanna hear 'Go.' To my right I wanna hear 'Irish.' "

"*Goooooo*," they shouted when he pointed to his left.

"*Irish*," they shouted when he pointed to his right.

"*Gooooo . . . Irish. . . . Gooooo . . . Irish.*"

The drummer—Derrick Fluhme, intramural hockey player and aspiring doctor—laid a martial beat beneath the chant. Sitting quietly beside him at the back of the stage was his roommate, Tom Carter, finance major and aspiring NFL cornerback. The computer had brought them together as freshmen, and their friendship had kept them together into their junior year. Football players at Notre Dame live in the same dorms as all the other students, not sequestered in the kind of separate athletic dorm that is the rule at most big football schools, though they do tend to room mainly with other players. When Tom Carter took the field on Saturday, putting his skills on display for a national TV audience, his roommate would be cheering with the crowd in the stands.

"*Gooooo . . . Irish. . . . Gooooo . . . Irish.*"

Joining in the cheers were a number of adults who didn't seem at all embarrassed about sharing so vocally in this display of student passion. Many were alumni, in fact, back for the big game, but many others were alumni only in dreams—the subway alumni, the descendants of those early fans who had streamed up through the subway exits whenever Notre Dame came to Yankee Stadium to play Army.

"Ladies and gentlemen," Somerville said, "the head coach of the Fighting Irish—*Lou Holtz!*"

At the west end of the quad, a full moon was rising over the Rockne Memorial—the athletic facility, better known simply as the Rock, built in honor of the coach who first made Notre Dame a national powerhouse. Displayed in glass cases inside are footballs from memorable games, including the 1909 win over Michigan; nearby is a map with an X marking the spot in Kansas where the plane carrying Rockne crashed in 1931. A bronze bust of Rockne stands watch in the lobby like that of a statesman, the broad, flat nose burnished to a high shine by the many hands that have rubbed it for luck.

"One of the great things about this university," Holtz said, "maybe the greatest, is that it's a university based on faith. You have to have faith in God, and in the Lady on the Dome. You have to have faith in yourself, too. People will try to tear you down, but you have to have a belief in yourself— and you've gotta have plans, and our plan against Michigan is to boot 'em in the mouth, knock 'em in the dirt, and kick the living daylights out of 'em."

Holtz left the stage quickly as the crowd chanted his name: "*Lou! Lou!*

Lou!" At the foot of the steps he turned to a beaming Mike Somerville and promised to return again. "You can count on me every year," Holtz said.

"*Here come the Irish! Here come the Irish!*" the crowd was chanting as Somerville took back the mike.

"I could die tomorrow and I'd be a happy man," he said.

In the lunchtime sunshine of the Friday before the big game, several thousand students herded themselves into a wide, orderly line stretching up to the front doors of Stepan Center, a geodesic dome that hovers on the northern fringe of the campus like a memory of the 1960s. A small plane flew lazy circles overhead, towing a banner that read "NO DRAFT DODGERS FOR PRESIDENT." The crowd was dotted with campaign signs favoring both sides of the coming election, the first one ever for most of these new voters, but only Bill Clinton was scheduled to speak here this afternoon. Other signs announced the presence of protesters for whom only one issue mattered: "Abortion Kills Children," "Equal Rights for Unborn Women." Some of the "Stop Abortion Now" signs had been hastily altered to read "Stop Clinton Now." Students from the campus Right to Life group offered pamphlets entitled *An Open Letter to Bill Clinton*, the text of which had also appeared this morning in *The Observer*, the student newspaper.

"Are you not aware that the blood of innocent human life cries out to heaven for vengeance against us?" asked the letter. "We beg you in the name of God and human decency to open your heart to the needs of our pre-born brothers and sisters and to listen to their cause as explained by your fellow Democratic governor, Robert Casey of Pennsylvania." Casey, whose son was a Notre Dame senior, had spoken on campus about his prolife views the previous semester. "Mr. Clinton, we are praying that you may see the true humanity of our fellow pre-born human beings, and that you will adjust your position to reflect a humane stance."

The letter was cosigned by the group's copresident, Claire Johnson, who was already inside, awaiting the arrival of the candidate whose defeat she prayed for. She had been arrested seven times at prolife protests, mainly for blocking access to abortion clinics, and she spoke of her brief jail stays with the same moral certainty as the early civil-rights workers. Today she planned to protest only with her voice, not her body, and she expected to spend the night in her room in Farley Hall, not in the custody of the St. Joseph County sheriff. She was a biology major in the honors program, but her grades had slipped out of med-school range because of the time she devoted to her cause.

"It doesn't take much biology to know it's a baby," she said. "It's basic science, it's not a value judgment."

Claire's slight and shy exterior—and her efficient, almost ascetic demeanor—camouflaged the ferocity of her beliefs. Her face had a way of switching suddenly from a wide youthful grin to a stone mask of stern resolve, without stopping anywhere in between. Her commitment to the prolife movement had blossomed at Notre Dame, and though her parents supported her views, they did not entirely share her activism. Some of her colleagues in the Right to Life club also had more measured attitudes: They would hold signs and pray, but blockading an abortion clinic—or publicly challenging a presidential candidate, as Claire planned to do today—was further than they wanted to go.

"They say they're prolife, but they do nothing about it," she said of the Notre Dame administration, whose welcome of the prochoice Clinton she saw as an example of what she called "their hypocrisy" on the abortion issue. "It's their way of kissing up to him. I'd like to see them make a statement against abortion. I'd like to see an attempt to make known the Catholic teaching on abortion."

For Chris Setti, the Clinton visit was an occasion for celebration, not protest. He and his two coleaders in the College Democrats—Andrew Holmgren and Andrew Runkle—had been sprinting around campus for days like junior advance men, helping to lay the groundwork for the big event, and today they had donned jackets and ties in honor of the candidate who had helped revive their moribund political club. Last year they had had just five companions in the College Democrats; three hundred had signed up so far this fall, and the first meeting was standing-room-only. All three were sophomores, an early sign, they hoped, of a political shift on a campus that had been faithfully Republican for a generation. As Catholics grew richer, and retreated deeper into the suburbs—secure members of the professional class Notre Dame had helped build—their politics, in the classic American pattern, moved to the right; and their children absorbed their conservative views. Though the campus-precinct results were an imperfect indicator—since many students used absentee ballots to vote back home—the last Democrat to win here was George McGovern.

"I feel more at home now," said Chris Setti, whose father was a Teamster in Los Angeles. The Democrats had spent most of the night helping to transform Stepan from a concert stage—a campus band, Victoria's Real Secret, had opened for They Might Be Giants the previous evening—into a political arena. Their efforts had earned them seats right next to the stage today. "Somebody came up to me in the dining hall and said, 'Hey, you're in the College Democrats.' I kinda shied away at first—I thought she was gonna hit me—but she wanted to join."

The hall was packed and sweaty under the high, concave ceiling, shadowy all around except where the bright lights were trained on the stage, pulsing with enough energy to sustain the illusion that the world did in fact revolve around Notre Dame, as some here would like to believe. Poker-faced Secret Service agents scanned the crowd. Scores of reporters and photographers stood on risers, blocking the view from the rear. Notre Dame would be a national dateline twice this weekend—the front page tomorrow, the sports page on Sunday. Maybe two thousand students had squeezed in, and a thousand or more were stranded outside, listening on the loudspeakers. Two campus spaces that would have held a larger crowd were previously engaged this afternoon: a women's volleyball game was scheduled for the basketball arena; and the fieldhouse was hosting the Quarterback Club luncheon, an intimate gathering of two thousand football loyalists who were at this moment listening to Lou Holtz speak. "The Notre Dame football team is not the most important thing," he was telling them. "The most important thing is really and truly being part of the Notre Dame spirit."

The Democrats started to chant, clapping in unison to keep the beat. *"Here we go, Clinton, here we go. . . . Hey hey, ho ho, George Bush has got to go. . . . Read our lips, no more Bush. . . ."*

They erupted in a touchdown cheer when they spotted Clinton among the fistful of politicians filing onto the stage. *"We want Bill. . . . We want Bill. . . . We want Bill. . . . We want Bill."*

Father Malloy took the podium to make the introductions. "The tradition of presidential candidates addressing the Notre Dame–St. Mary's community began in 1952, when my predecessor, Father Ted Hesburgh, invited Dwight Eisenhower and Adlai Stevenson to campus. Both accepted his invitation, and since that time no national election has passed without one or more of the presidential or vice-presidential candidates appearing here."

As Clinton stepped to the microphone, a giant Notre Dame seal loomed behind him, and four flags stood at attention beneath it, representing the four republics that intersected here today—the United States of America, the Vatican, Indiana, and Notre Dame. The red leather chairs on the stage were silently occupied by allies meant to secure safe passage for a Southern Baptist in this unfamiliar territory—Joe Kernan, the mayor of South Bend,

and Tim Roemer, the local congressman, both Domers and both Democrats; Evan Bayh, the governor of Indiana; Ray Flynn, the prolife Democrat
who was mayor of Boston; Harris Wofford, senator from Pennsylvania and
former Notre Dame law professor. The cheers faded, leaving room for the
jeers to rise, and it was soon clear that not all the opposition was coming
from the College Republicans who were waving Bush signs and shouting,
"Four more years."

"Abortion kills children!" somebody yelled.

"What about the babies?" Claire Johnson asked loudly. She was sitting
near the stage, too, not far from the College Democrats, in the section reserved for the Center for Social Concerns, the campus clearinghouse for a
wide variety of student service programs. "We're a fringe group there,"
Claire said later about the Right to Life group. "It's not like they exclude us,
but we feel we're not really accepted there."

"Prolife!" shouted a voice farther back in the hall.

The Republicans kicked in with some more *"Four more years,"* and the
din swelled enough to keep Clinton mute. The Democrats responded like rival fans across a football field, unleashing a raucous chorus of *"We want
Bill"* that drowned out the right and cleared some space for Clinton to
speak.

"We know that, in this room at least, our supporters can win the cheering
contest," Clinton said.

When presidents and candidates come to Notre Dame, they tend to in-
sert themselves into one chapter or another of its distinctive public story.
Jimmy Carter spoke of peace when he came, using the 1977 commencement
as the occasion for the first major foreign-policy address of his presidency;
he was a decade ahead of the rest of the country that day when he said that
America had lost its "inordinate fear of communism." When Ronald Reagan came in 1981, making his first trip out of Washington after he had been
shot in an assassination attempt, he slipped into sentimental reminiscence.
"I'm going to mention that movie Pat O'Brien and I and Notre Dame were
in, for it says something about America," said the old actor, who had played
George Gipp, the doomed football hero, in the 1940 movie *Knute Rockne—
All American.* "There will come times in the lives of all of us," he said, after
wading deep into the old football-is-life metaphor, "when we'll be faced
with causes bigger than ourselves and they won't be on a playing field." Reagan came back in 1988, for the unveiling of a stamp honoring Rockne, and
was moved to an even higher plane of rapture. "If they want to see the good-

ness and love of life of this generation, the commitment to decency and a better future, let them come here, to Notre Dame."

George Bush had been here just a few months earlier, using his commencement speech to fire the first shots of what became the Republicans' Family Values campaign. "At the heart of the problems facing our country stands an institution under siege, and that institution is the American family," he said, speaking to an audience comprised mainly of intact, affluent white families. "Whatever form our most pressing problems may take, ultimately all are related to the disintegration of the family."

So Clinton came to launch a counterattack—his first formal response to the Republican convention that had taken Bush's commencement remarks as its guiding theme—and he made deft use of the ammunition Notre Dame itself provided. Several careful weeks in the making, this was meant to be a "defining speech," according to Clinton's chief strategist, James Carville—a chance to show that Republicans had no monopoly on religious belief.

"I was then and remain today deeply drawn to the Catholic social mission," he said, recounting his own college days. He was a graduate of Georgetown University, Notre Dame's chief intellectual rival in Catholic America, but when he wanted to deliver a major campaign speech he came here, thus earning Notre Dame numerous bragging points on the unofficial scorecard the two schools kept.

The crowd stayed mostly quiet as Clinton name-dropped his way through a litany of people meant to serve as sponsors for his bid to be considered an honorary Catholic—Sorin, Hesburgh, Holtz (who was coach at the University of Arkansas when Clinton was the state's attorney general), Al Smith and John F. Kennedy (who both carried Arkansas when they ran for president), even Sister Mary Amata, his second- and third-grade teacher at St. John's School in Hot Springs, Arkansas. But when he reached the heart of his speech, the part about "the values behind my vision of America," the dissenting voices rose again.

"All of us must respect the reflection of God's image in every man and woman," he said.

"What about the babies?" Claire Johnson asked, loud enough for him to hear.

"Respect life," somebody else shouted.

"And so we must value their freedom, not just their political freedom but their freedom of conscience—in matters of philosophy and family and faith."

The crowd stood with a rousing ovation that silenced the protesters. Clinton went on about freedom of religion, separation of church and state, "the wonderful diversity of the American tapestry," and then he turned and aimed straight at Bush.

"That is why, like so many Americans, I've been appalled to hear the voices of intolerance that have been raised in recent weeks, voices that proclaim that some families aren't real families, some Americans aren't 'real Americans,' and what this country needs is a 'religious war.' " The crowd cheered loudly. "America doesn't need a religious war. America needs a reaffirmation of the values that, for most of us, are rooted in our religious faith."

He cited Martin Luther King, Jr., Mario Cuomo, the American bishops' pastoral letters on the economy and the family. He quoted the Bible like a preacher, recounted his tenure with his church choir, and discoursed on humility, the same topic that had occupied the dorm-Mass homilists. And he triggered a fresh round of exclamations whenever he ventured anywhere near the moral territory the prolife protesters considered their own.

"Echoing down the ages is the simple but powerful truth that no grace of God was ever given me for me alone. To the terrible question of Cain, 'Am I my brother's keeper?'—the only possible answer for us is God's thunderous, 'Yes.' "

"Children die!"

"Prolife!"

"If we truly believe that children are God's most precious creation," he said over the insistent shouts of a standing heckler, "then surely we owe every child born in the U.S.A. the chance to make the most of his or her God-given potential."

As the crowd rose to cheer, putting the heckler back in his seat, Claire Johnson sat and fumed in silence, doubly appalled at what she was witnessing—a prochoice speaker sharing a Notre Dame stage with Father Malloy and a Vatican flag; an audience of her peers voicing loud approval of a candidate who stood in stark opposition to a fundamental teaching of the Catholic church. Chris Setti and his fellow Democrats stood and clapped with joy, counting the votes already and dreaming of Election Day.

Clinton was appealing—successfully, by the sound of it—to those Catholics who at some level remained inbred parish Democrats; who hadn't yet completely abandoned the party loyalties of generations past, when the term "Catholic Republican" was almost an oxymoron; who might disagree with his stand on abortion, but who were still moved by the secret liberalism at the heart of their faith; who heard in the Gospels what he said he heard, too: a call to social action. Despite its prosperous Republican veneer, Notre Dame still harbored a large bloc of potential Clinton voters, and the College Democrats hoped to flush them out by November.

"I want an America that does more than talk about families—I want an America that values families," Clinton said, to another standing ovation.

The protesters stayed mostly silent for a long stretch as Clinton sketched a rough outline of one of his policy goals, a national service program for young people. He was hitting all the right notes now, echoing a theme that ran deeply through a campus where 60 percent of the students do some kind of volunteer work, and 10 percent of each graduating class forgo jobs and graduate school to do a year or more of service. "Talking about service here at Notre Dame is the classic case of preaching to the choir," he acknowledged, and he ran through the list: the Center for Social Concerns, the alumni-sponsored summer-service projects, the Center for the Homeless.

The applause lines were piling up high, and mostly unchallenged, as Clinton neared the end of his forty-five minute speech—high enough, in fact, that he decided to attempt an unscripted leap right into the hearts of the crowd, to connect with them at a level that transcended the some-of-my-best-friends-are-Catholic pandering he had indulged in earlier. He was talking about what he called America's "crisis of spirituality and community," telling a story about a recent visit with Florida hurricane victims and the volunteers helping them, when he left his prepared text to tell the story of another recent visit, with a woman in Cedar Rapids, Iowa, who had adopted a baby with AIDS.

" 'Governor, I respect this debate that's going on in our country about life,' " he said, quoting her. " 'But how I wish we would all reach out and help the children who are living.' "

The audience erupted with the day's loudest ovation, the amen roar of a congregation hearing an unspoken truth finally spoken aloud. Clinton ended a few lines later, and the protesters were completely submerged by the cheers. He had won the larger crowd, too: "One of Clinton's most substantive speeches of the campaign," *The New Republic* judged.

A crush of students mobbed Clinton as if he were a star quarterback as he left the stage. Chris Setti came away with a treasured handshake. "I would've been ashamed of Notre Dame if there had been no protesters," he said of the prolife voices that had been raised against his candidate. "They should be here to voice their opinions. But once they're in the hall they should stop. At that point it's like a lecture—if a philosophy teacher happens to be prochoice, you don't stand up and shout, 'What about the babies?' "

Clinton slowly worked his way outside and along the ropeline to the motorcade, compulsively answering policy questions and engaging in mini-debates, ignoring the signs and scattered taunts of the prolife protesters who shadowed him the whole way. Claire Johnson, carrying a sign that said "Abortion Stops a Beating Heart," fixed a cold glare on him, but his eyes never gave hers an answer. "I was within two feet of Hillary at one point," Claire said later. "She did everything she could to avoid looking at me, so I know she saw me. She was afraid of me."

When the crowd was finally dispersing, and the motorcade was safely on its way to the airport, one campus cop turned to another and let out a sigh of relief. "All right," he said, "now we get ready for the football game."

"Welcome one, welcome all," Dan Wagner shouted into the microphone, wearing a green leprechaun suit and addressing a crowd five times the size of the crowd Clinton had addressed, "to the inaugural 1992 Notre Dame pep rally."

The capacity crowd in the basketball arena had risen in greeting when Wagner led the band onto the floor, clapping and cheering and singing the fight song, and they would follow his lead now as they would follow a priest's. The Dillon pep rally the previous evening was just a practice run for this, the main event—the tent revival that convenes here the night before every, *every,* home game. Between the two big games on campus this week-end, Clinton and Michigan, many voices would be left hoarse by Sunday.

Notre Dame football weekends are tightly scripted extravaganzas that set the standard for football weekends everywhere, unfolding with a powerful, almost inevitable familiarity that derives from their faithful repetition of tra-ditions accumulated over the decades. Because they were designed by people with an attachment to sacramental rituals, it is no accident, then—as Father Thomas O'Meara, a chaired theology professor, has insightfully written—that they so closely echo the shape of a Mass. The pep rally, he suggests, is the penitential rite: "an examination of conscience . . . [a] confession of im-perfection [that] is immediately followed by a second, positive confession that looks to the future, to tomorrow's game. Forecasts of what might hap-pen, what should occur on the field, flow into convictions about success."

Wagner led the sinners out of the desert and into the promised land.

"Last year, many of you may remember, there were some people who said that Notre Dame didn't belong in the Sugar Bowl."

"*Booooooo!*" the crowd answered, directing their enmity toward all the anti-Domers who had grumbled that Notre Dame's last bowl bid came less for its record (9 and 3, mediocre by local standards) than for its rich TV contract with NBC.

"Some said that Notre Dame didn't even deserve to go to any bowl at all. You're probably familiar with the joke that was going around: What's the difference between Cheerios and Notre Dame? Well, Cheerios *belong* in a bowl."

"*Boooooooo!*"

"Well, Notre Dame did not beat Florida—Notre Dame *annihilated* Florida," Wagner reported, and the hosannas followed. He had stood on the sidelines in New Orleans for that game, the last of his first season as the leprechaun, and cheered his team on as they staged a dramatic second-half comeback to upset heavily favored Florida. "What's the difference between Wheaties and Notre Dame? Wheaties is the breakfast of champions—Notre Dame is the *team* of champions. Notre Dame doesn't mess around with breakfast, because tomorrow, at twelve-thirty in the afternoon, we're gonna have *Michigan* for *lunch!* Ladies and gentlemen, let's give a big warm welcome to your team, our team, the *University of Notre Dame Football Team!*"

Scores of muscular young men, starters and walk-ons alike, filed out into the seats on the arena floor, freshly showered after practice, packed tightly into their street clothes, moving with the nonchalant swagger natural to athletes accustomed to hearing their actions greeted by cheers. The crowd stood and applauded, more for what the team might yet do than for what it had done already. Expectations were high this year, despite Holtz's attempts to lower them with his usual Lord-I-am-not-worthy routine. Notre Dame was ranked number three in the nation today; the formidable Michigan team, now at number five, was one of the chief obstacles blocking the road to a national championship this season.

The pep-rally liturgy usually includes at least one selection from the Old Testament of Notre Dame lore—a speech from someone who can link yesterday with today, often an old player, bearing glorious tales of campaigns past—and tonight it was Paul Hornung, the 1956 quarterback and Heisman Trophy winner.

"To these young men sitting behind me, this day, this game, tomorrow is why they decided to come to Notre Dame," Hornung said. "This is what college football is all about."

Wagner moved on to the New Testament readings, introducing several brief exhortations from current players. "I hope you all wear your green tomorrow and get fired up for us," said Rick Mirer, who had deferred becoming a millionaire by passing up the NFL draft last spring and returning instead for his senior year.

The band rolled out the big guns of the "1812 Overture," a signal that the gospel according to Holtz was at hand, and the fans responded with their traditional salute—arms swinging up and down in unison, thumbs and index fingers extended to form thousands of little L's, all chanting *"Lou . . . Lou . . . Lou,"* a mass movement that appeared uncomfortably near bowing idolatry.

"The greatest any individual could ask is just to be the coach at Notre Dame," Holtz said. "I'm certainly no legend. I didn't come here to be a legend."

Holtz used that line a lot, about not being a legend, but he well knew that a legend is exactly what the fans expected him to be. Notre Dame believes in its legends as deeply as the Catholic church believes in its saints—the exemplary figures whose deeds inspire devotion and awe. Priests, brothers, and professors are all part of the Notre Dame litany, but more visible from afar are the football heroes. The requirements for beatification here are high— Notre Dame has more national titles, more Heisman winners, more Hall of Fame members than any other school—and it helps to have a miracle or two along the way. A second national championship would probably do it for Holtz, earning him a secure place alongside Rockne, Leahy, and Parseghian, the other coaches who won more than one title.

"I'm glad to see Rick Mirer come back—I'm glad to have the leprechaun back also," Holtz said, and Wagner acknowledged his own cheers with a short bow. A steelworker's son from a western-Pennsylvania mill town, Wagner was among the minority of current Domers who still fit the classic up-from-steerage, first-to-college profile of students from decades past, and he was generally rated as the best leprechaun in recent years.

"I don't know of many things in this world which would motivate a fifty-six-year-old man to put on a mask and play a game of football, but I would do so if I had the opportunity to play Notre Dame." Under his Tom Sawyer thatch of hair, Holtz has an Abraham Lincoln face; his years at Notre Dame have helped etch lines in it as deep as those the Civil War left in Lincoln's. At five feet ten, 152 pounds, Holtz is dwarfed by his players, but he was once a linebacker at Kent State, a team that never faced the likes of a Notre Dame. "But, ladies and gentlemen, only one thing would be a greater incentive than to be able to play Notre Dame—and that would be to be able to play *for* Notre Dame."

The occasion was solemnized by the singing of the alma mater—the whole crowd swaying slowly together, back and forth, row by row, arms draped around one another, Holtz and his coaches, Wagner and the cheerleaders, the players, the students, the fans. Down on the floor with the band, Rachel Stehle rocked from side to side with each deliberate note, trumpet raised, reverently sounding the hymnal cadence. Halfway up the stands, the freshmen from Keenan Hall sealed their Domer bond as they stood and joined the song, and those who stumbled over the as-yet unfamiliar words could look to Patrick Lyons for guidance: He had sung the alma mater at many previous pep rallies as a visitor, in the company of his father, but this was the first where he had sung it as a student, in the company of his peers. Way up in the back, the freshmen of Zahm Hall, Keenan's enemy and neighbor, slipped and squished against one another, having just endured a dorm initiation rite that included wading through the library reflecting pond, singing "Twinkle, Twinkle, Little Star," and diving into a mud pit and screaming "I love Zahm," all while wearing bedsheet togas. To clear the sob from its throat, the arena then broke into yet another rendition of the fight song.

The fight song escaped the pep rally with the departing crowd and blew through the campus all night and into the next morning. It blared tinnily from tape players in the RVs that had colonized the parking lots. It tooted annoyingly from specially rigged car horns. It was whistled nostalgically by young alums on their way into Senior Bar, the low-slung brick building near the stadium—unmarked and anonymous, often known instead as Senior Bank—where they packed in alongside their younger selves. It was sung softly and sweetly by two off-key Keenan freshmen, lying on their backs on their narrow beds, lubricated by several beers from their first room party. And it blew like reveille all through the clear, bright hours before kickoff, making sure that no one would, or even could, sleep through the big game.

The morning air smelled like lunch, not breakfast—bratwurst, burgers, hot dogs, and beer. The tailgaters laid out their portable feasts, unloading six-foot subs, raw-vegetable trays, cheese cubes, Triscuits, tortilla chips, salsa, onion dip, bottles of vodka and Bloody Mary mix. The dorms grilled meat at the temporary concessions they set up all along the quads. A long, hungry line waited outside the Knights of Columbus, where the steaks for their famed steak sandwiches were cooking fragrantly over fires built in bisected oil drums. The early game time, 12:30 p.m., apparently granted a special dispensation for prenoon drinking. To accommodate those fans for whom a tailgate party held deeper, more troubling implications, the Center for Social Concerns was hosting the regular game-morning meeting of Alcoholics Anonymous.

"Memories, anecdotes, myths and rituals multiply as more and more people arrive on campus and the narratives of people's lives unfold," writes Thomas O'Meara, who characterizes the morning before the game as the Liturgy of the Word. "Devotion to Notre Dame exists because celebration needs a cause, something bigger than life. Football at Notre Dame caught national attention in the first place because the immigrant underdogs won, and those victories seemed transcendent."

So many alumni come back for every home game that Notre Dame doesn't bother to designate a homecoming weekend. (The demand for tickets was rising—there were sixteen thousand tickets available to alumni for the Michigan game, and forty-two thousand requests, the most yet for a regular-season game—and so was the pressure to increase the supply of seats in the stadium.) Flags flying from car and RV antennas announced class years, and mini-reunions convened. The alumni, real and imagined, sat beside their tailgates in Notre Dame lawn chairs, wore upon their heads Notre Dame tam-o'-shanters and Notre Dame golf hats, emblazoned messages like "IM4ND" on their vanity license plates, dressed their little daughters in Notre Dame cheerleader outfits, wore garish plaid pants without shame, pasted shamrocks and leprechaun tattoos on their cheeks, and stood in long lines at the bookstore to buy more T-shirts, sweatshirts, running shorts, jackets, scarves, and assorted other Notre Dame regalia. The standard wardrobe came in three colors—blue and gold, the official colors, and green, the unofficial one.

The fight song grew in volume as game time neared, finally exploding into a brassy tidal roar when the band crammed onto the steep steps of the Main Building for their pregame concert. Rachel Stehle stood with the trumpets, proudly wearing the shiny new band uniform that had raised tears in her mother's eyes earlier; her parents didn't have tickets to the game, but they had driven out anyway to see her debut here on the quad. (They would have to watch the game and the halftime show on the big TV screen in the Joyce Athletic and Convocation Center, better known as the ACC, across the street from the stadium.)

Just next door to the band concert, in front of Washington Hall, Lou Blaum and his fellow Guardsmen were acting as if they were guarding the queen—standing at attention in full-dress glory, statue-still, faces fixed in granite as the returning alumni Guardsmen conducted the traditional inspection. "They're not supposed to smile, no matter what," one spectator explained to his young son. The old Guardsmen tried their best to crack the composure of the current Guardsmen. They got right in the faces of their successors, close as Marine sergeants. They fiddled with their hats, their capes, their kilts. Lou fixed his gaze somewhere in the distance as one old Guardsman stroked a Bic disposable shaver along his chin and neck. His mask never wavered.

The Irish Guard's official reason for being is to run interference for the band, and the crowds along the route to the stadium were large enough today so that the job was more than just symbolic. Marching with quick, high, precise steps, they led the band down the main quad, past the business school, the statue of Sorin, the law school, the engineering school, the art museum, and then down into the stadium tunnel, where they waited their cue to take the field. Fans fell in and marched behind them—"a long entrance ceremony," O'Meara writes, "like that at the offertory of the Mass."

The NBC truck that had been parked outside the stadium for days, a semitrailer crammed with electronics and trailing thick wires, was finally plugged in. It completed the circuit that powers Notre Dame football—the vast alternating current in which Notre Dame feeds on the wide national attention, and the nation feeds on Notre Dame's aura, the electricity racing between the two poles, gaining speed, rising in wattage, building to a white heat by game time. Carrying a Fighting Irish battle flag, Dan Wagner and the cheerleaders sprinted onto the field, claiming it for those who soon followed—the Guard, the band, and, finally, the team. The players' midnight-blue jerseys displayed no names, neither team nor individual, just numbers and a small "ND" logo on the sleeves. Their gold helmets caught the sun, glowing as brightly as if a spotlight were trained on each one. "There is no chance of rain," the announcer said when giving the forecast. The Goodyear blimp occasionally provided some slow-moving shade.

Notre Dame Stadium dates to 1930, Rockne's final season, and it still reeks of that era—a complex, elusive blend of wood smoke, damp wool, fallen leaves, worn leather, and dust. It is built of two million weathered yellow bricks and it holds at least that many tales. The tier of arches high up on its exterior open into deep, old shadows that look as if they might swallow you whole into the past. Looming directly behind the end zone, on the side of the fourteen-story Hesburgh Library tower, is the 132-foot-high mo-

saic of the risen Christ, arms extended toward heaven as if signaling the
result of the ultimate scoring drive: "Touchdown Jesus," they call it. The stadium is an intimate coliseum (population 59,075 on autumn Saturdays)
with no purpose beyond football; no moatlike running track separates the
fans from the field. The bleachers are nothing but worn, narrow wooden
planks that the students rarely use for sitting. The older portion of the
crowd was up standing on them, too, by the middle of the first quarter,
when tailback Reggie Brooks bounced off five would-be tacklers, cutting
and spinning and dashing, covering twenty yards in which each yard looked
as if it might be the last, before finally collapsing over the goal line for the
game's first score. They were up again at the end of quarter, when Tom
Carter of Dillon Hall stopped a Michigan drive by deftly employing his
forty-three-inch vertical leap at just the right moment, soaring across the
end zone and intercepting a pass bound for star receiver Derrick Alexander.

The student section of the stadium, the corner nearest the Dome, was a
block of forest green today. Most of the students were wearing identical
T-shirts—a fund-raising project for student activities, featuring on its back
both a portrait of Lou Holtz and, looming behind him, a rendering of
Mount Rushmore in which the presidents' heads were replaced by those of
the four other coaches who won national championships (Rockne, Leahy,
Parseghian, and Dan Devine)—and when the band played the "1812 Overture" for the Lou chant at the end of the third quarter, their waving arms
looked like the tentacles of some vast, algae-covered sea creature. The lingering remnants of the chant were abruptly silenced by the first play of the
fourth quarter. Tom Carter and Derrick Alexander were in the end zone
again, and the ball was in the air. Carter dashed across the sesquicentennial
logo painted on the grass, but this time he was too late. The thirty-yard
touchdown pass put Michigan up, 17–7.

Notre Dame fought back to tie the game with two quick scores—a field
goal and a two-yard touchdown run by fullback Jerome Bettis—but with
less than two minutes left, Michigan had the ball and was driving again.
The whole stadium leaned visibly nearer the action—from the players down
on the sidelines all the way up to the VIP seats above the press box, where
Father Malloy was hosting several trustees and assorted other heavy-hitters.
The twin white domes of the sprawling Joyce Athletic and Convocation
Center across the street—the basketball arena under one dome, the fieldhouse under the other—peered over the lip of the stadium like a pair of un-
blinking, all-seeing eyes.

With sixty-five seconds left, Patrick Lyons abruptly roared his approval, exulting with his fellow Keenanites as their dormmate, cornerback Jeff Burris, intercepted a Michigan pass. Victory was now eighty-nine long yards away. "I figured that was one time the Notre Dame mystique was going to come through," Tom Carter said later. "There was no question we were going to win." The crowd wanted a long, dramatic pass—the kind that could put the Irish within field-goal range, or maybe even score a touchdown; the kind that, as Holtz well knew, could also be picked off, losing the game as fast as it might win it. Holtz called a run, then another, and the boos started. The clock ticked down, the last time-out not yet called, and the boos grew. Two final desperation passes failed, and the game ended at 17–17, Notre Dame's first home-field tie in twenty-three years. Touchdown Jesus hovered in the distance beyond the goalposts, arms raised in vain, signaling the final score that never came. Scattered boos followed Holtz and the team off the field. The line between sinner and saint is very fine in the minds of the harshest, most demanding fans.

"It just doesn't feel like the game should be over, and I don't know how you are supposed to feel," Holtz told reporters. "It was a crazy game that has left me with an empty feeling."

The fans shared his puzzled emptiness. Football games usually end with a Judgment Day finality, the kind of black-and-white pronouncement that Catholics are familiar with. A tie is something like Limbo, a place the church doesn't talk about much anymore. At one level, the season was already over: Perfection, Holtz's oft-stated goal, was unattainable now; the national title would be that much harder to win; original sin was revealed.

"What are we supposed to do?" Patrick Lyons wondered. In all the games he had attended with his father, he had never seen a tie, and he now stood on the same uncertain ground as his less experienced floormates. "Do we celebrate or not?"

As the stadium emptied, the sanctuaries quickly filled. Masses are offered at Sacred Heart and the dorm chapels immediately after every home game, and the pews are always as packed as the bleachers. One of the day's readings was from Exodus: "With that, the Lord said to Moses, 'Go down at once to your people, whom you have brought out of the land of Egypt, for they have become depraved. They have soon turned aside from the way I pointed out to them, making for themselves a molten calf and worshiping it, sacrificing to it and crying out, "This is your God, O Israel, who brought you out of the land of Egypt." ' " On the quiet lawn outside the library, a large and fierce bronze statue illustrated that very scene—the wrathful Moses upon his descent from the mountain, his foot crushing the head of the golden calf, his left hand carrying the Ten Commandments, his right hand pointing heaven-ward toward the only God his followers should be worshiping. The statue is widely known as *"We're Number One" Moses*—the upraised finger makes the hulking, glowering prophet resemble a triumphant lineman after a big game—but today the prophecy proved inaccurate.

Down in the South Quad, amateur quarterbacks pretended to be Rick Mirer, throwing deep, trying to win the big game that had slipped away. "I'm open, wide open," one receiver called, darting up the evening lawn. Undefended, he caught it easily.

4

The procession started at ten-thirty in Sorin Hall, eleven students and the president, marching out into the cool night and north across the tongue of land that separates St. Mary's Lake from St. Joseph's Lake. Father Malloy led, walking briskly, wearing sweats like all the others. He carried a bag of basketballs—a gift from sportscaster Dick Vitale, who had two daughters here—and the keys to the seminary gym. The other side of the lakes, behind the Main Building, is more thickly wooded than the pruned campus, and more thinly explored by students—the domain of the once and future members of the Holy Cross religious community. Tucked into this quiet corner of Notre Dame are the graves of the priests and brothers who built it, marked by small stone crosses planted in lines as straight and uniform as in a military cemetery. No stone, whether for Sorin or for the brother who worked as a cobbler, is larger than any other. Some of the older stones have settled far enough into the earth to obscure the inscribed birth names of the brothers, leaving visible only the names they took when they made their vows: You have to bend and part the grass to see that Brother Romuald was christened in 1849 as Daniel Moran. They all lie buried in the order in which they fell, one cross after another, year upon year. Most of today's priests and brothers can point out the stone that marks the first funeral they attended after joining the community, and whenever they pass by this family plot they silently count the number that have accumulated in the years since, watching the line of crosses creep like a shadow across the open grass, slowly approaching the unknown plot where they, too, will one day rest.

Malloy left the path before it reached the cemetery, veering off through the woods toward the seminary. The gym was dark and empty until he unlocked it. He made this trip most Mondays and Wednesdays at this same hour, keeping a standing appointment known as Monk Hoops. Presiding over this full-court session gave him certain advantages over the other campus amateurs. He never had to wait for a court to open. He didn't have to sit if his team lost. He could always be shirts in these shirts-versus-skins games.

"Sorry, Monk," said Kerry Madden, a senior from Keenan Hall, after stealing the ball from Malloy and sinking a fast-break lay-up.

As a teenager back in Washington, D.C., Malloy had spent so much time on the neighborhood courts, sinking jump shot after jump shot, that he was called "the mayor of Turkey Thicket." His teammates at Archbishop Carroll High School included John Thompson, now the coach at Georgetown, and Tom Hoover, who went on to play for the New York Knicks. In his senior year, they didn't lose a single game. He was, then and now, a guard.

"Always," he said about his natural role on the court. "My whole life."

He stood against the yellow wall at courtside catching his breath, the high windows above him filled with night. Shirts were up, 10–6. He was, as always, the last player on his team to come out for a substitute, and he waited impatiently for his turn to rotate back in.

"This guy's a fine athlete, but he doesn't have much experience," he said, pointing out a teammate with a tentative shot.

Recruited by fifty colleges out of high school, Malloy chose Notre Dame for practical, not sentimental, reasons: It was Catholic, it had an engineering program, and it wasn't in his hometown. He crashed out of engineering after one semester and soon landed in English. His college basketball career never quite soared either: His game—slow of foot, sharp of shot—didn't fit the team's needs. His best year was as a sophomore, when he played in eleven games, averaging 1.7 points and 0.8 rebounds, and earned a monogram, Notre Dame's version of a varsity letter.

"My game is adapted well to age," he said. "I was always a good shot, more a finesse player, and I've managed to keep my eye."

Back in the game, he swished a pair of long jump shots, then found himself under the basket, trying to stop Kerry Madden from scoring. Malloy's height—six feet four, taller than most of the other players—often made him a *de facto* forward or center, forcing him farther inside than a natural guard normally likes to go. Kerry spun around him and scored.

"Nineteen–sixteen," called Malloy, who was always the official scorekeeper. The game was to 21, and shirts were still up.

Malloy spent the summer after his junior year with a group of student volunteers in the central-Mexican city of Aguascalientes—distributing food, working in a health clinic, building a parish center, and, ultimately, discerning a vocation. It was atop a mountain there, at the shrine of the Basilica of Christ the King, amid the icons and the discarded crutches of healed pilgrims, that he felt "a sense of certitude about what I wanted to do, what I was being called to do." ("Monk" is a nickname from childhood, bestowed upon him not for any religious reason, but simply because it rhymed with "Bunk," the name of a neighborhood friend's older brother.) Back for his senior year, he applied to join the Holy Cross community.

Malloy pulled down a rebound, then passed it long to a teammate, who laid it in for the win, 21–16. "New game," he announced.

Young Holy Cross priests are encouraged to study for graduate degrees beyond the seminary, and Malloy earned several—a pair of master's degrees from Notre Dame (one in English and one in theology, which, on top of his bachelor's, make him a rare Triple Domer) and a Ph.D. in Christian ethics from Vanderbilt. He taught theology, got tenure, was appointed an associate provost, then took his place among the other bright, young Holy Cross Ph.D.'s in the line of potential presidential successors who had accumulated over the long decades of Hesburgh's reign.

"Sixes," Malloy called after sinking a twenty-five-foot jump shot to tie the second game at 6–6.

Under Hesburgh's strong hand, Notre Dame had grown in the public mind from a football team into a university. "Our student body had doubled," he once wrote about the school he inherited in 1952, "our facilities were inadequate, our faculty quite ordinary for the most part, our deans and department heads complacent, our graduates loyal and true in heart but often lacking in intellectual curiosity, our academic programs largely encrusted with the accretions of decades, our graduate school an infant, our administration much in need of reorganization, our fund-raising organization non-existent, and our football team national champions." He bolstered its academic reputation, lifted it out of the Catholic ghetto, ceded governance to a lay board of trustees—but it still remained a family business, as the cemetery stones silently attested. When Hesburgh finally stepped down in 1987, the search for a new president was restricted, by charter, to a tiny gene pool—the few dozen priests in the Indiana Province of the Congregation of Holy Cross who had a Ph.D.

"Good shot, Kerry," Corey Babington cheered as Kerry Madden, his friend and teammate, hit a jumper over Malloy's in-you-face defense, winning the second game 21–19.

Because Hesburgh had never groomed an heir apparent, the trustees were left to conduct a search, not a coronation. In Malloy they found a candidate of the middle generation, younger than such other candidates as Ernie Bartell or Dave Burrell, older than Michael McCafferty or Thomas Oddo. He lacked the administrative experience of Dave Tyson or Bill Beauchamp, but he had the academic credentials that would earn him easier entrée into the elite, degree-conscious world of university presidents. He was also the only candidate with a monogram, thereby combining in one person both sides of the Notre Dame story, and demonstrating how much self-confidence the school had gained since the day in 1952 when an angry Hesburgh, determined to transcend the jock-factory image, refused to pose with a football for the photographers who covered his appointment as president.

Drawn in again from his guard's perimeter, Malloy got caught in a crush of bodies under the basket and emerged wincing, calling for a substitute. He walked in quick circles, alternately clutching his hand tightly and trying to shake the pain out of it. A few sideline minutes concluded that the hand was just jammed, not broken. "I've been lucky with injuries," he said. "It's mostly because of the way I play."

"My legs are gone," Corey Babington said, joining him at courtside.

"My hand's gone, so we're even."

Everything about Hesburgh was so large that any successor, even one who stood six feet four, was bound to seem small by comparison. Hesburgh had counseled seven presidents and four popes; collected enough honorary doctorates to earn a place in the *Guinness Book of World Records*; spoken loudly and internationally for the causes of civil rights and human rights; emerged as the nearest thing America had to its own pope ("In any properly run church," Father Andrew Greeley once wrote, "Theodore Hesburgh would be a cardinal archbishop"); and reinvented Notre Dame as decisively as Sorin had invented it. When Malloy took over, Hesburgh gave him a special gift: He disappeared for a year. He took a round-the-world trip with his equally long-serving second-in-command, Father Edmund Joyce; Ted and Ned, they called themselves, like an old vaudeville team.

"Let me see if I can shoot the ball," Malloy said after skins had won again, by the same score, 21–19. He swished a few and pronounced himself fit. "One more game, to eleven."

Hesburgh had ruled the place like a benevolent dictator for thirty-five years, and his departure left a power vacuum under the Dome that several competing factions rushed to fill. Some in the Holy Cross community thought he had given away too much of Notre Dame to forces outside the order, and they wanted the family business back in the family; some on the faculty thought they deserved more of a say in how things were run; and Malloy was now the target they all fixed on.

"Go back to basics," an annoyed Malloy advised a teammate who, in attempting an NBA-style no-look pass, had thrown the ball away. Shirts were up, 4–3, and he wanted them to stay up. There is a varsity intensity in Malloy's devotion to basketball, as anyone can attest who has endured his elbows under the boards. He doesn't like to lose.

"If you play basketball with somebody who's decently good a time or two, you find out a lot about their character," he said later—about a person's affinity for teamwork, the size of his ego, his capacity to handle anger and success, the depth of his work ethic. His own game, he said, reveals "that I'm competitive, that I like to play within the rules, that I enjoy having a central role within a team concept—I like to take the last shot to win, things like that—but that I don't lose my temper, and that I have a pretty even demeanor during the course of the game."

"I got it," Kerry Madden said, calling a foul on the president. His drive up the lane had been seriously impaired by Malloy's long arms. When shirts got the ball back, Malloy rolled off a pick and, falling forward toward the basket, sank a Larry Bird bank shot.

The basketball court was a place of rare clarity for Malloy, where the rules were unchanging and the motives of the other players were always easy to read. Earlier this evening, he had met with the faculty senate, with whom he had established a wary truce since their threatened no-confidence vote last spring. He had been making the rounds of all the academic departments, fielding their requests and complaints: They all wanted more money, more positions, more facilities. He had logged marathon hours at the meetings of the Colloquy for the Year 2000, the massive self-study team he had recruited to help envision the school's future. Although the Hesburgh era was receding ever further into history—Malloy was starting his second five-year term, as voted by the board of trustees—the current president was still being measured against his predecessor: in judging Malloy, his critics tended to see him as both too little like Hesburgh (for exhibiting a shortage of vision) and too much like Hesburgh (for wielding an excess of authority).

Malloy brought the ball upcourt, looking as if he had no intention of giving it away. He found a hole, drove the lane, and pulled up short to launch a soft twelve-foot jumper. Shirts won, 11–9, evening the series at two games apiece.

It was after midnight when they finally left, locking up the gym and trooping back between the lakes. Malloy's gait was quick and predatory: He has the tall man's habit of keeping his head slightly dipped, as if he's never quite sure how much clearance he has. Upon entering the dorm, the players each gently touched the feet of the Sorin statue in the hallway, a habit as ingrained in the men of Sorin Hall as reaching for holy water upon entering a church; the old president's feet were as shiny as the old coach's nose on the bust in the Rockne Memorial. Malloy still had two or three productive hours left in him before he would pull out the small single bed—it did double duty as a couch in a room that did double duty as a study—and finally go to sleep; when you live among students, it's hard not to keep their hours. He had a book to finish for the Freshman Seminar he was teaching: *The General in His Labyrinth* by Gabriel García Márquez. Looking up from the quad outside, you could see that the lights were also still on in the office suite Hesburgh now occupies on the thirteenth floor of the library that wears his name. Hesburgh, like Malloy, is also on an undergraduate schedule, and he works late into the night up there, keeping up his correspondence and attending to the business of the various boards and committees he sits on. He sees the Dome mainly from the outside now, framed in flood-lit golden splendor in the large picture window beside his desk; he rarely ventures into the administrative chambers beneath it, leaving Malloy a wide lane to maneuver in.

"When you come to a new crossroad, what kind of choice you make often depends on the kind of things you've seen in the past or been taught," said Corey Babington, Monk Malloy's backcourt opponent, sitting now at the supper table in the room of Keenan Hall's rector, Brother Bonaventure Scully. "Life is one big circle, and if you stay in that circle too much, you can get trapped in your own world."

Scully got up to replenish his guests' plates with the meal he had prepared—salad, beef stew, chicken and rice. Squeezed around the table were six students who had come to discuss their service projects from the previous summer. Directed by the Center for Social Concerns, and supported both by scholarships and the wide network of alumni clubs, they had, along with 120 of their peers, fanned out across the country to shelters, halfway houses, hospitals, social-service agencies, and parish centers in poor neighborhoods. Scully was an official debriefer, prodding them with questions that led them deeper into the lessons behind their actions. Corey Babington had worked in a transitional home for homeless men in Oakland; his friend Kerry Madden was at a parish recreation program in Indianapolis.

"Some people don't notice there are other people in need or suffering, or they know it and they don't want to acknowledge it," Kerry said.

Conversations like this, and students like these, were what kept Scully, sixty-five come January and a rector for a dozen years, from contemplating retirement just yet. Notre Dame interested him not for its football team—he usually gave his tickets away—but for its reservoir of bright young people willing to do good works. His mission was to convert as many as he could to the cause of social service. A one-man placement agency for volunteer positions, he always knew of someplace, somewhere, that needed somebody to help somebody else.

"How did you feel about leaving?" Scully asked.

"They said I was going to feel sad about leaving, and I did," Kerry said.

"I wouldn't say sad, or unfulfilled either; somewhere in between," Corey said about ending his service project and returning to school. "It's hard to get used to not being able to help someone."

One person he had been able to help, though, was himself. Corey's junior year had seemed at times as if it might be his last. He had spent the fall semester back home in Racine, Wisconsin, stranded by cash problems, working double shifts in a machine shop to earn enough to return. Depressed, his pride challenged, he was determined to disprove those who said he was finished at Notre Dame. As a black man on an overwhelmingly white campus, he had worked hard to make a place for himself here, and he didn't plan to give it up without a fight. "In most of my classes, I'm the only African American. It's kinda like, 'Man, I wish there were more of us here,' " he said. Tall and well built, he was—like his friend Kerry and every other tall, well-built black man at Notre Dame—often assumed to be a varsity athlete, even though his career was limited to Monk Hoops and intramurals. "I don't use that as an excuse. I kinda knew what I was getting into."

Corey made it back for the spring of his junior year, but he wound up on academic probation. Then came his summer-service project, when "everything flipflopped." A science-business major, he was thinking about graduate school, pharmacy possibly, or maybe a shot at the music business: He was also known as MC Bones, the premier rapper on campus; Kerry was his partner, the DJ who sampled the beats. Their latest collaboration was "The X Factor," an original rap about Malcom X. Onstage, Corey found an eloquence that sometimes eluded him in class and in conversation: His stutter disappeared when he became MC Bones, and he sped through his raps without ever tripping.

"As soon as my project was done, I felt a whole lot stronger about my values, like nothing could hold me back," he said in the group now. "You just feel like you can do anything."

"What do your friends say—are they interested?" Scully asked.

"I get the feeling that people don't really want to know," somebody said.

"Or they want to know how it makes them more marketable."

"They say, 'That's nice,' because they're well groomed in how to be social. They're not gonna say, 'That sucks.' They say, 'That's nice; go your way, now.' "

"Even our own friends, who see that stuff every day," Corey said of his circle back home, "I hear so many of us say, 'Me, me, me,' and 'I, I—I gotta get mine.' They don't have a concept of sharing. They don't know how much more you can gain by sharing."

"I think sometimes Notre Dame can get to be a bubble."

"I think a large portion of America needs a good dose of seeing what life is like beyond TV, beyond their own homogeneous neighborhood."

"That's so hard to do, because of the way society was developed since World War II," said Scully, the eternal city boy. "We build walls around places."

Scully assigned them to do some more thinking on paper. "Did your service experience lead you to questions about God's will in relation to the limits, suffering and problems faced by those you worked with?" asked the short essay question on the yellow sheets he passed out. "Did the experience challenge your understanding of God's will in relation to your own life, suffering and limitations?" They would discuss the answers at their next session.

"It's easy for us to think we're never gonna be in a suffering situation," Scully said. The "we" was an old teacher's habit; he really meant them more than himself. "People my age just think, 'How's it gonna come? What kind of suffering will it be?' "

Tom Morris took the next transparency from his bulging manila folder and laid it on the overhead projector, carefully concealing with a sheet of paper all but the first line.

"No gym-rat basketball player ever grew up to be president of anything," he read, and the class wondered where he was headed. The subject was epistemology, the theory of knowledge, and they were exploring the border territory between belief and truth, appearance and reality.

"Monk is a gym-rat basketball player," Morris continued, moving the paper on the projector to reveal the next line on the transparency. Everybody makes certain propositions about reality, he had been saying; but if you string them together, he was asking now, do they necessarily lead you to knowledge?

"Soooo," he said, uncovering the final line with the flourish of a magician waving a cape, "Monk will never grow up to be president of anything."

Because Monk had obviously grown up to be president of something, Morris' point was clear. "It's not a sound argument," he said. "It lacks truth in one of its premises."

Morris tries, in Philosophy 101, "to be responsible to the highest level of work in the field, so I could defend it before the American Philosophical Academy, but also to be accessible to the least prepared of the freshmen." He had first taught the intro course almost a decade earlier, as a young assistant professor with just thirty students. He had eighty students the second year, then 120, then three hundred, until the university finally imposed some limits: Enrollment now was determined by how many teaching assistants were available to lead the weekly discussion groups that supplemented the lectures. Some freshmen, alerted by their older siblings but shut out by the registrar, clamored to get in; Morris only had room for about 180 this semester. His scholarly writings had won him respect from his peers—his 1986 book, *The Logic of God Incarnate,* is considered one of the major works in his field, the philosophy of religion—but his lectures had made him a campus legend. A full professor now, he continued teaching intro each year, long after he could have begged out of it, because it provided a base from which to wage his populist campaign "to get as many people as possible to philosophize about their lives."

In the fall of 1987, the goal had been to get as many freshman football players as possible to philosophize about their lives: Twenty-nine of them were in his class that semester. "I saw more big people than I'd ever seen in one place before," he said about the first lecture. "I thought, 'Boy, do I have a reputation I don't want to have?' " Hoping to spark some intellectual excitement among the new recruits, the athletic department was steering them toward professors who, like Morris, had won teaching awards. But the excitement that followed the first exam was the wrong kind: Faced with questions like "What does Soft Determinism claim about freedom and inner psychological states?," most of them punted. "Twenty-six of them failed," Morris recalled, "with scores the likes of which I'd never seen before. One guy got a zero. He worked the whole hour and got a zero." Morris convened review sessions—"the below-C-level club, to help keep their heads above water"—and he gave them "the academic equivalent of a locker-room pep talk."

"These guys were staring down the barrel of failure for the first time in their lives. They were local heroes back home, and here they were in their first class in college and they're looking at F's." His strategy was to appeal to their strengths. "I told them, 'You all play a complicated sport. Number one, you have a great deal of natural intelligence or you wouldn't have made it to this level. Number two, you're teachable. Your coaches teach you. You have complex playbooks that you have to learn. Number three, you have self-discipline. You make it through all those grueling practices. These are all transferrable qualities. They can be transferred from the football field to the classroom.' " The second test asked them, among other things, to "present and discuss two of Hume's objections to the teleological argument," and though nobody emerged as the next Immanuel Kant, the F's did turn into C's, and the D's became B's. "These are the future philosophers of the NFL. These guys can nail these questions."

Patrick Lyons could nail them, too. Sitting near the back of the auditorium with his fellow freshman Keenanite Vishal Pahwa, he was just out of reach of the Snickers bars Morris sometimes sent sailing into the seats, but his notebook caught and held all the key ideas. He had collected some A's on the short essays that were due each week—Descartes's *Meditations* and Plato's *Crito* were recent topics—and discovered that his talents inclined more toward the philosophical than the mathematical. "Calculus is my nemesis," he said. He had tested too high for his own good, an arts-and-letters refugee misplaced among the engineers and science majors in Calc 126.

Slouched down in his seat, the preferred posture among his male peers, and wearing the obligatory baseball cap, Patrick took notes as Morris discoursed on the problem of human freedom. "Is all of life a play that is written in advance?" Morris wondered aloud. "Are we just mouthing lines we have been given? Or do we have freedom?" He unveiled a new word on the projector: Determinism. "I was caused to do it," he explained. "Just like a computer, just like a robot. Nature, heredity, my environment—they punched all the right buttons so that I had to do it. I was a puppet."

Nature, heredity, and environment had punched the buttons that brought many of these students to Notre Dame, and at first glance it seemed as if Patrick was part of that deterministic clan—his presence here foreordained from the moment in 1964 when the man who would become his father, a Notre Dame sophomore, met the woman who would become his mother, a St. Mary's freshman, on the bus to the Purdue game. The pull of Notre Dame on the children of alumni is so powerful that a quarter of each entering class is generally composed of them. It can be a rich, nurturing connection—the continuity between generations, the sense of belonging to an institution larger than yourself—but it can also be suffocating. Some alumni children come to Notre Dame only because it would be unthinkable to their parents if they didn't. Some come and try to do nothing more imaginative than replicate their fathers' experiences; the coed era isn't old enough yet to include many who try to replicate their mothers' experiences. Some feel unequal to the challenge—their insecurities fed by the knowledge that the admissions standards for alumni children are slightly lower than for other applicants—and never quite make the place their own. Some use their legacy mainly as a license for excessively boorish behavior.

"Genuine human freedom seems to involve various possibilities for action," Morris said, and that was a better characterization of Patrick's path here than the rigid model of determinism.

Patrick's father was deeply devoted to Notre Dame, but not to the point of insisting that he come here. The decision was his own, and he was already finding for himself a version of the Domer experience that was not overshadowed by his father's. He had the self-confidence that comes from knowing the place well—all those football weekends had taken care of that—but not the smug, possessive reverence that inhibits any attempt to reimagine it. He had quickly become one of the LaFortuneites—the diverse crew that spent long extracurricular hours working for the various clubs and organizations that inhabit the LaFortune Student Center. He was already a regular in the second-floor offices of student government, where he had found an appreciative audience for his graphic prowess on an Apple Powerbook; his connections had helped score him seats at the Bill Clinton speech. The first issue of *Notre Dame Today*, the student-government newsletter, came straight out of his computer, earning him the position of layout-and-design editor. He had gained entry to the circle surrounding the student-body president, Greg Butrus, and he was scoping out candidates for the spring elections. "It's better for me to be in the background, whispering in people's ears," he said. He flinched slightly now, along with the rest of the class, as Tom Morris—in the midst of ruminating about what God's role is in determining what happens next in life—took the cup he was sipping from and calmly started to turn it over. Everyone in the class—Morris included, it seemed—assumed that not even God could stop the water from spilling now.

"I think God has nothing to do with whether I'm drinking water at this moment or not," Morris said as he upended the cup. His surprise was feigned, but the students' was genuine when the cup proved empty, spilling nothing, as if stayed by a higher power—a stunt designed to make the class wonder, for a brief, almost transcendent instant, whether God did in fact have something to do with whether or not Morris was drinking water at this moment.

You can hear the echo of Tom Morris' earlier self—the lead guitarist who, before his Ph.D., played in a string of rock-and-roll bands—in the shape and style of his lectures: He might slash like Keith Richards, or meander like Jerry Garcia, or even, on days like this, soar like Eric Clapton, hitting notes that ring with a pure and startling clarity. Instead of droning on with a windy, obscure exposition of the principle of universal causality, he prodded the students with questions from their own lives. "Raise your hand if you ever had a dream that turned out true," he said, and maybe three-quarters of the class did. "What kind of world do we live in if you can have a dream tonight and it's a true picture of next week?"

He spoke without condescension to the minds he knew his students had—half formed, fuzzy, easily seduced by portents and sentimentality, a tangled underbrush of undergraduate longings—not the minds he wished they had. His accent traveled a few states deeper into the South as he captivated them with the story of a friend's grandmother who had foretold his future once, right down to the color of his wife's hair (blond) and the number of his children (two). "Am I being given a picture of what will happen regardless of what I do? Or of something that will happen unless I act?"

Having wooed them with talk-show epiphanies, he hit them with philosophy again—unwrapping their soft ideas to find the hard substance within. "You can deny God foreknowledge," he said, placing on the overhead a list of some theological challenges to determinism. "Maybe God only knows all the possibilities of what might happen, not what actually will happen."

He moved on to the second challenge. "Maybe God is somehow outside of time," he said, pushing God offstage, behind a curtain, removed from the linear chain of causality that seems to characterize human life. "Then God's knowledge of the future is not a fact before your act, so it's not behind your actions, it's not constricting your actions."

He ended class with a third challenge, which hung expectantly in the air as the students gathered their things and hurried out to beat the lunch lines. "God knowing what you'll do," he said, "doesn't *cause* you to do it."

Patrick Lyons headed toward North Dining Hall with Vishal Pahwa, who was thinking about the speech he had to make tonight. He was running for Keenan's seat on the freshman council of student government; Patrick was his backer and adviser. Steve Sabo was the floor's original candidate in the race, but a premature campaign ad in *The Observer*, placed by an overeager Patrick, had resulted in his disqualification. "I'm just gonna tell 'em I'm not a politician," Vishal said about his speech.

They passed a face that looked familiar. "Hey, you live in Keenan, don't you?" Vishal asked, offering his hand and his pitch. Patrick, silent, looked on with approval.

The copresident of Pasquerilla West put her hands over the hands of her teammates as they broke out of their huddle with a collective grunt. *"Hurt Chicks!"* they cried. Jenny Tate then lined up in the backfield and, after the ball was snapped, took the handoff from the quarterback and sliced through a hole up the middle, gaining almost ten yards before a defender finally grabbed one of the flags that hung from a belt around her waist.

"All right, Tate!"

"Nice run, Tate!"

The offense was running smoothly in practice today, just as it had in the last two games. The PW Purple Weasels were undefeated so far in women's interhall football, with victories over Knott and Pasquerilla East, and their chances seemed good of reaching the goal that had eluded them last season—a shot at the league title. The championship game is always played in the stadium, on the varsity's turf, but to get there requires many hours on the amateur fields behind Stepan Center.

The daily athletic migration at Notre Dame starts as classes end in the middle of each afternoon: Students spill out of the academic buildings in the center of campus and stream toward the gyms and playing fields on its outer rim. The varsity athletes troop east across Juniper Road to the twin-domed ACC and the wide complex of sports facilities it anchors; the rest fan out to intramural practices, pickup games, and solitary workouts. At this school where athletic ability has always been prized, athletes have always been abundant. Back at the turn of the century, before Rockne had even enrolled as a freshman, about half the students played on interhall sports teams; by the 1920s, more than three-quarters were competing, Rockne was bragging about "the best intramural program of any school in America," and some dorm football teams were playing, and beating, other colleges' varsities. The numbers are almost identical now: 82 percent of the men, and 80 percent of the women, participate in organized recreational programs. Coeducation didn't dilute the sports culture of Notre Dame, only broadened it: Many of the women were, like the men, varsity heroes at home in high school, and it seems that a higher-than-usual number of them are the ball-tossing daughters of fathers who have no sons.

Jenny Tate resumed her position in the backfield, ready for the next snap. Back in high school, her sports were basketball, track, and tennis; here her athletic skills were reserved for her intramural dorm teams. She had turned down Harvard for Notre Dame ("I didn't feel at home there"), preceded here by her brother and an uncle. Her home was on the plains of western Kansas, in the remote town of Garden City, where her father was a rancher and her grandfather had presided over the murder trial chronicled in *In Cold Blood*; South Bend, to her, was not the boring backwater it was to some of her classmates. "I'm really enjoying the whole college experience, so I'm trying to prolong it," she said. She was a junior now, but her double major, accounting and English, would probably keep her here for another two years.

Jenny rolled to the left behind the quarterback, who also happened to be her roommate, and, without breaking stride, deftly caught the pitch with one hand. In a game it would have been another first down. The shouts of the other Purple Weasels were drowned out by the tackle grunts and shoulder-pad slams of the men's dorm teams practicing on the next field.

By game time, a few days later, the men were gone, and the women had the field to themselves. "Here we go, Weasels, here we go!" the PW fans chanted in the Sunday dusk at Cartier Field, the weekday-practice home of Lou Holtz's team. Before the Weasels' defense went in, they got some final instructions from their coach, a senior from Flanner Hall.

"When they're in I-formation—everyone know what that is?—they usually run to the strong side of the field," he said. "Megan, if they run trips, you're blitzing."

Farley's Finest, wearing the red flags, were the opponents today, and the Weasels, wearing the yellow flags, went at them as if they were the Michigan Wolverines. Notre Dame's stay-hall residence policy—you stay in the same hall as long as you stay on campus—has created a shadow system of fraternities and sororities: Dorms, the core communities of student life, though tamer and less exclusive than most Greek societies, are objects of similar affection and devotion. They are sources of identity, guardians of bonding rituals, and they inspire their members to take to the playing fields to defend their honor. The men's dorms, with a 130-year head start, have a larger store of accumulated traditions, but intramural sports have helped give the women a chance to catch up.

"C'mon, hold 'em, Weasels!" the fans urged.

The women's teams play flag football—not tackle, like the men—but they sometimes play it with such intensity that it seems as if they, too, should be wearing helmets and pads. It was the occasional violence of the games that kept away Laurie Brink, PW's pacifist rector. She usually welcomed anything that generated this much dorm spirit and unity—anything at all, in fact, that helped women make a place for themselves on a male-dominated campus—but she rarely came out to cheer the Weasels on. She didn't like to watch the women smash into one another.

"Why's there no flag on that?" the PW coach yelled at the official after a Farley defender leveled the Weasels' runner. "That looked like a real good tackle to me."

Neither team had scored yet, and the first half was in its final two minutes, when Jenny Tate caught another long pass—a high, tight spiral right on the money—that moved the Weasels within reach of the goal line. Her roommate had maybe the best arm in the league ("She's in the running for the Heisman," their coach said, although Siegfried's sophomore quarterback was looking strong, too), and she used it again on the last play of the half. A third roommate—cheer, cheer for room 322—caught the pass in the end zone.

"All the way, PW, *woooooooo!*"

The second half was a defensive standoff that did nothing to change the score. The game ended with a 6–0 Weasels victory, pushing their record to 3 and 0. The team converged into an exultant mass of purple T-shirts.

"We are the Weasels," they sang, to the tune of "We Are the Champions," as they headed back home toward the dorm. "No time for losers, 'cause we are the Weasels!"

On the dim, gray morning of the Purdue game, the sky was streaked with drizzle and Lou Blaum's heart was filled with clouds. Only five Irish Guardsmen—the five rookies who had been chosen by Lou and the other, veteran Guardsmen a few weeks earlier—stood at attention in front of Washington Hall for the ritual pregame inspection, somber, still, and tall in their kilts and capes and bearskin hats. Stripped of their regalia like cashiered soldiers, the five veteran Guardsmen were left to mingle instead with the returning alumni. Lou, like the others, wore an Irish Guard sweatshirt and a mask of disappointment. As he fiddled with the low brim of a rookie's high hat, his own head was bare to the rain, protected only by his tight crew cut.

"They were out to get us, no matter how," Lou said about the Office of Student Affairs, the authorities responsible for abruptly ending his career in the Irish Guard. The ruling had come from under the Dome earlier this week, with little warning and no chance for appeal: The five veterans were dismissed from the Guard, the five rookies placed on probation. "There was an attitude they didn't like about the Guard."

The stated reason for the disbandment—the second such action in five years—was "alcohol violations and improper conduct." The unstated reason was that, in the eyes of the administration, the Guardsmen were behaving too much like an exclusive fraternity, and too little like a part of the band; they had once again ventured too deep into their own mythology, a quasi-ROTC brotherhood of private traditions and public partying. The suspension hit Lou especially hard: Just as he was the shortest member of the Guard, barely topping the six-foot-two minimum height requirement, so was he the quietest, the least likely to accompany his fellow Guardsmen out for a night of drinking.

"I was the one at the Northwestern game," Lou said indignantly, referring to an alleged incident of public debauchery that had apparently sparked the administration's action. At a tailgate party at the season opener in Chicago, according to an anonymous source quoted in *The Observer,* one Guardsman was seen pouring a bottle of alcohol down the throat of another Guardsman, whose head was propped back against a tree. "I had the flu, and it was a bottle of Seven-Up. If anyone tried to force anything down my throat, I'd have beaten him up."

In a long letter to *The Observer* published the day before, Lou and his dismissed colleagues had decried the allegations about forced drinking as "heresy and blasphemy at its best," railed against the unjustness of their "manipulative, cowardly, unprofessional conviction," and proudly declared "that we will always be Irish Guardsmen at heart." This morning, they could only stand aside and watch when it was time for the five rookies to march off and collect the band for the parade to the stadium.

The rain picked up as the band, finished with their pregame concert, climbed down the steps of the Main Building and fell into formation. The fans could duck under the spreading arms of the big magnolias for shelter, but the band had no place to hide. Rain trickled down the long blue coat Rachel Stehle wore over her uniform, and it glistened in droplets on her trumpet, washing away her hopes for a reprise of the glorious Michigan weekend. Being in the band—as she was learning today, as she had already learned in practice every day, trying to keep up with all the new steps and new turns and new songs for ninety intense minutes as the director exhorted her and her colleagues to "Make a sound! Make a sound!"—was not all sunshine and pageantry. "In my band back home, I was the hot trumpet," Rachel said, but so was everybody else here, which meant that it was easier to hear now if she missed a note or two. "I think I've gotten better, though."

By the middle of the first quarter, the rain was accelerating into a silent, steady downpour, the Notre Dame offense was bogged down in the mud, and Rachel was sodden on the sidelines, longing for her dry room back in Siegfried Hall. The concessionaires had long since sold out of rain gear, and garbage bags were being pressed into service as ponchos. The only people in the stadium who weren't drenched were the sportswriters and officials in the press box, and the priests and brothers in the sheltered seats beneath it, a section reserved for the Holy Cross community. "You can see how the separation of church and state works here," one priest said. The game was a strenuous test of faith for the fans—a miserable day and a weak opponent, Purdue, who hadn't beaten the Irish since the Faust years—and most of them passed: Few seats were empty. To the true believers, every Notre Dame game is an important Notre Dame game. Just as there are six holy days of obligation each year for practicing Catholics, so are there six equivalent days for practicing Domers—the six home games each season.

At halftime, most of the crowd retreated beneath the stands and lined up for coffee. Rachel and her bandmates slipped and slid in the same mud that had confounded Reggie Brooks and the other Notre Dame running backs, doing their best to keep their turns sharp in a routine that few people were around to watch. The rain drummed a separate, steady rhythm on their white hats, it made the fingering slippery on their instruments, and it kept the applause thin when their show was over. The sun got a bigger hand when it appeared in the middle of the fourth quarter—with Notre Dame up 42–0 and any suspense about the outcome long since drained from the game—but it was soon hidden by clouds again. When the Irish Guard lined up to lead the band out of the stadium at game's end (48–0 was the final score), the sky was still the same leaden hue as Lou Blaum's mood. Lou could only watch from a distance as the five rookie Guardsmen marched out the tunnel and into a future that no longer included him.

"It's a real heartbreaker," he said.

Sweeping out of his Main Building office, bound for his next appointment, Monk Malloy passed under the unblinking eyes of all his predecessors. The walls of the wide third-floor corridor he hurried through were lined with the age-darkened portraits of the sixteen Holy Cross priests who had presided over Notre Dame before him, most of them clad in the imposing black cape and biretta that were once standard features of the order's habit. Malloy wore a simple black suit over a black shirt and a white Roman collar; the absence of color made him look even paler and grayer than he already was. His position meant that he usually had to dress like a priest now, on a campus where the priests—his prepresidential self included—usually dress like professors. The tall, dim halls under the Dome are plagued by the kind of shadows that suggest it's always raining outside, but when Malloy pushed open the heavy front door today he found an afternoon ablaze with autumn.

He trotted down the wide steps—traditionally off-limits to undergraduates back when he was one—and headed across the sunny Main Quad toward Crowley Hall. The trees were loud with leaves of orange and yellow and red, their final cheer before the long gray winter silenced them. In the faces of the students, the change in seasons had already come: As they crossed the quad between classes, many of them wore the dark, hunted look that signaled the approach of midterms. Scrawled on the asphalt walkway was a series of chalk messages, left by a small group of graduate students protesting the lack of a campus day-care center.

"No Birth Control AND No Child Care?" one asked.

As president, Malloy was faced with issues that had barely been dreamed of when he was a student. In the early 1960s—when the unusual size of Hesburgh's vision and drive had become apparent, and the standard six-year presidential term limit had been lifted to accommodate it—Notre Dame was just emerging from its boys'-school slumber, gaining academic respectability and shedding some of the disciplinary habits (11:00 p.m. lights-out, morning-Mass checks) that had earned it a reputation as a "Catholic West Point." Graduate students were few, just over a thousand, and potential day-care clients even fewer. Notre Dame's stature in academia had risen considerably since then, and it was eager now to secure its place among the ranks of the nation's elite universities—in the same tier, perhaps, as Duke and Brown. Large stone monuments had been erected at the campus entrances proclaiming it "A National Catholic Research University," but just what that meant, or how it might be achieved, was still not entirely clear.

Malloy veered into Crowley Hall, a building that had, like him, started out in engineering. It had since housed departments from every school but business—chemistry, law, architecture, and psychology, each one leaving for larger quarters as it, and the university, grew. Music was the current tenant, and the department's faculty were gathered in a classroom, waiting to meet with the president. Malloy sat next to the piano.

"We don't feel we get adequate funding for what we do."

"Year after year, we see students who want to go to Notre Dame, who get into Notre Dame, but who get no aid. We need to get merit scholarships."

"The library is inadequate—that's a gentle word for the situation."

"Tchaikovsky is catalogued in three different spellings."

Malloy absorbed it all, nodding inscrutably, encouraging more. Music was the sixteenth stop on his tour through all the academic departments this semester—a journey meant to sharpen his insights into an institution that was in the midst of an unusually intense bout of self-examination. Because Malloy was eager to listen (even the critics who considered him an autocratic leader conceded that, although they were suspicious about how much he actually heard), and because the faculty, after thirty-five mostly silent years under Hesburgh, were eager to talk, the big questions about Notre Dame's identity and its future were being debated openly, and loudly. More than one hundred people—faculty, administrators, staff, and students, tapped by Malloy to serve on the various Colloquy committees—were spending many long nights in the library's penthouse conference room, trying, in his words, "to determine the priorities and needs for the next stage of the university's development." For the first time anyone could remember, a faculty group had formed to discuss just how Catholic Notre Dame ought to be. The faculty senate was monitoring the progress of the April Accords—the agreement, reached after their threatened vote of no-confidence in Malloy last spring, that was intended to give them a larger voice in the governance of the university.

"I'd like to stand up so I can see everybody better," Malloy said when the chorus of wishes and complaints had ended. He unfolded his long body and stood beside the piano. His boyish haircut—short and tight on the sides, full and tall on top—accentuated his height. He spoke, as is his habit, without a prepared text. Small groups like this are his best forum; his articulate ease often evaporates in front of larger audiences, leaving him sounding stiff and distant. His voice is nearer a pediatrician's—calm, even, soothing, unflappable—than an orator's. What he told the music department was the same thing he had told the other departments, which was the same thing he had also told the board of trustees at their recent meeting—that times were tight everywhere in higher education, and Notre Dame was no exception.

"One of the things I would remind you of is that life is not fair—not that I think that's a good thing," he said. "The university is not equitable. You make less than the faculty in business and engineering—that's just a function of competitive conditions."

He painted them a portrait-by-numbers of the university, in which some of the numbers showed how far Notre Dame had come, and others showed how far it had to go. The endowment was up (to $720 million, the fifteenth largest among the nation's universities), and so was the average faculty salary—$57,000, which went a lot further in South Bend than it would in Cambridge or Palo Alto. (Malloy's own salary was $200,000, which went directly to the Holy Cross community.) The physical plant had grown (seventeen new buildings, thirty-two buildings renovated, ten buildings expanded in the last decade). But applications were down (seventy-six hundred for eighteen hundred spots, down from a peak of ten thousand in 1989).

"If you ask me why they were so high that year, it was probably because we were in the top twenty-five in *U.S. News* and we won the national championship in football."

Like the Catholic gentry it has nurtured, Notre Dame aspires to keep climbing higher in America, and in the world where it wants to be, the *U.S. News & World Report* rankings—based on academic reputation, financial resources, selectivity, and student satisfaction—mean more than the Associated Press football poll. The failure to crack the *U.S. News* top twenty-five again—the most recent survey put it at twenty-six—was more troubling to many people at Notre Dame than the drop in the AP poll (from third to seventh) after the Michigan tie. Its ambitions, the survey showed, still outpaced its resources and its traditions. Sorin, boldly and hopefully, had called his tiny new school a university, but in reality Notre Dame was, for most of its first century, more adept at turning orphans into blacksmiths at its Manual Labor School than it was at grooming scholars in its nominal graduate school. Its soul was always that of a college, the place where a Catholic boy went to gain entry to the professions or the business world. It lacks the deeply entrenched research culture of other, larger universities—the kind that employ legions of professors who never gaze upon an undergraduate, the kind that collect Nobel Prizes the way Notre Dame collects Heismans. It receives less research money than the universities it likes to refer to as its "peer institutions," most of which have, as it does not, large, grant-attracting medical schools.

"They bring in $15,000 more per student a year than we do," Malloy explained—the result of higher endowments, more gifts, more research dollars. "We end up spending $10,000 less per student than they do."

The solution, of course, was more money; the problem, also of course, was where to get it. Raise tuition? It was, at $18,000, about $4,000 less than Notre Dame's chief competitors, but it was an illusory bargain: Financial-aid resources were so much thinner here that it was actually cheaper, if you demonstrated sufficient need, to go to a more expensive school—Duke, for instance, or Georgetown—where the aid packages were more generous. A big tuition hike would leave too many would-be Domers outside the gates. Dip into the endowment? Run a deficit budget? Neither option was palatable at a school that retained the frugal habits of a Depression-hardened immigrant.

"The Notre Dame way," Malloy said, reaching the final option, "and it's always been the Notre Dame way, is to bring in additional sums of money from fund-raising."

Underlying all the institutional reflection at Notre Dame this year, the debate about its character and its future, was the knowledge that the next big fund-raising campaign, the one Malloy was alluding to here, would finally push the total endowment past the billion-dollar mark—an amount so huge, so far removed from Sorin's cash-poor beginnings, that it was hard not to wonder just what kind of school all that money might buy. The Colloquy was sketching the new blueprints, and Malloy outlined some of the recommendations they had been discussing: more financial aid ("We should meet 100 percent of the demonstrated financial need of the students"); 150 new faculty positions; ten new buildings, including a performing-arts center

that the music department was eagerly awaiting; five new doctoral programs, including one in music; a beefed-up library; a replacement for the
campus bookstore, which is much more proficient at selling Notre Dame
T-shirts than it is at selling actual books.

"Nobody has to remind me of that need," said Malloy, whose own tall
bookshelves hold a collection that rivals the bookstore's. "But I would remind you that the paraphernalia part of the store puts lots of money into the
operating budget that we can't afford to lose."

Nor could Notre Dame afford to lose the loyalty of the people who buy
all that paraphernalia—the alumni, who want Notre Dame to stay the way
it is in their golden-hued memories, an intimate place of familiar greetings
between students and professors; the unaffiliated Dome-lovers, who are
drawn here the way European Catholics are drawn to Lourdes, and who
want it to be a rare outpost of truth and beauty in a fallen world; and the
students, who don't want to be left behind as it continues its academic ascent. Malloy said again now what he had said many times before—that
Notre Dame was, is, and always will be primarily an undergraduate institution—but in fact it was the undergraduates who felt the university's growing pains most directly. When teaching loads were lightened, to give faculty
more time for research, one result may have been more publications in
scholarly journals, but another was more crowded classes and more graduate students teaching them. "The declining quality of undergraduate education" was the subject of the two most recent reports submitted by the
student government to the board of trustees, and it was a persistent theme
in campus grumbling. The conservative student magazine had just taken a
nasty public swipe at a professor in the government department—one of
the most crowded departments of all, since it was where a lot of students
landed after organic chemistry persuaded them that maybe they ought to be
lawyers rather than doctors—claiming she neglected her class in favor of her
research.

"The students do have the best interests of the university in mind, I'm
convinced," Malloy said. "But when they say they want smaller classes and
more faculty, they don't say they're willing to be charged $2,000 more each
year to cover it."

The same debate was being repeated throughout the realms of higher education in America—Malloy himself had spoken on the subject at a large
conference Notre Dame had recently hosted, "Storm over the University"—
and it hinged largely on a single issue. "The question is," Malloy said, "what
are the proper responsibilities for the faculty?" Having posed it rhetorically,

Malloy expected no answer—which was fortunate, since the assortment of
opinions on the matter would have consumed the rest of the day, and he
was due now at his next departmental meeting, number seventeen on his
list. The philosophy department—home to some of his sternest critics, a department that declined to participate in the Colloquy process—was waiting
in the faculty lounge in the library. Malloy gathered up his papers and hurried out of the music building, his stride long and fast as he crossed the
campus.

Even after forty years among the insects, George Craig could still get excited about mayflies—tiny creatures that remained adolescent and unformed for even more of their lives than students did, swimming through
ponds as nymphs for two years or more before all emerging at the same
moment for their single day of adulthood, a swarming orgy of mating, egg-
laying, and death. "If you're one day late, you're out of the gene pool," he
said, his voice rising in wonder and awe. "Their internal clocks must be ac-
curate to that day."

He sat at the front of the entomology lab in the basement of the biology
building, facing nine students whose clocks, internal and otherwise, had
managed to get them up for an eight o'clock class on a Monday morning.
Seniors mostly, they were perched attentively on their stools along the lab
tables. The walls had no windows, only large diagrams of insect bodies.
Dead specimens were entombed in shallow glass cases, pinned and labeled
in orderly rows, a collection that gave the room the air of a Victorian
museum.

Craig was discussing some of the evolutionary mechanisms for the isolation of a gene pool—gamete incompatibility, genome incompatibility, hybrid sterility. The law of natural selection was a special passion of his—he
was, after all, a man who celebrated Charles Darwin's birthday each year,
and who kept in his office a stone he had plucked from a pathway at Darwin's home in England—but he was soon led to a new subject that moved
him just as deeply: the achievements of his former students. Another isolat-
ing mechanism, he explained, was hybrid breakdown, where the immediate
offspring of two different species is fertile but later generations are sterile,
and he illustrated it by citing the work of one of his protégés.

"He's now the world authority on insect nervous systems," he said with a
father's pride, "and he sat in the same seat you're sitting in."

In his thirty-five years on the Notre Dame faculty, Craig had spawned a large brood of biologists who, like him, study small creatures. Every year—and there was no reason to think this year would be an exception—at least one of his undergraduates went on to graduate school in entomology. Up on the third floor, in the maze of humid rooms that constitute his Vector Biology Lab, he did the work that had secured his standing as the nation's leading expert on mosquitoes and the diseases they carry. Down here in the basement, he focused on what he still considered the proper responsibility of the faculty—the teaching of undergraduates.

"The rule in a university is, the higher you rise, the less you see undergraduates." Craig had risen very high—an endowed chair, thirty-five years of continuous research funding from the National Institutes of Health, election to the elite National Academy of Sciences, the only Notre Dame professor so honored—but he tried to remain an exception to the rule. "Teaching undergraduates can be an awful waste of time—many are called, few are chosen. But they're Notre Dame's greatest talent pool. Maybe kids like this occur elsewhere, but I don't think so."

Craig was part of the old guard who revered Hesburgh ("the greatest man I will ever know"), but was skeptical about Malloy ("lovely man, bad administrator"). Though he embodied what Notre Dame aimed for in its future—the renowned researcher who was also a gifted teacher—he was also among the loudest voices defending its past. "We have areas of excellence, but we're so far away from being a research university that we embarrass ourselves when we talk about it. Undergraduates are getting a bad deal at Notre Dame now. That report"—the recent student-government report on the state of undergraduate education—"was good, but it missed the target. What it couldn't report was what's in the hearts of assistant professors who've been told over and over again that time spent with undergraduates is wasted."

A veteran iconoclast, Craig had rhetoric as large as his reputation. Up on his desk now was a copy of a letter he had just sent to Malloy, suggesting that a proper way to celebrate the university's sesquicentennial would be to recognize the research efforts of some stellar undergraduates—Craig, naturally, had a few in mind—and to provide some funding to get more of them into the labs. "My emotional commitment to this university is beyond words." A college wrestler himself once, back at Indiana University, he is a devoted fan of all Notre Dame sports, not just football. "I even watch cross-country. I follow them all, because they're our kids and they're competing against other kids. It's like a medieval morality play. I want our kids to win." Hovering amid the mosquito memorabilia in his office is a portrait of Knute Rockne.

"Are you all over twenty-one?" Craig asked the class now, before yielding to the student whose turn it was to give the insect-of-the-day report. Today's specimen was the lovebug, a small, short-lived fly that is shameless in its mating habits.

"Pretty much, they'll fly in this position for three days, which is almost their entire lives," said Dana Ciacciarelli, passing out copies of a drawing that depicted a male and female in awkward flight, connected end to end. "Then the females break away, lay their eggs, and die."

Dana was among the dozen or so undergraduates who had joined Craig on his annual trek north to Wisconsin at the end of last semester. Notre Dame owns a seven-thousand-acre wilderness retreat at Land O'Lakes, on the border of Michigan's Upper Peninsula, that is home to twenty-seven lakes, a favorite fishing spot of Hesburgh's, and an environmental-research center, a favorite teaching spot of Craig's. For two weeks, he watches his students' curious minds roam through a lab far larger than anything the biology building on campus can offer. Swarms of mosquitoes, of course, are native to Land O'Lakes, but lovebugs, as Dana pointed out, are not. They congregate mainly along the highways of the Deep South—lured, it seems, by some strange, seductive elixir produced by the interaction of the vehicle headlights with the exhaust fumes.

"It mimics the organic matter they lay their eggs on, so they're attracted to it," she said.

"If you've ever driven in Georgia or Florida or Alabama when large clouds of these things are flying around, you know that they get all over your car," Craig added. "The females splat all over your windshield, and cleaning it is no small problem."

"The males have bigger eyes," Dana said in conclusion, "presumably for searching for females."

Craig took over again, describing for the class the architecture of an insect abdomen. In a discipline increasingly in thrall to bigger and faster machines, to tissue grinders and other elaborate instruments of genetic technology, Craig retains his faith in the observations you can make with your own eyes. He finds the round stories hidden within the flat data, and by the time he got through the eleven basic segments of the abdomen and finally reached the telson, the flap that marks its posterior, he also somehow reached the saga of the cockroach—among the earliest of all insects, unchanged for 350 million years, one of natural selection's greatest triumphs.

"When we're all gone in a burning atomic pile, probably the last thing left on earth will be a cockroach." This was the kind of fact that moved him deeply, providing as it did still more testimony in behalf of his most endur-ing belief. "How could you not believe in evolution when you see this stuff? It's so overwhelming."

"That's how you fill in the hydrogens around a cyclohexane ring," Geoff Slevin said, using what looked like pieces from a giant Tinkertoy set to build a stick-and-ball model of the molecule in question. "The chair configuration is more stable than the boat configuration."

Though he was just a senior chemical-engineering major, Geoff stood at the head of the lecture hall with an easy assurance, addressing the class with the authority of a professor. The dozens of students in the tiers before him listened closely as he spoke. Sophomores mostly, they were just now slog-ging through the minefield he had already crossed—organic chemistry—and they came to these weekly review sessions with the hope that he would help draw them a good map. A midterm was imminent, and their attention tonight had a quality of dread in it.

"Where does it go stereochemically? Hydrogen goes to the least substi-tuted part of the ring. . . . All right, what's that boron, what are we gonna get? . . . This is just peroxide in general, any kind of peroxide. . . . Any ques-tions about cyclohexane? . . . We're gonna bang through this stuff to get to some reactions, which are the heart of the test."

Geoff volunteered to lead these reviews because he was grateful that someone had volunteered to lead them back when he was taking organic chemistry as a sophomore. He did well in orgo then, and he continued do-ing well in physical chemistry, analytical chemistry, thermodynamics, trans-port phenomena, and all the other required courses for chemical engineers, compiling a 3.6 average that was, he said, "almost golden for a job." When Dana Ciacciarelli—his girlfriend, to use a word he usually avoided—was in Wisconsin with George Craig, he was in Texas, on a coveted summer intern-ship with Exxon. In a grim year for job prospects—the worst in two decades, according to national surveys—he had made the earnest, gray-suited trek to the career-placement office in the library basement more often, and more successfully, than most of his classmates. Interviews with Procter & Gamble and ARCO had gone especially well.

The second of eight children, he grew up in a rambling, old house in Peru, Illinois, where his father was a radio broadcaster. "My father always dreamed of coming here, and I'm living his dream. He sees me here and he cries." Geoff was a loyal, four-year Stanford man; his brother was a sophomore in archrival Keenan. Hanging in his room was an Illinois license plate that read "I AM ND," a door prize from an alumni-club function that he couldn't actually bring himself to attach to his car. "It seems a little vain," he said. (The preferred usage here is "WE ARE ND.") "It's also somewhat gaudy for a Ford Escort."

Geoff and Dana had first met while working in the dining hall as freshmen, but their courtship got off to a fitful start. He had a girlfriend back home; she wasn't interested in acquiring a steady boyfriend so early in her college career. She tried to use a party in her room as an occasion to set him up with one of her friends; he used it instead to ask her to a Stanford dance. After two dates, she stopped returning his phone calls. Back for sophomore year, he asked her to the first Stanford dance of the semester, and she—older and wiser now, no longer afraid of being tied down too young—accepted. They had been going out together ever since.

"Notre Dame women get a bad rap. They're smart, they have self-respect, and when you're eighteen, nineteen, twenty years old, the last thing you want is a girl like that."

The review students watched closely now as Geoff drew on the board a diagram of the type that filled their textbooks and their nightmares. "All right, this is a TTQ, a typical test question," he said. "Name this molecule." Organic chemistry stands at a fateful crossroad in the lives of college sophomores. More than any other class they'll take, it has the power to shape their futures. You need at least a C to keep your chances of getting into medical school alive. Tensions rise and nerves fray with so much at stake, and the material, which is difficult enough, can begin to feel overwhelming. Geoff led them through the problem with calm logic: "Start by looking at the longest chain. . . . Which has the largest molecular weight? . . . Come across this double bond." He then gave them the answer he hoped they had already reached themselves: E–5–cyclohexyl–4–ethyl–1,4 hexadiene.

"It's really easy once you see it, although seeing it the first time is sometimes hard."

It was still hard for him sometimes, too. Earlier this week, he and his partner had pulled a marathon all-nighter to finish a report for their required chemical-engineering lab class—logging on at the computer cluster at seven-thirty on Monday evening, fortifying themselves with vending-machine pretzels, and then finally logging off at one-thirty on Tuesday afternoon, just before it was due. "Freshman year, all I did was study. I pulled a 3.8 both semesters, but I didn't like the kind of person I'd become." He had since found a better balance—volunteering at the pediatric ward at Memorial Hospital, "holding the kids, letting them know they're loved"; becoming a regular, along with most of the other seniors, at the $2.50-a-pitcher nights every Tuesday at Coach's, an off-campus sports bars whose walls were a portrait gallery of old Notre Dame football heroes; leading these review sessions.

"Draw this molecule," he said, writing another TTQ on the board: 4–methyl–2 hexene. "Any questions about that? It's not too complex."

They did have some questions about it, though, and their questions continued even after the session officially ended. They clustered down around Geoff as he worked patiently through their list. When the last student was gone, Geoff put his baseball cap back on his ROTC-short hair and headed out of Nieuwland Science Hall—which had been built partly with patent royalties from Father Julius Nieuwland, the Holy Cross priest and chemist whose work led to the development of synthetic rubber. He had a test tomorrow in music, a rare elective in an engineer's course load, and he still had some symphonies to listen to.

"They're scared to death that if they don't pass there's no med school, no $200,000-a-year salary, no fancy car," he said about the review students. "They just want reassurance, mostly."

The view from the rocking chair tonight—the one that let Brother Bonaventure Scully look out through his always open door and into the eyes of anyone entering Keenan Hall—was as bright as the Fourth of July. The corridor was hung with streamers and balloons, festooned in red, white, and blue for the dorm's fall semiformal. The original plan for the dance's theme was "Top Ten Reasons Why Zahm Sucks," although it wasn't clear just how the rivalry with the neighboring dorm would translate into hall decorations. One of the reasons was "We have Brother Bonaventure and they don't," but Scully dissuaded the students anyway. He suggested a political-convention theme instead—an idea that appealed to the students because it was cheap and easy, and to him because it might get them to think, however briefly, about the world beyond Notre Dame.

"People at Notre Dame can be very microscopic—they think Notre Dame is the only world they're part of." Scully himself had just returned from a hard trip to the world beyond—to the funeral of a young medical student, a former Keenanite, who had died of cancer. Scully had been in touch with him all through his illness, and had spoken to him not long before he died. "At times like that, I'm glad I'm not an atheist."

As the dorm filled with people and noise, it became clear that, convention bunting aside, the party in question tonight was not the political kind. A constant stream of traffic moved through the halls—Keenan men and their dates commuting from the scattered room parties, where the alcohol was, down to the basement lounge, where the food and the DJ and the dance floor were, and then back up again. The stairwells echoed with an unfamiliar sound in this all-male preserve—the click of high heels and the rustle of stockings. Whenever a room door opened, a sudden roar would escape, like a cheer erupting in a stadium. Downstairs, the DJ played a song by The Cure, "Friday I'm in Love."

Keenan's semiformal was just one of the fifteen on campus this weekend, the peak of the fall social calendar. SYR is the more familiar name for these dances, an acronym for "screw your roommate": By tradition your roommate was supposed to set you up for the night, and by tradition that also meant your chances were good of getting a date-from-hell. Each dorm is allowed two hall-wide dances a semester, one SYR and one formal. Because they are prohibited on football weekends, and are undesirable around exam times, they tend to cluster into weekends like this, when the whole campus finally seems to have a date.

The rituals preceding the kickoff of an SYR weekend are, in contrast to those preceding a football weekend, largely private and quiet. All through the late afternoon, young men lined up at the florist in the basement of the LaFortune Student Center to buy flowers for their dates—a carnation if it was casual, a rose if it was more serious, whether actually or only hopefully. On their way in and out, they mostly ignored the folk dancers on Fieldhouse Mall, a performance that was part of the Multicultural Fall Festival; the only folk dances that interested them now were the ones they would do tonight to the accompaniment of "Brown-Eyed Girl," "Paradise by the Dashboard Light," and all the other timeworn favorites that constituted the obligatory soundtracks of most local parties. In the expectant evening hours, the Main Quad was quiet enough so that you could hear, rising from the music building, the faint strains of the weekly practice session of Voices of Faith, the student gospel choir. "My mind's made up," they sang, over and over again, "no turning back." In the dorms, you could hear, rising from behind the closed doors up and down the halls, the steady drone of showers and blow dryers.

Couples started crisscrossing the quads sometime after ten, when the Sacred Heart bells had finished their nightly rendition of the alma mater. The men mostly wore the standard SYR uniform—blue blazer and khakis (job-interview suits were reserved for formals). The women's wardrobes were more varied, but short, tight, and black were common elements. The status of each couple's relationship could be measured by the distance they kept between them as they walked: The certified boyfriends and girlfriends marched in tight, arms-around-shoulders lockstep; the kinda-sorta-maybe-almosts walked as close as they could without actually touching; the blind dates and the chemistry-class acquaintances were separated by a wide and wary gap, the women with their arms crossed in front, as if to ward off the chill. Rooms grew cramped and sweaty, windows flew open, stereos blasted out: R.E.M.'s "It's the End of the World As We Know It (And I Feel Fine)," Frank Sinatra's "Love and Marriage."

For most of its life, Notre Dame had done its best to prohibit just these kinds of activities, enforcing a code of behavior so rigid that the result was, as Hesburgh once acknowledged, "a kind of cross between a boot camp and reform school." Students, as was their nature, craved freedom and pleasure; the priests, as was their job, gave them discipline and virtue. Sorin had promised parents that the students were "never left, either day or night, without a prefect," and he was quick to expel anyone found in the officially off-limits, and thus presumably sinful, districts of South Bend. Drunkenness was grounds for dismissal, and in the 1870s Notre Dame became the first Catholic college with a campus chapter of the Total Abstinence Society, a national temperance group. "The discipline is paternal," the university cata-logue declared in 1908, "and aims at giving young men the fullest liberty consistent with earnest study and manly Christian character." According to the 1938 student manual, "the ideal of the University" at Notre Dame meant "a college home in which young men who value clean character even more than a well-stored mind associate with their fellows under the influence of gentlemen." Up until the early 1960s, the main light switch in each dorm was turned off at eleven each night; everybody had to be in his dorm by the midnight curfew (it was extended to 12:30 a.m. on Saturdays, to give them time to get back from St. Mary's); and female guests were permitted in the rooms only on football Saturdays, for an hour before and after the game, with the door open.

The wide sweep of the 1960s made these rules seem unnaturally narrow and petty, and they were gradually relaxed. By the 1970s, dorm parties were being lubricated by kegs in the rooms and cocktail bars in the corridors. But the administration eventually tightened its grip again, and its announce-ment in 1984 of a revised, more restrictive alcohol policy sparked a raucous march on the Main Building that evoked—in size, at least, if not in seriousness—the campus antiwar protests of 1969 and 1970. The students drinking at tonight's SYRs were well aware that any violation of the implicit rule at the heart of the current policy—don't throw up in public—could land them in the dreaded office at the east end of the Main Building's third-floor hallway, waiting for a Student Affairs official to hear their confessions and assign them their penance; more than half of all the discipline cases handled there were alcohol-related. The shadow of authority reached off-campus as well: Local police had raided several student-apartment complexes and bars already this semester, issuing almost two hundred citations for underage drinking.

At midnight in the southeast turret of Sorin Hall, a crush of bodies moved in the lucid orange light to the beat of "I'm Free," the Soup Dragons' remake of the old Rolling Stones song. In the northeast turret, by the pale light of his desk lamp, Monk Malloy sat working on a speech. It was the annual President's Address to the Faculty, to be delivered next week to an audience that was, at this hour, far away from any SYR activity. Last year he had used the Faculty Address to launch the Colloquy for the Year 2000; this year he was reiterating most of the same points he had been making on his rounds of departmental visits. "We have made great progress in the last two decades," he wrote, "but our budgetary base is simply too low."

Malloy had traded his black suit and collar for civilian clothes—chinos, V-neck sweater, button-down shirt open at the neck. He had spent the evening at a rehearsal dinner for the wedding he was presiding at tomorrow, and for which he still had to write a homily tonight. He also had a second homily to write, for the big Mass closing the year of sesquicentennial celebrations, and he had a book to read for his freshman seminar, Nadine Gordimer's *My Son's Story*.

"I close the door and I can't hear a thing," he said.

The next night, Saturday night, when the SYRs had moved into the women's dorms, Laurie Brink sat in her lookout chair in her room in Pasquerilla West, watching the traffic on the party-room-to-dance-floor circuit. Only clear drinking cups were permitted in the halls, so she could see what was in them, and any that weren't clear caught her eye quickly. "You say 'No drinking in the hall,' and if they say 'It's only Coke,' it probably is," she said about her strategy for separating the imbibers from the abstainers, the sinners from the saints. "But if they say 'OK,' you know it was alcohol." The identities of the passing men were not as readily decipherable, so differently were they dressed now from the way they dressed in her seminar class. "I didn't know some of them had hair," she said, so accustomed was she seeing them in their ubiquitous baseball caps. "They never take their hats off."

Women generally lavish more attention on SYR decorations than men, and tonight each section of PW was dressed up like a different board game—Life, Clue, even Candyland, a reminder of just how near to childhood college really is. "It's the biggest babysitting job of the whole semester," Brink said of the SYR. "You want them to have fun, but you don't want to let them know that you want them to have fun." She had already thwarted the intended fun of one room party, confiscating their supply of Jell-O shots—morsel-sized cubes of grape Jell-O, spiked with grain alcohol. "They were indignant. They kept saying, 'Well, what's the policy on Jell-O shots, anyway? It's not in *Du Lac.*' "

Two women came bounding up the stairs from the front door, barely able to contain their laughter. "Our dates were bad," one explained to a sectionmate who was on her way down.

"It was not good," the second concurred.

"I only went out with him because I know all his friends."

"Let's go celebrate."

In Walsh Hall, on the Main Quad, the SYR theme was old TV shows—*Fantasy Island, The Munsters, Sesame Street.* Down in the basement, where the DJ was playing the Village People's "Y.M.C.A.," the dancers formed the letters with their arms every time the chorus came around. Up in the *Hawaii Five-O* corridor, a Walsh woman and her date were in the middle of a heated version of what was sometimes known as a DTR (Define the Relationship), one of those intense, apocalyptic arguments about an entity that one of them really wasn't sure even existed in the first place—namely, "us."

"Would you come over here and talk to me?" the woman asked sharply.

"What am I supposed to do?" the man wondered grimly.

"This is so stupid. It's not gonna get resolved like this."

At 2:00 a.m., the witching hour of parietals, the exodus began—the men finally expelled from the women's dorms, spilling out all at once in crowds that recalled their great-grandfathers streaming up out of the subway exits at the old Notre Dame–Army games. They were left to wander across the quads, still searching for the promised land. Some had wrapped their neckties around their heads, the swashbuckler-prep look.

"Was her name Kristen or Kirsten?"

"No, don't go up there, that's LaFortune. You're lucky you found us— you'd never get back."

" 'Who knew?' What a great phrase—'Who knew?' "

"I started saying, 'Yeah, what of it?' and I started jumping on the record. Dude kicked my ass out."

"I'm so pissed, I'm so pissed right now, I'm so pissed."

In the shadows by the Center for Social Concerns building, a couple was locked in a deep clinch. Amid the good-nights at Pasquerilla West's front door, another couple stood shaking hands for much too long. It was the woman who finally broke the impasse, leaning over to peck her date on the cheek; he left, fairly loping, with a goofy smile on his face. Down in the South Quad, the walkways in front of Pangborn Hall were done up like Hollywood Boulevard—adorned with paper stars, each one inscribed with the names of a couple at the dorm's SYR tonight. A cold, thin drizzle had started to fall, and it was already blurring some of the stars, proving them as ephemeral as most of the couples they commemorated.

"Hey, here's ours," one man called to his date as he bent over to inspect their star. "How do you spell your name? Did they spell it right?"

6

Two by two, rank upon rank, the priests slowly appeared on the arena floor, dozens of them, hands folded, white albs flowing, a long, solemn line emerging from the tunnel for the entrance procession. The crowd this afternoon at the basketball arena in the ACC was smaller than a pep rally, and quieter. A cloud of smoke collected up beneath the dome, rising from the censers of the acolytes, not the cigarettes of fans. Great waves of triumphal music swelled from the student groups ringing the floor—the Concert Band, the Glee Club, the Chorale, the Liturgical Choir, the Folk Choir, the Women's Chorale. The procession moved up the center aisle toward the stage, where the altar was set, the priests bowing in pairs when they reached the foot of the steps and then moving off to their places on the side. Father Malloy was the last in line. His gait as he climbed to the altar was steady and deliberate, nothing at all like the bounding trot he used when climbing the steps to the Main Building.

"As we joyfully conclude the 150th anniversary of the University of Our Lady," he said in his introduction, "we renew within us the spirit and vision of Father Sorin."

Malloy, as the chief administrator of Notre Dame, also served, symbolically at least, as its chief priest—called to the altar whenever there was an occasion (and there were many) that required a big Mass. When a graduate student had died earlier in the semester—of an overdose of pills he was taking for depression, an apparent suicide—it was Malloy who presided at the funeral. When two members of the women's swim team were killed in a bus crash the previous winter, and weeping students flocked to Sacred Heart—

83

first for a memorial Mass, so crowded that the priests ran out of communion wafers, and then for a funeral—it was Malloy who led their prayers. He
made the rounds of Sunday-night Masses in the dorm chapels, and most
Mondays he said the daily lunchtime Mass at Sacred Heart. And today, using Sorin's chalice again, he was the presider and homilist at the Mass marking the end of the year-long sesquicentennial celebration.

"We're here to remember how small our beginnings really were," Malloy
said in his homily, and to honor the "courage and dedication and zeal of our
ancestors."

There were many times, Malloy told the crowd, when the chances seemed
slim that Notre Dame would ever reach its next semester, let alone its 150th
birthday. "There were years when it almost closed for indebtedness," he
said. A cholera epidemic in the mid-1850s killed dozens of students and
community members; to avoid a campus-clearing panic, many of the victims were buried quietly, under the cover of night. (Some Protestant opponents attributed the outbreak to Catholicism; Sorin blamed it on the marshy
breeding grounds around the lakes. He had the marshes drained, and the
plague lifted.) A fire in 1879 almost killed the school itself—destroying the
Main Building, four other buildings, and thirty-seven years of work in just
three hours. After surveying the damage, Sorin—sixty-five by then, and
wearing a long, white beard that lent him a prophetic authority—spoke
from the altar of Sacred Heart, which was spared by the flames. "If it were *all*
gone," he said, uttering a rallying cry that was soon emblazoned in Notre
Dame lore, "I should not give up!"

A large American flag hung from the high ceiling as Malloy spoke, a display that would have pleased Sorin. "The road to America seems clearly to
me the road to heaven," Sorin had written before leaving France for Indiana, and he embraced his new home with an immigrant's fervent, grateful
patriotism. He ended the 1845 academic year by declaring the Fourth of July
a school holiday and inviting local dignitaries to a campus ceremony that included a band concert and a reading of the Declaration of Independence. He
named Washington Hall after America's first president, and his political
hero. During the Civil War, he sent eight Holy Cross priests to serve as
chaplains with the Union Army. When the Main Building was rebuilt after
the fire, he commandeered a muralist from the Vatican and commissioned
a twelve-painting series depicting the life of Christopher Columbus for the
entrance hall. Among the priests and brothers who served as models for
the artist was Sorin himself. In the final panel, the deathbed scene, Sorin's
face is the face of Columbus, the man who had found America before he

did. "From the moment he landed on our shores, he ceased to be a for-
eigner," the archbishop of St. Paul once wrote about Sorin. "At once he was
an American, heart and soul."

Notre Dame arrived with the first big wave of Catholic immigrants to this
Protestant nation, and it grew as they grew, coming to embody their story,
and to serve as their capital, more fully than any other institution. The Holy
Cross order, unlike the Jesuits, had no long centuries of tradition trailing
them here from Europe, and no wide network of schools to diffuse their energies. They were free to build a new tradition in this remote, unlikely
place—a tradition rooted more in the New World than the Old. From the
beginning, Sorin conceived of Notre Dame as something beyond just a
school, with a presence and influence beyond just Indiana: American
Catholics, he hoped, would look to it as a kind of *ex officio* outpost of the
Vatican. His Notre Dame published *Ave Maria*, a popular devotional journal with a national readership; was a leading American distributor of holy
water from Lourdes; and even built its own Grotto behind Sacred Heart, a
rocky replica of Lourdes that now blazes with votive candles on the eve of
big exams and big games. It commemorated the Catholic past in Bishop's
Memorial Hall in the Main Building, a large collection of portraits, busts,
chalices, miters, croziers, documents, and assorted other artifacts of American church history; and it honored the Catholic present by bestowing an annual award, the Laetare Medal, on a leading American Catholic. Sorin, like
Hesburgh after him, rose to a position where he was accorded the respect, if
not the title, of a bishop. "I know of no other institution which, while it is so
thoroughly Roman in its doctrine, is so completely American in its spirit,"
the archbishop of Chicago said in his sermon at Notre Dame's Diamond Jubilee in 1917.

As part of this sesquicentennial year, all of the nation's bishops had converged on campus for their big annual meeting, a reminder that—despite
the sprawling, fragmented state of the modern church—Notre Dame still
stands at some unique juncture where Rome and America intersect. It remains, as Hesburgh liked to say, "the place where the church does its thinking," a place whose experience of the 1960s was shaped less by the Berkeley
Free Speech Movement then by the Second Vatican Council. It attracts
every stripe of Catholic—severe traditionalists from Opus Dei; vow-of-
poverty liberals from the Catholic Worker movement; vigilant prolife protesters; Pax Christi radicals who spill blood on missiles; Holy Spirit–seeking
charismatics; Thomas Merton mystics; Virgin Mary devotees who believe in
the visions at Medjugorje, the popular but officially unrecognized Bosnian

shrine; advocates of opening the priesthood to women and married men; worshipers to whom an ideal Mass is a lavish, smells-and-bells production in a gilded church, and worshipers to whom it is a simple liturgy in a spare chapel; and, maybe the largest contingent of all, moderate, prosperous suburbanites who watch the games on Saturdays, go to Mass on Sundays, usually vote Republican, use methods of birth control unsanctioned by the pope, and whose daughters, without their knowledge, sometimes have abortions. And all of them, to some degree, expect Notre Dame to reflect their vision of Catholicism. During the bishops' meeting, Cardinal John O'Connor of New York refused to stay on campus with his colleagues, retreating instead to an off-campus motel: He was protesting the university's decision to award the Laetare Medal to Daniel Moynihan, the New York senator whose public stance on abortion was in opposition to the church's.

After communion, Malloy led the congregation in a special rite of renewal—something along the lines of a renewal of marriage vows, except that here the objects of the pledge were, as he said, "the three ideas at the core of the university."

"We renew our commitment," they recited, following him in the program, "to freedom of inquiry and expression in the search for truth . . ."

". . . to belief which should widen, not narrow, our search for truth . . ."

" . . . to be a community which nourishes both inquiry and belief. . . ."

"May Our Lady, Notre Dame, pray for us, and may her Son sustain us in this resolve. Amen."

When they were finished, they sang, as always, the alma mater. "Someone once asked me," a campus priest recalled later, " 'When we sing this, are we singing to the Mother of God or are we singing to the university?' I said, 'Yes!' That's the only answer possible."

Sometime around the middle of each football season, a low, dense permacloud settles over South Bend like a bad mood—a claustrophobic ceiling that blocks the sun for days, even weeks, at a time. It made today the same color as yesterday, the same color, probably, as tomorrow, too: a drab, featureless gray. Claire Johnson wore only a Notre Dame sweatshirt and blue jeans against the morning chill. A small gold cross hung around her neck. She marched in a circle with maybe two dozen fellow members of the Right to Life club, saying the rosary aloud—a smaller, quieter showing than the protesters at the Clinton speech.

"Hail Mary, full of grace," they prayed in unison, "the Lord is with thee.

Blessed art thou amongst women, and blessed is the fruit of thy womb, Jesus. . . ."

They were in a small office plaza just east of campus, not far from a McDonald's hung with Notre Dame memorabilia. Most students who came out to this stretch of highway were lured by the Big Macs, a welcome respite on nights when the dining hall served the dreaded meatless baked ziti. Claire was drawn instead by a bland brick building that was home to the Women's Pavilion, South Bend's only abortion clinic. Friday mornings like this one, as well as Tuesday mornings and Wednesday afternoons, were what she called "kill days"—days when abortions were performed, and when the pro-life protesters tried to make themselves visible.

". . . Holy Mary, Mother of God, pray for us sinners, now and at the hour of our death. Amen. Hail Mary, full of grace . . ."

The protesters stayed on the street, off the clinic's private property, and out of the custody of the watching police. Claire had spent many hours in front of abortion clinics in several states, and she knew just what would get you arrested where. "South Bend is a difficult place to do rescues," she said. Her one local rescue—a tactic in which protesters try to prevent women from having abortions by blocking a clinic entrance—had cost her, she said, five days in jail. Next week she was due in court in Champaign, Illinois, to face charges stemming from a rescue operation she had participated in last spring: She and two other Notre Dame students were among seventy-three protesters arrested for blockading a clinic there on Good Friday.

"All we really want to do is make our presence known," she said of to-day's demonstration. "We want women going into the clinic to know that there are alternatives other than abortion."

Claire wanted to make their presence known not only at the clinic, but also on the campus, where, she believed, too little energy was spent on the issue of abortion. The equation was clear in her mind: The Catholic church opposes abortion, Notre Dame is a Catholic institution, therefore Notre Dame should, loudly and publicly, oppose abortion. "I think Notre Dame's probably as prolife now as it ever was, which isn't saying much." Like Cardinal O'Connor, she was outraged at the identity of the latest Laetare winner. "There's no justification for giving Moynihan a medal as an exemplary Catholic. He's on excommunication lists all over."

"Our Father, who art in heaven," they prayed now, "hallowed be thy name. . . ."

Claire was so immersed in prolife activities that she had almost left be-hind the life of a student. She had missed the SYR at her dorm, Farley Hall, for an off-campus meeting. Her classwork was piling up—a lab to finish for physics, vocabulary to learn for German, reading to do for theology, terms to memorize for her two biology classes, vertebrate physiology and cell biology. "It's more important to me to follow my conscience and be a good Christian than to be a student." She was planning to join some more rescues soon, and she was just starting work on her big project for the year—helping to bring to campus a national prolife conference, sponsored by the same group that had sponsored the Champaign rescue, CALL, Collegians Activated to Liberate Life, based in Madison, Wisconsin.

"I think about leaving a lot—I'm not sure this is where God wants me to be right now," she said. Staying at Notre Dame would keep her on her tentative career path—to teach biology in high school, or, perhaps, to work in a diocesan prolife office. Leaving would free her to plunge full-time into a prolife activist group, like CALL. "If He doesn't want me here at Notre Dame, I'll go."

A man crossed the parking lot from his car to the clinic entrance, presumably to join a woman already inside. "Get her out of there," a protester shouted. "We can help you find a different way."

The man responded with silence, the sound that lingers in the middle of most discussions about abortion at Notre Dame. Many words are spoken about the issue here, but few are really heard: Too many minds are already made up, and the implicit moral weight of the institution itself lies too heavily on one side. The landscape of opinion is actually as varied here as anywhere else, but the rhetoric is so polarized, the language so harsh, that it has cut a wide gorge between the sides that seems all but unbridgeable. "You can't debate belief," one prochoice professor explained.

The voices on the prolife side are far from unanimous. Few are as extreme in their views, or their actions, as Claire. Some are hard-liners—opposed to any abortion, any time—who want their beliefs translated into law, but who are also opposed to the militant strategies of the rescue movement. Some walk the line that Mario Cuomo drew in the landmark speech he made here on the issue in 1984: They believe abortion is wrong, but they do not believe that gives them the right to make it illegal. Some take what they call the "seamless-garment" approach: You can't be against abortion, they believe, if you are not also for a society that—in its policies on health care, day care, maternity leave, job protection, and other related issues—values and aids a woman's decision to have children. Some are public in their beliefs—offering prayers for the unborn, for instance, during the general intercessions at the dorm Masses—and some are private.

The voices on the prochoice side mostly stay private. Student polls usually show a pretty even split on the issue, but you wouldn't know it from the letters column of the student newspaper, *The Observer*: Prolife letters predominate, and any writer who offers a prochoice opinion is quickly met by a wave of rebuttals. A letter that chided the prolife protesters at Bill Clinton's speech as "rude, intolerant and immature" was soon answered by another defending them as "true Roman Catholics" exercising "their first amendment rights at a Catholic university by asking for the redress of 27 million dead children." The six women interviewed by law professor Teresa Phelps for a recent law-review article—all Catholic, all members of the Notre Dame academic community—all identified themselves as prochoice, but they were speaking under a shield of anonymity: Faculty members are often wary of broadcasting views they fear could hurt them in tenure and promotion decisions, despite administration assurances to the contrary. "What language can one find," Phelps wondered in her article, "The Sound of Silence Breaking: Catholic Women, Abortion, and the Law," "that balances the critical values in the abortion controversy without either mindlessly mouthing the position taken by the Church hierarchy or sounding hopelessly secular?"

By midmorning, the protesters were drifting away from the Women's Pavilion. Their strategy is to arrive early, before the day's first patients, and then try to dissuade the entering women from having abortions, or else steer them instead toward Pregnancy Life Line, the abortion-alternative group in the building next door. They claimed one save for the day—a woman who, they said, left before having an abortion. "It encourages us to continue doing what we're doing," Claire Johnson said, getting ready for a long walk back to campus (she had no car).

"Maybe I'm kidding myself, but I don't think Notre Dame students come here," she said. "Not that Notre Dame and St. Mary's students don't have abortions, but I don't think I've ever seen one here." She may not have seen them—maybe they came when she wasn't there, or had faces she didn't recognize, or successfully concealed themselves when passing the prayer vigil—but some of her classmates did in fact come to the Women's Pavilion, and they came for reasons very different from hers.

Even after the Clinton visit—the epic event that had put them at center stage for a brief, euphoric moment, and had made them feel, for once, like a legitimate campus organization—the local chapter of the College Democrats still maintained its nerve center in the modest quarters of room 309 in

Cavanaugh Hall. This was the room that Vice-President Andrew Runkle shared with a cast-off couch, a battered recliner, a fish tank (the pair of white mollies were named Bill and Hillary, the black pair were Al and Tipper), an ample collection of R.E.M. CDs, two real roommates, and two semipermanent squatters—fellow Vice-President Chris Setti, who lived down the hall, and President Andrew Holmgren, who technically lived in Fisher Hall but might as well have had his mail delivered here. Room 309 was where they plotted their strategy, prepped for their debates, wrote letters to campus journals, and took requests for campaign buttons, stickers, and posters. It was where they talked about George Bush in the past tense. It was where they hatched the plot whose results they were now sharing with their fellow College Democrats at a meeting in the Center for Social Concerns.

Andrew Holmgren stood on the auditorium stage and started the videotape. "We went to a prolife meeting to voice our opinion that you could be both prolife and pro-Clinton," he explained as the TV monitor showed a local news report about the guerrilla action the Democrats had recently staged. Several members of Collegians Activated to Liberate Life had come to campus to speak to prolife students, and several members of the College Democrats had—quietly, with no invitation or notice, having informed only the TV crew of their intentions—joined the audience. In the middle of the meeting, when the Democrats stood to challenge the prolife speaker, the TV lights went on. "I think I can be prolife and vote for Clinton and still go to heaven, believe it or not," one woman said, captured on tape for the evening news.

The invasion of the CALL meeting had represented a payback of sorts for the prolife heckling at Clinton's speech, and the tape of it ended to a round of cheers from the members at tonight's meeting. The Right to Life group had greeted the action with a different sound: a "publicity stunt" is what they called it in a full-page ad in *The Observer*, "a bold move to silence whose who do not share their political views." "We will not be silenced," the ad vowed.

It was a small, sweet victory for the Democrats, but, as Andrew Holmgren reminded them now, it was still too soon to celebrate. "I'm a little disappointed in the numbers tonight," he said, his measured voice shaped by a broad Boston accent. The group's first meeting of the semester had been standing-room-only; tonight, with the glamour and excitement of Clinton's visit long since dissipated, only a few dozen seats were occupied. "Now more than ever, we need to show our numbers."

Chris Setti joined him onstage to discuss the group's pre-election plans—a rally on Fieldhouse Mall, a voter-registration drive, a pizza party to watch the televised Clinton-Bush debate, a debate of their own with the College Republicans. Andrew Runkle stayed offstage, his preferred venue.

"It should be like watching Notre Dame play Purdue," Chris said of their upcoming debate, hoping for a similar rout.

Chris and the two Andrews—Holmgren and Runkle—were, unsurprisingly for Democrats, a diverse trio. Holmgren was the calm, unflappable history major who, unlike many history majors, wasn't too interested in law school. He had a goatee that came and went through the year—it was gone right now—and he usually got the recliner in Runkle's room. Chris was a wired, fast-talking government major from California, closely tied to the Center for Social Concerns crowd. He was taking Italian this year, hoping to learn it well enough to speak it with his father, who had learned it as a boy in Italy. Runkle was a premed in the honors program who had spent some time on *The Observer*'s police beat. His dry wit was the element that leavened the mixture. The three tended to travel together, even when not on party business. They were frequently sighted off-campus at Chili's, Chi-Chi's, and Taco Bell. In South Dining Hall recently, in the company of some friends, they had gathered around a long table near the large *Last Supper* mural and, draped in bedsheet togas, assumed the positions of Jesus and the disciples. For their next group photo they planned to attempt a Nativity scene.

Holmgren turned the meeting over to the members, asking for suggestions. "When they put up those crosses," one student offered, referring to the annual prolife ritual of planting a campus lawn with small white gravemarkers, "why don't we put coat hangers on them?"

So radical was the suggestion, so far outside the bounds of normal daily discourse here, that it triggered an audible gasp in the room. To be a Democrat at Notre Dame was not necessarily to be prochoice, and the group was not given to such militant gestures. "Some people want it to be a prochoice club," Chris said later, "but that can't happen." They quickly moved on to safer suggestions, like more window posters for the dorms.

Holmgren ended the meeting with a call to arms, reminding the troops that, for the first time in a generation at Notre Dame, a Democratic victory might actually be within reach. "I honestly believe we can win the campus," he said, before opening up the T-shirt sales. The shirts were emblazoned with a red-white-and-blue Clinton logo. "Wear it under something," he said, gently taunting them. "Be brave. Show how gutsy you are as Democrats."

Kevin Kuwik was still reeling from the coat-hanger remark when he came up to buy his T-shirt. "Can you believe he said that?" he asked no one in particular. Though only a freshman, he had already tasted more politics than most of the other members. He came to it by birth, hailing from the steel towns near Buffalo, where his grandfather had owned a bar and his father was an Erie County legislator who ran on three ballot lines: Democrat, Conservative, Right-to-Life. His last name was all Polish, like his father, but his first name was all Irish, like his mother. "I personally don't like stereotypes, but I still really think that the Republican Party is the party of big shots. The Democratic Party is not necessarily just middle-class, but it is middle-class-oriented."

As Chris and the two Andrews headed back to room 309, Kevin walked across the dark campus to his room in Fisher Hall. He had papered his ceiling there with football photos clipped from the newspaper, and hung the wall with pennants: Buffalo Bills, New York Yankees, Dallas Cowboys, and, most important, Notre Dame. On the wood of his loft bed he had written the scores of the varsity games so far this season: The recent Stanford score was the hardest to write, a shocking 33–16 loss that had killed any lingering hopes for a national championship.

It was a football weekend—the trip he made out here for the Air Force game when he was a freshman in high school—that had sold Kevin on Notre Dame. "I said, 'Dad, I'd really like to come here,' and he said, 'All right, if you start saving right now, maybe you'll have enough money for bus fare.' " He came up with the grades, and the Army came up with the money. In return for an eight-year commitment to serve as an officer in the Army Reserves, he got a full, four-year ROTC scholarship to Notre Dame. "I was militarily clueless. No one in my family is in the military." When his freshmen classmates were busy unpacking their stereos back in August, he was learning the Army alphabet, tossing practice grenades, and traversing a rope bridge strung across a corner of St. Mary's Lake. He spent the big SYR weekend at Field Training Exercises at Fort Custer, Michigan, eating corned-beef hash from an MRE packet, an appetizing Meal-Ready-to-Eat ration. At six-forty-five tomorrow morning, an hour that most students don't know even exists, he would be at PT, Physical Training, running laps and doing push-ups.

Hanging at eye level on the wall Kevin's desk faced was a yellow Post-it note with a single word printed on it: "FOCUS." "But if I'm looking at it, then I'm not focusing." He was majoring in mechanical engineering—he hoped to fulfill his reserve duty in the Army Corps of Engineers—and carrying the same heavy course load that had once convinced Monk Malloy to switch majors to English. He had to keep a 3.0 average to keep his scholarship; so far he had seen only one grade that wasn't an A.

"It was the first thing I didn't do as well as I wanted on," he said of his last physics test. He got a 48 out of 50 on the first test, but only a 41 on the second. Physics was the book open on his desk now. Stacked nearby were the books for his other classes—calculus, engineering concepts, theology, and Brother Bonaventure Scully's Freshman Seminar. When the physics was finished, he still had some reading to do for Scully's class—*The Violent Bear It Away*, a short novel by Flannery O'Connor.

"She gets your attention with stories," Scully said in class the next morning about O'Connor. He had relocated the seminar from a classroom in DeBartolo to the basement lounge of Keenan Hall, the dorm where he was rector. "And inherent in her story is a theme. That's the way she lives, thinks, and sees—she's not trying to convert anybody." He was helping them unearth the deep vein of religious faith that lay beneath the strange and dark surface of O'Connor's work. "What Flannery O'Connor believed was that the presence of God works in the least expected circumstances."

The discussion moved around the room and through the cast of characters in *The Violent Bear It Away*. "He used him as a chance to regain this lost son, and to take him in as his own," Kevin Kuwik said of one character.

"I thought that he was resisting baptism," said Kathleen Bergin, who was sitting across from Kevin, about another. "It just so happened that he killed him while he baptized him."

Kathleen, like Kevin, had been up early that morning—reporting to her job in the dining hall at seven to chop vegetables for two hours—and that night, after Scully's class and all her others were done for the day, she, too, found herself talking politics, but at a forum less partisan than a College Democrats meeting. Her dorm was Pangborn, right next door to Fisher; it was the newest women's dorm on campus, having undergone a sex-change operation over the summer. Her room was in the basement, which the men had called Skid Row, but the women had dubbed The Dungeon. Her door was open, and in these days before the election, that was an invitation to a political debate. Opinions drifted in and out.

"I think Clinton's promising way too much. He's trying to please too many people."

"I really want to vote for Perot."

"I think Perot is a joke. I laughed so hard at that last debate."

"The thing with Bush is that he doesn't want to do anything for anybody, and Clinton wants to do everything for everybody."

"I'm afraid this election is who's the best of the worst."

Kathleen had already voted by absentee ballot, for Clinton. "I'm prolife, but I'm not so prolife that I don't understand Clinton's position. There are so many other things you have to look at, you can't just go on a single issue."

Her father had been raised on a ranch in Nevada and came to Notre Dame on a ROTC scholarship. He returned to Reno after he retired from the Army as a lieutenant colonel. Though she went to the same small Catholic high school he had, she was reluctant at first to come to the same college. Once she got here, though, Notre Dame had quickly won her over. "At the first football game, it was like, 'We're at Notre Dame, I can't believe it. It doesn't get any better than this.' "

The discussion moved in stages up to the first-floor TV lounge, out across the quad toward LaFortune; the Acoustic Cafe was in session in the basement there tonight, a popular weekly forum for student performers.

"He reminds me of Kennedy."

"I think taxes are gonna go up, and the middle class is going to take the brunt of it."

"Clinton said the upper class are the ones who will feel it."

"I'm sure the middle class will be affected."

"Bush just looks like a tired old man. It's so pathetic."

"I can't see George Bush remembering what it was like to be a college student. That was like fifty-seven thousand years ago, in the Stone Age."

"I don't want to get out in the real world and have nothing there for me. That scares me."

They stepped down into the LaFortune basement, where the uncertainties of politics were soon washed away by the more reliable rhythms of an acoustic guitar.

"She has amazing legs. She runs like every day."

"I hate like all the cliques and stuff, so I refuse to be part of one. I'm sort of part of a bunch of different cliques."

"He likes me. I know you don't think so, Mary, but he really does."

Father Bill Seetch was making his Friday-night duty rounds through the dorm where he was rector, Flanner Hall, and the conversations he passed—in the hallways, the stairwells, drifting out of open doors—were concerned with matters other than politics. Fridays are the loudest nights on campus, the week's pent-up energy exploding in a sudden burst that Saturdays usually can't match. Seetch, as was his custom, had taken the elevator to the eleventh floor and was making his way down by foot. The display of his collar reminded the students that this campus, unlike most others, had not been abandoned at night by adults. He found a traffic jam blocking the hall in front of one packed room party.

"Ladies and gentleman, are you going someplace or coming someplace, or are you going to say a rosary here?" He poked his head into the sauna heat and summoned the host from across the wall-to-wall crush. He had to shout even to be heard. "I want you to cut the population in half in the next ten minutes."

Growing up near the airport in Cleveland had given Seetch a high threshold for loud noise, but the years he had spent in Arizona—teaching religion and English at a Holy Cross high school, and falling in love with the spare and silent desert—had given him an appreciation of quieter moments, too. In Flanner he tried to keep the volume at some healthy equilibrium. The two tower dorms—Grace, next door, is Flanner's identical twin—are home to fully a quarter of all the men who live on campus, a bubbling cauldron of testosterone so huge and ominous that it makes the rectors' jobs there among the most daunting on campus. Seetch, in his second year at Flanner, had found that his easy, endearing "Hey Fahdduh" style fit the building well.

"No chipping in the hallway," he said to a woman who was, inexplicably, carrying a golf club. "Putting's allowed, but no chipping."

"Watch this boy, young lady," he said, looking through an open door into a room where several couples were gathered, addressing a woman who was sitting on a man's lap. "He's got more moves than a can of worms."

"What happened to the gentlemen who actually live here?" he asked four women who were dancing alone to Tom Petty in one room.

"They've got other girls they like better than us," one answered.

"Lovely ladies like yourselves? What's wrong with them? I'll have to go slap them around."

"Thank you, Father."

"Michael, you owe me fifty bucks," he informed one resident he found carrying an open beer in the hall.

"Now, this is what I call a nice social gathering," he said upon finding three roommates who were busy watching the guppies mate in their fish tank.

"He's fine, Father," a freshman in another room said, reporting on the condition of his drunk, sleeping roommate. "I just rolled him over."

"I don't make it personal," Seetch said later of his disciplinary style. "I just tell them that what they're doing isn't gonna work here."

He was fond of referring to his charges as "lads," the same word coach Frank Leahy always used when referring to his players. "I have different degrees of dealing with the lads," he said. The first degree was a warning. "I'll invite them down for a friendly fireside chat. I'm in the chair, they're on the couch." Next was the Chair of Shame. "I'm leaning forward on my desk and they're sitting in front. I had two in here the other day, they were so nervous I almost came out and wiped the chairs after they left." Student Affairs was the last stop. "Sometimes you have to let them wear the big black hat."

Back in his room, he got a call from the campus police: Two freshmen, roommates, had been caught fighting outside, both of them drunk. "They'll get the Chair of Shame."

Though the size of the dorm was a liability on Friday and Saturday nights, it became an asset on Sunday afternoons, when the interhall football games were played. The 520 residents constituted a large recruiting pool for Seetch, who in addition to serving as Flanner's rector was also its coach. He had played football in high school, and rugby as an undergraduate at Notre Dame, and though his frame had since drifted toward the far side of lineman size, he still loved to be on the field. He was also the chaplain for the varsity hockey team and the Bengal Bouts boxers, but his duties there did not extend to charting strategy and calling plays.

"Their linebackers do most of the tackling," he said to one of his assistants. "We'll have to get our guards out to block."

Keenan's team was playing Dillon, and Seetch was on the sidelines scouting. The Keenan players were in gold pants, the varsity castoffs they had earned the right to wear this season when they won the league championship last season. Flanner had already beaten them, 13–0 in the season opener, but Seetch expected to see them again in the playoffs.

"We beat 'em on the line," he said of the first win. "We're not as big, but we get across the ball quicker. If we get good enough blocks, we can pop someone for five yards."

"Keep your feet, keep your feet, keep your feet!" one of Keenan's student coaches yelled onto the field. Brother Bonaventure Scully was on the sidelines, too, but his support was moral rather than technical. "Get your pursuit angle!"

Helmets and pads cracked loudly on each play. The men play full-contact tackle football, not flag or touch, and the games unfold with a ferocity that seems an innocent relic of a less litigious age. Most of the players are veterans of high-school varsities, and many are good enough to have played on college varsities at schools smaller than Notre Dame. Each team's field style is an amalgam of sandlot memories and old high-school playbooks.

"I didn't notice any pulling or trapping, just straight blocking," Seetch said. "They run a quick pitch, like we do."

As the clock ticked down near the end of the first half, Keenan hit three quick passes in succession, one of them ending in a tackle so hard it sent the receiver to the sidelines wondering just what day it was.

"What was the score of the game yesterday?" asked the EMT who was summoned to examine him.

"I don't remember who we played," he answered, an unmistakable sign that something was amiss. A mild concussion was the diagnosis. He was put into a neck brace, immobilized, and loaded into an ambulance. His teammates lined up for a field-goal attempt.

"Thank God for that tree," Seetch said as the ball hit a branch that tipped it through the goalposts. "Like a bumper shot in pool. That's what God put the tree there for."

Similar miracles had not attended the recent Stanford game, which Seetch had also watched from the sidelines. Invited to join the varsity for the day, he had blessed the team in the locker room and stood with them on the field. He had seen many games at Notre Dame Stadium—from the bleachers in the student section; from the folding chairs up past the last row in the farthest corner, where the seminarians always sat; from the Holy Cross seats beneath the press box—but this was the first one he had seen from the same angle as Lou Holtz. It was not a pretty sight. "My mother called up and said, 'You were on the sidelines. Why didn't you do something?' "

He could do something about his own team, though. When Keenan finally won, the players gathered into a huddle and said an "Our Father." Seetch collected his notes and headed back to Flanner, armed for this week's practice. Victory, he knew, depended on something more than prayer alone.

7

Just before nine on game-day morning, just as the fans were groping through the first of their prekickoff rituals, the players were arriving at church for theirs—the traditional team Mass. They filed out of the team bus and into the Basilica of the Sacred Heart, through the arched Gothic doorway that was built as a memorial to Notre Dame's World War I dead. Inscribed in the stone above their heads as they entered was the legend "God, Country, Notre Dame." They were dressed in neat, dark suits as if headed to job interviews—which, in a way, they were, given the number of NFL scouts who would be watching today's game. The team used to spend the nights before home games in the seminary across the lake, to shield themselves from the general campus uproar, but more recently they had been traveling to the Holiday Inn in Plymouth, twenty-five miles down the road. Lou Holtz drove up separately in his tan Mercury Cougar, alone.

"Good morning, men," he said as he breezed inside.

As big as the players were, as fearsome as they would look once they exchanged their suits for uniforms and lined up against Brigham Young, they were dwarfed by the soaring interior of the church. From the outside, Sacred Heart resembles the kind of small cathedral you can find anchoring dioceses in midsized cities all over the Midwest—a blocky exercise in the nineteenth-century Gothic Revival style, designed not by an architect but by three members of the Holy Cross community, whose training was more spiritual than structural (a priest, a brother, and Sorin himself), and built of the same modest yellow bricks as all the other old buildings at the campus's core. It grows larger and grander once you get inside, though—lavish with gold, ornate with murals, and rising heavenward as if loosed from the grip of the brick exterior. High above the players' heads, saints floated on clouds, and angels hovered against a starry background. The morning light slanted into the empty nave through the tall stained-glass windows. The dust motes caught in the sun's path were spotlighted in rainbow hues, like the floating stars a fullback sees after taking a sharp hit. More than ten thousand people would pass through Sacred Heart today, an obligatory stop on a visitor's itinerary, but now it belonged to the team alone; guards outside gently informed the curious that the church wasn't open yet, at least not for them. All around Sacred Heart, the building that was the true center of Notre Dame, the noise was swelling, as the crowds cranked up toward game volume; while all around the team inside, the young men who were the true center of the weekend, the silence was rising, a high and heavy hush that offered a welcome sanctuary before the roar of the stadium.

The players set down their bags and walked slowly into a small chapel in the apse behind the main altar—the Lady Chapel, where a large statue of the Virgin Mary hovered over an elaborate, angel-bedecked Baroque altar that swirled and swooped in a frenzy of gold flourishes. The altar—wishfully attributed to Bernini, the architect and sculptor of the Vatican, but actually attributed to one of his followers—was purchased by Sorin in Rome and installed in time for a massive 1888 celebration that marked both the consecration of Sacred Heart and the fiftieth anniversary of Sorin's ordination as a priest. Later that same year, Notre Dame's football team, in just its second season of intercollegiate play, celebrated its first victory, a 20–0 win over the Harvard School of Chicago. Earlier this season, the team Masses had been held in Keenan Hall's chapel, and for many years before that in Pangborn, off-limits now since its gender switch. Today was the first time the team had gathered in Sacred Heart: After the Stanford loss, any extra help was welcome.

The seats in the chapel faced one another across a central aisle like a scrimmage line. "God gave different gifts to different people," the team's chaplain, Father James Riehle, said in his homily. Back in the late 1960s and early 1970s, Riehle had been a stern dean of students, the school's chief disciplinarian. He and his cigar were now a familiar fixture on the sidelines at practices and games. "Take a look during this Mass at each other. Compare yourself with someone who plays another position. Compare yourself to someone who might be a little faster or stronger than you are, but who might not be able to catch a pass the way you can. You all have talents unique to yourselves that you can be proud of. But you need each other. We all have our role to play. And the thing that bonds you together is the love you have for each other."

The team Mass—mandatory for all players, whatever their religion—is a Notre Dame tradition that dates back to the era when most of the players were, as they are not now, Catholic. They had Mass at home, on the road, even in the middle of the trip to the Southern Cal games, the train stopping for a moment in the desert when the priest consecrated the bread and wine. The wire services gave wide play to a story about the religious devotion of the "manly Notre Dame football players" after they stopped for Mass at a Lourdes replica in Albany while on their way to West Point for the 1921 Army game—a public display of faith that helped earn them the allegiance of Catholics everywhere.

What made the Notre Dame story so compelling in the 1920s wasn't just that they had Rockne and Gipp and the Four Horsemen, or that they kept winning games and collecting national titles—but that they were, openly and proudly, Catholic, and that their rise to prominence coincided with the rise of Catholics into the American middle class. They became the "us" in the great "us-versus-them" battle that American Catholics waged with the Protestant establishment, and every time they beat a school like Princeton they struck a blow for the cause. Al Smith might lose the election, but Notre Dame won the game. Anti-Catholic prejudice was still widespread in America in the 1920s, and Notre Dame became one of the chief weapons against it. When the Ku Klux Klan staged a big march in South Bend in 1924, Notre Dame students went downtown to fight them; the Notre Dame football team fought a wider foe on an even larger field. Rockne's players upended the ugly caricature of Catholics that many Americans held—strange, Latin-mumbling, Old World relics beholden to Rome—and showed that theirs was a religion not just for frail old women in veils, but also for burly young men in shoulderpads.

Football and religion got so tangled up in each other at Notre Dame that it became hard to tell where one began and the other left off. The games held a sacramental significance for American Catholics, and each new season took on the quality of a Crusade. On Fridays in autumn, children in parochial schools prayed for victory; on Saturdays, nuns sat beside their radios, fingering rosary beads; and on Sundays, priests recapped the score at Mass. "The world is beginning to realize the source of Notre Dame's brand of sportsmanship," wrote Father John O'Hara, the school's prefect of religion, after Rockne's team won the national championship in 1924. "[It] is a red-blooded play of men full of life, full of hope, full of charity, of men who learn at the foot of the altar what it means to love one another, of men who believe that clean play can be offered as a prayer in honor of the Queen of Heaven. Notre Dame football is a new crusade: it kills prejudice and it stimulates faith." O'Hara—who later served as Notre Dame's president, and then as the cardinal archbishop of Philadelphia—gave religious medals to players before games and encouraged them, as well as their nonvarsity classmates, to receive daily communion: According to his calculations in his weekly *Religious Bulletin,* the more students taking communion during the week before a game, the greater the chances of a win on Saturday.

Seated now just a few steps from the small side chapel where O'Hara lay buried, the team listened as Father Riehle continued his homily. "This team is united by the things that bring you together—the love you have for this school, this unique place, and the love you have for each other," he said. "We can't worry about ourselves too much. Sometimes we need to say to ourselves, 'Yes, I am unique, but I need something to help me rise above selfishness.' A team does that. When we open our hearts to the tremendous grace God gives us, then love will bring us together."

Sitting quietly in the back of the chapel, rosary beads in hand, was Moose Krause, the seventy-nine-year-old legend-in-residence, who had played under Rockne, coached under Leahy, and served for decades as Notre Dame's athletic director. Sitting in the front was Lou Holtz, who, as a grade-schooler under the tutelage of the Sisters of Notre Dame, had marched in and out of St. Aloysius School in East Liverpool, Ohio, to the strains of the "Notre Dame Victory March"; and who now tried, as O'Hara had urged, to make the early Mass here on weekdays, too. (Although piety is welcome in a Notre Dame coach, it is neither a necessary nor a sufficient condition for the job: Rockne was a Lutheran, though he converted in 1925; Parseghian was a Presbyterian, and stayed one; Faust was a regular at Sacred Heart and the Grotto, but that didn't help him when the losses kept mounting.)

"This is my body," Father Riehle said, holding up the host at the consecration, "which will be given up for you."

Sitting on the side was Tom Carter, who, like many of his teammates, had been raised Baptist. "We're all going to the same place," he said, "we're just going by different paths." He had come to Notre Dame "because of its tradition. When you tell people you go to Notre Dame, there's a whole new light on their faces. You tell them you go to Florida State"—where he was also recruited—"and they say, 'That's a good school,' but if you tell them you go to Notre Dame, they go 'Oooooh!' "

Because so many players are not Catholic, the central ritual of the team

Mass is not really communion, which is closed to them, but the sign of peace, which is not. The players all rose and embraced, as if at a homecoming. The sanctuary echoed with the buzz of greetings and the thud of hands slapping hard, muscled backs. Tom Carter made a point of seeking out his closest friends on the team—John Covington, his partner in the defensive secondary, linebacker Demetrius DuBose, tight end Irv Smith. "That's the part we all look forward to," he said. "We're not afraid to express how we feel about each other. We say we love each other."

Father Riehle stood by the memorial-door exit after Mass, with the team's student manager by his side. The players lined up as if for communion. In Riehle's hand was a small, round gold case that contained—according to the authentification papers that accompanied it, issued by the Vatican and written in Latin—a piece of the True Cross, the crucifix that Jesus died on. Resting inside the case on a red velvet cushion, shielded behind glass, were two tiny splinters of wood, arranged in the form of a cross. All the players but one—Karmeeleyah McGill, the team's lone Muslim—bent to kiss the relic. As they left, the manager handed out small medals: Today's supply had St. Gerard on one side, the Virgin Mary on the other.

In the locker room before the game—a brick-walled space as simple as Sacred Heart is elaborate, behind a blue door marked only with a single, weighty word, "Varsity"—Riehle blessed each player individually, as he would again at halftime and at game's end. They then knelt and held hands as he led a "Hail Mary." "Our Lady, Queen of Victory, pray for us," he concluded. "Notre Dame, Our Mother, pray for us."

The players had one final devotion to make before they took the field. On their way down the narrow steps that led out of the locker room, headed for the dim tunnel that led out to the sunlit stadium, they each in turn touched—or punched, banged, caressed, slapped, or stroked—the gold sign that hung on the yellow brick wall above them. "Play Like a Champion Today," it commanded.

"We begin today on the New Testament," Larry Cunningham, the chairman of the theology department, told the freshmen in his section of Theology 100. "But first I want to tell you how far the influence of Notre Dame extends."

Cunningham often illustrated his lectures with stories—seventy-five straight minutes of Biblical exegesis at nine-thirty in the morning can have a numbing effect on a roomful of eighteen-year-olds, as he well knew—and he opened today's class by telling one on himself. He had been away at a conference over the weekend, staying at the Trappist monastery in Gethsemani, Kentucky, where there was no television on which to watch Notre Dame play BYU. Having gone to sleep not knowing how the game had ended, he rose at three-fifteen and joined the monks in the chapel for vigils, their first prayers of the day. A monk he knew from previous visits spotted him. "He leaned down next to me and whispered in my ear, 'Notre Dame beat the stuffing out of those Mormons.' " The score, he learned, was a decisive 42–16. A Notre Dame victory, it turns out, is loud enough to penetrate even the cloistered silence of a monastery.

He tossed a piece of chalk in the air for emphasis, caught it, then leaned back against the blackboard and led the class out of Indiana and into the ancient Middle East. The day's subject was the historical context of Jesus' birth, a story that involved successive invasions of Assyrians, Babylonians, Persians, and Romans.

"What do we call Persia today? What country is it?" Cunningham asked a student in a Navy ROTC uniform, whose ears turned as red as his hair as it became apparent that he didn't know the correct answer: Iran. "A few years ago, you could've been on a ship fighting near there."

With his red face and his shock of white hair, Cunningham is occasionally mistaken for Pat Moynihan, and though he differs with the senator on some issues, he does share with him a personality that blends intellectual erudition with political acumen—a useful mixture in the theology department, one of the university's prime battlegrounds. Until well into the Hesburgh era, the department was a bastion of the old Catholic ghetto, dedicated to preserving Catholic traditions in a Protestant nation. Guided by faith and obedience, not inquiry, it was staffed entirely by Holy Cross priests, and its courses were often little more than catechism recitals. It had since evolved into a widely respected academic department that produced original research and offered a diverse range of classes. Half its members now were lay, a quarter were not Catholic, and Holy Cross priests were guaranteed nothing: "Publish or parish" was their new guideline. Though the department had, according to Cunningham, "no radical prochoice marchers," it was perceived by conservatives as excessively liberal. It had strayed too far afield, they believed, and neglected its duty to teach official church doctrine.

"I think it's hard for people who aren't at Notre Dame to understand just how Catholic this place is," Cunningham said. "And all the fractures and partisanships you have in the Catholic church, you have here at Notre Dame."

Cunningham was the first theology-department chairman who was not—though he once had been—a priest. He was nearer the center, and lower in profile, than his predecessor, Richard McBrien, whose left-leaning views and plain-spoken habit of going on camera to disagree with the pope had earned for him—and by extension the department and the university, too—the wrath of the Catholic right. "I tend to be more 'on one hand, then on the other hand.' I don't like controversy. I'm interested in the history of how saints function in the church. My views on St. Francis of Assisi aren't likely to get me on *Nightline*."

McBrien had lured Cunningham to Notre Dame from Florida State University, his home for most of his academic life. "My chairman said, 'I suppose, if Notre Dame wants you to come to their department of theology, it's like Jesus calling you to heaven.'" He was prolific both at scholarship—sixteen books, regular contributions to *Commonweal* and other journals—and at gaining the trust of his colleagues: They had chosen him to represent the College of Arts and Letters on the Provost's Advisory Committee, the group that was expanded in response to the faculty's demands last spring for a larger voice in tenure and promotion decisions. He also sat on the Colloquy subcommittee that was drafting—and redrafting and redrafting—a mission statement for the university, trying to summarize in a few paragraphs Notre Dame's distinct reason for being. And he made a point of teaching a freshman section, a task he could have easily assigned elsewhere. "I love those fresh notebooks and freshly sharpened pencils."

Theology 100, like Philosophy 101, is a required class for every student, but Cunningham, like Tom Morris, tried to make it shine as if it were an elective. The main text, naturally, was the Bible—the blue-jacketed Catholic study edition lay open on the desk before each student—and so far this semester they had been through Genesis, Exodus, Samuel, Kings, Psalms, Isaiah, and Hosea. Today their Bibles were open to Paul's first Letter to the Corinthians—a text that gave Cunningham a chance to trace the development of the church in the first decades after the death of Jesus, and to examine the split between Paul and his fellow disciple Peter.

"There was one big problem," Cunningham said. "What was the relationship going to be between this new Jesus movement and the parent religion from which it came, Judaism?"

Peter's side, as Cunningham explained, believed that Christianity was a refinement of Judaism, and that to be a Christian meant that you must also be a Jew. Paul's side believed that Christianity should be more than just a faction within Judaism, that it should instead be a universal religion open to Gentiles. "Paul said, 'I need to straighten Peter out,' sort of like Lou Holtz putting a headlock on that official," he said, referring to Saturday's game, when an angry Holtz had charged the field and draped his arm around an official's neck, demonstrating the holding violation he believed he had seen but the man in his grasp had missed. Though Holtz lost the call, he, like Paul, won the game, which was, of course, the larger battle. "It was a watershed moment in the history of Christianity."

The infrastructure of the early church, Cunningham continued, included nothing on the scale of Notre Dame, but was instead limited to small groups of people meeting in one another's homes. "There's a cliché that the early Christians gave these big Billy Graham rallies, but it really grew just by the multiplication of these small assemblies." Within a generation of Christ's death, Christianity had spread all along the Mediterranean, to Rome, Spain, Corinth, Turkey, and northern Greece. By A.D. 100, it had reached the Black Sea. What united the far-flung adherents of this new religion was the story they all believed in—the death and resurrection of Jesus—and the rituals they developed to commemorate it.

Cunningham was digressing on the prevalence and meaning of rituals when the ROTC student spotted a chance to atone for his earlier lapse. "A handshake, that's a ritual behavior. Why do I use my right hand?" Cunningham asked.

"It's your sword hand," the student offered.

"Yes," said Cunningham, clearly pleased at hearing the right answer. "It means 'I come in peace, without my sword.' "

"I don't believe the world needs another Duke or Northwestern. It does need a Notre Dame that's great in its own way. Its Catholic character is what makes Notre Dame unique. Our quest should be to build a great *Catholic* university, for which there are no blueprints. To simply copy the great secular universities is to abandon that quest."

"It's a flawed notion to think that Notre Dame will always be a Catholic university as long as there are undergraduates praying in the Grotto at midnight. It's a feature of the undergraduate experience, but it doesn't have to do fundamentally with the intellectual life of the university."

"The worry is that someday Notre Dame is going to become some kind of intellectual ghetto."

It was not so much a debate as a conversation, a few dozen professors gathered in a conference room tossing around big ideas, and when the participants had finally settled on a name for their new group, that was just how they described it: the Conversation on the Catholic Character. They had sprung up last spring, an informal byproduct of the Colloquy, assembling regularly to discuss a deep, difficult, and potentially divisive question: What was the relationship between Catholicism and Notre Dame, they asked, and how should it manifest itself? Having outgrown the faculty lounge in the library, they were now meeting in the Peace Institute—the more familiar name for the new building that holds the Hesburgh Center for International Studies, on the southern edge of campus. The professors packed in tightly around the long rectangle of conference tables, with the overflow clustered in seats to the rear. The bright and placid white room was dominated by a large painting of a violent demonstration in South Africa. Outside tonight, on Notre Dame Avenue, you could see all the way up the wide, straight alley of trees, clear through to the Dome: The leaves that had earlier blocked the view had fallen, like sins cast off at confession, signaling the arrival of the long, penitential South Bend winter.

"I believe that faith has nothing to fear from the life of the mind, in fact is enhanced by it, and that the intellectual community has nothing to fear from faith."

"Are there any kinds of limits of discussion at a Catholic university? What is the relationship to faith in disciplines where its doctrines aren't obvious?"

"How do you reconcile academic freedom with church authority?"

They were an old and familiar batch of questions at Notre Dame, having been asked with a similar intensity—and answered, to a point—back in the 1960s, an era when Notre Dame's ambitions came into conflict with its traditions. Spurred by Vatican II (with its emphasis on expanding the role of the laity in church affairs) and by his own grand vision of Notre Dame's future (with its emphasis on achieving academic respectability), Hesburgh was moved to do something that would have been unimaginable to all the Holy Cross priests and brothers who had come before him: He gave their school away. In 1967, over the objections of some of his colleagues within the community, he transferred control of Notre Dame from the Congregation of Holy Cross to a predominantly lay board of trustees. It was, in his later view, the greatest accomplishment of his thirty-five years as president, and it represented a critical step in Notre Dame's evolution from a small sectarian college into a leading national university. He took another step later that same year: After meeting with other Catholic-university officials at Land O'Lakes—the same place where George Craig takes his young entomologists each summer—he issued a declaration of independence from Rome. "[The] Catholic university," the Land O'Lakes statement said, "must have a true autonomy and academic freedom in the face of authority of whatever kind, lay or clerical, external to the academic community itself." But it must also, the statement continued, "be an institution . . . in which Catholicism is perceptively present and effectively operative." Just what that meant at Notre Dame for the next twenty years was determined largely by Hesburgh himself. What it meant now, however, was up for grabs.

As Notre Dame reached toward the highest rungs of the American academy, some people on campus worried that it was leaving behind its Catholic identity. They raised the specter of Vanderbilt, Duke, Yale, and a host of other elite schools—all once religiously affiliated, all now resolutely secular—and they wondered aloud if Notre Dame was on the same path toward secularization. To join that exclusive community of the mind, they asked, was it necessary first to lose your soul?

"Some departments are more Catholic than others because of what they're about. One result, then, is that the Catholic character resides in a small group of people."

"I think the statement 'There is no Catholic physics' is a red herring, because you have to answer, 'No, there isn't,' and the discussion stops."

"There may not be a Catholic physics, but there may be questions a Catholic physicist would ask, like 'What is the relationship of cosmology to belief?' "

"What I'd like to defend is a person doing particle physics and *not* relating it to cosmology. He's finding out about the world in his work, and there's no need to say to him that he needs to make some cosmological argument."

"It just isn't really clear how Christianity bears on these subjects."

It was the kind of discussion that you weren't likely to hear at one of the secular schools they feared becoming, and its very existence here tonight— on a campus that featured a chapel in every dorm, a crucifix in every classroom, a Knights of Columbus chapter right on the South Quad, a small battalion of priests, brothers, and nuns in residence, and a statue of the Virgin Mary overlooking it all—seemed proof that Notre Dame's Catholic character was still in good health. What worried them, though, was the unspoken question: Who will do this when we are gone? In 1970, 66 percent of the faculty were Catholic; today it was 58 percent; and only 42 percent of the new professors hired this year were Catholic. In the end, then, the Conversation was really about jobs: Who would get hired and promoted? Who would constitute the Notre Dame faculty of the future?

"Catholicism should enter into the equation just like teaching talent or research talent."

"When we're interviewing candidates, we should ask them this question: Notre Dame is a Catholic university; how does your work fit into that?"

"We need to have more patience in hiring, especially in affirmative action for Catholics."

The mission statement that Larry Cunningham co-wrote for the Colloquy had addressed the same issue, and stirred similar questions. Through all the drafts of the statement, one clause had remained constant: Notre Dame's Catholic identity, it asserted, depended upon "the continuing presence of a predominant number of Catholic intellectuals." But what number did "predominant" equal? And who was counted as Catholic? Was it everybody who checked the box on the application, or was it just those who went to Mass every Sunday? Were nonbelievers not welcome?

"I think many faculty members feel threatened by this conversation. They're threatened by the hierarchy of the Catholic church—because a hierarchical structure violates the idea that the most powerful ideas prevail, not the most powerful people."

"For people who didn't get into the loop early, it sounds like a religious sect is forming."

"I don't think it's subversive."

"Catholicism's not just a creed, it's a culture, a way of life."

"The faith of many people is internalized. They give examples by doing, not proclaiming. Don't exclude those who are silent."

"There are strong reasons why some women feel alienated from the Catholicity question."

The Conversation was open to all faculty members—students were largely unaware that Catholicity was the subject of any debate at all—but those who actually came to the meetings tended to be those who were already sympathetic to the cause. The philosophy department, which had within it a distinctly conservative streak, was well represented, while the theology department was not. It was an informal, independent group, with no official ties to the administration, but among its lead organizers were two popular young Holy Cross priests—Bill Miscamble from the history department, Tim Scully from government—who were on everyone's short list as likely potential successors to Malloy.

"I think we should consider inviting some people from the administration, like Monk and Tim O'Meara."

"I think that's a terrible idea."

"We aren't trying to influence anybody but ourselves."

The discussion continued at a postmeeting reception out in the lobby, but it didn't end when the wine and cheese were gone. It seeped into conversations far removed from the Conversation itself, over coffee at Decio Commons and Allegro, lunch at the faculty club and the Morris Inn, dinner at the Carriage House and the LaSalle Grill, and every other place where professors and administrators met.

"That word 'predominant' upsets people, because what they hear in it is 'dominate,' " said longtime provost Tim O'Meara, the first layman to hold that job. His was the desk that tenure and promotion files landed on. "When I say 'predominant,' I don't mean it should be from the top, I mean it should be from the faculty. I'm not saying you need to have a lord and master who dominates from above. You can't expect us to re-create *Going My Way* with Bing Crosby. I think there's a radical transformation occurring now in the life of the church, not because of structures like Vatican II, but because of the people. The question is: What is our role here?"

"I don't think we have to mill around and create some concept called 'Catholicism'—it's already there," said law professor Charles Rice, the affable, crew-cut ex-Marine who served as faculty adviser to both the Bengal Bouts and the Right to Life group, and who opened each of his classes with a "Hail Mary." His model for Notre Dame was contained in *Ex Corde Ecclesiae*, the recent Vatican document that declared "fidelity to the Christian message as it comes to us through the church" as one of the "essential characteristics" of a Catholic university. "If I were El Supremo and I were running the place, I'd make sure every student coming in here had the opportunity to receive authentic exposure to the philosophical traditions of the Catholic faith."

"If I were running things at Notre Dame," said Father Richard McBrien, who was lying low now, in the middle of a long sabbatical to revise his massive book, *Catholicism*, and edit the *HarperCollins Encyclopedia of Catholicism*, "I would say that, if we succeed in one thing in the four years that undergraduates are here, we've got to teach them what Catholic social doctrine is all about. We have to get them to the point where they either reject it and they reject the church, or they accept it. They have to see that they need to take a stand in life—whether to use their resources and talents only for themselves and their families, or whether they see them as gifts to be put at the service of others. That's the real test of the Catholicity of Notre Dame. It's not a question of 'Shall I continue going to Mass on holy days of obligation?' That's child's play. That isn't why they put Jesus on the cross."

"People want to redefine what it is to be Catholic," said chaired philosophy professor Ralph McInerny, the author of fifteen scholarly books and several dozen novels. His current projects included a book on Aristotle and St. Thomas Aquinas, and *Down by Six*, the seventeenth installment in his popular Father Dowling mystery series and the first to be set at Notre Dame: The plot involved a retired canon lawyer attending a meeting on campus on a football weekend. "To be a Roman Catholic is to be a Roman Catholic—either you're in or you're out. Now, we're talking about religious belief as if it's some kind of impediment. It's almost as if Catholicism is what you do in church, and then, when you go into your classroom or your office, there's no difference between what they do here and what they do anywhere else. I think that's a big loss, I really do. My sense is that we've got something we ought to be celebrating instead of apologizing for."

The day's scarce light was quickly fading, the cold sun sinking invisibly somewhere behind the permacloud, as the varsity and its attendants made their way toward the practice field behind the ACC for the regular 4:00 p.m. session. Lou Holtz rode out in a golf cart, accompanied by the chaplain, Father Riehle. He waved as he passed the inevitable cluster of fans at the gate. Tom Carter walked out in full uniform and pads, his gold helmet tucked under his arm.

The weather was perfect for playing football indoors—on the artificial turf under the warm and welcoming roof of the Loftus Center—but Saturday's game would be played outdoors, and so, barring rain, would today's practice. The players split up by position, running through their separate drills with the assistant coaches. Tom Carter and the other defensive backs practiced pass coverage, cutting and backpedaling like Fred Astaire in hyperdrive. Holtz roamed the field, twirling his whistle. He wore his trademark blue Notre Dame cap over a blue jacket and chinos. No one called him anything but "Sir" or "Coach," a title they invested with the same weight they might have given to "Captain" or "Father." Young men almost twice his weight instantly downshifted from full-tilt attack mode and hung their heads in abashed silence whenever he spoke.

"Do it the right way," Holtz barked, in a tone that made the wrong way seem not to be an option at all.

"That ain't it, that ain't gonna do it. You gotta keep that hip up."

"Hey, men, you push off your left foot, your inside foot. That's better, that's better."

Standing with the small crowd on the sidelines—sportswriters, scouts, and student managers mostly—was one spectator whose only credential for being here was his overriding obsession with Notre Dame football. His name was Jimmy Zannino, but everyone knew him as Jimmy Z. His job was night cook at the Oak Room, the public cafeteria in South Dining Hall, but his vocation was as the Ultimate Fan—a thirty-seven-year-old man who not only possessed, to the nth degree, the almost childlike awe and devotion Notre Dame often inspires in its followers, but who had turned it into a lifestyle. He was such a familiar figure now that he could breeze right through the gate and into practice like part of the team.

"Little does he know that I just flip burgers," he said about the student manager who guarded the entrance with a clipboard and the official guest list. "I'm a nobody."

Zannino stood far back from the action, staying out of everyone's way, trying not to do anything that might cost him his privileges, careful not to push too near the edge of his dream. It had taken him his whole life to get here, and he didn't want to leave now. He grew up in central Pennsylvania, a Notre Dame fan in the heart of Penn State country. Both his parents worked in a shirt factory, and both were diehard Notre Dame fans. On game days, his mother would cook up vats of pasta and meatballs, and family and friends would gather to root for a school none of them had ever seen in person.

"All my life," he said, "whenever I watched a Notre Dame football game and they showed pictures of the Golden Dome, for some reason I got goose bumps, I got a lump in my throat, I felt like I wanted to cry. I felt like there was a magnet drawing me here. Now I look back and—I don't want to spook you—I realize that all my life the Lady on the Dome has been calling me here."

A year and a half ago, he was working in a Chambersburg supermarket, feeling low about his mother's recent death—his father had died when he was fourteen—and his breakup with his girlfriend. He went to church alone one night and, in the candlelit shadows, knelt before the statue of the Virgin Mary. "I asked her to give me a sign, some kind of sign, showing me what she wanted for me." The next day's mail brought his copy of *Blue & Gold Illustrated*, a newspaper devoted to Notre Dame football. He quit his job, sold what he owned, paid what he owed, packed his bags, and, with $300 in his pocket, started driving west in his battered 1975 white Oldsmobile. When he came down the ramp off the interstate and saw the Dome for the first time, he pulled over, got out of the car, sat on the hood, and cried.

"I felt like my grandparents must have felt when they saw the Statue of Liberty for the first time."

Like most immigrants, he had a rough landing. "God was telling me, 'If you want it bad enough, you gotta show me.' " He slept in his car, subsisted on that month's Burger King special (three burgers for $1), and got a job changing dirty sheets at a motel. He searched in vain for work on campus, prayed nightly at the Grotto, and kept asking himself: "Am I worthy to be here?" He befriended the Holy Cross brother who lived in the ACC and handled the sports equipment, and he went to an open practice to see "the gods I'd always worshiped." He found a room in a house with two law students and then, finally, got the job in the Oak Room, a favorite late-night haunt of hungry players.

"The next thing you know, I'm like 'Jimmy Z' to all the athletes, and I'm making burgers for Tommy Carter," he said. "I do believe in miracles. I believe wholeheartedly that the Blessed Mother is looking over my shoulder. She's my family now. She's adopted me."

"At first we were a little intimidated by him," Tom Carter said later of Zannino, whose faith can appear as fanaticism to the uninitiated. "But he's real cool. He's a guy who just loves Notre Dame. That's just Jimmy Z."

The players were scrimmaging now on the two adjacent fields—the offensive starters on one field, the defensive starters on the other, each going up against the second and third teams and the walk-ons. Video cameras watched from a tower between the two fields, recording the action for later study: In football, it didn't really happen if it's not on tape. The grass was worn and patchy, stomped down to dirt by months of practice. The plays unfolded quickly, the squads moving up and down the field at a pace nearer to soccer than football. Their speed and strength—the explosive runs, the fierce hits, the lightning reflexes—were magnified when seen from such a close angle, undiminished by the deep and dwarfing distances of the stadium. Holtz was on the offensive field.

"Block his ass, it'll be a new experience," Holtz advised a lineman. "Why the hell didn't you stick his ass in the chest?"

"Nice pattern, good job."

"Who in the hell has him? Get your ass in there."

"That your man? You get his ass."

A pack of players trailed the offense up the field, waiting to be called in for a down or more. Before each snap, a student manager scrawled the play's code name on a board and held it up so everyone on the offensive side of the ball could see what was supposed to happen next: "LIZ 301 WG PETE," the board read, or "RIP TRPS EMPTY 900 LEON," or "DBLS RT 901 CURL." Off in the dark distance, the faint bells of Sacred Heart tolled the hour.

"Where the hell's our flanker?"

"I'd like the fullback a little deeper."

"Why in the hell can't you do what we ask?"

On the defensive field, Tom Carter played as hard against the practice squad as he had against BYU. He was a junior now, one of the team's quiet leaders, and he knew what mistakes cost. In training camp as a freshman—a blue-chip recruit from St. Petersburg, ranked among the top hundred in the nation—he had felt the wrath of Holtz, in full view of teammates he had scarcely met yet, when he misread a pass play he was covering. He started six games that year, until he got beaten on a fifty-yard play-action bomb against Navy. He spent the rest of the season as a reserve. He came back as a sophomore to lead the team with five interceptions and log more game minutes than any other player. As a unit, the defense had gotten off to a shaky start this season—"ND," the critics were saying, now stood for "No Defense"—and in the week before the BYU game, Holtz rode hard on the secondary in practice, leading them through extra tackling drills and coverage drops. They responded with three interceptions, shutting down the vaunted BYU passing attack. Tom had one of those interceptions in the game, and he picked off another one now in practice.

"All right, T.C.!" Jimmy Zannino applauded.

Watching from the sidelines near Zannino were several NFL scouts, who had a professional interest in the proceedings. They had been showing up regularly at practice for the last few weeks, sizing up potential employees, much like the corporate recruiters who were frequenting the career-placement office, just across Juniper Road, in the Hesburgh Library. Today's batch included the Bengals, the Chiefs, the Vikings, and the Falcons. Though Tom Carter was only a junior, they eyed him closely, on the chance that he might forsake his senior year and enter the draft early. He had the kind of skills—

4.35 in the forty, forty-three-inch vertical leap, 350-pound bench press—that could make him a first-round pick. He was determined to finish his degree ("If I were just interested in playing football, I would've gone to Miami or Florida State"), and he was on track to graduate, with a finance major, in a total of three and a half years, but he had other concerns, too: The only child of a single mother who worked as a bank teller, he wanted to pay her back for all she had done for him.

"Agents call you up all the time and blow smoke up your behind, telling you you're the greatest thing since sliced bread," he said. "It sticks in your mind. I stay up all night sometimes, staring at the ceiling, thinking about the money. It weighs on my mind a lot."

Tom's territory was usually the wide side of the field, where the fleetest receivers roam, and his game assignment was usually to shadow the opposition's best man, while the rest of the secondary played zone. Cornerbacks have a high-risk job—either you beat your man or he beats you, and all the world can see—that tends to turn them into cocky gunslingers. Tom's style, quiet and confident, was nearer that of a sheriff. He was among the handful of players who roomed not with other players, but with civilians, four of them squeezed into three small rooms in Dillon Hall. One room was devoted to sleep, stacked high with bunk beds; one was devoted to study, crammed with desks; and one was devoted to leisure, equipped with stereo, TV, and refrigerator, and furnished with a battered couch and a recliner that Carter often occupied in the weary aftermath of big games, accepting congratulations from dormmates until he finally dropped off to sleep amid the din of celebration.

Carter hung back now on the practice field as some linemen punctuated a tackle by unnecessarily piling on the runner, one of those moments when the controlled violence of the game threatened to veer out of control. Voices were raised, and the bottom of the pack disintegrated into a wrestling match. "Get your ass up off the ground and cut this bullshit out," an assistant coach yelled, peeling one player from another and exiling the main offenders to the sidelines. "We fucking coach, you guys play. You guys fucking play."

On the offensive field, the starters had reached the end zone again. "Turn it around, put it on the ten," Holtz instructed, pointing them down the field again.

"You've gotta get outta there a helluva lot earlier than that."

"Get your ass up or get it gone."

"I told your ass what to do. You screwed our ass up last Saturday. You know what you do on 196?"

"Any questions on anything else we're doing?"

It was nearing six-thirty, the evening chill was deepening, and the players were eager to get to the training table in North Dining Hall. Jimmy Zannino was in no hurry, though: He wasn't due at work until eight.

"We'll stay here until we get it done," Holtz declared.

Though they remained divided on the larger issues, the Democrats and the Republicans appeared united tonight on a smaller one: what to wear to a debate. Chris Setti and Andrew Holmgren wore blue blazers as they took the stage in the library auditorium, mirroring their counterparts from the College Republicans. Chris, in gray pants, was the only one who wasn't also wearing the standard-issue khakis that usually complete the uniform. As they stood at their podiums, making their opening statements in behalf of their candidates, it was hard to shake the impression that they had somehow gotten lost while on the way to pick up their dates for an SYR.

"Twelve years ago, Ronald Reagan asked the American people a simple question: Are you better off now than you were four years ago?" Chris said, referring to a presidential campaign that had unfolded the same year he made his first communion. "When I ask you now if you're better off today than you were twelve years ago, can you honestly say yes?"

Though the Democrats had been more visible as an organization this semester, the Republicans remained more visible as a philosophy, as was apparent in the muted response to Chris's question. He was trying to appeal to the economic fears of the students themselves, who were facing an uncertain job market after graduation, but they were still wrapped up in the economic success of their parents, many of whom were in fact better off now than they had been twelve years ago. Affluence ran high at Notre Dame (at a recent political forum in Keenan Hall, one student had defined "middle class" as a family with $200,000 in savings) and conservatism ran deep: When Sinéad O'Connor tore up a photo of the pope on *Saturday Night Live* earlier this semester, the student senate passed a resolution asking NBC to issue a formal apology and a statement of regret. Just today *The Observer* had endorsed George Bush, "the best choice in this confusing race."

The format of the debate was borrowed from the actual presidential debates—the debaters fielded questions from one another, from a panel of professors, and finally from the audience. The answers were similarly borrowed from the presidential answers. Most of the people in the auditorium were electoral virgins—voting for their first president, voicing political views that would, for the first time, actually count toward something—and their dialogue here tonight had about it a touching and innocent quality of faith—in the rightness of their candidates, the power of ideas, the possibility of change.

"Do you believe Bill Clinton has the moral authority to send people to serve our country in the military?"

"Sometimes I think it's more patriotic to tell your country they're doing something wrong than to blindly follow it."

"Bill Clinton says he's profamily, yet he's pro-abortion."

"How can you justify George Bush as prolife when he allows the inner cities to fall prey to drug wars?"

"We have to get people to get up off their butts and start working. Let the free market solve the problems that government can't."

"What we've seen for twelve years is a trickle-down economy, and it just didn't trickle down. If it had, we wouldn't be in the economic downspiral we're in now."

"Quayle's been getting a bad rap from the press."

The Quayle line raised a big cheer from the Republicans in the crowd, who easily outnumbered the Democrats. Kevin Kuwik launched a question from the back row that was intended to help the Democratic cause—it was about George Bush's inability to work with Congress—but it backfired in favor of the Republicans. "I think gridlock would be better than letting Bill Clinton have his way in Congress," the Republican debater parried.

The longer the debate went, the wider the opinions diverged, and the louder the rhetoric grew. "In America you can achieve things. You work hard and you get to keep what you make," the Republican boasted.

"But right here in America now, there are middle-class people, poor people, who don't have that option," the Democrat implored.

"Regardless how they mask it, it all boils down to—they're trying to redistribute wealth."

"I wish you'd go out there, I wish you'd understand, there are people out there who are really hurting, people without jobs, people being thrown out of their houses," Andrew Holmgren finally pleaded, running out of time, and answers.

Andrew and Chris left the stage looking winded and slightly shell-shocked, the clear losers if the debate were graded by audience reaction alone. "Man, that was a hostile crowd," Andrew said. "I don't think there's a real awareness of how bad the job market is out there."

The crowd was friendlier the next day at a festive College Democrats rally on Fieldhouse Mall, an event for which the College Republicans had no re-buttal. A campus band played James Brown, and the Democrats felt good about their chances on Election Day. In volume and visibility at least, the Democrats had already won; it could no longer fairly be said, as it had been recently, that "ND" stood for "No Democrats." In votes, though, the contest would likely be closer: A few days later, Bush won the mock election staged by student government, which left Chris Setti muttering darkly about ballot stuffing and nervously reassuring himself that it wasn't for real yet.

On Election Day, Chris got to the polling place in the ACC just as it opened at 6:00 a.m., cast his first vote for a president, then hopped in a car with several other College Democrats and started driving south. By seven that evening, they were in downtown Little Rock. They watched the returns come in with the vast open-air party that had assembled there, cheered wildly when Clinton was declared the winner, listened raptly as the new president-elect made his victory speech, then climbed back in their car at 2:00 a.m. and started driving north.

Andrew Holmgren didn't make the road trip—he had a test to study for, and twenty-four hours in a car wouldn't help matters any—but he found plenty to celebrate right here at Notre Dame: When the local returns came in, it was their man on top. The College Democrats had finally reached ex-actly the goal that had seemed so distant last spring but had kept getting nearer and nearer ever since Clinton's visit in September—the first Demo-cratic victory in the campus precincts in two decades. Success, however, had a down side: With no campaign to distract them now, they would have to resume their roles as students.

"Man, I've got a lot of work to catch up on," Andrew said, shaking his head in resignation.

Outside the ACC on the eve of game day, amid the crowd filing in for the pep rally, a dozen or so Boston College fans collected into a circle and began singing their school's fight song, "For Boston." A modest enough display of loyalty, it was greeted here by stares of disbelief. Most visiting fans tread lightly at Notre Dame, giving wide berth to the local legends—whether out of deference to the ghosts of Rockne and company, or out of fear of provoking the wrath of Touchdown Jesus. Boston College, though, apparently paid little heed to the "God Made ND #1" bumper stickers that dotted the parking lots. The only other Catholic college that plays Division 1-A football, it is run by the Jesuits, an order that—when measured by its saints, its schools, and the sheer breadth of its achievements—outranks almost any other, including the Congregation of Holy Cross. The two teams had met just three times before, with Notre Dame the winner each time, but the BC Eagles were riding a 7–0–1 record now and ranked ninth in the nation, just one spot behind the Irish. The Eagles seemed convinced that, this season at least, God was rooting for them for a change.

As the chastened remnant of the Irish Guard led the band onto the arena floor, Lou Blaum watched from a distance, a disappointed exile. This weekend should have been a sweet coda to his boyhood dream, because it was at an earlier Boston College game that he had sat in the stands with his father and, enthralled by the squadron of tall men in kilts, decided he would march with the Guard one day. He eventually did, for a little more than a season, but now he was back in the stands, his career cut short when the Office of Student Affairs dismissed the five veteran Guardsmen the week before the Purdue game. Although he remained bitter about the dismissal, his attention had shifted now to a larger goal. Like many seniors, Lou approached his dorm mailbox these days with an anxious mixture of hope and fear, waiting for the responses from the medical schools he had applied to. His premed career had started poorly—a 2.2 average in the first semester of his freshman year—but he survived orgo as a sophomore, scored well on the MCATs, and climbed back up to a 2.998. "I'm one of those people who have to work for their grades." This was a tight year for med-school applicants—the numbers were way up, after slumping for a few years—and he had already collected several rejections. He was still waiting to hear from his first choice, Thomas Jefferson University in Philadelphia, the alma mater of both his father and his grandfather. On his recent visit to Jefferson, he ended up showing his interviewer a photo of the Irish Guard. "He asked about the kilts." But Lou, by Guard covenant, could not tell him what everybody wanted to know: Just what did the Guardsmen wear beneath them?

The band marched onto the floor behind the five remaining Guardsmen, stirring up the crowd with the fight song. The band uniforms are a simpler affair than the Guard's regalia, but it had taken two separate attempts to shorten Rachel Stehle's pants to the proper length. They fit her now as well as she fit the band. "I totally feel like I belong," she said. "I would've been devastated if I didn't make it." Having committed her trumpet parts to memory, she marched tonight, as she had since the BYU game, without sheet music. The fans clapped and sang along, having committed their parts to memory, too. "These crowds are unbelievable. I went back home for homecoming and it was like, 'Oh my god, it's so small.' "

As thrilling as football weekends still were to Rachel, the weekday practices were sometimes a grind. "At times I want to quit, I'm just sick of it. But it's hard to imagine my life now without band. It's just so much a part of my life." She had fallen into the student habit of ordering pizza at midnight with her floormates and skipping breakfast, and she found it a challenge sometimes to rouse herself for her 8:00 a.m. theology class. Since she had no hometown honey ("I made sure of that"), she was sort of seeing—"hanging out with" was the technical term—a guy from Morrissey Hall. She planned to major in psychology, then go on to graduate school "to study behavior."

"*We are BC!*" the small Boston College contingent was chanting in the middle of the pep rally now, exhibiting behavior so unexpected here that the Notre Dame fans were momentarily silent, as if pausing to study it themselves.

"*We are ND!*" they finally responded, following the lead of Dan Wagner, the leprechaun, raising the volume as they chanted, until the Boston College fans were forced to retreat into silence.

"*Let's go, Eagles!*" the visitors tried again, later in the program.

"Now, wait a minute, just hold on a second," Wagner replied. "You may remember a slogan from a few years ago, 'Catholics versus Convicts.' " He was referring to the bad-blood rivalry with the University of Miami, a since-suspended series of battles that were as much cultural as they were athletic. "Well, tomorrow it will be 'Catholics versus Catholics.' We will be the same, alike in every manner. But remember this—we *will* differ from Boston College, because Notre Dame has *classssss!*"

Wagner bit down on that last word long and hard, practically hissing, wielding it like a sword against the heretics who had entered the temple. It was a word that carried great weight here—because class is exactly what Notre Dame has always embodied to American Catholics, who for so long felt they had precious little of it; and class is what was conferred by extension on all those who rooted loyally for Notre Dame's football teams. Once uttered tonight, it became a mantra for the remaining speakers to echo.

"Wherever you go, whatever you do, if you associate yourself with Notre Dame, act with class," Lou Holtz said, half turning toward the cluster of Boston College fans up in the stands behind him, barely concealing his disdain, "and tomorrow afternoon, we will annihilate Boston College."

As the band invoked the solemn ritual of the alma mater, the visitors chanted *"Go BC,"* perhaps sealing their fate in the process. Barely ten minutes into the first quarter the next day, Boston College was down 21–0, and the Notre Dame fans were taunting *"Overrated!"* Even at 37–0, the Irish wouldn't let up, embarrassing the Eagles with a fake-punt play on fourth down. Tom Carter and the defense were impregnable, yielding only a last-minute touchdown that let BC avoid a shutout. The game ended at 54–7, but the clashes continued off the field—well-lubricated trash-talking between Eagles fans and Irish fans that escalated into shoving matches and flared into fights, keeping the bouncers at the off-campus bars busy deep into the night.

"It was as bad as the Miami games," a weary administrator said on Monday, wading through the disciplinary wreckage of a victory weekend.

The players gathered into a huddle as their coach led them in a pregame prayer. "Hail Mary, full of grace," they recited together, "the Lord is with thee. . . ."

"Our Lady, Queen of Victory, pray for us," Father Bill Seetch concluded.

"Cocks on three," he then instructed, and they all joined hands in the center of their circle.

"One, two, three—*go, cocks!*" they exclaimed as they broke, in a collective voice that was somewhere between a shout and a grunt.

As the Flanner Hall Cocks strapped on their helmets, Seetch donned his cap—emblazoned with the name of the team whose name his team had borrowed, the University of South Carolina Gamecocks. "The emphasis, unfortunately, is on the second half of the name, and on the sexual innuendo. I'd rather go with something like the Flanner Philistines, but they're not buying it."

The interhall football season had reached the playoffs, a time when some teams stoked themselves up by convening pregame breakfasts and watching *Wake Up the Echoes*, the devotional film history of Notre Dame football that has been known to raise tears in grown men's eyes. Flanner was still undefeated, 5 and 0, matched up in this semifinal game against Keenan, the team they had beaten in the season opener. The winner today would play the winner of the game that had just ended, Zahm Hall, for the championship—not on this distant field behind Stepan Center, but on the sacred turf of the stadium itself. The women's championship game was in the stadium, too, but Jenny Tate and the Purple Weasels of Pasquerilla West wouldn't be playing there this year. They had been undefeated until they met the Siegfried Slammers in the final game of the regular season. They lost, 26–6, and then lost again to Siegfried in the first round of the playoffs, 25–7.

"Push, 'em back, push 'em back," Seetch exhorted his team now from the sidelines.

"Watch the screen and the draw."

"Good cover, gentlemen."

"Good run, Mike."

Flanner was in Keenan territory when their quarterback, scrambling for a first down, slid out of bounds and collided head-first with the down marker.

"I gotta go in, Father," the quarterback pleaded—slipping automatically, perhaps inevitably, into win-one-for-the-Gipper mode—after Seetch told him he was out of the game.

"Let's have a little talk," Seetch said, putting an arm around the despondent quarterback's shoulder and gently steering him away from the field, explaining all the way why it might not be such a good idea to play with a concussion.

"But I gotta play, Father. This is for the championship."

At halftime, Seetch changed the game plan, ditching the conservative, Lou Holtz–style ground-control strategy that had so far gotten them no closer to scoring than a missed field-goal attempt. "Their backs can't keep up with our receivers, so we're gonna start throwing," he told the players huddled around him. On the other side of the field, Keenan's rector, Brother Bonaventure Scully, kept clear of the huddle, and let the coaches do the talking.

At game's end, Seetch called the team into a final huddle and tried to console them. The new passing attack had in fact kept them moving up the field, but it never got them quite far enough. Their last pass of their last drive was batted down near the goal line by a defender. Keenan won, 3–0, earning a return appearance in the championship game. " 'Nothing in his life became him like the leaving it,' " Seetch said, quoting *Macbeth* as he tried to lift the downcast heads around him. "We left well. It was a good ride we had this season. We gave them a scare."

They said another "Hail Mary," then joined their hands again in the center of their circle for the final time. "Cocks on three. One, two, three—*Cocks.*"

"Raise your right hand," Tom Morris told the students in Philosophy 101, and two hundred right hands went up in the air. "All right, put it down. Now lift your left leg. Come on, this isn't Simon Says, I promise. This is an experiment."

They had left behind Plato, Descartes, and the other familiar landmarks of an introductory philosophy class and were wandering now in territory usually mapped by daytime talk shows and the *Weekly World News*—with Morris discoursing on apparitions, psychics, Shirley MacLaine,, xenoglossy (the ability to speak in languages you never learned), automatic handwriting, and memories of past lives. The subject this morning was life after death, and on his way to exploring the philosophical implications of an afterlife, Morris first stopped to examine the evidence of its existence, however spurious and light.

"What if I told you that heart attacks tend to happen between 9:00 a.m. and noon, and they tend to cluster right around this class time." He usually sprinted through his ideas when he spoke in class, but now he was accelerating toward panic speed. "As soon as I tell you that, you begin to feel very strange. This is peak heart-attack time, remember. As you try to take your pulse, you feel worse and worse." The whole class was practically hyperventilating by now. "You check your heart—put your hand over your heart—you're feeling stranger and stranger, when suddenly—everything goes black." All the lights went out at once in the windowless auditorium, leaving only the dim green Exit signs to challenge the darkness. "You're leaving your body now. You're going down a long dark tunnel. Suddenly, at the end of the tunnel, you see a being of light." The flashlight he turned on himself revealed a face covered by one of the eerie Lou Holtz masks sometimes worn by devoted fans on football weekends. "The being says to you, 'It's not your time yet. You must return to your body. You must return to Notre Dame.' "

This stunt was designed to help the class feel a near-death experience, rather than just imagine one, and it was in keeping with the advice Knute Rockne once gave a professor who complained about apathetic students: "Make your classes as interesting as football," he said. It was also in keeping with the advice Morris himself gave to his teaching assistants, one of whom had played the role of God by killing the lights at the right moment: "Remember, the classroom is a DRAMATIC ARENA," he had written in the guidelines he handed out at the start of the semester, "and your fifty minutes with a class is your pedagogical WORK OF ART for the week."

"Does this stuff prove there's life after death?" he asked, after all the students had safely returned to their bodies. It didn't, of course, but it did lead to the question that would occupy the next few lectures. "What is at the pinnacle of the universe?" he asked next. "Where do we got our idea of God?"

It would have been an unusual question to hear in a philosophy class at most American universities, but at Notre Dame—where the department has a strong, and rare, interest in the philosophy of religion—it was at the core of the course. On his overhead projector, revealing one line at a time, Morris divided humanity into three categories. Theists, he explained, are those who "believe in some kind of divine reality"; atheists are those who don't; and agnostics are those who aren't sure.

"We're gonna ask, 'Who's right?' " he said. "My guess is, in this room we have people in all three of these categories."

Sitting near the back, Patrick Lyons from Keenan Hall counted himself pretty strongly among the theists these days, having lately been on a Notre Dame Encounter, one of the popular weekend retreats offered by Campus Ministry. "It was the first religious thing I did by choice, and I was sort of tricked into doing it," he said. Greg Butrus, the student-body president, had encouraged him to go on one, and—before he knew exactly what was involved—he agreed. "I signed up first, then I figured out it was religious. I thought it was gonna be all guitars and granola and Birkenstocks—it was the last place I wanted to be. I decided I was gonna be the cynical outsider."

When Patrick first came to Notre Dame, he, like many of his fellow students, went to Mass mainly by habit; by the time he left, Notre Dame hoped, he would instead be going by choice. "Notre Dame is a great place to lose your faith," Father Hesburgh liked to say, "because it's a great place to gain it." Students can hardly help confronting their beliefs here, so deeply ingrained is religion in the campus culture—from the daily Masses in the dorm chapels to the earnest, half-drunk arguments about St. Thomas Aquinas that you can sometimes overhear in Senior Bar. The rote, examined faith of childhood is a casualty of many college educations, killed off when restless young minds are first exposed to a larger world of new ideas, and new questions; but at Notre Dame a path is laid to lead those minds toward the more thoughtful, mature faith of adulthood. "I like Notre Dame," Norman Mailer once said after a visit. "You can say the word 'soul' there, and no one snickers."

The Notre Dame Encounter had sent Patrick and fifty-five other students—fourteen from each class—to the Fatima Retreat Center, across St. Mary's Lake, for two days of small-group talks, big-group talks, gather-in-a-circle-and-bare-your-soul talks, Masses, songs, and skits that weren't nearly as goofy as he had expected. At the reconciliation service, all the participants wrote their sins on a piece of paper—flash paper, actually, though they didn't know it yet—then touched it to a candle and watched their guilt explode and burn away. "I found a whole other side of myself that I didn't know before. I have like no doubt at this point that God exists."

Nor did Patrick have any doubt about his party affiliation. "I truly believe that no thinking Catholic could ever vote Republican," he said that evening at WVFI, the campus radio station. He was keeping company with his floormate, Steve Sabo, who was doing a turn as DJ. "If they thought about it, there wouldn't be anywhere near as many Republicans here as there are."

As the song ended—Soundgarden's "Slaves and Bulldozers"—Steve signaled for silence and spoke into the microphone. "All right, that was definitely the definition of grunge music from Seattle," Steve said as he cued up the next disc, U2's "Until the End of the World," "Even though people like them, they're still alternative."

"You say 'all right' too much," Patrick advised when the "ON THE AIR" light was off. "Be more confident."

Notre Dame has two student radio stations—WSND-FM, broadcasting from the clock tower in O'Shaughnessy Hall, and playing mostly classical music; and WVFI-AM, broadcasting from the third floor of LaFortune, and playing the kind of music that appealed to Steve but not to Patrick, whose tastes ran more to Paul Simon, Eric Clapton, and the other usual suspects. At a school whose soundtrack is dominated by the likes of Steve Miller and Billy Joel—on a campus where black is the color of old priests, not young bohemians—WVFI is a rare outpost of alternative culture. Its audience is tiny—its signal is carried on the university's power lines, and can only be received within campus buildings—and most of those listeners, it seems, tried out for DJ positions. Steve placed seventh among two hundred candidates, earning a slot as a fill-in.

"Here's 'The Day I Was a Horse,'" from *The Way of the Vaselines*."

The small, glassed-in studio was lined with records and discs, the walls hung with record-company posters—Eleventh Dream Day, the Melvins,

Helen Keller Plaid. Dutifully logging each new track on the playlist, Steve served up a string of songs by Screaming Trees, Smashing Pumpkins, the Smiths, Sugar, and a host of other bands that to Patrick all sounded like undifferentiated guitar noise. Their political tastes were almost as divergent as their musical tastes—Patrick voted for Clinton, Steve for Perot—but they remained the fast friends they had become on orientation weekend. They had spent the week of fall break at Patrick's home near Milwaukee, and they would soon be spending Thanksgiving there, too.

"All right, Mudhoney's one of my favorite bands, so I can't help playing another song by them, so bear with me."

"You've gotta stop saying 'all right.' "

"All right, all right already."

"If you have a four with a little two up here, that means four times four," Mike Somervile explained to a girl who fit far more comfortably than he did in the small school-desks where they both sat. "If it's a little three, that means four times four times four. That's called an exponent."

When he was on campus, the math he did was usually more complex—accounting and finance were among his classes this semester—but when he went off-campus, he spent more time on the basics. Twice a week, for an hour or so before dinner each Tuesday and Thursday, Mike came here to St. Hedwig's Outreach Center with a group of student volunteers to tutor children who lived a few miles, and several worlds, away from Notre Dame. He charmed this small audience with the same easy wit that had made him the natural choice to emcee the Dillon Hall pep rally back before the Michigan game.

"How many times does three go into three?" he asked, pointing at the next problem in the old math book. The faces in the book's illustrations were, like the faces of the tutors, all white. The children were all black.

"Once."

"How many times does three go into six?"

"Twice."

"That's it. You're stylin'. You're all over this stuff."

For most of its history, Notre Dame tried to keep its students out of South Bend—sending priests to patrol the bars, pool halls, and other establishments that might tempt a young man's baser instincts; turning over letters with a local postmark to the prefect of discipline, whose aim it was to quash any romances with the local girls; screening proper movies in Washington Hall on Saturday afternoons so the boys wouldn't need to make the two-mile trip to the downtown theaters, where, of course, they might see improper ones. Now it tries to get its students into the city, hoping they'll find there a place to exercise their nobler instincts. St. Hedwig's Outreach Center is an old house attached to an old Polish parish in downtown South Bend; the neighborhood is better known to most students for Tippecanoe Place, a plush restaurant popular for entertaining visiting parents and important dates. The center is meant to be a stable refuge in the often unstable lives of the children it serves. It relies heavily on student volunteers, who play games with the kids, take them on outings, and help with their homework.

"What do you think you do first here?" Mike Somerville asked, pointing to the next problem in the book: $(72 - 6) \times 1$.

"You do seventy-two–take–away–six first."

"So what's that?"

"Sixty-six."

"Times one?"

"Sixty-six."

College students, by nature, are inclined to think they can change the world, but Notre Dame students are more inclined than most actually to try. The inescapable lesson here—repeated by priests and rectors, professors and fellow students—is that ideas mean little if not accompanied by deeds. Evidence of their efforts was everywhere, and it spanned the political spectrum. Hanging on kiosks and bulletin boards all over campus now were posters, produced by Patrick Lyons on his Apple Powerbook, that announced "ND for the Homeless Week"—a series of events that included dorm meetings with guests from the Center for the Homeless, a 135-bed downtown shelter that Notre Dame was largely responsible for founding and funding. Planted in the wide lawn in front of the library last Sunday were eighteen hundred small white wooden crosses—"one cross for each aborted child in South Bend each year," according to Claire Johnson from the Right to Life group.

Though volunteerism is a pervasive ethic at Notre Dame—two-thirds of the students do some kind of service at least once during their four years—radicalism is not. There is a distinct element of upper-middle-class guilt in the service work here, an inability "to see the difference between charity and justice," according to Father Don McNeil, the Holy Cross priest who runs the Center for Social Concerns. "We have a heck of a time trying to get them to really see the structural causes beyond the surface problems." Many students work in shelters and soup kitchens, some hang portraits of Dorothy Day in their rooms, but few return to their three-car-garage suburbs preaching revolution. Student participation had climbed lately in one-shot programs—two hundred had applied for one hundred spots on the fall-break Appalachian Seminar—but it had dipped slightly in the ongoing trench work, the regular volunteer sessions with the retarded, the elderly, the hospitalized, the poor, the kids at St. Hedwig's. About 15 percent of the students volunteered regularly, more women than men, more from the College of Arts and Letters than from Business, Engineering, or Science.

"The first thing you want to do is everything in parentheses," Mike Somerville said, moving to another problem: $(99 \div 9) - (3 \times 2) - (7 - 4)$.

"Eleven," the girl said, biting her lip in concentration, calculating with her pencil, "take away six, is five, take away three, is two."

"That's the toughest problem on the page, and you did it with no sweat," Mike said. Her homework done, she was working on math now simply because she liked it. "And that's a seventh-grade book. You're doing next year's homework already."

"I'm gonna go to high school and then college."

"Big-time."

"You gonna still be going to Notre Dame if I go there?"

"No, probably not," said Mike, who was already a junior. "I'm sorry."

As a high-school senior, Mike hadn't been sure he'd be going to Notre Dame until he came here on a visit. Stranded by snow delays in the Cleveland airport, waiting in line to buy a hot dog, he met a Holy Cross priest who gave him the big Domer pitch. When they finally landed in South Bend, well past midnight, the priest offered him a ride to campus. He closed his eyes, following the priest's suggestion, as they drew near. "Then he told me to open my eyes, and I saw this huge golden dome at the end of Notre Dame Avenue. There was snow on it, and I got chills looking at it. I told people the next day that I met the greatest guy, a priest by the name of Father Hesburgh, and they all looked at me funny. I had no idea who he was."

Mike was collecting his share of A's now in the College of Business ("I liked the idea of a suit and a briefcase"), but he still hadn't declared a major. He was weighing two options: marketing, the only business class to catch his interest so far; or psychology, which would mean switching into Arts and Letters. "I like to do well, and I work hard, I've always worked hard, but it gets to me sometimes how some people act like there's nothing else to life—like, if they don't get an A, their whole life is shot, they're not gonna make any money, they're not gonna get a job. I want to say to them, 'Hey, it's not your life, everything's gonna be all right, you've really got to relax. You're young, you have limited responsibility, you're at Notre Dame, you're doing something right. Have some fun.'" Because he would be spending the spring semester at a program in London, he was interviewing early for a resident assistant's job next year. "It'll be good to get away from here for a while." But it would also mean missing the interhall hockey season, the Badin Hall stand-up comedy contest (he was the defending champion) and the kids at St. Hedwig's.

"These kids have two and a half strikes against them," he said, when the session was over and the two worlds had parted again. "A lot of them don't have people in their lives they can count on. I make sure I'm here every Tuesday and Thursday regardless of what I have going on in my life, so they know they have somebody."

The last few arrivals picked their way through the congregation, stepping gingerly through the cross-legged crowd that covered the floor, searching for a seat. The only chair in the chapel was the one reserved for the celebrant, Father Joe Ross, who waited for everyone to settle in before starting the Mass. The chapel inside Morrissey Hall had once been as cluttered and encrusted as the façade outside—the tall, crenellated pile of college-Gothic flourishes that looms over the far corner of the South Quad like an old horror-movie castle. But soon after Ross became rector, he and his students had stripped it clean of everything but God. A large crucifix hung over the raised platform where the altar once was, and a simple altar stood on the floor where the pews used to be. High, rounded arches and whitewashed walls the texture of stucco gave the chapel a vaguely Moorish air, a desert refuge migrated to these cold northern climes. It was a spare, contemplative chamber now, with plenty of room for its most important element: a couple of hundred young worshipers.

They all knew him as Joe—he didn't like to be called "Father"—and they packed Morrissey's chapel whenever he preached. He never wore a collar, preferring T-shirts and jeans instead, but his eyes marked him unmistakably as a priest: They had the rare quality of seeming to see near and far at once, of being able to look deep within you while still holding in their gaze the wider view above and beyond. Even when he smiled, he often clenched his brow like a fist, and he kept his dark hair as short as the Trappists whose monastery he liked to visit for retreats on school breaks. He kept his mattress on the floor, and a U2 poster on his wall. On Tuesday nights, he led a group of dorm residents over to the seminary gym for a round of basketball. Like Malloy, he was a guard, but unlike him, he hadn't played for, or even gone to, Notre Dame. He was a product of the Jesuits, a graduate of Loyola Marymount in Los Angeles, and, briefly, a high-school teacher before joining the Holy Cross community.

" 'While some people were speaking about how the temple was adorned with costly stones,' Jesus said," Ross said, as he stood to read from the Gospel of Luke, " 'All that you see here—the days will come when there will not be left a stone upon another stone that will not be thrown down.' "

His voice had a small, persistent rasp in it, as if still hoarse from previous exhortations. When he spoke from the pulpit, he often spoke like a man walking along the edge of a sheer, steep cliff—a tone that encompassed both the thrill ahead and the danger below, well suited to the apocalyptic vision of today's Gospel.

" 'Nation will rise against nation, and kingdom against kingdom,' " Ross read. " 'There will be powerful earthquakes, famines, and plagues from place to place; and awesome sights and mighty signs will come from the sky.' " Jesus was warning his followers of the trials they would face—persecution, prison, even death. " 'You will be hated by all because of my name, but not a hair on your head will be destroyed. By your perseverance you will secure your lives.' "

Because the text was so direct, so unequivocal in its meaning, Ross was free to use his homily not to dissect it, but to underline it. "Imagine going into Sacred Heart church on a football weekend," he said when everyone had settled back down again on the floor. "It's full of visitors and tourists, all sort of craning their necks to be able to see all the paintings and all the gold, all sort of oohing and aahing at how awesome this thing is. Now, imagine if you found yourself there, and this sort of rumpled character walks up the middle aisle, up the steps to the altar, and then in the most powerful voice insists, *This will all be destroyed!* "

What Ross was telling his audience now, what Jesus had told his then, was that they needed "to live for God alone." Faith was more than just "costly stones" in the temple, in the Gospel's words, or "a crucifix in every room in DeBartolo," in the homily's. "Tonight we got a wakeup call, like those people milling around admiring the temple," Ross said, speaking in waves that rose and fell like distant thunder. "Are our decisions really driven by faith, or are we just trying to get good jobs?"

Today's Gospel gave him the perfect platform from which to declaim one of his favorite themes—that the beliefs you profess in church for an hour each Sunday should shape the actions you take everywhere else the rest of the week. "We have to focus ourselves on Jesus—nothing else matters. No job, no GPA, no good looks, no athletic kind of macho. None of the lies our culture tries to sell us matter at all." The stakes Ross outlined were high, the choices stark. "Let's not stand around gawking, and saying how beautiful the church is. Christianity is not a spectator sport. Get in it. The wakeup call comes to all of us."

Before continuing the Mass—which had almost reached the point where the Liturgy of the Word gives way to the Liturgy of Eucharist, where speech give way to deed—he sat for a moment and let his rising message drift back down to earth. Ross was one of the top box-office draws on the Sunday-night Mass circuit, preaching the kind of homilies, and celebrating the kind of liturgies, that students rarely heard back in their home parishes. But as Morrissey's rector, and as a Freshman Seminar teacher, he had other pulpits, too. His students in Morrissey were among the core volunteers at St. Hedwig's. The students in his seminar, which had a reading list built around the theme of liberation theology, centered their discussions on two big questions: Can a Christian be wealthy? Can a Christian go to war? After participating in protests against the Persian Gulf War, Ross went to all the ROTC students in his dorm to explain why he was opposed to the war, and to hear why they were not.

But there was also a rigid streak in Ross that occasionally made him unpopular with some students. Rachel Stehle ran into it while carrying a bowl of Jell-O shots to a Morrissey party back in October—an encounter she later commemorated in a poem she hung amid the blown-up "Calvin and Hobbes" comics on her dorm-room wall:

> "Stop," he screamed, "what's in that bowl?"
>   (if only then we'd have sunk in a hole.)
> "Just Jello, sir," was our meek reply
>   but HE knew from that look in our eye.
> "I'm sorry, I have to take them away."
>   OH NO—what were our friends to say?

Rachel and her friend served their sentence—twenty hours of community service—by working on the recycling van. Tonight she was standing near the altar as the congregation joined hands in a long, sinuous chain to say the "Our Father."

"Let us take a generous moment to share a sign of Christ's peace," Ross said, smiling as he did, because he knew what he was unleashing. These moments grew more generous as the year wore on—a dense, lingering reunion scene worthy of an airport arrival gate, punctuated by bear hugs and high-fives that rivaled the football team's Mass.

"It's like being pastor of a parish where the parishoners are all living in the same building," he said later, after walking the few steps to the small dorm room that was his home, his rectory.

9

Mass was canceled at Sacred Heart today, and guards were posted at the doors to detour worshipers down to the chapel in the basement. Bright lights were shining inside, but the pews were mostly vacant and the altar was unattended. A large movie camera was set up over near the sacristy. A small crowd was clustered around the bank of tall director's chairs behind the camera, watching the last take of the scene they were shooting, and planning the next one. The basilica was doing brief duty as a movie set, its soaring interior busy with people who were more interested in how it looked than in what it meant. A makeup artist touched up the faces of the actors. The church's face had been attended to several years earlier—a $7-million restoration that left the gold gleaming, the soot-darkened murals and windows shining, and the critics complaining that the money would have been better spent on less opulent projects. In the glare of the movie lights now, the gilt arches and column capitals seemed to drip like regal stalactites.

"Slate . . . Roll sound . . . Action!"

The name of the movie was *Rudy,* the story, based on a real person, of a boy who—despite his height (five feet six inches), his dyslexia, his doubting friends and family, his lack of any great talent either on the field or in the classroom—wanted so badly to play football for Notre Dame that he finally did, for twenty-seven seconds when he was twenty-seven years old, as a walk-on who sacked the enemy quarterback on the last play of the last game of his senior year. It was a medium-budget Hollywood feature from the same writer-director team that had earlier made *Hoosiers,* another triumph-of-the-underdog sports saga set in Indiana. In today's scene, Rudy had failed yet again to get into Notre Dame, his third rejection so far, and he had come to church to wonder why. The screen Rudy (played by Sean Astin, better known as Patty Duke's son) sat in a pew looking glum. The real Rudy (whose seldom-used given name is Daniel Ruettiger) sat in a director's chair looking giddy. It had taken him six years to convince Hollywood to turn his life into a movie, longer than it had taken him to get into Notre Dame in the first place, and now that they were here he rarely detached himself from the proceedings. He habitually referred to the director as "Coach." He habitually referred to Notre Dame as "bigger than life," "a slice of heaven," "a mystical place." He came here in the Hesburgh era, when women were in the classroom and change was in the air, but the Notre Dame he believed in, the Notre Dame the movie depicted, was the Notre Dame of the Rockne era—a male-dominated citadel of sports and prayer, the solemn grail of working-class dreams.

"My father—the only pleasure he had, the one joy he had, was listening to Notre Dame football games," said Ruettiger, forty-four now, who grew up in a small house in Joliet, Illinois, with thirteen brothers and sisters. His father was an oil-refinery superintendent. "It was religion, it was like a Protestant-versus-Catholic type feeling."

While the crew reassembled the scene for another take, three men in black priest's suits waited back near the big gold altar for their cue. Two of them were real priests playing themselves in a brief cameo, Ted Hesburgh and Ned Joyce. The third was an actor (Robert Prosky, better known as Sergeant Jablonski in *Hill Street Blues*) playing a fictional priest—Father Cavanaugh, Rudy's kindly, white-bearded mentor.

"Hey," Ruettiger called to a crew member who had failed to remove his baseball cap upon entering the church. He sounded as indignant as a pious curate. "The hat—off."

"Roll sound . . . Action."

The priestly trio ad-libbed some background chatter as they strolled down the aisle together. "Excuse me," Prosky said to his companions when he spotted Astin, and he stopped to talk: Hesburgh and Joyce kept on walking.

"Cut."

The crew had been filming at locations all over campus for weeks—the Grotto, the dining hall, the seminary (the expanse of empty rooms and the view of the Dome had earned it the role of Rudy's dorm), the practice field, the locker room, the quads. Because the movie was set in the early 1970s, students working as extras grew sideburns, combed their hair badly, and donned wide bell-bottoms and other fashion relics of the era. Rudy's climactic sack, and his triumphant ride off the field on the shoulders of his teammates, were staged at halftime of the Boston College game, with 59,075 fans as the cheering backdrop. Movie money had spruced up an obscure off-campus bar, filled it with Notre Dame memorabilia, rechristened it Corby's in honor of a legendary but defunct local nightspot, used it to shoot a brief scene—Mike Somerville earned $100 for the eighteen hours he spent on the set as an extra that day—and in the process created a hot new student hang-out. Cameras had even made it inside Corby Hall, the big rectory adjacent to Sacred Heart, where some of the older priests could still remember the last time a movie was shot on campus.

Hollywood had courted Notre Dame many times in the past (when Rockne was killed in an airplane crash, he was on his way to California to sign a $50,000 deal to play a football coach in a movie for Universal), but only once before had Notre Dame said yes—for *Knute Rockne—All American*, the misty-eyed 1940 hagiography starring Pat O'Brien and Ronald Reagan. Warner Brothers had originally slated Jimmy Cagney for the title role, but Notre Dame exercised its veto power to keep him out: Cagney was a public supporter of the Loyalists in the Spanish Civil War; the Catholic church sided with Franco. Pat O'Brien, on the other hand, was "a family man of high character," according to a university official, with "a large following of Notre Dame people throughout the country." The movie was so successful at propagating the Notre Dame football legend that the university, fearful of being typecast as nothing but an athletic department, spurned all other football-movie proposals for the next fifty years. (In 1964, it even went to court in an unsuccessful attempt to stop Twentieth Century-Fox from showing *John Goldfarb, Please Come Home*, a rude farce in which an Arab king's football team somehow managed to beat Notre Dame, whose players are depicted as a rowdy bunch of sex-starved drunks.) The movie people needed Notre Dame's approval to film on campus, but university officials rejected the *Rudy* proposal several times before finally seeing a script that showed interest in something more than just those final twenty-seven seconds. Even then, not everyone thought it was wise to grant permission to the producers.

"Rudy doesn't exactly embody the nobility of spirit we like to encourage in our students," one official said, referring to Ruettiger's spotty postcollege career. "It's just another football movie, and that's just what we don't need."

"I felt my story would inspire people," Ruettiger countered. After graduating with a degree in sociology in 1976, he never quite found a place for himself in the world as certain as the one he had left behind at Notre Dame.

He sold disability insurance door-to-door, started a cleaning business, sold cars. A brief marriage ended in divorce. When he decided to shop his life around to Hollywood, he found year after year of closed doors, but he kept knocking with the same persistence that had once earned him a spot on the varsity. He finally sold the movie rights for $200,000. When shooting began, he was a caretaker at the condo complex near campus where he lived amid a sprawling collection of Notre Dame football relics. After the movie was finished, he hoped to find work as a motivational speaker. "It's everybody's story. It's everybody who has obstacles, it's everybody who has dreams."

"*Action.*"

". . . and on top of that, we've got to do all our own cooking, and we've got to do all our own laundry, and we're not very good at that either," Hesburgh was telling Prosky now, referring to his motor-home retirement trip with Joyce. The real priests kept on walking again as Prosky peeled off, but this time they continued around the rear of the church and back up the opposite aisle to the encampment behind the camera, their final take completed.

"*Cut.*"

After stepping down as president, Hesburgh continued living in the same room in Corby Hall that had been his home since 1949, but his presence on campus was as understated and quiet as his movie cameo. He said some Masses in the dorm chapels, spoke to a few classes, heard confessions occasionally at a Notre Dame Encounter. He traveled widely to meetings of the many boards and committees he sat on; last time he checked, he had 248,000 frequent-flyer miles on USAir alone. "Every time you turn around, there's something you forgot you belonged to," he said. Sometimes, at a Corby Hall dinner, after regaling the young seminarians with old stories, he collared Joe Ross and tried to convince him, unsuccessfully so far, to go on for a Ph.D. Though a great admirer of Sorin, Hesburgh did not model his retirement after him: Sorin remained the *de facto,* behind-the-scenes leader through the twenty-seven years, and five successors, between the end of his presidency and the end of his life; Hesburgh still had strong opinions about how the place should run, but he kept them mostly to himself. His word had been law for too long to be heard simply as advice now—so he didn't offer it, and he wasn't asked for it, at least not in public.

"I had my say, and I had my time on the throne, and I'm out. The worst thing in the world would be for me to try to edge my way back in." He had been in the Main Building only five times in the last five years, by his account, and spoken only three times—two of them in response to direct questions—at trustees' meetings. "I have a very good deal with Monk. I just said, 'I'll give you one piece of advice and that's "Be yourself and forget Hesburgh," and no more free advice. If you want to talk about something, you know where I am.' "

The likeliest place to find him is up in the suite of offices on the thirteenth floor of the library, which looks out over the Dome and the church, not the stadium. He has a museum's worth of mementos up there, walls full of books, a tiny chapel where he says Mass daily, often with only Father Ned Joyce for company. He keeps students' hours, staying up until 1:00 or 2:00 a.m., with the campus radio station—the classical one, not the rock-and-roll one—playing in the background as he works. He answers letters, works the phone, offers counsel. He riffles through the vast Rolodex in his mind, putting the wide and loyal network of Notre Dame people, money, and causes into service of one another. Students often make the pilgrimage up to see him, bearing copies of his books to be inscribed.

"Thank you, Father," Ruettiger said now, reverently clutching the book Hesburgh had just signed for him—*Travels with Ted and Ned*, an account of the trip that had been the subject of the earlier movie chatter. "I'm a huckster at heart," Hesburgh said of his brief, unscripted screen appearance. "I got a plug in for the book."

Prosky was sitting in the pew beside Astin now as the crew continued the tedious exercise in cubism that a movie shoot is—trying to capture an object from many angles at once, over and over and over again. They had to be out of the church by early evening: A wedding rehearsal would take over then.

"Son, in thirty-five years of religious studies, I've come up with only two hard, incontrovertible facts," Prosky told Astin, in a line he would repeat many times today. "There is a God, and I'm not Him."

The chair at the head of the long table disappeared under Monk Malloy when he lowered his sprawling, rangy body into it. He unfolded his great wingspan and locked his hands behind his head, crossed his legs widely, and tipped back to an angle of precarious repose. In order to make it to the conference room at the appointed hour of 7:00 p.m., he had reluctantly switched off the close final moments of the Chicago Bears game that had been playing in the background on the TV in his adjacent office. He wore a sleeveless argyle V-neck sweater over a blue button-down shirt. The walls were lined with framed color photos of the campus that had been taken in seasons more flattering than the cold, blank November lurking outside tonight. The Main Building was dark and empty all around this one lighted room.

"Tell me about the cabaret as a place, and as a concept," Malloy said.

"The cabaret is a place where people could come and leave their problems behind," offered one of the eighteen students arrayed around the table in the most comfortable chairs they would ever sit in on campus. "They could be happy. They didn't have to worry. They could block out all their problems, but at the end all the problems came out."

Malloy had taught a Freshman Seminar section every semester since his second year as president. It met on Sunday nights—two classes combined into a single two-and-a-half-hour session—because that was the time most likely to find him on campus. Although his schedule required frequent use of the university's small airplane—meetings, conferences, courting calls to potential donors, speeches throughout the vast archipelago of alumni clubs and satellite organizations—he gave the impression of being around more than his famously peripatetic predecessor had been. ("What's the difference between God and Hesburgh?" the old joke went. "God is everywhere. Hesburgh is everywhere but Notre Dame.") The seminar kept him updated on the state of the student mind, and it provided an outlet for his voracious reading habit. He consumes 150 books each year, putting eight of them on the seminar's reading list each semester). Two movies were also on the syllabus, one of which was *Cabaret*, the musical set amid the ominous decadence of prewar Berlin.

"That's one level," Malloy said. "What other way does it function?"

"It's like going through life, almost—putting a performance on, for yourself, for everybody around."

"OK, that's a second level—the metaphor that one plays a role in life, in history."

"I kinda think the cabaret was a way of showing the deterioration of society—how it led to the Nazi takeover, how it led to society's downfall."

"You can go to the cabaret, you can have all this happiness and fun, but beyond these doors evil lurks."

By this late point in the semester, the students knew him as "Monk," and he was more at ease with them than he was with most faculty members. Malloy does not share Hesburgh's love of the public stage, preferring instead the private rooms of his life. Living in a dorm, teaching a seminar, he is able to remain at least partly what he was before he became president. His classroom style showcases the qualities that are often hidden in more presidential arenas—the quick, dry wit; the engaging gift for conversation; the ability to employ his wide learning without pretension or pedantry; the empathetic interest in asking questions, rather than just answering them. He guided the discussion like a point guard, pushing the ideas up and around the floor, keeping the whole class in the game, leaving no one to molder on the bench, tossing no-look passes to the unsuspecting when necessary. His natural talent as a teacher makes him a worthy inheritor of his room in Sorin Hall: The longtime previous occupant was Paul Fenlon, the last of the bachelor dons, the unmarried lay professors who lived surrounded by their books and their students in the dorms.

"What was the Nazi salute?" Malloy asked one student. "Why don't you stand up and show us?"

"Heil Hitler," the student said, thrusting her arm up.

"What does that evoke in you, seeing that?"

"It scares me," another student said.

"Why?"

"Because of what happened."

What gave the exchange a special resonance was its timing, coming in the wake of the loud furor over a recent column in *The Observer*. Headlined "Jewish Slave Law must be abolished before it destroys," the column was actually a demented letter of the type all too familiar to most opinion-page editors—a hateful screed from one of those basement-office conspiracy theorists who dispatch their missives wholesale to the nation's newspapers, most of which have enough sense to deposit them directly in the trash. It came from New Mexico, from someone who had no connection at all to Notre Dame, and it was disturbing less for its assertions—easily discredited ravings about "global Zionism" and the "debt/tax slavery money system instituted by the Jews"—than for the implications of its publication: Apparently, none of the student editors knew enough about what anti-Semitism looked like to recognize it when they saw it. Among the deluge of outraged letters that followed was one from Malloy; it was the first time since he became president that something in *The Observer* had made him mad enough to write in response. "This species of bigotry and hate, whether in print or in deed, is anathema to everything this university stands for and will not be tolerated here," his letter declared.

"What happened?" Malloy asked.

"The Holocaust."

"What's the connection?"

"It's a symbol."

"Of what?"

"Hitler's power."

"It's like a Notre Dame pep rally, would you say? It's kind of like the Lou thing?"

"It's a lot more intense."

"If everyone here in class did what she did, all synchronized, would that scare you more?"

"Yeah, definitely."

Malloy's seminar, in both its makeup and its material, was meant to explore a world beyond the insular Notre Dame of *Rudy*. The authors included Shusaku Endo, Nadine Gordimer, Toni Morrison, and Elie Wiesel. The students represented a similar ethnic rainbow—Chinese, Indian, Hispanic, African, Irish, German, Italian, and more. Malloy's instructions to the freshman advisers who suggested candidates for the class were simply to divide the sexes equally and make the mixture interesting. One seat was usually reserved for a varsity athlete: Rick Mirer and Heisman runner-up Raghib "Rocket" Ismail were among his former students. This semester it was Jeremy Akers, an offensive tackle with an uncommon pedigree: He was a graduate of St. Albans in Washington, D.C., Al Gore's alma mater; his mother was Karen Akers, the singer and actress; his father was a lawyer. "It's more diverse than Notre Dame probably will be in the next ten or twenty years," Malloy said about his class, "but it may resemble what it will look like sometime beyond that."

Malloy's idea of what a class, and a university, should look like was shaped by what his world looked like when he was growing up in the nation's capital. The eldest of three children in a family of modest means—his father was a claims adjuster for the transit company, his mother a secretary—he learned to see beyond race at the neighborhood playground, where blacks and whites met on the basketball court as equals. His high-school team was a rare study in integration for its time, the late 1950s—three blacks and two whites who won fifty-five straight games, were ranked first in the nation, and united the city behind them.

The football team at Notre Dame was similarly mixed, and similarly successful, but Malloy wanted to inject some diversity into the crowd that cheered it on. He raised the amount of financial aid available to minority students—helped by proceeds from the $37-million NBC football contract—stepped up recruiting efforts to bring minority students to campus, and hired counselors to help them once they got here. Minority enrollment had climbed during his tenure, to about 14 percent of the undergraduate population. Hispanics—the fastest-growing segment of the American Catholic church, the natural inheritors of the Notre Dame dream—have accounted for most of the new faces. Notre Dame now holds much the same promise to a Mexican immigrant's daughter in Weslaco, Texas, as it did decades earlier to an Irish immigrant's son in Scranton, Pennsylvania. Black students, however, athletes excluded, have proved a tougher sell.

"What's a good negative thing that can bring us together?" Malloy asked, launching an impromptu exercise meant to show how a demagogue like Hitler can lure a nation toward evil. After tapping a student as their leader, they chose a cause: Up with the young, down with the old. In deference to Malloy, the upper age limit was lifted to fifty-two.

"OK, we need a TV station and a newspaper."

"We're gonna take over *The Observer*."

"No, *The New York Times*. Think high."

"You can only wear jeans—no ties."

"Free education for party members."

"Where are you gonna live?"

"In a big palatial mansion surrounded by girls."

"What do the women get out of this?"

"Free cosmetics."

"Uh-oh, I sense bickering in the party."

Black students didn't arrive at Notre Dame in any numbers until the 1960s, and they have been trying ever since, with mixed success, to feel at home here. To protest the scarcity of black players on the football team, fifty black students marched around the field at halftime of the 1968 Georgia Tech game, carrying banners that read "The Day of the All-White Backfield Is Over" and "Hey, Ara [Parseghian], Black Is Beautiful." Scattered jeers and several tossed liquor bottles greeted them from the stands. When some fans gave them the finger, the protesters answered with the black-power salute. In 1969, when the black population was only 1 percent of the student body, the Afro-American Society asked that it rise to 10 percent by 1972. The first goal was more easily achieved than the second: Blacks accounted for three-quarters of the starters on the varsity this year, but only 4 percent of the student body.

Malloy agreed that the number of black students should be higher, but there were forces larger than Notre Dame at work here—historical, cultural, religious—that prevented any quick or easy fix. African Americans have a long and bitter history with Irish Americans, the ethnic group that still dominates Notre Dame—from the Civil War draft riots (abolition, the Irish feared, would mean hordes of freed slaves fighting them for jobs at the bottom of the economic ladder) through the school-busing protests in Boston. They did not mix often then, and they do not mix often now. The white-flight suburbs are heavily represented at Notre Dame, and many white students arrive here having never been acquainted with a black person. On a campus so hugely white, black students have sought shelter among one another, carving out a largely separate social network. They usually skip the SYRs in favor of their own dances and parties, which feature less beer, more Anita Baker, and no Meat Loaf. They stayed away from Stepan Center when the headliners were the Spin Doctors—the contemporary band that most resembles campus icon Steve Miller—but flocked there for the Def Comedy Jam. They staged their own show at Washington Hall, *Black Images*, which most white students were unaware of: Corey Babington and Kerry Madden provided the finale, a Babington-original rap, "You Want a Damn Degree?," to the tune of Naughty By Nature's "O.P.P." And since most of the black students are not Catholic, they were doubly outsiders here, lacking the religious ties that allow many other minority students—Hispanics and Filipinos especially—to find some common ground with the majority. The members of the Baptist Student Union must go off-campus to worship: No non-Catholic Christian services are permitted at Notre Dame.

In 1991, frustration ran high enough among minority students, blacks especially, to spark a semester of protest. "[T]he vast majority of Notre Dame's traditionally underrepresented Ethnic Americans have been alienated and made to feel like step-children in this family known as Notre Dame," declared an open letter from a new campus group, Students United For Respect, better known by its onomatopoeic acronym, SUFR. Demonstrations were staged, demands were issued—a policy to deal with racial harassment, more financial aid, a multicultural center, more minority faculty, required courses in black and Latin American studies. Testy exchanges filled the letters pages of *The Observer*: One writer parodied SUFR's demands by calling for the establishment of a mandatory Irish Studies program, and the banishment of the Fighting Irish emblem, which "wrongfully portrays the Irish as the partying, fighting type." Anonymous callers left racist phone messages. Finally, more than one hundred students converged on the registrar's office in the Main Building for a sit-in. "N.D. really means No Diversity," one of their signs said. They dispersed after eleven hours, and a meeting with Malloy. Some demands were answered, some were not—the proposed multicultural center was a particular source of friction—and a task force on cultural diversity was appointed. Rarely had it been more apparent that Notre Dame was "a community in transition," as Malloy later wrote in his own open letter to a community that was far more comfortable instead with tradition.

Passions had since cooled, and SUFR had faded away, but the larger issues persisted. "So why do people hate Jews?" Malloy asked his class now, having given them a brief survey of the beliefs and practices of Judaism. ("It's amazing how little they know about it," he said later.)

"Basically because they see people with different practices from their own, and they're afraid of that," one student said. "They think it threatens their position."

Malloy ended the class with a question he left unanswered, hoping it would lodge in their minds until next Sunday. "Can any society," he asked, "accept an indefinite number of refugees who are different, ethnically and culturally?"

"I wanna ask you one question," Dan Wagner the leprechaun shouted up at the standing-room-only pep-rally crowd, his voice adopting the cadences of a TV preacher. "I say, 'Do you *believe* in Notre Dame? Do you *believe* in your university? Do you *believe* in the Lady on top of the Dome?' Say '*Amen!*'"

"*Amen!*"

"Say '*Amen!*'"

"*Amen!*"

"Say '*Amen!*'"

"*Amen!*"

The sweet and heavy aroma of nostalgia hung thickly in the air tonight, a sense of finality that left the crowd poised somewhere between celebration and loss. Tomorrow was the last home game of the season—the last game, too, of the series with Penn State, which was leaving to join the Big Ten— and every moment of the weekend's proceedings was encrusted with extra layers of sentiment and meaning. The fans were drinking in the scene a bit more deeply than usual, because they knew that what they saw and heard and felt here now would have to sustain them until at least next fall, and perhaps much longer.

"I'd like to introduce the seniors," Lou Holtz said, "who will be going down the tunnel for the last time tomorrow."

By name, position, and hometown, Holtz called on all the senior players to stand and be recognized, walk-ons and All-Americans alike. The biggest cheers went to the stars—Reggie Brooks, Rick Mirer, and especially

Demetrius DuBose, the linebacker and cocaptain who had choked up during his brief remarks earlier. In this arena at least, as on the playgrounds of Malloy's youth, the crowd, overwhelmingly white, seemed to make no distinctions based on race, only on ability.

"There are no Irish, no Italians, no Germans—there's just Notre Dame," Creighton Miller told a much smaller crowd gathered for dinner in the adjacent Monogram Room after the pep rally. Each home-football weekend, NBC treated some of its sponsors to a VIP version of the Notre Dame experience—game tickets, campus tours (Jenny Tate of the PW Purple Weasels was often their guide), ample food and drink, and after-dinner speakers like Miller, the All-American halfback for Frank Leahy's first national-championship team in 1943. The last of a storied family that had sent six players to Notre Dame, the son of one halfback (Red Miller) and the nephew of another (Don Miller, one of Rockne's Four Horsemen), he went on to Yale Law School, and a career as an attorney in Cleveland. "Part of our philosophy here is that you don't have to be an All-American. You may not have made the traveling squad, you may not have earned a letter. There aren't first-stringers or third-stringers, there's just Notre Dame."

Miller was followed by Tom Morris, a regular at these affairs. "I'm proud of you all, that you didn't get up and leave when you heard I was a philosopher," he said before launching into a typically animated talk on one of his favorite themes of late: "What is the Good Life, and what does it mean to live the Good Life?" Wielding an overhead projector and some of the same transparencies he used in class, he led the sponsors on a seductive little philosophical journey—raising the big rhetorical questions ("What ultimate good should we pursue? What should be the defining good of our lives?"); discoursing on the intellectual, aesthetic, and moral paths to fulfillment; defining what he called "the two basic human spiritual needs," the simultaneous needs for both "a sense of uniqueness" and "a sense of connectedness."

"Why are people so attached to the university?" he then asked, a question many of the guests were probably asking themselves about now, having just witnessed their first pep rally. "Because people need to feel a sense of union with something larger than themselves."

As he spoke, the stadium across the street—larger in every sense than anybody on campus, now or then—was sitting silently under a thin blanket of new snow. The locker room was busy with the corps of student managers, preparing the equipment for tomorrow. Out in the high, cold shadows of the concourse beneath the stands, the helmets were getting their weekly coat of gold paint. The paint contains real gold dust mixed with lacquer, and when it emerged in a cloud from the spray gun it hovered like an incongruous spot of sunlight. Occasionally, a couple of the managers would wander down into the tunnel and out onto the field, the stadium rising around them like the walls of a secret valley, shrouded in white, luminous in the night. Some, reverently, crossed the goal line onto the varsity's turf, leaving ghostly tracks in their wake.

By game time, snow was falling again from the low, heavy sky—slow, fat flakes that swirled in the wind and obliterated all memories of the T-shirt sunshine that had graced the season opener against Michigan. Penn State was another black-shoe team with no names on their jerseys and little flash in their offense, and, seeing them lined up against Notre Dame on this cold, muddy field in this old brick stadium—a scene as gray and grainy as an old newsreel—it was easy to imagine that the year was 1943 again, with Creighton Miller in the backfield and Frank Leahy on the sidelines. Tom Carter started his game with a strong statement on behalf of the Irish defense: On Penn State's first pass attempt, he hit their tight end so hard that the ball popped out into teammate John Covington's hands for an interception. But as the first quarter wound down, Tom fell down, slipping on the snowy turf and getting beat for a forty-six-yard gain. A touchdown soon followed, but not an extra point. Patrick Lyons, Steve Sabo, and all the other freshmen from the second floor of Keenan Hall cheered wildly up in the stands as their hallmate, fellow freshman Bobby Taylor, leaped high enough to block and kick, a play that would later return to haunt Penn State. The half ended tied at 6. Notre Dame's offense had only managed to get within field-goal range of the end zone.

A third field goal came in the third quarter, putting the Irish up 9–6, and the defense kept Penn State from getting near enough to answer it. The poor footing that had been Tom Carter's enemy earlier ended up as his ally, causing Penn State's star receiver, O. J. McDuffie ("the best I've ever played against"), to slip twice, and drop two long passes. The sky cleared briefly, patches of grass emerged from beneath the snow, and the sun's surprise cameo appearance was greeted by applause. Spirits were high when the band played the "1812 Overture" for the traditional arm-waving Lou salute at quarter's end.

But the snow returned in the fourth quarter, and with it came the Penn State offense: A field goal tied the game, and a touchdown put them ahead. With barely four minutes left in the game, Notre Dame was down by seven—it would have been eight if not for that blocked extra point earlier—and sixty-four yards away from a chance at victory. With twenty-five seconds left, they were three yards away, and their fate rested on one last play. On fourth-and-goal, Rick Mirer dropped back, the crowd held its breath, fullback Jerome Bettis rumbled out of the backfield and across the middle, the ball went up, the crowd froze, the ball came down safely in Bettis' arms, the crowd erupted.

The touchdown was a necessary but not sufficient condition for victory, leaving the score at 16–15, Notre Dame still trailing. Nobody wanted a tie, not when they could still taste the bitter and ambiguous residue of the Michigan game, so the only real option now—strategically, psychologically, morally—was to attempt a two-point conversion for the win. Rick Mirer dropped back again, looked at his first receiver, covered, his second, covered, his third, covered, before finally spotting Reggie Brooks—a gifted runner, but a questionable receiver, having caught just one pass in his entire collegiate career up till now—in the far-right corner of the end zone. Mirer launched the ball, and the crowd launched their "Hail Mary"s. Brooks leaped, his fingertips reaching, his horizontal body sailing so deep into the corner that most of the crowd was left straining in vain to see whether the pass was good or not. After a tiny instant of uncertainty, the official raised his arms, a triumphant gesture immediately repeated in every corner of the roaring stadium. After a longer moment of celebration—some fans rushed the field while there was still time left on the clock, a disorderly outburst of a type rarely seen on campus outside the immediate vicinity of alcohol—Penn State got the ball back to attempt its own miracle in the few remaining seconds. Three passes fell incomplete, and the score was inscribed in legend: Notre Dame 17, Penn State 16.

It was the kind of storybook ending that caused some Notre Dame fans to believe in divine intervention, that shamed even the Hollywood version of *Rudy*, and that unleashed mighty streams of joy. The crowd spilled out of the stands and onto the field, unimpeded by the guards until they tried to pull down the goalposts. Mud-caked players wandered among them, holding their scarred gold helmets aloft in salute. Relic-seekers ripped up the turf from the spot where Brooks had caught the fateful pass. The face of the crowd was one vast mask of wonder, both at what they had just seen and where they were now standing. They mostly just wandered and gaped, occupying the field in a way that, though it didn't seem purposeful, did seem necessary. Granted this special dispensation, they were reluctant to leave.

After playing the fight song one last time, Rachel Stehle and her bandmates stood in stoic formation, waiting for a path to clear. Lou Blaum could only watch from the crowd as the tall, black bearskin hats of the five remaining Guardsmen bobbed ahead of the band toward the exit. Many of the fans fell in beside and behind the band and streamed up through the players' tunnel, directly under the watchful gaze of Touchdown Jesus, whose upstretched arms were still signaling that final, improbable score.

"What a difference one point makes," Lou Holtz told the sportswriters.

Rachel Stehle was back on the field the next morning, playing a smaller fight song with a smaller band for a smaller crowd. Her dorm's football team, the Siegfried Slammers, was playing the Wild Women of Walsh for the interhall championship, and she and eight bandmates had brought their instruments to help create the proper atmosphere. The NBC truck, its interest limited to the varsity, had already packed up and pulled out for the season. The few hundred fans in the stands were mostly friends and dormmates of the players on the field. Siegfried's quarterback proved as troublesome to Walsh as she had to the Purple Weasels, completing a twenty-five-yard pass on her first attempt, an eight-yard touchdown pass soon after, and eventually leading the Slammers to a 13–0 win.

"S-I-E-G-F-R-I-E-D," the fans chanted as the miniband played the "Victory March" again.

"*Rudy, Rudy, Rudy,*" the extras in the end-zone seats chanted, prompted by the film crew that was here to shoot a stadium scene today.

"*Zahm sucks,*" the Keenan fans chanted when their team, the defending champions, took the field for the men's final. Brother Bonaventure Scully, Keenan's rector, stood down in front, holding last year's trophy under his arm.

"*Rudy, Rudy, Rudy,*" the extras chanted again—coincidentally, but annoyingly—when a Zahm runner plunged over the goal line.

"*Shut up!*" a Keenan fan shouted at them. "No one's gonna see it."

"You can't win 'em every year." Scully shrugged as he yielded the trophy at game's end. The final score was 14–0.

"*Rudy, Rudy, Rudy,*" the extras chanted again, cheering for a game that existed only in the imagination. More than two thousand of them sat in the stadium all afternoon, watching the same six plays unfold over and over again, cheering on cue.

"I wouldn't have missed it for the world," said Jimmy Zannino, short-order cook, ultimate fan, and eager extra. He was still high from yesterday's game. "That was the greatest play of my entire life. I'll relive it as long as I live. After the game, I just sat in the stands and cried. I cried as hard as I ever cried in my whole life."

"*Rudy, Rudy, Rudy,*" the extras chanted, the real Rudy chanting along with them. Here to film his cameo turn, he was seated in the stands behind Ned Beatty, the actor playing his father.

"This is the most beautiful sight these eyes have ever seen," Beatty said tearily again and again as the camera rolled, each time acting as if it were the first time.

All through the day, sporadic cheers rose up incongruously from the stadium, accompanied by amplified instructions from the movie people, who constituted perhaps the largest collection of male ponytails ever sighted locally.

"This isn't real life," a voice declared between takes, floating eerily above and across the campus. *"This is the movies."*

The battalion commander slipped quietly out of Lewis Hall—once home to visiting nuns, now the largest women's dorm—and set off across the sleeping campus. Fellow cadets emerged from all the other dorms, joining the stream that flowed toward the varsity's practice field in the Loftus Center. Their midnight-blue dress uniforms camouflaged them against the early-morning darkness. They walked briskly but crisply, trying not to disturb the creased-and-polished packages they had just assembled so carefully before their mirrors.

"Good morning, Miss McCurdy," Captain James Pattison said, greeting the commander, the chief among the cadets this semester.

"Good morning, sir," Allison McCurdy said, returning his salute.

The 287 Navy ROTC cadets stood straight and silent on the Astroturf, assembled in close ranks for a formal inspection at 7:00 a.m., an hour when most of their classmates were still reclining comfortably in the at-ease position. Each row snapped from parade rest to attention when Pattison approached. Allison and the other ranking cadets accompanied him, inspectors today rather than inspectees.

"Your cap's all messed up," Pattison told a freshman, tugging gently on its brim. "The anchor's not centered."

"You look pretty good."

"You've got good polish on the tops of your shoes, but you've got mud around the soles. Get a toothbrush and work on that."

"Your tie's not right."

"Captain likes a dimple in his tie," Allison explained in an aside.

Allison was shorter than most of the other cadets (five feet four), but she had more stripes on her uniform now than any of them (six). In a unit that is 90 percent male, she was only the second woman to serve as battalion commander. She oversaw all the battalion's activities, ran drills, wrote evaluations on all the cadets. "After three years, I'm kinda thought of as one of the guys," she said. Red-haired and freckled, she had a soft voice that was an inaccurate measure of her command authority. "I expect a lot, but I'm not a screamer. I learned that a lot of respect can come from leading by example. If you're always setting a standard, you can get a lot of respect that way."

Her father was a Navy captain who planned to retire next summer, soon after commissioning his only child as an ensign. Her grandfather was a professor at Penn State, the school she had originally expected to attend. "Notre Dame was a reach school for me." She came with the kind of three-year scholarship that puts great pressure on a freshman: if she got a 3.0 in her first year, which she had to pay for, ROTC would pay for the next three years. She got a 3.1, including an A from Brother Bonaventure Scully in her Freshman Seminar class. A biology major, she was waiting now to hear from the seventeen medical schools she had applied to.

As Pattison moved through the ranks, Allison backtracked to the row where a freshman cadet had fainted, falling out of formation. "When you tense up, your knees lock and it cuts off the blood flow," she explained. "You have to remember to flex your knees."

Because so many of Notre Dame's civilians keep their hair above their ears—by choice, not by command—the ROTC cadets only stand out on the days when military activities require them to be in uniform. One of every twelve students is in training to become an officer in the Army, Navy, Air Force, or Marines, a number so high that the campus sometimes resembles a service-academy annex. The Navy unit is the nation's largest—Texas A&M has more cadets, but Notre Dame has the most scholarships and commissions the most officers—and the deepest-rooted locally. During World War II, the Navy all but took over the campus, turning it into a Midshipmen's School that trained almost twelve thousand officers, and kept Notre Dame financially afloat at a time of sinking civilian enrollment. All the dorms but Sorin and St. Edward's became barracks, the dining hall became a mess hall, the South Quad became a parade ground.

"A large number of them use it as a way to pay to go to Notre Dame," Captain Pattison said of the ROTC scholarships, which are awarded through a national competition. If you earn one, you can take it to any participating school that will accept you. "I think Notre Dame stands out as a traditional, values-oriented university—at least it's perceived that way—and the military tends to attract people who hold those beliefs. It appears to me to be a natural relationship."

Pattison worked his way through the sophomores and juniors and into the seniors. While the Navy stood still, the Army ran laps around them, sweating through their Physical Training session. Kevin Kuwik from Bonaventure Scully's class jogged in tight formation with his chanting squad, wearing a black "Fightin' Irish Battalion" T-shirt.

"Good uniform," Pattison complimented one cadet.

"You're wrinkled in the back."

"He has the best-looking shoes in this platoon, and maybe in this company," he said of another cadet, turning to face executive officer Joe Carrigan, Allison's second-in-command.

"A lot of people took hits on shoes," Joe noted as the company was dismissed. This was for him, as it was also for Allison, the last inspection before he rejoined his fellow cadets in the ranks. New student officers would soon be installed, and the extra stripes he had to relinquish would become a memory in his scrapbook, enshrined beside his latest treasure—a photo of himself holding a gold helmet in the varsity locker room the night before the Penn State game. A friend who was a student manager had gotten him inside for a visit. "The reason Reggie Brooks caught that pass is because I was holding his helmet in the locker room the night before."

10

The snow arrived after dinner and lingered through the evening, collecting softly up on the Dome and the spires of Sacred Heart, slowly dusting the wide and frozen quads, lightly crowning with white halos all the outdoor statues, from Sorin down near the entrance circle to Moses up beside the library. It fell gently onto the sills of the dorm windows, where the students watched it like eager schoolchildren. By tradition, the first big snowfall each winter is marked by a massive snowball fight, the larger, newer North Quad battling the smaller, older South Quad for possession of the campus. It was one of the few happy rituals left to anticipate now in a semester that had dwindled down to its cold, gray husk. Papers were due and exams were looming. The computer clusters were busy, and the library was full—not just the sprawling second-floor study area, where the cruising scene sometimes rivals the Linebacker Lounge, but also the carrels squirreled away in the upper reaches of the tower. Football was finished, the regular season having ended in Los Angeles when Tom Carter leaped high in the end zone to intercept a last-minute USC pass and preserve a 31–23 Notre Dame victory. The *Rudy* filming had wrapped up, the movie people decamping before the deep chill set in. The sesquicentennial celebrations were history. (The actual anniversary of Sorin's arrival here fell on Thanksgiving, when the campus was all but empty, and it was marked only by a single rose left anonymously on his grave in the community cemetery.) Tonight the snow stopped before it was deep enough to sustain a skirmish. By morning, it had been cleared from the walkways, leaving only the thin patches of ice that made the footing uncertain this time of year.

"Why were these Christians persecuted?" Larry Cunningham asked, but only rhetorically, much to the relief of the drawn and weary freshmen in his theology class. Their hacking coughs punctuated the lecture. The campus was deep in the grip of the collective postnasal drip—physical, intellectual, emotional—of semester's end. The cold weather made everything seem brittle, from the branches of the elms to the nerves of the students. Cunningham peered bemusedly over the top of his half-glasses, his snow-white hair a premonition of the deeper winter yet to come. "It was connected to the virtue of *pietas*—the love and fear that children had for parents, that parents had for the state, that the state had for the Roman gods. The Christians wouldn't show any outward signs of *pietas* to the Roman gods—they thought it was a form of idolatry. For them it was a matter of principle, but to the Romans it looked like an act of treason."

They had traveled back almost two millennia this morning, to an empire where the small, new religion of Christianity was considered a subversive threat to the state—a hard concept to grasp now at a school where crucifixes hang beside flags, where the stadium pregame ceremony includes the recitation of an excerpt from the Declaration of Independence, and where the baccalaureate Mass at graduation each year closes with the blessing of a giant Stars and Stripes. Cunningham took them down into the catacombs and out into the less familiar districts of Rome. "Our vision of the place is that it was made of marble, with everybody walking around in togas talking about Cicero. But in plain fact, most of Rome looked like a shantytown." It was a highly combustible shantytown, he added, half of which burned to the ground in A.D. 64; the emperor Nero ("a crazy megalomaniac," in Cunningham's description) blamed the fire on the Christians, using it as justification for the first wave of official, brutal persecution. In the classroom, as in his writings, Cunningham speaks with an easy, unthreatening authority that makes ancient history seem like current events: His name is engraved on a plaque outside Monk Malloy's door in Sorin Hall, as the winner of an annual teaching award named for the room's longtime previous occupant, bachelor don Paul Fenlon.

"The ideal type of Christians in the first two centuries of Christianity were the martyrs," Cunningham explained. Because Christianity was a religion under siege so often in its early years, because the cost of being a Christian could be so high, a special place was reserved in its ranks for those who paid for their faith with their lives. "They were the ones who gave public witness to their beliefs."

Back in his office after class, Cunningham fielded questions from Kevin Kuwik about a different type of ideal Christian, one who lived in this century, Thomas Merton. Kevin was working on his final paper for Brother Bonaventure Scully's Freshman Seminar, trying to tie together the three writers the class had read this semester—Willa Cather, Flannery O'Connor, and Merton. Although Kevin was in a different Theology 100 section, he knew that Cunningham was the best source on campus for insight into Merton. Cunningham's most recent book, just out this fall, was an annotated collection of Merton's writings; on his desk now were photocopies of Merton's handwritten journals, which he was editing for publication. Kevin asked Cunningham about Merton's transformation from a worldly Columbia University student into a Trappist monk, about the depth and breadth of his spiritual experience, about the power of his writings, about the conflict in his life between solitude and involvement.

"If you have a deep sense of the reality of God and concern for the world that Christianity preaches," Cunningham said, as Kevin quoted in his paper, "you will ask yourself, 'How do I fit into the larger plan of making Christ present in the world?' Thomas Merton said, 'I'm a monk. How do I make monastic life witness to the depths of what I am learning in prayer, while at the same time trying to be an agent of reconciliation?' "

When Kevin arrived at the next meeting of his Freshman Seminar, taking his place on one of the overstuffed rec-room chairs in the basement of Keenan Hall, he brought with him what Scully had asked all the students to bring—a favorite quote from Merton. Scully used the quotes, collected aloud from around the circle, to start the discussion.

" 'If we are ever going to have peace, we will have to hate war more than we do now,' " offered Kevin, the Army ROTC cadet.

" 'Man is truly alive when he is aware of his ability to decide for himself— this is the beginning of a true life,' " Kathleen Bergin said.

" 'I am in a condition of ecstasy over the universe,' " somebody else quoted, questioningly. "How could he be in ecstasy over the universe? He thinks we're going to annihilate ourselves into piles of radioactive dust."

"I think he's fascinated by that fact—that it's such a struggle for humans," Kevin suggested. "The human condition isn't perfect. You have to overcome that."

"There's a lot of good in human existence, and it's something to get excited about," Scully added.

"We never stop to think of ourselves as humans," Kathleen Bergin said, continuing the discussion of Merton's ecstatic condition. For her paper, she had interviewed a religious-studies professor at St. Mary's. "We're so caught up in our busy lives and our busy schedules that, when we do stop to think of it, it's amazing."

Back in his room, guided by the little yellow "FOCUS" sign over his desk and accompanied by the semester's readings, Kevin started work on his paper, which he titled "God, Others, Self—Life According to Cather, O'Connor and Merton." "To me, this course was an exciting journey towards discovering what life really is about," he began. "In keeping with this theme, I gained insight into the three vital ends of our life—our standing with God, self and our fellow brethren on the earth." Twenty pages later, after sections exploring Cather ("Search for Self"), O'Connor ("The Shocking Awareness of God"), and Merton ("Bringing God to Others"), he reached his conclusion.

"Thomas Merton serves to show that self-introspection and reaching for God is not all that there is to life," he wrote, extracting from his semester some wisdom that might help shape the life of a young Domer. "While these two factors were certainly cornerstones to his experience, the ultimate fulfillment shines through in how he took the meaning he found in examining himself and spiritually engaging with God and sought to enlighten and aid others with it."

It was the night of Flanner Hall's Christmas Formal, and Father Bill Seetch was in full Holy Cross regalia—short black cape draped over the long black buttoned-to-the-floor habit. When he put on the black soufflé-shaped biretta, retrieving it from among the baseball caps on the hat rack in the corner of his room, he looked as if he had stepped out of one of the old photos that hang on the walls of Corby Hall. Joining him in the upbound elevator were several women whose outfits were similar in theme but different in execution.

"Your skirt's almost as long as mine," he said to one woman, whose black dress stopped above the knee, not below the ankle.

As usual, Seetch rode all the way up to 11, the top floor, the start of his trip down and around through a dorm that had, like him, dressed for the occasion. Each floor has two sections, and each section had decorated its halls according to how it filled in the blank in the dance's theme, "It was a _____ Christmas." The winners would be announced later: $200 for the section with the best decorations, $150 for second place, $100 for third. Accompanying Seetch on his rounds were the guest judges: Patty O'Hara, the vice-president of student affairs, who had welcomed the freshmen at orientation; Father Peter Rocca, a Holy Cross priest who was one of her assistant vice-presidents; and Bill Kirk, another assistant vice-president, whose duties during football season included scanning the stadium's student section from the press box for signs of illicit drinking. The official guests tried to look unofficial and unobtrusive, but most students along their path froze like deer in headlights, looking guilty in spite of themselves.

"Arriving at Notre Dame," read the poster at the entrance to section 11B, the *Star Wars* section tonight, complete with black lights and aluminum-foil stalactites, "Luke found an elite group of young men willing to skip their classes to learn the way of the Force."

"We'll have a gay old time," said the wall in the *Flintstones* section, quoting the theme song that was playing in the background.

"Strictly heterosexual," someone had clarified.

In section 3B, the *Fantasy Island* section, the residents had recorded their Notre Dame fantasies on a poster. "Coed Dorms," it wished, "Kegs in the Hallway, No Classes on Fridays, Drinking Age 18."

Downstairs, on the dim dance floor, a sea of couples swayed to "You've Lost That Lovin' Feeling" by the Righteous Brothers. In Seetch's room, after scores were tallied and notes compared ("I'd be willing to trade *Star Wars* for the *Flintstones*"), the winners were chosen: 11B *(Star Wars)* in first, 9B *(Flintstones)* second, 6A *(Dracula)* and 2A (New York City) sharing third. Though the student-affairs officials had done nothing but walk through the building, their mere presence alone had the effect of keeping the party in line, allowing Seetch to cede control to his assistant rectors and, *mirabile dictu,* get to sleep at what was for him an uncommonly early hour. He was due at Lou Holtz's house at eight-thirty the next morning to say a special Mass for fifteen visiting football recruits.

At the other end of campus, Father Joe Ross and his RAs were gathered in his Morrissey Hall room like generals in a bunker. The big event in Morrissey tonight wasn't a Mass, where Ross could exhort the students toward good deeds, but an SYR, where he could only hope to prevent bad ones. Before venturing back out to patrol the noisy, crowded dorm, the RAs joined Ross in a huddle, hands joined in the middle of the circle: "One, two, three," they chanted as they broke, stoking themselves for the task ahead. "Duke sucks." The perceived smugness of Duke's dominant basketball team—the defending national champions, due here later in the season to play an unranked Notre Dame team—inspired some local fans to root against them, in much the same way that fans on other campuses rooted against the perceived smugness of Notre Dame's dominant football team.

"You want to find him in the next fifteen minutes and tell him that's not interesting," Ross instructed an RA who had a troublesome reveler at large in his section.

This was the last loud, late night before quiet hours and midnight parietals became the rule of the dorms, and nobody was eager to see it end too soon—except Ross, whose preferred pastime at this hour was a round of euchre in his room with several students. The walls seemed to throb all around him; the old dorms like Morrissey don't absorb an SYR as easily as a tower like Flanner. With no elevators to ferry people to and from the room parties, the stairwells became a danger zone: He had already dispatched one woman to the hospital after she fell hard enough to require stitches. The dance floor was in the entrance foyer, and as the 2:00 a.m. deadline arrived it was still as packed as the stadium on game day.

"Tell that DJ if that music doesn't fade in ten seconds, I'm gonna rip his lungs out," Ross told an RA, who did. When Eric Clapton's "Wonderful Tonight" ended in a mass, slow-dance clinch, so did the SYR.

The crowd streamed out of the dorm, across the quad—the women creeping carefully along icy walks that were treacherous to their high heels—and into South Dining Hall for the traditional Morrissey postdance breakfast. On another campus, the couples might instead be going to breakfast ten hours from now, emerging starry-eyed and sated from their coed dorms; but here the ritual was foreshortened, the middle section, in theory at least, omitted. They filled their plates with pancakes and took their places at the long tables under the high ceiling. Ross stood on the sidelines, making sure that the food did not become ammunition. When the men at one table stood up on their chairs, the rest soon followed.

"Fight on for Morrissey," they sang, to the tune of the USC fight song, "The black and gold for victory."

"On the first day of Christmas," the women from section 2A of Pasquerilla West sang several nights later, closing their social season on a quieter note, "my rector fined me for—letting a guy into 2A's bathroom."

The dorm's residents sat cross-legged in their study sweats on the floor of the first-floor lounge, gathered for the PW Christmas special. Each section presented a skit; most of them were aimed at least in part at their rector, Laurie Brink, who sat in the audience laughing at herself. Tomorrow she would teach the final installment of "Books of Color," her Freshman Seminar; she wasn't teaching next semester, her last at Notre Dame before joining the Dominicans. She had already handed out the assignment for the final paper: "Can Notre Dame maintain its 'Catholic' character and tradition and accommodate a 'diverse' student body?" it asked. She had done some writing herself recently, too—a moving personal essay in the student weekly, the *Scholastic*, that explored the intertwined issues of abortion, which she knew as a counselor, and adoption, which she knew as a daughter. "[W]e as a community haven't created an environment where the choice for life is easier than the choice for death," she wrote. "Ending abortions will not do that. It is not a change of law we need but a change of heart." As she watched now, she gently rocked the newborn daughter of a visiting friend.

The singers from section 2A counted all the way up to the last day of Christmas, each new entry eliciting knowing, slightly guilty laughter from their dormmates at remembered sins large and small. "On the twelfth day of Christmas," they sang, "my rector fined me for—

> "Breaking parietals,
> Putting tape on my room door,
> Rollerblading in the dorm,
> Leaving the front door open,
> Social gathering on a weekday,
> Getting locked out of my room,
> Losing the kitchen key,
> MAKING JELL-O SHOTS!
> Leaving late for the formal,
> Three quiet hour warnings,
> Passing out on the dance floor,"

and then, the whole crowd joining in for the final partridge-in-a-pear-tree line, "Letting a guy into 2A's bathroom!"

The male singers from the Glee Club arrived soon after, bearing a selection of more traditional Christmas songs. It was midnight, and PW was the last stop on their annual caroling tour of all the women's dorms. All through "Deck the Halls," one member waded through the audience with a sprig of mistletoe, bestowing kisses with each "fa-la-la" and aiming toward the corner where Dan Wagner, the leprechaun, sat with his fiancée, Jen Avegno, the RA on 3B. They had met at a Sunday-night Mass sophomore year in Flanner Hall, Wagner's old dorm. "At the end of Mass, when they said, 'Are there any announcements?,' I stood up and said, 'My name's Dan Wagner and I really need a girlfriend bad. I'm serious. I'll cook, I'll clean. My number is . . .' The rector [of the dorm] was mad, but Jen and her roommate came up and asked, 'Do we apply here?' " They had gotten engaged last spring, and they were getting married next spring, just a few weeks after graduation. With the mistletoe hovering over them now, they kissed, to a round of cheers and applause from the crowd.

"Fa-la-la-la-la," the Glee Club sang, "la la, la, laaaa."

"I want to tell you the story about the Hessian fly," George Craig was saying to his entomology students, who had managed to get to the basement lab in the biology building—the one with the sticker on the door that boasted "Entomologists Get the Bugs Out"—for one last 8:00 a.m. lecture. Hanging in the corner was a white insect suit and a specimen net. "It's a parasite of wheat, and it was first found in Long Island, New York, during the American Revolution. The claim is that it was introduced in the bedding brought with the Hessian mercenaries."

The flies, he told them, are tiny (a wingspan of barely four millimeters), dangerous (they wiped out the entire Long Island wheat crop), and resilient (they overwinter as maggots in the wheat stubble), but they are not invincible: Their lifespan is only three or four days, and if you wait to plant your wheat until their brief season is over—the fly-free date in South Bend, Craig said, is September 22—your crop will be safe.

"So the question is, when are we going to run out of the need for entomologists?" asked Craig, whose fervor for his subject was evangelical, and who saw in the Hessian-fly story yet one more reason why it was important to study the vast and complex world of insects. "Never."

Dana Ciacciarelli, sitting at the middle lab bench, took close notes as Craig spoke. There was little that Craig didn't know about insects, and there was little that his exams didn't ask. He was equally demanding in the lab portion of the course, sending the students out with cyanide jars, nets, and plastic bags to assemble large specimen-collections. Some students had made road trips to Kentucky to find new insect trophies for their collections; Dana had hunted locally for hers, which included representatives from sixty different families so far. "This is actually a pretty decent breeding ground," she said of the campus.

Dana was applying to graduate programs in entomology now—Michigan State, Wisconsin, Purdue, Oregon State, Kansas State, and Notre Dame, too. "I'm kinda ready to move on, though," she said. Complicating the decision was the unresolved question of whether her boyfriend, Geoff Slevin, would still be her boyfriend after graduation, and, if he was, where he would be. The air was leaking out of the bubble now for the seniors, especially those involved in long-standing relationships, exposing them to a future where time was no longer suspended, and reverie was no substitute for action. It was the season when some men were frequenting jewelry stores, seeking diamonds appropriate for a Christmas engagement; when some women were rehearsing gentle elegies that included phrases like "too young," "my freedom," and "see other people"; and when Dana and Geoff were hovering somewhere in between. The view was clear and happy at the moment—she had spent fall break with him and his family in Illinois—but it was cloudy and uncertain when they looked too far ahead.

"The U.S. Navy sprayed DDT and blasted the hell out of the flies," Craig was saying now, in the middle of a story set in Egypt, where houseflies were spreading a virus that caused blindness in humans. "Six months later, the flies were back up again. By the next year, they were resistant already."

Craig scanned the class with the same look that a lawyer uses on a jury, confident that he had just presented a crowning piece of evidence in behalf of his argument—that human power was as nothing next to the power of nature. "We're on a treadmill, and what's that treadmill called?" he asked with a flourish. "Evolution. Man comes up with ways for controlling insects, and insects come up with a way to get around it."

Long after class and late into the evening, Dana was still busy doing work for Craig. Trying to finish a research paper from her summer stint with him in Wisconsin, she was perched at a terminal in the DeBartolo computer cluster, punching in the data she had collected on the frogs of Land O'Lakes. Geoff Slevin sat a few screens away with his lab partner from Chemical Engineering 459, trying to finish their final report. The other seventy-six terminals in the long, loud room were occupied by seventy-six other students trying to finish their own deadline projects, and the lounge outside was crowded with dozens more hoping to hear their names called soon from the waiting list. The soda and snack machines were working overtime. The screens flashed with random bits of information from every corner of the university.

"The situation in Sarajevo . . ."

". . . greenhouse gases . . ."

". . . Gertrude Stein's view on . . ."

". . . production was increased."

"Engineers get to do this all the time," said Geoff, a veteran of many late-night computer sessions, surveying the scene like a professional among the amateurs. The rigorous workload tends to breed in engineers a boot-camp hardness, and a suspicion of other, presumably softer academic disciplines. "These business guys get all excited—'Like, wow, it's 3:00 a.m.' Their professors let them do it once a year."

Geoff shared some M&Ms with Dana, then returned to his partner. "I learn engineering, he *knows* engineering. He's more the theorist, and I'm more the clean-up guy." He expected to be up most of the night finishing the lab report, and to be up for several more long nights soon finishing the rest of his work: He still had hundreds of pages of reading to catch up on before exams. The sophomores in his organic-chemistry review sessions were on their own now. "They've either given up or they've realized I can't help them now."

A year from now, engaged or not, Geoff was likely to be deeper into the rhythms of adulthood than most of his classmates. The unpredictable cycles that drive the engineering job market had made this a banner year for chemical engineers, with starting salaries pushing toward $40,000. (The aerospace engineers, by contrast, were less lucky: Flying high a few years ago, when today's seniors were career-shopping freshmen, they were all but grounded now, with scant job prospects.) In a hard major with a high casualty rate, Geoff had managed to stay near the top of his class, which now put him near the top of the recruiters' interview lists. He had been on twenty interviews so far, more than most of his classmates, and though he had also collected his share of thank-you-but letters, he expected to have a choice of job offers before graduation. He was scheduled to tour a Procter & Gamble plant in Iowa City over Christmas break.

"Remember, we've got to go over to Fitzpatrick and bang out the numbers," Geoff said to his lab partner. The big mainframe, the domain of the hard-core engineering computer jocks, was next door in Fitzpatrick Hall, where the upperclassmen sometimes taunted the freshmen by breaking into their programs and disrupting their screens. They would invert the text, or turn it into static, or, favorite of all, cause it to melt away into oblivion, and in the process cause the freshmen to melt in their seats. Later, chastened victims would gratefully realize that their work itself was not damaged, only their nerves and their pride. By 1:00 p.m. tomorrow, Geoff and his partner would need to have all their numbers in line, and be ready to make their presentation in class. "He's from Alabama, fortunately," he said of his partner, "so he talks slower, and we can waste some time."

As the hours ground on, some of the nonengineers, the giddy all-nighter novices, closed up shop. "Meet me for breakfast?" one student asked a friend as he left. "Promise me?"

"Promise," the friend declared, blessing himself. "Swear to God."

"Swear on the Dome?"

"Swear on the Dome."

Allison McCurdy sat at the front of a large lecture hall in DeBartolo that was pitched as steeply as an anatomy theater in an old horror movie. Looming up before her like a craggy blue mountain was the entire Navy ROTC battalion, all sitting straight and attentive in their dress uniforms, gathered here for the end-of-semester change-of-command ceremony. Captain James Pattison, their commanding officer, was at the podium.

"I want to congratulate Midshipman McCurdy on an outstanding semester," Pattison said. "She has been a strong leader who knew what she wanted to do and went forth to do it. Those of you in the underclasses who aspire to leadership positions in the battalion should study how and what she did."

Allison took the podium from him with a speech she had timed at eight minutes. "I must admit that I stand here today feeling some regret, but mostly a lot of relief," she said. "I enjoyed my stint as battalion commander not just because I had power, but because I enjoyed making decisions and learning to be a leader."

She thanked Joe Carrigan and the rest of the staff, quoted from Dr. Seuss *(Oh, the Places You'll Go)*, and recounted events of the semester, from freshman orientation to the midnight study breaks in the ROTC building during exams. It had been her best semester yet, both in and out of uniform: Despite her duties as commander, she was earning the highest grades of her college career, dean's-list bound for the first time. Looking up from her text and scanning the battalion, she took special note of her fellow seniors, whose first service assignments depended in part on what she thought of them. One of her duties had been to rank them from one to seventy, "the most difficult thing I was asked to do this semester."

"Leading your peers presents unique challenges that do not exactly parallel those found in the fleet as a division officer or platoon commander," she said. "In a way, I think it is more difficult, because you are faced with leading your friends. There becomes a very fine line between friendship and the number of stripes you both are wearing. Sometimes it is hard to retain a strictly objective view."

"I will now read my orders," Captain Pattison said, putting his cap on and standing when the applause for Allison had ended. "You will stand relieved of your duties as the midshipman battalion commander. Congratulations on a job well done."

"I am ready to be relieved," Allison said, putting her cap on and standing off to the side at parade rest.

After Pattison had read his orders to the battalion commander he had selected for the spring semester, he turned again to Allison. "I relieve you, ma'am," he said, saluting.

"I stand relieved," she said, returning his salute. "Sir, I have been properly relieved as the midshipman battalion commander."

"Philosophers don't have roadies," Tom Morris explained to the class as he rolled onto the stage an unorthodox teaching aid—a Peavey electric-guitar amp. He strapped on a white Fender Stratocaster and plugged in. "A guitar-playing philosopher, it's kinda like a heavy-metal nun. It's an oxymoronic category."

Morris had been a guitarist long before he was a philosopher, and he hadn't shed that first role when he assumed the second. After playing lead guitar in several rock-and-roll bands in high school and college, he went on to Yale. While studying for his Ph.D., he played daily on his own to clear the thickets of Wittgenstein and Kierkegaard from his brain. When Notre Dame's football team won the national championship in 1988, he wrote and recorded what he called "the first major rock-and-roll fight song," "The Fightin' Irish Are Back":

> If you know the game of baseball,
> You know about the Hall of Fame.
> And if you know the game of football,
> You know about Notre Dame.
> But if you've come to doubt the legends
> That so often get retold,
> We're gonna bring back the Gipper
> And bring back the Rock, and roll.

The guitar was as much a part of his identity now as his bow tie, and because he had earned enough stripes within the academy—as a tenured full professor with an astonishing proliferation of scholarly books and articles on his vita—he could bring it into class without fear of professional reprisal. The weight of the amp (150 pounds) and the strain on his back had led him to retire it for a couple of semesters, but popular demand led him to bring it back now.

"Use your imagination, and move back to the time when I was twelve years old and I had just bought my first guitar," he said, ineptly strumming a beginner's chord. He went on to pluck the few, simple notes of the *Peter Gunn* theme. "That was my biggest achievement when I was twelve."

But then he stepped back and showed them what he had learned in the subsequent years, launching a fast, pyrotechnic solo that showcased his fluency as it betrayed his age: It sounded nearer the Allman Brothers than it did to Pearl Jam. The final note set off a wave of cheers and applause. Most of Morris' students were happy to follow him on detours like this, but in the course evaluations they completed at the end of each semester, sprinkled among the "you-changed-my-life" paeans, he sometimes heard a few grumbles from those who would have preferred more philosophy, and less performance art.

"Now, how do you get from point A to point B?" he asked, trading the guitar for another instrument he played expertly—the overhead projector. "How do you get from not being able to play chords to being almost able to play?"

Morris had one more class left before the semester ended, but he was already starting his summation, wrapping all the big ideas into small, neat packages the freshmen might hang on to long after they had sold or lost their copies of Descartes's *Meditations*. The guitar solo was his way of luring them into a lecture on the philosophy of success—the subject of the business talks he had been giving lately, and of a book he was now writing that he hoped would find an audience beyond his fellow Ph.D.'s.

"We need to have a clear *conception* of what we want," Morris said, offering the first of his "Seven C's of Success." His rhetorical strategy owed much to Lou Holtz, whose own corporate speeches earned far more money than Morris' (and mentioned Aristotle far less often), and who served as the first example today of the first "C" of success. After Holtz lost his job as an assistant coach at the University of South Carolina in 1967, he sat down and—as Morris told the class, repeating a familiar story—wrote a list of 107 goals, which included becoming head coach at Notre Dame and winning a national championship. He had reached number 92 already, and was planning to add 93 next summer, when he rafted through Hells Canyon on the Snake River. "That shows you the power of articulation. When you talk about your goals, you clarify them."

Morris' journey through the remaining six "C"s included stops to visit Einstein; Faulkner; the Book of Proverbs; Rudy Ruettiger; his own father, a fifty-year smoker who was now battling lung cancer ("Habit is the second-strongest natural habit in human life," he said; "only one power is stronger—imagination"); and his recent incarnation as a *Winnie the Pooh* pitchman. ("You can always tell your good students," he had said in his thirty-second TV spot. "They know their *Pooh*.")

"A strong *confidence* that we can attain that goal . . .

"A focused *concentration* on what it takes to reach the goal . . .

"A stubborn *consistency* in pursuing our vision . . .

"An emotional *commitment* to the importance of what we are doing . . .

"A good *character* to guide us in our choice of goals, and in our means to those goals . . .

"And a *capacity* to enjoy the process along the way," he concluded. "The best way to think of success is not as a destination, but as a process."

For his final performance, he played only the overhead, but he whipped the transparencies across it at a speed that approached his lightning guitar solo, racing through the semester, and the history of philosophy—belief, truth, goodness, free will, determinism, materialism, death and afterlife, the existence of God, the problem of evil. He was trying to lead the students up to a height from which they could see it all unfold at once—the wide, clear landscape of ideas.

"Your world-view as a whole is a map, whereby you steer through life. But is your map correct? It can't be correct if it's not coherent. Do your beliefs cohere? Are your actions consistent with the beliefs you affirm? Are your emotions consistent with your beliefs and values? That brings us to the focal question: Is philosophy practical?"

His answer, of course, was little in doubt. "Philosophy involves a search for the deepest truths about you, about the other people around you, about the physical world in which you live, and about the nature of ultimate reality. To the extent that you find some of these truths, you acquire wisdom. So, if among the goals for your life is a better understanding of yourself, then I can't imagine anything more practical than philosophy." Notebooks rustled as students tried to keep up, and the auditorium echoed with a crescendo of epiphanies. "Everybody is an artist, and everything you do is a stroke on the canvas—it contributes to the work of art that is your life. And without reflection on the deepest questions, we're unlikely to make that work of art the best that it can be."

He was sprinting now, his breath short, his voice rising. "The most important thing I was ever taught in the entirety of my formal education, which spanned twenty-two years, I was taught on the first day of first grade. The teacher wrote this sentence on the blackboard, Miss Anders of the Durham Academy in Durham, North Carolina"—and he placed the last transparency of the semester on the overhead, reading it loudly, twice, for emphasis—*"Life is not what you want it to be, it is what you make it."*

"That's it for me," he said after a coda of farewell, and he was answered with an even louder round of applause than had greeted his solo in the previous class—one of the rare moments in history when, appearing on the same stage, a philosopher had outplayed a guitarist.

Just as classes were ending on the semester's last day, the seasons' first big snow, as if on cue, was starting, and by midevening enough had fallen to arm two teams for battle. The campus snowball fight started when an advance party from the South Quad—the perennial underdog in these contests, given its smaller population—staged a fatalistic first strike against the North Quad, trying to pin them back against Haggar Hall, the psychology building. But reinforcements soon arrived, pulling on boots and gloves and pouring out of the dorms, launching a heavy aerial barrage that overpowered the southern invaders as decisively as Notre Dame's offense had overpowered Purdue—driving them all the way back across campus, through Fieldhouse Mall, through the God Quad (in the center of campus, overlooked by Sacred Heart and Mary on the Dome), finally trapping them against the Rockne Memorial, where, backs against the wall, their only option was surrender. To the relief of the campus police watching from the sidelines, the casualties were limited to a few black eyes: A few years earlier, snowballs had shattered some stained-glass windows in Dillon Hall's chapel. The virgin field of snow was now a rough-terrain map, pockmarked by the stampede. Reluctant to return to their studies, the combatants stayed out to play when the fight was over. Men and women tackled one another, laughing and shrieking and rolling in the snow—a rare exhibition of physical contact between the sexes on a campus where public displays of affection are usually limited to hand-holding walks around the lakes.

The new blanket of snow seemed to muffle the campus, which settled into a stretch of monkish silence that wouldn't lift now until exams were past and a new semester had begun. Lights burned late in dorm windows, each one marking a private series of anxious deadlines. The library was open around the clock, and the Campus Ministry office in the concourse offered free coffee, tea, and hot chocolate. The earnest study routines were broken only by a few raucous outbursts—the Alumni Hall streak through the second floor of the library; the Keenan naked run around campus; the midnight pancake breakfast, in the dining hall on the night before the first exam, that degenerated into a wild food fight.

"I'm getting kinda stressed," said Rachel Stehle, who spent seven hours in the library making little progress on a paper about *Heart of Darkness*. "I'm getting ready for the break." A few days after Christmas—when she hoped to get the silver trumpet her father had promised her if she made the band— she was flying to Dallas, where Notre Dame would play Texas A&M in the Cotton Bowl and the band would play the fight song for the New Year's Day audience on national TV. "I am so excited, I can't wait. There're four freshman trumpet girls, and we're all gonna room together."

Lou Blaum would have to watch the Cotton Bowl from a distance—only the five rookie Irish Guardsmen were marching in Dallas—but he had something else to be excited about. "I was just lying down to take a nap," he said, recalling a recent 3:00 p.m. phone call from his father, who had just gotten the letter: Thomas Jefferson, his first choice for medical school, said yes. "I ran down the hall in my underwear."

Kathleen Bergin was finished with Brother Bonaventure Scully's Freshman Seminar—her final paper, like Kevin Kuwik's, earned an A—but not, unfortunately, in calculus. "I need to do well in my math," she said, and if she did, she would have an easier time enjoying her Christmas break back home in Nevada. She was, like Rachel Stehle, leaning toward psychology as a major. "I've decided not to go into business. The only reason I was considering it was the practicality of getting a job, but I got to thinking that I wouldn't be very happy in business. Even if I have a harder time finding a job, it's worth it if it's something I'll be doing my whole life."

Mike Somerville had already switched from business to psychology, but now he was planning to switch back to business. He had said goodbye to the kids he tutored as a volunteer at St. Hedwig's, finished his last round of interviews for an RA's job, and brought most of his things back home to New Jersey at Thanksgiving: His spring semester would be in London. "I've got like two boxers and three shirts I keep wearing over and over again," he said. "If I ace all my finals, I could end up with a 4.0."

"It's an easy B," Patrick Lyons from Keenan Hall said of Tom Morris' Philosophy 101. "A moderate A." When the teaching assistants passed out the final exam, Patrick scanned all the questions—five short essays, two long. "Present two major theodicies in their most extreme forms, raise two objections against each of them, and state a more moderate form of each," the last question asked. He went back to the beginning and started writing his answer to the first question: "Lay out the positive response that can be made to the question 'Is philosophy practical?' "

"Here's Nordy Hoffmann, folks—he was sergeant-at-arms in the Senate until the bad guys took over," Colonel John Stephens said to the small crowd standing outside the church, announcing the arrival of another mourner, an old teammate of the man they had all come to bury. "An All-American."

"The greatest All-American is inside there," Hoffmann said, pointing through the doors and into the sanctuary. "Moose."

Old coaches, old players, old bishops, old priests, and assorted other notables from Notre Dame's old guard were gathering at Sacred Heart on this cold, gray morning for the funeral of Moose Krause—whose career had reached from Rockne to Holtz, and whose smoke-filled office in the ACC was, until just a few days ago, as rich a trove of local lore as the Heisman-filled Sports Heritage Hall just down the corridor from it. At seventy-nine, he had seemed in good health, apart from the shuffling gait of an old lineman. He spent the last night of his life at the athletic-department Christmas party, wearing his trademark cowboy hat and puffing the fat stogie that was all but surgically attached to his fingers. He went home, went to sleep, and didn't wake up. Several students hurried past the church now on their way to exams, glancing at the scene with a bewildered curiosity, as if it were some detached, private ritual wholly unconnected to their experience of Notre Dame.

"Here's Angelo Bertelli, folks, one of our Heisman guys," Colonel Stephens announced from the steps. He was working the door like a bouncer, letting the honorary pallbearers in first while keeping the rest of the mourners out, performing much the same gatekeeper role for Krause in death as he had for him in life. When Krause became emeritus athletic director after thirty-two years in the job, Colonel Stephens—his associate director, and the former commander of the Army ROTC unit on campus—became his emeritus factotum, the short and salty sidekick to Krause's gentle, looming bulk. He had been planning a big bash for Krause's eightieth birthday in February.

"Johnny Lattner, folks," he said, announcing another Heisman winner, and then another, "Paul Hornung, folks."

When the church was filled, the long procession of priests started up the aisle, fifty in all, including Father James Riehle, the football-team chaplain;

Father Bill Seetch from Flanner Hall; Hesburgh and Joyce and their two successors, Malloy and Father Bill Beauchamp. The last priest in line, the presiding celebrant, was the eldest son of the deceased—Father Edward C. Krause, a Holy Cross priest and a professor of theology at Gannon University in Erie, Pennsylvania.

"My dear father and all his wonderful friends and associates in the athletic department always looked back to the Rock," the younger Krause said when he took the pulpit for the homily, "to Coach Rockne, for inspiration and for the principles that would sustain the finest traditions and highest standards of this university in intercollegiate athletic competition. The athletic tradition at this university has endured because it was built on a stable foundation: on the Rock and on what he believed, what he lived for, how he lived and coached, his philosophy or, we might say, his theology of the game—and the game of life."

Recruited by Rockne, Moose Krause came to Notre Dame from the Back of the Yards neighborhood on the South Side of Chicago, where he grew up in an apartment over the family butcher shop. The son of Lithuanian immigrants, he was known as Edward Walter Krauciunas until he met a coach who was impressed by his size but stumped by his name. He was a freshman in the spring of 1931, when Rockne—at the height of his powers, undefeated for the last two years, winner of back-to-back national titles, just finished with his first season in the new stadium his success had made necessary—died in an airplane crash in Kansas. Rockne's funeral was on Holy Saturday, the day before Easter, right here in Sacred Heart. Loudspeakers in the church spire broadcast the service to the throngs gathered outside. CBS radio carried it live to millions more nationwide.

"The lessons one learns on the playing field from a good coach, like Rockne, Leahy, Parseghian, Holtz, and a host of others," Father Krause said today, paraphrasing Father Hesburgh, "are every bit as serious as any lessons you might learn in books or a classroom—integrity, teamwork, discipline, courage, humility, perseverance, leadership, and how to have fun and laugh together."

Krause was an All-American in both football and basketball, and Notre Dame's only member of the National Basketball Hall of Fame. He came back to campus a few years after graduation and never left, serving as head basketball coach, Leahy's line coach, athletic director, roving goodwill ambassador, and all-around mythic figure—the third part of the trinity that included Hesburgh and Joyce. He was admired as much for his personal qualities as for his athletic achievements, the prototype of what is known locally as "a Notre Dame man," a term of respect that is not bestowed lightly. He prayed the rosary daily, beat alcoholism, was a soft touch to anyone who asked anything of him. After his wife was left brain-damaged by a car accident, he visited her at least twice daily in the nursing home, spoon-feeding her meals. On their fiftieth wedding anniversary, his son presided as they renewed their vows.

"Nothing was more important, in my father's estimation, for the future of this institution and everything he lived for and gave his life to," Father Krause said, "nothing was more important than that Notre Dame's religious and sacred purpose survive and thrive. He understood this could only happen at the interior of Christ's church, founded on another rock, the rock that is Peter."

Before the funeral, Krause's body lay in state for two days in the Lady Chapel in Sacred Heart, the same place where he had joined the varsity just a few weeks earlier for their pregame Mass. In the open casket with him were a cigar, his cowboy hat, and his Knights of Malta medal, an award for Catholic laymen that Krause valued as highly as a Heisman.

"He fought, as Paul says in the epistle, to the finish line," Father Krause said, extending the New Testament reading into an athletic metaphor, "right up to the final whistle, a Notre Dame trait if there ever was one—and count how many times this quality of soul has allowed us to snatch victory from defeat, as in the Penn State game four weeks ago."

At the end of Mass, one of Krause's grandsons, a student at Notre Dame now, stood at the lectern and read what has come to be known as the Rockne prayer, though Rockne wasn't its original author. "Dear Lord," he prayed,

> "In the battle that goes on for life,
> I ask for a field that is fair,
> A chance that is equal with all in strife,
> The courage to do and to dare.
>
> If I should win, let it be by the code
> My faith and my honor held high.
> If I should lose, let me stand by the road,
> And cheer as the winner rides by."

Before they all sang the alma mater, Malloy offered a brief presidential farewell. "I can think of no greater tribute to Moose than to say that he was a gentle, kind, and giving person, that his magnetism was a kind of magnetism for goodness, for making people feel better about themselves," he said. "May Moose rest in peace."

A chill drizzle fell on the foothills of flowers around the gravesite in Cedar Grove cemetery, a short walk down Notre Dame Avenue—within sight of the Dome, and within earshot of both the bells of Sacred Heart and the cheers of the stadium. A large arrangement of yellow gladioluses in the shape of a football wore a small ribbon that told who had sent it: "The Rockne Family," his children and grandchildren. The pallbearers—Holtz, Parseghian, and Colonel Stephens among them—struggled with the heavy, flag-draped casket, setting it into place

The mourners around the grave were mostly men long past their playing days, and in their faces you could see the familiar outlines of black-and-white varsity portraits taken decades earlier, when the cheers were still louder than the echoes. They were as likely now to be reunited at funerals as at football games. They had started as boys together, bonded by a game, but now they were old men, separated by time and age and death. The same week that Krause died, they lost two others from among their ranks—Jack Elder, a swift halfback for Rockne's 1929 national champions, and Hugh Devore, a teammate of Krause who later served as an interim head coach. With each passing friend, their Notre Dame faded further into the dim distance of newsreel memories.

Taps was sounded—Krause had served in the Pacific in World War II— and a Marine honor guard fired a twenty-one-gun salute. After the flag was solemnly folded, and the last prayers were said, the service was officially over, but the farewell still seemed incomplete. A moment of uncertain silence passed before someone started singing, joined so quickly by the rest of the mourners that it was hard to trace the song to its source, though some said later it was Krause's younger son, Phil.

> Cheer, cheer for old Notre Dame,
> Wake up the echoes cheering her name. . . .

Any hats that had already been put back on were quickly taken off again. The voice was the low, gruff, tuneless rumble of men unaccustomed to singing in public, and it found in the fight song shades of meaning that were lost under the layers of brass in the game-day version. The pace was slow and mournful, a dirge rather than a march. Though it had the feel of an old, inevitable ritual, it was completely spontaneous: Father Riehle, the team chaplain and a veteran of many team funerals, said later that he had never heard anything like it before.

> Send a volley cheer on high,
> Shake down the thunder from the sky.
> What though the odds may be great or small
> Old Notre Dame will win over all. . . .

The gentle rain mixed easily with the silent tears that rolled down the cheeks of the singers. The fight song—a sturdy and familiar vessel for their emotions—had coaxed out their grief from the reluctant corners where it often hides in the hearts of men: It gave them a language for their sadness, a memory of their joy. As eternal as the song had always seemed to them, they had reached an age at which they knew they would not be singing it forever. The triumph they were celebrating as they sang now was a triumph beyond the stadium, beyond Notre Dame, a triumph they all hoped to share in one day.

> While her loyal sons are marching
> Onward to victory.

SPRING

11

The song rose from the dense crowd of worshipers like a prayer, up through the middle shadows of the Morrissey chapel, slow and heavy, reaching toward the high, distant ceiling, carried by the off-key, self-conscious murmur of reluctant male singers—the same voice that had been heard at Moose Krause's grave. Father Joe Ross stood in the midst of the Sunday-night congregation, singing along with the students. Back from several weeks of Christmas break, they were celebrating their first Mass of the new semester. According to the academic calendar, it was now spring—though an act of faith was required to see it that way, when all the world still seemed locked in the death grip of the long winter darkness. The gray slush that had closed the last semester—covering the slippery quads, sloshing inside all the exam-addled student brains—was gone now. Fresh snow was falling through the cold night outside the chapel.

"I will sing, sing a new song," they all sang. "How long, to sing this song. How long, how long, how long, how long, to sing this song."

The song was U2's "40," a Morrissey favorite, its lyrics borrowed from the 40th Psalm. "He set my feet upon a rock, made my footsteps firm," they sang. "Many will see, many will see and fear."

"According to the church's calendar, we are in Ordinary Time," Ross said, opening his homily. "And it feels very ordinary to me."

As a preacher, Ross has a gift for starting you up a road you think you know, then leading you to a place you've never been—a rhetorical journey that forces you to see the familiar from an unfamiliar angle. He recited a litany of the ordinary: classes, annoying roommates, the South Bend winter; then Somalia, Yugoslavia, a Morrissey RA with cancer.

"Young people still get sick," Ross said. "Very ordinary stuff. Yet, in tonight's readings, we hear God appointing Jesus to be *extraordinary*."

Back home in California for Christmas, Ross had missed the funeral of a beloved member of the Holy Cross community whose determinedly ordinary life was extraordinary in its devotion to God—Brother Cosmas Guttly, who died two weeks after Moose Krause, and two months after celebrating his ninety-ninth birthday. Brother Cosmas was a widower of forty-eight when he made his vows, a Swiss-born precision machinist who helped build an atom smasher for the physics department, and later served as the sacristan of Sacred Heart. "I have had a happy life," he said at his final birthday party, at Holy Cross House, the community retirement home across the lake, not far from the cemetery where his stone cross was now the last in line, "a life of Masses, a life of prayer."

"God chose him and he said 'yes' to an extraordinary life," Ross said, referring first to John the Baptist, the subject of tonight's Gospel, and then to Martin Luther King, Jr., whose birthday it was today. "He . . . said . . . *yes*."

Ross was rising onto his toes now, like a man at the back of a theater stretching to see the front. His arms—folded earlier within his vestments— were flung wide, gathering in the congregation. "The great joy and challenge of Christian life is that *we* get the same call from God—be *extraordinary* and rid the world of sin. And the world desperately needs us to shake off ordinariness."

But Notre Dame was stuck in the long purgatory between football and spring now, and ordinariness, as Ross knew, was a hard thing to shake off. With no more games to fill the stadium, or the imagination, a large hole was opened at the center of campus, and Ross had his own ideas about how to fill it. "How awesome would it be if we really studied with an eye toward service, always asking, 'How can my accounting, my engineering, lift up people and not just profits?' " he wondered aloud. He encouraged them to volunteer at the Center for the Homeless, to help tutor the schoolchildren at St. Hedwig's. Earlier in the evening, he had led a discussion session with some participants in the Urban Plunge—a Center for Social Concerns program that sends hundreds of students to inner cities all over America during Christmas break, immersing them for forty-eight hours in the life of the poor.

"Let's crack the complacency!" he said, cranking his homily up to the speed of a pep rally. "Let's be different! Let's break the routines—of video games, of complaining, of excessive drinking, of comparing ourselves to others in grades, looks, sports, of jokes that bash women or gays or Jews or blacks."

What filled the chapel in the pauses between his thoughts was not quite silence: His words disturbed the air like friction, generating a buzz just below hearing. "Let's not bore God with ordinary lives," he said, reaching his final stop. "Let's excite God, and the whole world, with the extraordinary lives we are called in Christ to live."

Bundled against the kind of cold he had never felt in his native Florida, Tom Carter slipped out the back door of Dillon Hall and hurried across the snowy campus to his afternoon class in DeBartolo Hall—"Investments Theory," a requirement for all finance majors. To most of his classmates, Finance 370 was still a speculative exercise, an exploration of financial markets, securities, analysis, options, futures, and other high-capital features of a world that wasn't yet theirs. To him, though, it had more practical implications: A few weeks earlier, he had announced his intention to forsake his senior season as a defensive back and enter the NFL draft early, a decision that would probably make him a millionaire by semester's end.

"I was thinking about coming out before she told me about losing her job," he said, referring to his mother, who had worked as a bank teller. Tom's announcement had surprised most Notre Dame fans, whose early-draft speculation had focused mainly—and also correctly, as it turned out—on his teammate, junior fullback Jerome Bettis. "She kept saying she's all right, she's all right, but I kept thinking about Chris Zorich." Zorich, another only son of a single mother, had returned home to Chicago's South Side on the day after the last game of his senior season, the 1991 Orange Bowl, to find his mother dead of a heart attack, gone before she could enjoy the rewards of his pro career. "If I did come back next year, what if I got hurt? It could be a million lost instead of a million gained. Nothing is promised for tomorrow."

Tom's varsity career had ended at the Cotton Bowl on New Year's Day, under cold, gray skies that helped Dallas do a fair imitation of South Bend. For this one game, his gold helmet, like all his teammates', wore a small decal that said "MOOSE" in place of the one that said "IRISH." On the field that day, the defense built a wall that wouldn't fall, holding Texas A&M to a mere 145 yards of total offense as Notre Dame plowed under the previously undefeated Aggies, 28–3. Late in the second half, the game all but over, Tom

leveled an Aggie receiver with such force that it raised a collective, empathetic *"Ooooh"* from the crowd. When the final polls came in, Notre Dame
was voted the number-four team in the nation.

On the sidelines that day in Dallas, Rachel Stehle had shivered along with
the rest of the band, and played the fight song on her old brass trumpet. A
new silver trumpet had been waiting for her under the tree at Christmas—as
her father had promised—but she left it home in Ohio when she flew south
for the Cotton Bowl. "You wait till you know you're good," she explained.
For Rachel—who was less interested in football than in the occasion it provided for marching with the Notre Dame band—the trip was as memorable
for the off-field activities as for the game itself: the New Year's Eve party, the
dance club, the three-story mall, and the ice rink attached to the hotel. "All
the trumpets went ice-skating together," she said.

Back on campus now, Rachel was quickly discovering that her spring
course schedule would offer her no reprieve after a trying fall. "I thought I
was gonna flunk out of every class," she said, but she didn't, managing to
pull out a respectable 2.8 grade-point average. "I'm not upset about that."
What she was upset about, though, at least at first, was the reading list for
her Freshman Seminar: Shakespeare, more Shakespeare, nothing but Shakespeare. "I was going to walk out of there and cry. It's not that I don't like
Shakespeare, it's just that I find it really hard to understand."

Bundled against the kind of cold she knew all too well from the frigid
Lake Erie winters back in Sandusky, Rachel slipped out the side door of
Siegfried Hall and, careful to avoid the icy spots on the walkways, headed to
her seminar. Her footing was firmer once she was inside the classroom,
surer than she had expected after the first class meeting. Her professor, as it
turned out, was adept at translating Elizabethan poetry into colloquial prose
that made sense to a modern student's ears; and her mother, a fifth-grade
teacher and herself a veteran of a college course in Shakespeare, had sent
along some old helpful notes. Her philosophy class, however, remained a
dense, frozen thicket. "Nobody understands anything he's doing," she said
of the professor; she hadn't been lucky enough to get Tom Morris in the
Philo 101 draw. "He said we'd have to go back and start all over again."

The sky was low and heavy as Rachel walked back to Seigfried Hall in the
late afternoon, her class day ended. Lights in the dorm windows were beginning to flick on, glowing yellow against the gray predinner gloom. Rachel
looked heavenward in frustration: The cloud cover meant that her astronomy homework would have to be postponed yet again. The class assignment

was to plot the moon for eight nights, using the small observatory on the roof of the Nieuwland Science Hall. But in a South Bend winter, the moon can be an elusive object, and it was starting to seem as if the project would require the entire semester to complete. "It just hasn't been clear at all," she said, sighing.

"A little fur and she'd look just like Ivan the Terrible," Andrew Runkle said from his perch on the couch in room 309 in Cavanaugh Hall, home office of the College Democrats. He had skipped organic chemistry this afternoon to watch the inauguration of the candidate whose visit he had helped organize, and whose hand he had shaken, back in September. On the TV now, Hillary Rodham Clinton had all but vanished beneath her unfortunate blue hat.

"We shouldn't think our mission is accomplished yet," said Andrew Holmgren, the group's president. He had left halfway through his constitutional-law class, and was now settled into the worn recliner that was his reserved seat here. "The question is how to organize a political club without an election."

"Just in time," Chris Setti said, winded by his sprint from Italian class, arriving as Clinton raised his right hand to take the oath of office. Chris remained standing, his engine, as usual, revving a bit higher than his fellow Democrats'. They watched in silence as power was passed from one party to another, from one generation to the next. The only other sounds in the room were the gurgles from the steam heat and the bubbles from the fish tank, where the mollies—Bill and Hillary, Al and Tipper—swam, unaware of their namesakes' fortunes.

"That's the end of Republicanism, boys," Chris said wishfully after Clinton had finally become president. "I'm sorry, but Bush must just feel awful. In the span of one moment, he went from being the most powerful man in the world to being no better than me."

They fell silent again when Clinton took the podium, the Capital dome rising behind him in the cold, sharp sunlight, as bright today as the Golden Dome that rose behind Cavanaugh Hall. "Each generation of Americans must define what it means to be American," Clinton said, earning a nod of assent from three representatives of the youngest generation to have voted for him. Though pitched for a wider, more secular audience, his inaugural address sounded many of the same themes—community, responsibility, sacrifice—as his campaign speech on campus. "I challenge a new generation of young Americans to a season of service, to act on your idealism by helping troubled children, keeping company with those in need, reconnecting our torn communities. . . . In serving, we recognize a simple but powerful truth: We need each other and we must care for each other."

"I never actually watched one of these before," Andrew Runkle said when Clinton was finished. "I never cared before."

"I thought it was excellent," Chris Setti added, "but I remember seeing a speech of Kennedy's and that was awesome."

"A lot of phrases he used in the address were similar to JFK's phrases," Professor Peri Arnold said to his students in Government 404, "The American Presidency," not long after the speech. "What message was Clinton sending to the electorate through that address? What kind of sense of himself and his presidency?"

It was a large class, stacked several score high in a steep DeBartolo lecture hall, but Arnold tried to engage it like a seminar, using the inaugural speech as an occasion for intellectual analysis, not partisan cheerleading. The students were mostly senior government majors, many of them bound for law school in the fall, with a sprinkling of graduate students, who tended to be both more liberal and more voluble. The aim of the course, as Arnold described it, was "to understand the nature of the presidency in the American regime"—which was also the aim of his scholarly work over two decades at Notre Dame, and of his big, reputation-making book, *Making the Managerial Presidency*. From his classroom, the view on Clinton was longer and wider than it was from room 309 of Cavanaugh Hall.

"He's not going to forget the people," one student offered. "He's going to be a populist president."

"He's a Yale graduate; how populist can that be?"

"But isn't he really just this small-town boy from Podunk, Arkansas, who grew up calling hogs or whatever?"

"There was definitely a message of change and newness."

"When you read previous inaugural addresses, it sounds like they all believe they're entering the year one," Arnold said. "They all talk about great winds of change, as if today were a fundamentally different day than yesterday was."

Arnold's own distinct speaking style is shaped by a precise formality and colored by generous shades of irony. Thick glasses and a brushy mustache sometimes make his face appear impassive, but the tone of his voice is as explicit as an arched eyebrow. As a scholar of the presidency, he was called upon often by *The Observer* for comments during the election season. As a Jew, one of only a few dozen on campus, he was later called upon to meet with some *Observer* editors in the outraged wake of the "Jewish Slave Law" letter. "We asked them," Arnold said, recalling the meeting, " 'Would you print something that encouraged the killing of African Americans?' and they said, 'Well, no, no, we'd never do that.' Well, in effect, that's what you printed about Jews. I don't think that it's institutional anti-Semitism. There's a lot of civility here, and we're at a stage in American society where anti-Semitism is no longer good manners. But that it could happen here shows just how insular a world our students come from, where there's no dialogue between different religions."

Under Arnold's direction, the discussion moved away from currents of this week's politics and back into the deeper tides of history—to the Articles of Confederation, when the king-shy colonists designed a government with little executive authority, and the Constitutional Convention, when the founders changed course and created a stronger office of the presidency. The question now, and the question for the rest of the semester, was how that office evolved; how it came to encompass both Franklin Pierce and Franklin Roosevelt, both Ronald Reagan and Bill Clinton; and why the nation expected so much more from Clinton now than it had from George Washington two centuries earlier. Arnold used the overhead to display a survey that showed Clinton's current approval rating, which was far higher than his actual vote total.

"Now, there's a vote of confidence, but is it a vote of confidence in Bill Clinton?" Arnold asked. "I don't think so. This is, at the very least, a vote of confidence in the presidency. We Americans, naïve fools that we may be, see these moments as new beginnings. We start again. It's my obligation to hint at bitter endings, not just happy starts."

"With what Clinton did, I feel like I have to leave school now," said Claire Johnson, who went to Washington during inaugural week to protest, not celebrate. With sixty-one other students from Notre Dame and St. Mary's, she made a twelve-hour bus trip to join the demonstrations marking the twentieth anniversary of the *Roe* v. *Wade* decision. They marched to the Supreme Court behind a huge banner, so wide it took seven people to carry, that declared, "HUMANS ARE PERSONS TOO!" That same day, in an action Claire called "cruel and spiteful," Clinton fulfilled a campaign pledge by lifting the gag order that had barred federally funded clinics from counseling patients about abortion. "That makes it a moral imperative to take a serious stand now. If we don't have hundreds and hundreds of people doing something now, we're going to have killing for twenty years."

Claire took her stand immediately, peeling off with two other Notre

Dame students to participate in a rescue at a Washington abortion clinic. She was arrested—her ninth so far—and fined $50, which she had no intention of paying. "We managed to keep the clinic closed for most of the day." Back at Notre Dame, she switched from protest to prayer, joining a special prolife Mass at Sacred Heart—where not long before, and not without some grumbling, the bells had rung as part of a simultaneous national chorus of bells in honor of Clinton's inauguration.

"Immaculate Mary, your praises we sing," Claire sang along with the congregation as the entrance procession moved slowly up the center aisle of Sacred Heart. "You reign now in heaven with Jesus our king."

The procession trailed a cloud of incense as it passed Claire's pew, approaching the altar. It included several priests and acolytes, the Knights of Columbus with their plumes and swords, and two men carrying the Missionary Image of Our Lady of Guadalupe—"an exact photographic replica," according to the accompanying literature, four feet wide by six feet tall, "of the original Miraculous Image which Our Lady left on Blessed Juan Diego's tilma [a cactus-fiber cloak] in 1531." Our Lady of Guadalupe—the Virgin Mary as she appeared to a converted Aztec Indian in Mexico 460 years ago—had been adopted as a special patron by some devout members of the Catholic prolife movement, and the Missionary Image had been traveling among them across the country, making appearances at protests, prayer services, and Masses. It was displayed on a corner of the altar all through Mass—Mary standing alone, draped in a blue cloak, head bowed, and hands folded in prayer. After Mass, it was moved back to the Lady Chapel, where a long line of people waited to venerate it.

"Our Lady of Guadalupe," one older woman prayed softly as she stood before it, "Patroness and Protectress of the Unborn, pray for us."

The next morning, the Missionary Image was outside the abortion clinic near campus, with maybe two dozen people gathered around it in a tight knot, praying the rosary. The temperature was below twenty, and light snow was swirling in the air.

"Hail Mary, full of grace," they prayed, Claire among them, "the Lord is with thee. Blessed art thou amongst women, and blessed is the fruit of thy womb, Jesus. . . ."

Brother Bonaventure Scully sat in the middle of the dim, empty auditorium, looking more weary than amused. For almost three hours now, he had been watching the men of Keenan Hall trying to be funny, and he still had two more hours to go. Rehearsals were under way for the Keenan Revue, his dorm's annual attempt to lighten up the winter, and he was getting his first glimpse of the skits. What the students sought from him tonight was not his theatrical advice—they ran the show from start to finish—but his imprimatur. The Revue, like most college humor, tended toward the outer limits of good taste; Scully was the border guard who tried to keep it in line.

"Given the university's rules, called *Du Lac,* why would you act in direct contradiction to those rules?" the student in the spotlight asked now, directing his question at a witness who sat at attention with a towel wrapped kiltlike around his waist. The skit was titled "A Few Guard Men"—a parody of *A Few Good Men* in which the defrocked Irish Guard took the place of the loyal Marines. The Guardsmen were on trial before "the high court of Student Affairs," charged with forcing a freshman recruit "to drink ten bottles of Mad Dog."

"I joined the Guard because I wanted to live by a certain code," the witness replied, "a code which challenges me to exhibit my superiority over the student body at all times."

"And what is that code?"

"Guard . . . Band . . . God, Country, Notre Dame."

"Why did you order the Code Mad Dog?" the lawyer asked the next witness.

"Listen, pal," he sneered, doing his best clenched-teeth Jack Nicholson imitation, "I get on that field every Saturday in my skirt and hat to protect a hundred band members in their faggoty blue uniforms while 59,075 of you sit pretty up in the stands, drinking your goddamn warm beer, watching those pathetic cheerleaders and that stupid-ass leprechaun!!!"

The verdict, of course, was never in doubt. "I find all four Guard members guilty and order them dishonorably discharged from the Guard," the judge declared. "They are hereby relieved of their skirts and from now on will wear pants like the rest of us."

After each skit, cast and crew looked discreetly toward Scully, whose inscrutable half-grin was the equivalent of the white puff of smoke from the Vatican when a new pope is chosen. Auditions in the Keenan basement had whittled 120 skits down to the thirty onstage tonight; Scully had already vetoed one, "Fun with Latex," and suggested toning down several others.

"I try to say to them, 'Why don't you do some skits about some real issues—like tuition going up, or the whole research-versus-teaching question?' " Scully said.

But they preferred the broader targets—alcohol, sex, *Rudy,* the dining hall, the laundry service, video games, engineers, the infirmary, Notre Dame women, St. Mary's women, women in general. Keenan's Glee Club contingent took aim at SYRs and parietals now in their rendition of "In the Still of the Night."

> It was tiiiime
> For roma-ance
> Navy blue blazer
> And khaki pa-ants.

They met, they danced, they swooned, they walked back to her room, and then,

> It's almost twoooo
> You know what that me-eans
> The only fireworks
> Will be in my dre-eams.

> I didn't knoooow
> What to do-oo
> She wanted to kiss me
> I wanted to . . . shoo doop, shoobee, whooaahhh!
> At the ennnd
> Of the ni-i-ight. . . .

And the singers all brought their hands together before them like angelic choirboys in prayers.

> At the end
> Of the niiiiiight.

When they sang it again a few nights later, decked out in tuxedos and facing a packed house, they heard the kind of cheers usually reserved for varsity athletes. The Revue had started in the 1970s as a strictly in-house diversion, staged in the basement, where Scully's Freshman Seminars now met, but it had since attained the aura of a genuine campus event, so popular that no space on campus could hold it any longer. Because Washington Hall was too small, and the ACC too big, it had migrated across Highway 31 to O'Laughlin Auditorium at St. Mary's. Tonight was the third night of its run, the Saturday finale, and the crowd was dressed for Broadway and stoked for a big night out. A Keenan SYR would follow the final curtain—a special dispensation had been granted, extending parietals until 3:00 a.m.—so the hall was thick with blue blazers and black dresses, the basic dating uniforms. Down near the front were several rows of nonstudents—faculty, staff, administrators, parents, and assorted other interested adults, including Angelo Bertelli, the 1943 Heisman winner, who was on campus this weekend for an Alumni Board meeting.

What made a Revue ticket such a hot commodity was more than just the school-play lure of seeing your friends onstage. It was a don't-miss spectacle that crammed into a single evening almost as many only-at-Notre-Dame moments as a football weekend—a mixture of near-professional talent and amateur nerve that offered sharp-eyed commentary on campus life. It was also a rare chance to watch men bonding by wearing women's clothes together in public. At its worst, the Revue was a crass collection of drag-show misogyny and cheap jokes about sex (or the lack thereof). At its best, it was the underground newspaper the school didn't have—a forum where the sacred and the profane met on equal terms, built on the premise that, at a place where tradition and ritual run so deep, humor is sometimes the straightest path to understanding.

"You said it, Phil," one student said to his partner as they sat side by side at a table in the spotlight. They both wore Middle Eastern headdresses, and they spoke with the exaggerated up-and-down cadences of sportscasters. "Jesus Christ really came to play ball, and has proven himself to be the savior for the New Testament team."

The skit was titled "Old Testament Football," and they were narrating the offstage game between the Old Testament Torahs and the New Testament Miracles. The score was tied late in the fourth quarter, and the Old Testament had the ball.

"On the other side of the ball, the tailback Moses had been parting the Miracles' defense like the Red Sea."

They swapped the call back and forth as the Old Testament moved the ball up the field.

"It appears that a slight drizzle has started up, and that should prove beneficial to Noah in the backfield, who always seems prepared for a rising storm."

"It looked like Job had some room to run, but the Lord stuffed him in his tracks and it appears that Job is hurt. He's holding his left leg. If it's broken, it'll be the sixth fracture he's sustained today."

It was the irreverent flip side of the reverent team Mass, further proof that football and religion are inextricably linked here. The Old Testament's quarterback—David, who had taken the starter's job from Goliath—passed now to Moses, who looked as if he had a clear path to the goal line.

"Lazarus made the touchdown-saving tackle! You know, Phil, he seemed dead out there in the first half, and reports have it that Jesus said something to him during halftime. We don't know what, but he has really come to life here in the second half."

A fumble by Moses at the three-yard line ("He apparently cannot reach the promised land") left the New Testament with a long field to cover, and a short time to do it in—a situation not unlike Notre Dame's at the end of the Penn State game. The Virgin Mary had taken over at quarterback from Judas, who had thrown sixteen interceptions.

"Mary, in shotgun formation, Bartholomew split left, there's the snap, Mary rolls left, *nails* Jesus on the *cross*-ing pattern for the big gain. *Oh myyy!*"

The New Testament team was down to their final play, their last chance to score. "Shotgun to Mary, who fades back to throw. Scrambling, she stiff-arms Jeremiah to avoid the pressure. The Virgin Mother rifles one deep into traffic. Oh, the New Testament is going to need a miracle one—*and they get one! Touchdown Jesus!* The Mother-Son combo connects for an immaculate reception!"

"Hail Mary, what an arm!"

"Mom really smoked that one in there," Jesus told the sideline reporter after the game.

Although the Revue was a guest this week at St. Mary's, it was as rude to its host as it was to everyone else—maybe even a bit ruder, given the number of jokes about SMC (short for St. Mary's College, pronounced "smick") chicks. St. Mary's is slightly younger than Notre Dame (founded by the Sisters of the Holy Cross in 1844) and much smaller (eighteen-hundred students), and it has the kind of complicated relationship with its brother school—a mixture of love and hate, distance and intimacy—that is inevitable when siblings live so near each other for so long. Notre Dame and St. Mary's almost merged in 1971, going so far as to sign a public letter of intent, but they called it off before they reached the altar: Notre Dame wanted more than St. Mary's was willing to give. Notre Dame went coed; St. Mary's retained its identity, making its stand as one of the shrinking band of Catholic women's colleges. Traffic passes briskly between the two schools now—classes, Masses, parties, football games, clubs, and activities—but so does wariness. The vast, looming bulk of Notre Dame, swaggering in its heavy cloak of myth and history, tends unfairly to overshadow St. Mary's— a school that, with its small classes and tight student-professor bonds, actually embodies the old Notre Dame ideal better than today's Notre Dame does; and that ranked higher in its category in the *U.S. News & World Report* survey this year (second among Midwestern regional universities and colleges) than Notre Dame did in its. Notre Dame students—men and women alike, as susceptible to SAT snobbery and brand-name cruelty as any other adolescents—have an ugly habit of looking down at their St. Mary's peers: St. Mary's women, the crude stereotype goes, wear skirts and seek husbands; Notre Dame women wear sweats and seek careers; and Notre Dame men are torn between the two.

> I hate SMC butts and I cannot lie,
> You other Domers can't deny
> When a girl walks up with a pretty big waist
> And something bigger in your face
> You get queasy.
> Man, it's real easy
> To see that this chick is sleazy.

The blaring rap music was Sir Mix-A-Lot's "Baby Got Back," transformed here into "SMC Got Back" and accompanied by a chorus of large Keenan men, bumping and grinding in drag. Patrick Lyons—whose other contribution to the Revue was the show program now in everyone's hands, produced on his Apple Powerbook—was wearing a bra and slip. Four of Keenan's varsity football players—Jeff Burris, Bryant Young, Brian Hamilton, and Bobby Taylor—vamped and pranced across the front of the stage, squeezed into short, tight skirts. The rap ran through a string of stinging couplets that rhymed such elegant terms as "waist reduction" and "liposuction," "llama" and "big mama," "chick" and "ugly-stick."

> A word to the wide-load SMCs that are makin' me sick.
> I gotta tell you real quick
> That the Notre Dame girls
> Are, mmmmmm, not the most attractive
> Or active.
> No need for a prophylactic.

A much smaller act, though, was the evening's biggest hit—an "Ode to Patty O'Hara," the vice-president of student affairs and the chief disciplinarian on campus, as sung by Tim O'Neill, one of the singers from the earlier "In the Still of the Night." He sat alone at a piano, expertly playing a medley of hits by Notre Dame's chief pop icon, Billy Joel. He started with "Piano Man," strolled through "The Stranger" and slipped into "She's Always a Woman."

> She can kill with a smile, she can wound with her eyes.
> And she'll ruin your night, if you unzip your flies.
> She'll bust down the doors, as you're partyin' hard,
> Just 'bout the same as she did with the ole Irish Guard.

Although many administrators attended the Revue, O'Hara usually stayed away—not because she disapproved (actually she liked it, she said), but because she didn't want her presence to disrupt the proceedings, causing students to muffle their laughter and glance guiltily in her direction whenever her name came up, as it often did. "He actually called to see if I minded," she said of O'Neill. She told him she didn't. "I think I'm pretty fair game." By now, O'Neill had rolled into the inevitable "Only the Good Die Young."

> I say, come on, Patricia, don't let us wait,
> The Notre Dame girls start much too late.
> I'd rather go to St. Mary's and find a quick date.
> They are much more fun.
> Well, the parietals rule has just got to go,
> But no need to worry, we've got Honor Code.
> Just give us a chance, and Patty we'll show
> That nothing will go wrong,
> Because only the good die young.

He blazed through the lightning piano solo of "Angry Young Man," moved straight into "Movin' Out," and finally ended with the emphatic "My Life."

> We're in college and we can take care of ourselves.
> We don't need you to worry for us 'cause we're all right.
> We don't want to be told at two o'clock to go home.

We don't care what you say anymore, this is our life,
Go ahead with your own life—and leave us alone!

The crowd cheered the way people cheer when they hear somebody say exactly what they would like to say, if they only could.

12

Perched in the far corner of the South Quad, Lyons Hall is a more restrained study in Gothic masonry than the dorm next door, Morrissey Hall—its central feature not a thrusting tower like its taller neighbor, but a wide, graceful arch that opens onto St. Mary's Lake like a window into the placid past. When the weather warms, the lawn that slopes down behind it to the lake becomes Lyons Beach, a haven for sunbathing students. Lyons Hall was built in the 1920s, part of the construction boom financed by Rockne's lucrative football franchise, and it was home for many years to the legendary Frank O'Malley—the most luminous of all the bachelor dons, "Notre Dame's Mr. Chips," who came as a freshman in 1928 and stayed as a revered English professor until 1974, when he was buried in the Holy Cross community cemetery, one of the few laymen so honored. As part of the sesquicentennial celebrations the previous year, several hundred of "O'Malley's Boys," as they called themselves, had gathered at a special conference on campus to honor the memory of "The Master," the teacher who had, both in formal daytime lectures in the classroom and in informal evening seminars at the bar of the LaSalle Hotel downtown, guided them toward truth, toward God, through literature. Lyons is a women's dorm now, among the first converted after coeducation, and on this bright winter afternoon, when the sun was ready for spring but the chill air was not, this monument of the old Notre Dame was the staging area for an attempt to usher in a new Notre Dame.

"Life is not a game," Stephanie Gallo said, reading the motto she had inscribed on a poster-sized piece of paper. "It's your future."

In a small, crowded lounge on the first-floor of Lyons, on the eve of the election campaign she hoped would make her Notre Dame's first female student-body president, Stephanie stood at a flip chart and led a meeting of her assembled precinct captains. The words on the large white sheets were printed in letters as bold as her voice, and her ambition. She had flow charts, mission statements, diagrams, campaign themes and slogans ("Putting Notre Dame to Work")—the kind of presentation, corporate in structure but collegiate in enthusiasm, that a sales manager might use when trying to whip up the regional reps. It was an approach befitting a government major who planned to go on for an M.B.A.

"We're not discounting Keenan," she said. "They say there's still hope for Keenan."

Student elections are notoriously territorial, dorms usually voting loyally for their own candidates, and one of Stephanie's opponents was Dave Reinke, the copresident of Keenan Hall. The third major candidate was Frank Flynn, the president of Stanford Hall and the roommate of deposed Irish Guardsman Lou Blaum.

"The South Quad is our strength—we can't let it slip up. . . . You think we can get Dillon? . . . Do you know anything about Alumni's opinions? Or Pangborn, or Fisher?"

The election had been taking shape behind the scenes for months already—tickets forming, alliances building, power bases consolidating—but the actual campaign, governed by bylaws that were Thomistic in their complexity, would last only a week, starting at one minute past midnight tomorrow, when all the candidates' poster-hanging squads would race out to claim the best locations. At stake was a suite of offices on the second floor of LaFortune, a raft of patronage positions, access to the corridors of power under the Dome, and control of roughly $400,000 of student-activities money. Flynn had the inside edge: He was the candidate with the closest ties to the current administration. Earlier, he had asked Stephanie to be his running mate.

"I told him I'd rather lose running for president than win as vice-president," Stephanie said. "For so long, women at Notre Dame have been compromising what they believe in and what their capabilities are and settling for second position, and I just couldn't do that."

Because Notre Dame had always been such an insular, all-male preserve, a closed society dominated by priests and athletes, it had no place ready for the women it finally allowed inside the gates two decades ago. For 130 years, the only women on campus were support staff and nuns—who worked as domestics in the early years, cleaning and cooking and sewing, and who came to study at special summer sessions in later years. Contact with younger laywomen was limited largely to strictly supervised visits at St. Mary's, and the occasional, unsupervised spring panty raid. When the first 325 female undergraduates arrived in 1972, they found that the bathrooms in a couple of dorms had been remodeled but the campus culture had not. Women arriving today soon find that the larger renovations are still under way. Until just this year, only men could send their laundry to the campus laundry service; the women had to do their own, in the laundry rooms that only their dorms are equipped with. The infirmary has no staff gynecologist, and it does not routinely dispense contraceptives. For many years, women were not allowed on the golf course, and women sportswriters are still not allowed into the locker room after a football game. There are no women among the dozens of figures on the library's immense Touchdown Jesus mosaic. There are only two among the campus's outdoor statuary—Mary atop the Dome, and, in front of O'Shaughnessy Hall, the Samaritan woman speaking to Jesus at the well: the Virgin and the adulteress. The women's athletic program is large and successful—eleven varsity sports and sixty-seven scholarships this year, compared with the men's thirteen sports and 146 scholarships (ninety-three of them in football)—but fan support for even the winningest teams is small. Though more than 40 percent of the students are women now, it still feels in many ways like a boy's school.

"A lot of girls do shrink back," Stephanie Gallo said. "Guys are obviously intimidated by girls who are more aggressive or smarter than they are. I've seen plenty of smart girls who act stupid." As measured by high-school grades, Notre Dame women were in fact smarter than the men: The administration's slow-growth policy on coeducation kept a cap on the number of women accepted each year, and resulted in higher admission standards for them than for the men. This year was the first year that the proportion of women in the freshman class (44 percent) actually equaled the proportion in the applicant pool. "I'm not a feminist by any means, but being in class with all these guys—it's like I have to prove myself."

As copresident of Lyons Hall, she sat on the Hall Presidents Council, and watched in frustration as the men on the council almost inevitably took over the meetings. She also sat on the student senate, where she was one of just three members to vote against the resolution condemning Sinéad O'Connor for ripping up a picture of the pope on *Saturday Night Live*. "I didn't think it reflected the whole student-body opinion," she said. Two years earlier, when she was a freshman, a Lyons hallmate had run for student-body president, the first woman to do so, and lost—a campaign that taught Stephanie an important strategy lesson.

"It's suicide to run only on women's issues," she said. "I'm not going to run on a feminist platform."

Successful campaigns usually focus on one or two specific issues: The current administration had run largely on the issue of "study days," a proposal to set aside two class-free, catch-up days before exams. (They won, and study days became part of the calendar.) To run on the big issues—coed dorms, parietals, the alcohol policy, the issues that students actually have strong opinions on, and that student government has little say in—is quixotic, counterproductive, and divisive. Stephanie ticked off her platform now for the campaign volunteers—an organized alumni network for jobs and internships; a slimmer student-government budget; a textbook-leasing program; a twenty-four-hour eating spot in the LaFortune basement.

"Everyone right now is worried about what they're gonna do after graduation," Stephanie said, explaining her main issue. "The seniors all have wailing walls of rejection letters tacked up in their rooms. Notre Dame represents the best alumni network in the country, but we're not maximizing it."

Stephanie's twenty-first birthday was just a few days off, but she would have to forgo the traditional Domer celebration—a night of legal drinking at an off-campus bar—until after the election. The next week would be a marathon of campaigning—meeting the voters door-to-door, and the other candidates at a formal debate. She turned now to an important question of strategy.

"How many bathroom stalls are there in each dorm?"

The posters she was passing out had consumed the bulk of the budget— her campaign had spent $149.44 so far, just shy of the $150 limit—and she encouraged her troops to deploy them wisely. The 250 large yellow posters were for bulletin boards, hallways, and other high-traffic spots. The six hundred smaller green posters were for lower-traffic areas, which in the women's dorms meant the doors of the bathroom stalls.

"I don't know about the men's bathrooms," Stephanie said. "Where's the best spot?"

"Above the urinals is where the high visibility is," offered her running mate, Chris Browning, the copresident of Sorin Hall. The key to a successful poster, he reminded them, was eye-level placement.

"OK, 12:01 tomorrow night, eye-level—that's all you have to remember," Stephanie said. "And go to Mass on election day. Five minutes of praying is two hours of campaigning."

Teresa Ghilarducci stood in the well at the front of a tiered classroom in DeBartolo, showing her students how to sketch a portrait of an elusive, shifty beast: the United States economy. Floating on the blackboard behind her was a small cluster of words chalked in white, the residue of whatever class had met here earlier: "Ethics," "Politics," "Human Beings," "Theory of Everything." To make her next point—how the National Income was broken down—she turned to the board and started writing: wages and salaries (73.2 percent), proprietors' income (8.2 percent) . . . To make room for the rest of her list, she had to erase the older, broader message. It vanished from the board, but it remained somewhere near the center of her approach to her subject.

"How many of you folks here want to work for yourselves when you grow up?" she asked, trying to show them how proprietors fit into the economy. Only three students out of twenty-five raised their hands. "Ten years ago, I think more hands would've been raised."

The class was "Intermediate Macroeconomic Theory"—Econ 302, a requirement for all economics majors—but it was Ghilarducci's aim to cover the territory where theory and reality intersected. Her first lessons in economics had come as one of two children of a single mother in California: Food stamps, welfare, and Medicaid kept the family afloat at times. Her later lessons were at Berkeley, where she earned all her degrees. Her field was institutional economics ("where politics and history matter," she explained), and her position was on the left ("but the spectrum goes beyond me to Marxists and radicals"). Her chief interests were labor unions and pension funds: *Labor's Capital: The Economics and Politics of Private Pensions*, her first book, had just been published to wide acclaim among her peers.

"What are you doing here?" she asked the class, using their own experience to illustrate an important economic distinction. "Would you consider this consumption or investment? If you're here because it's as much fun as playing poker or going to Florida, it's consumption. If you're here because you expect it will yield a return over a long period, then it's an investment."

As a tenured female professor, Ghilarducci was an unfamiliar sight to many of her students. Notre Dame had no women at all on its regular faculty until 1965, and it still lagged far behind most of its peer institutions: Women accounted for just 13 percent of the faculty now, and a woeful 4 percent of the full professors. Not quite two years earlier, Ghilarducci had become the second woman to get tenure in the economics department. There was still not a single tenured woman in the entire College of Business. The shortage of women meant that Ghilarducci was frequently called upon to serve on committees, panels, and assorted other gatherings that required a female voice.

"Among my woman undergraduates, I've seen no change in ten years in terms of their own ambition, their own self-esteem in the classroom," she said. "The knowledge that they are being looked at every single moment of the day hasn't dissipated."

Ghilarducci gave the women in her class—and the men, too—little chance to shrink into the background, drawing them into the lecture with a steady stream of questions. "In the 1980s, did that ratio go up or down?" she asked now, meaning the ratio between the nation's wealth and its income. She has a way of leaning forward, neck craned up and out, when she's looking for an answer, and nodding emphatically when she gets one. "Who said 'down'? That's right, and the hint is Rockefeller Center. What happened? It was sold to the Japanese. Our net worth went down."

Her own net worth went up recently—when Clinton was elected, and her book, with its proposals for reforming the nation's pension system, caught the attention of some key players in the new administration. She had written some memos for the transition team, and she made a short list of thirteen candidates for a position as an assistant secretary of labor. She did not, however, make the later, shorter list of four. A Washington appointment would have been a welcome victory not only for her, but for Notre Dame, which does not have the same clear pipeline to power as schools like Harvard and Georgetown: Bruce Babbitt, the new secretary of the interior, was as high as they had gotten recently.

"Now let's move on to the political economy—the role of government in a capitalist economy," she said. It was a subject familiar to the class from the recent pages of *The Wall Street Journal*, a required text for the course, where they had been following the debate over Clinton's economic plan. "Governments have always wrestled with the question of how much of a role they should play in promoting economic development."

She detailed some of the economic tools available: tariffs, trade restrictions, ownership and management of key industries, regulation, limits on

foreign investment, guaranteed demand (the Pentagon's buying sub-
marines, for instance), subsidizing research and development. "The biggest
source of research money for Notre Dame is . . . ?"

"The Navy," a short-haired student answered, correctly.

"I see we have some members of the Navy here," said Ghilarducci, who
has a soft spot for ROTC students. ("They're some of our best kids," she said
later. "They're usually the only working-class kids in my class.")

What helped draw her to Notre Dame was the department's unusual interest in the human side of economics, in research and teaching that focused
on subjects like poverty, labor, and developing nations. Within the university, the economics department is often seen as the liberal counterweight to
the conservative-dominated law school. "When I was at Berkeley, people
were always arguing about how to integrate their personal lives and their
political lives. Here the personal is political—it's a seamless garment, where
what you live is what you believe." Because of the distinct way in which
ideas and faith tend to fuse at Notre Dame, the debates on the great public
issues take on a different character than at other universities: When people
here make their stands, whether on the right or the left, their beliefs are often shaped by deep religious convictions, not transient political fashions.
"At Berkeley, people would talk all the time about Central America, but here
there were refugees from Nicaragua living in people's houses, and nobody
knew about it."

In class, Ghilarducci kept her politics anchored in economics, illustrating
her points with numbers, not polemics. She didn't hammer down on views
that were opposite her own, but tried instead to tunnel under them—using
figures rather than rhetoric to argue, for instance, that poverty is a failure
not of character but of opportunity. Her lectures were often shaded by gentle sarcasm and punctuated by a throaty laugh that might give the mistaken
impression that she was a smoker.

"And then there's something that exploded in the 1980s and is coming
back to haunt us now," she continued, reaching the end of her list. "Tax
concessions, loan guarantees, cash grants to businesses. The savings-and-
loan crisis is a direct result of our policy toward one industry—real estate."

What was left on the board when class was over was a series of formu-
las—$C = YD - S \equiv Y + TR - T - S$ and the like—a message harder to decipher than the words she had erased earlier. These chalk hieroglyphics were
clearly meant to say something significant about a key economic point, but
their meaning was lost without her voice there to explain them.

———

"Just because you have a vagina, that doesn't mean you automatically become a feminist."

"The system is a sinful, evil, deliberate, malicious effort to keep women powerless."

"I'm torn because I still identify myself as Catholic. Culturally, I still feel connected to the liturgy, the community."

"We have to rethink the whole issue of choice and abortion, how it fits into the larger system—of women's health care, of child care."

The exchange moved back and forth between the half-dozen women seated on the stage and the few score more seated, with a sprinkling of men, in the audience. It was already mid-afternoon on the annual Day of Women, an outgrowth of the Year of Women celebrations at Notre Dame two years earlier, a forum for marking the achievements and frustrations of female undergraduates at a school of men. They were gathered in the basement theater of the Snite Museum of Art, across the street from the stadium and one floor below the galleries where medieval Madonnas share space with contemporary abstracts. It was a dim, bunkerlike space, sealed off from the rest of the campus—a reminder that, for all the social-justice activism that flourishes aboveground at Notre Dame, you sometimes have to go underground to find the kind of feminism that at many other schools occupies the safe middle. The morning session had brought women from Notre Dame and St. Mary's together to perform their dances and display slides of their artwork. The postlunch panel discussion was ending now, making way for the poetry reading.

People, said Nietzsche, still hold the view that what is handed down to us by tradition is what in reality lies behind us—while it in fact comes towards us because we are its captives and are destined to it.

Beth Ann Fennelly stood at the podium reading "While It in Fact Comes Towards Us"—a poem that was inspired by an address Pope John Paul II once made to a Vatican audience of four thousand women who served as housekeepers to the clergy, "domestic collaborators in the priesthood"; a poem that implicitly explored one of the chief reasons why many women had a hard time finding a home at Notre Dame: because many women had a hard time finding a home within the Catholic church.

My first impression is," she read, quoting from the pope's speech in her poem, "women do have their place in the church!"

Women who come to Notre Dame face a weight of tradition that

women who go to Princeton or Yale or almost any other formerly all-male
school do not: the two-millennia-long tradition of a church run by men. Because Catholicism so deeply shapes the institutional life of Notre Dame, it
inevitably shapes the personal lives of women here, and not always in ways
to their liking. One result has been the evolution of a distinct brand of feminism, as concerned with questions of theology as with politics. When the
American bishops were meeting on campus last summer, so was the Committee on Notre Dame's Position on the Ordination of Women, a group
whose members included professors, priests, nuns and at least one nun-in-
the-making, Laurie Brink, the rector of Pasquerilla West. At their most recent meeting, one of Brink's PW students had spoken eloquently of the call
she felt to the priesthood, and the anger and sadness she felt because of her
inability to answer it.

The pope urged the women: Be happy that you can keep the residence
of the priest clean, and free him from material tasks which would absorb part of the time he needs for his apostolic labors. Such material
tasks are more suitable for female charisms. You could never thank the
Lord enough for giving you the grace of choosing to serve the clergy.

Beth Ann wore a jaunty orange flower in her black hat as she spoke.
Though not generally given to histrionics, she embellished her reading with
handclaps, shifting voices, a snatch of "do-do-do"s from Lou Reed's "Walk
on the Wild Side."

(i

found god

in myself

and she

is beautiful)

She repeated a line from the papal address like a chant, or the chorus of a
rap song: "more suitable for female charisms."

"THEIR CALLUSES ARE WEDDING BANDS TO CHRIST," she read as she neared
the end. "While it in fact comes towards us."

In the applause for her poem, from an audience largely sympathetic to
her views, Beth Ann heard a measure of approval that often eluded her on
the wider campus. She was among the minority of women willing to speak
openly in behalf of feminist issues, and the response she triggered some-

times included phone messages calling her, incorrectly, a lesbian. She was part of a group that collected more than a thousand signatures on a petition recently calling for the establishment of a Women's Resource Center on campus. "Some men come up to me and say, 'What about a men's resource center?' This whole university is a men's resource center." In a gender-studies seminar last semester, inspired by a landmark feminist document—the 1848 Seneca Falls Declaration of Sentiments and Resolutions—she had helped draft a similar declaration about life at Notre Dame. "We believe," it began, "that Mary on the dome should not be the only woman in a prominent, public position." It went on through twenty-nine more points, calling for changes large and small, global and local—more tenured women faculty; an equal number of athletic scholarships for men and women; equal coverage in *The Observer* for men's and women's interhall football; washers and dryers in men's dorms, not just women's; a campus day-care center; women in the Irish Guard; coed dorms; ordination of women as priests. "We believe parietals are a patriarchal institution designed to protect students from their own sexual weakness," it declared. "They suggest that men and women can not be friends between 2 a.m. and 11 a.m., thus emphasizing only the sexual relations between the sexes." The declaration appeared as a long letter in *The Observer;* the letter then appeared on a door in Keenan Hall, annotated by a yellow highlighter that marked what the occupant apparently considered the oddest points, and that declared his own incomprehension with a single scrawled word: "WHATEVER."

"I love Notre Dame, and it's because I love it that I think it's very important to be vocal about what's wrong with it," Beth Ann said. She had come to Notre Dame, she said, because her father, a Holy Cross graduate, "said he would pay for college if I went to a Catholic school." From the first day of her freshman year, when she heard the first of thousands of renditions of the fight song and its paean to "her loyal sons," she had been trying "to make other people feel as crazy as I was feeling."

Her feminism, however, did not translate into separatism. She was a regular at the parties at the Campus View apartments, the off-campus student refuge where she, and many other seniors, had moved after three years under the rule of *Du Lac* in the dorms. On game days, she could usually be found in the stadium. "People ask me, 'If you're a feminist, why do you wear makeup? Why do you go to the football games?' There is a part of me that thinks it's a crime that the main social event is a sport that's only played by men, with the women only on the sidelines going 'Rah-rah.' But I support it because I love the school. What good would it be to not go to the football

games?" Her poems had earned her wide respect within campus literary circles, and had made it safe for her now to enter Waddick's—the small coffee
shop in O'Shaughnessy Hall that was usually the province of gaunt grad
students with distant eyes and studied vocabularies, earnestly discussing
hermeneutics and phenomenology. "I was scared to go in there until I was a
senior."

Beth Ann prefaced her next reading with a quote from Norman Mailer:
"A writer must have balls." Called "Poem in the Language of the Oppres-
sor," it took as its central metaphor the letter "e" that is used to feminize
words like "blonde." "We are the daughters of the silent 'e,' " she read,

> Seen, not read, we write in "feminine rhymes."
> We speak in tongues, for our tongues cannot speak.

"It's good to use a pencil, because when you start out you're going to make
errors," Carolyn Callahan told her students as they bent busily over an accounting problem, her deliberately schoolmarmish tone reminding them to
show some humility in the face of a discipline she knew they hadn't fully
mastered yet. "All of us do."

In just a few months, these senior accounting majors would become real
accountants, earning a degree that was a surer, quicker ticket to gainful employment than almost any other at Notre Dame. They would fan out to
firms all across the country, trading their blue jeans for blue suits, working
for paychecks (in the $30,000-a-year range) rather than grades, calculating
numbers that represented real dollars rather than textbook exercises. But
first they had to get past Callahan, who saw it as her job to instill in them the
habits and methods of their new profession. Her brisk, precise delivery, her
crisp power suit, gave the classroom the feel of a corporate training session,
and gave the students a taste of the world beyond graduation. On the desk
before each student stood a name card emblazoned with the logo of Arthur
Andersen, one of the Big Six accounting firms that vacuumed up dozens of
Domers each year. Of the twenty-two students in the class, two were
women.

"OK, the worksheet should look like this; the target number is $190,000,"
Callahan said, using the overhead projector to show them the number they
were trying to reach at the end of the problem. "Your textbook doesn't do
this, but I do. I think it's always important to know what the target is."

Though she had a reputation as a demanding teacher, she was no more demanding of her students than she was of herself—largely because she knew how far off $190,000 or any other target sometimes was. Her father had worked in a factory, her mother as a dime-store clerk, and she had grown accustomed to hearing the phrase "first black woman" attached to her achievements. She was a parent with considerable work experience of her own (accountant in private industry, director of a social-service agency) before she earned her bachelor's degree—summa cum laude, like her master's. She went on for a Ph.D. in accounting and finance from Michigan State, and she won tenure at her first faculty appointment, the University of Massachusetts in Amherst. She was in her second year at Notre Dame now—drawn back to the Midwest by reasons personal (her ailing father in Ohio), professional (the accounting department was ranked sixth in the nation by a recent survey), and spiritual: She is among the small percentage of African Americans who are Catholic. She and her husband, regulars at Sacred Heart, served as gift-bearers during offertory at the big Mass that opened the academic year back in the fall. Her office, where a poster of Andre Dawson hangs over a shelf of *The Accounting Review*, has a clear, near view of the Dome, which she will lose, reluctantly, when the College of Business eventually moves into its new building.

"I really believe that I was trying to use the talents God gave me, and that what I was doing was pleasing to God," she said of her long climb through academia. "I have this sense of 'This is not just for me,' that I'm a trailblazer trying to open a whole new field for black women." As one of a tiny handful of black women on the faculty, and as the lone black woman in the College of Business, she was often called upon to serve beyond the classroom, both officially and unofficially: Father Malloy had recently appointed her to the new Committee on Cultural Diversity, the latest in a long list of extracurricular appointments. It was her duty, she believed, to lend what help she could to minorities and women who were climbing the ladder behind her, and though she did it gladly, she wished there were more people around to share the job with her. "No male I know with the kind of research load I have carries my service load. All the women I know have service and teaching loads that are higher than the men."

Callahan started a new problem on the overhead. "We do not see the capital or equity accounts of the subsidiary," she said. "The equity we do see is the equity of the parent."

She was teaching three separate sections of Accountancy 473 this semester—an advanced course in corporate financial reporting that, as she taught it, mixed technical instruction (how to handle mergers and acquisitions, for

instance, or parent-subsidiary relationships) with ethical guidance. The required texts included both *Advanced Accounting* and *The Seven Habits of
Highly Effective People.* Her intention was to explore not just the surface
techniques of accounting, but also the logical foundations and the moral parameters. The students were divided into teams ("It drives you to pull for
the group, and to put less emphasis on self-achievement"), and when making presentations the teams were required to dress as if their members were
speaking in a boardroom, not a classroom.

"So, when you take the CPA, it'll be very easy to proof the numbers on
your financial statements," she said, finishing the problem. Her features
were taut from her six-day-a-week running schedule; she shunned the middle distances when she competed in races, focusing instead on marathons.
"You have to be logical when you take the CPA exam. You have to follow
orders."

Over in the library basement, the students in the waiting room of the
career-placement office were dressed as nattily as Callahan's students on
group-presentation day. Periodically, an adult would emerge from the warren of tiny interview rooms, call the next name on the list, shake hands and
exchange pleasantries, then lead the young postulant back to a harsh fluorescent box barely bigger than a confessional for an earnest conversation
about the future.

"Nice to meet you," one interviewer said, greeting an interviewee. "First
door on the left."

Thirteen representatives from Arthur Andersen were here today, interviewing eighty candidates for three summer internships. (A particularly
heavy concentration of alumni at Andersen ensures a steady flow of Domers
through the recruiting pipeline.) They had already harvested the crop of
graduating seniors, having hired thirty-seven of them, including several
from Callahan's classes. Tonight they were planning to treat their soon-to-
be co-workers to a big group dinner.

At the pay phone in the corridor, a recruiter from another company was
reporting back to his home office. "I met with fifteen yesterday," he said,
sounding exasperated, "and ten so far today, and I haven't seen one Afro-
American."

The driver tossed the bundle of *Observer*s out of the back of the van and
onto the concrete steps of South Dining Hall like a teamster in an old
Warner Bros. movie, dropping the bulldog edition at a corner newsstand on

Broadway. As soon as he slit the bundle open, and before he could deposit the papers into the rack inside the door, students were peeling off copies to take into lunch with them. *The Observer* is a valued table companion in the dining halls at lunch, when students rushing between classes have little opportunity for the socializing that characterizes the evening meal. When they turned to the Viewpoint page in the middle of the paper today, they found, in place of the usual round of abortion letters, a boxed, boldfaced editorial.

"The Observer endorses Stephanie Gallo and Chris Browning," the editorial declared, "a ticket with solid ideas and a vocal willingness to cut down on Student Government excess."

"I was completely surprised," said Stephanie, who had heard about the endorsement before she actually read it. She was also completely thrilled, hoping it would give her an edge in the race for student-body president. She had expected *The Observer* to stand against her comparatively liberal views—it had, after all, endorsed George Bush in the other presidential election—but she had impressed its editors with her straight and candid performance in the candidates' debate a few nights earlier.

"Emerging from the field of candidates," the endorsement continued, "Gallo resisted the temptation to dodge questioners, and even went on the record saying her administration would advocate the recognition of a homosexual organization at Notre Dame." Gay students had been trying, unsuccessfully so far, to gain official recognition from the administration for their campus group. "The ticket's response to that question and others showed earnest convictions, a mix of pragmatism and idealism, and a dual confidence to get things done."

Stephanie was also surprised, less pleasantly, when the student magazine, the *Scholastic*, issued its endorsement. "We at *Scholastic* were truly amazed at the amount of time and energy which the ticket of Gallo and Browning put into their platform," wrote the generally more liberal campus weekly, which Stephanie had expected to be on her side. "In fact, the packet of information which they gave us was substantially larger than the press kit which we received for President Clinton's visit." But, despite their amazement, they endorsed one of her opponents, Dave Reinke. "*Scholastic* feels, however, that this ticket has two major flaws: their detailed knowledge of the issues bespeaks a great deal of inside knowledge that comes from working in student government, but also the lack of perspective that comes from spending too much time on administrative issues. Also, their commitment to multiculturalism, although laudable, seems to be leaning toward an extreme of Political Correctness which most of us would rather avoid."

Because the endorsements came smack in the middle of campaign week, a frenetic whirl of grass-roots electioneering, Stephanie had little time to ponder their impact. After dinner that evening, she set out again on her nightly round of dorm visits, carrying her appeal door-to-door until parietals closed the men's dorms to her at midnight. On every hallway bulletin board she passed, her bright-yellow posters competed for space with the posters of the other candidates. In one of the densely packed, wet-towel-smelling men's tower dorms, she stopped at an open door and knocked to announce herself.

"Hi, I'm Stephanie Gallo and I'm running for student-body president," she said.

The six men clustered in front of the television set barely looked up from their Nintendo game. After finishing her brief pitch, Stephanie continued down the corridor, her optimism flagging but her determination intact. One of the men rose to close the door behind her. From inside she could hear them laughing.

When the polls opened a few days later, Stephanie ran into another, more threatening speed bump. Some of her campaign volunteers had distributed flyers—fifty-five, to be exact—outside South Dining Hall at lunchtime—unaware that campaigning was supposed to have ended at midnight the day before, and that they were therefore technically in violation of the election rules. The ballot boxes were impounded at the end of the day, and an emergency student-senate meeting was convened to decide whether to count the votes or throw them all out and start over again.

"The time the campaign was supposed to end wasn't on the list of dates we were given," Stephanie argued.

The meeting dragged on for almost two hours, a tense blend of parliamentary deference and youthful indignation. Stephanie was the besieged, mostly silent center of the debate, her presidential ambitions hostage now to the solemn bylaw-fixation of the apprentice politicians in the student senate. In the end, only two of the six presidential tickets could recall being told about the ban on election-day campaigning, a sufficient level of uncertainty to convince the student senate that no campaign violation had occurred. Stephanie sighed in relief as the senators voted to open the impounded ballot boxes and tally the results. She sighed in disappointment as the numbers were posted: She had finished third, with 23 percent of the vote. Her showing was especially weak in the men's tower dorms.

"I thought we were so well organized and so well thought-out that people wouldn't think about the gender issue," Stephanie said. "I think if I had run a campaign like this at any other school I would've won. I don't think Notre Dame was ready for something like this."

The two top finishers—Frank Flynn, with 35 percent, and Dave Reinke, 32 percent—went on to a runoff. Stephanie endorsed Reinke, who had argued strongly in her behalf at the student-senate meeting. Two days later, by a fifty-four-to-forty-six margin, Flynn was the winner.

"I probably learned more about life in two weeks by losing than I would have by winning," she said. "I honestly believe that, if I had been elected, things would've changed. A lot of attitudes need to be changed here, and I see what I could've done—that's what makes me sad." She planned to retreat gradually now from the student-government activities that had dominated her extracurricular life, concentrating instead on becoming a resident adviser in Lyons Hall—the universe she hoped to influence shrinking from the whole, coed, often indifferent, occasionally hostile campus to the narrower, friendlier, female confines of her own dorm.

13

Glowing softly against the bitter winter night, wrapped all around in a white blanket of snow, the Log Chapel down by the lake looked much the way it must have looked 150 years earlier to Sorin and his band of brothers—a safe and welcome refuge in a hostile wilderness. It was already ten years old when they arrived, built by another French-born priest, Stephen Badin, whose ambitions for his modest mission station extended no further than serving as a small school and orphanage. Sorin and the brothers moved into the first floor, used the squat attic as a chapel, and started instead to build a university. Notre Dame now looms so large over the place of its nativity as to all but overshadow it. The current Log Chapel is a 1906 reconstruction—the original burned down in 1858—but it functions as more than just a symbol: It is host to seminarian Masses, charismatic prayer meetings, rosary groups, alumni weddings. Father Bill Seetch of Flanner Hall was saying Mass tonight for an all-male congregation maybe three dozen strong. The chapel was small enough so that their body heat made it feel something like a warm and close gym. Under the stone set flush in the center aisle lay the mortal remains of Badin, the first priest ordained in the United States. Resting on the altar was a pair of boxing gloves.

" 'See, I am sending an angel before you, to guard you on the way and bring you to the place I have prepared,' " Seetch read, from the Book of Exodus. To find an appropriate reading for tonight's Mass, he had jumped out of the usual lectionary calendar to the Feast of Guardian Angels. " 'If you heed his voice and carry out all I tell you, I will be an enemy to your enemies and a foe to your foes.' "

This congregation had been meeting almost daily for many weeks now, but tonight was their first visit to the Log Chapel. Their more familiar sanctuary was the humid boxing room in the ACC, where—dressed in sweaty gray T-shirts, not neat Mass clothes, hands clenched into fists, not folded in prayer—they jabbed at one another in a canvas ring under the watchful gaze of a huge portrait of the late Dominic "Nappy" Napolitano, the founder and guiding spirit of the Bengal Bouts. The Bouts are a throwback to the Bing Crosby days of parish boxing teams, when good kids learned how to defend themselves in a hard world. Like Notre Dame football, they reside at the corner where sports and religion intersect: The money raised from ticket and program sales goes to the Holy Cross missions in Bangladesh, a nation that, when the Bouts were born in 1931, was still part of Indian's Bengal region. More than $300,000 had gone to the missions over the years, and another $10,000 or so would probably go this year. The first round of fights started in three days.

"In a real sense, you gentlemen are guardian angels to a group of people who are desperately poor," Seetch said in his homily. "From the sweat and toil, the blood and tears, of what you do, many people are fed. A whole army of men have marched before you, and have been messengers of God's love and providence to the people of Bangladesh."

Seetch was the Bengal Bouts' chaplain, a duty he found especially welcome in the dregs of winter—when the football stadium was an icy void, the middling basketball team offered scant consolation, and February, as he often said, "feels sixty-three days long." The cabin-fevered students were starting to get on one another's nerves, and occasionally on his, too. Several had sat before the Desk of Despair in his room lately, and one had been remanded to Student Affairs after an epic parietals violation: His Valentine's Day weekend in the dorm with his hometown girlfriend had ended when they were caught in the shower together at noon. As Seetch spoke tonight, his voice was thick with his inevitable winter dose of bronchitis: It passes through the dorm as on a troopship, and it had been lingering in his system for two weeks now.

"This is a story my mom's family always tells," Seetch said in his homily, taking the boxers back to Cleveland in the Depression, when his grandfather had lost his job in the steam plant at the city water department. There were eight kids in the Gallagher family, and supper was often creamed corn over toast, but when a stranger came to the door one night asking for something to eat, he was invited in to join them. "My grandmother was in the back when he said goodbye and left. She ran out of the house with a sandwich for him, but he was already gone. Now, this was a rowhouse in the middle of the block, and there was no place to go. He had literally disappeared in only a matter of seconds. Later, my grandmother said, 'Did you notice how clean his hands were?' The next day, my grandfather got a job." He paused for a moment, leaving the crowd to wonder just where family legend ended and angelic intervention began. "You do a lot of work training for boxing, and a lot of times it hurts. But there's a higher motivation for you. It's not just for physical fitness—it's going the extra mile for someone else. And God will look after you as you look after them."

Sitting in the front row was Joe Carrigan, who had stepped down as executive officer of the Navy ROTC battalion, but who remained an officer of the Bengal Bouts club. The winner of his division as a sophomore, he had sat out the next year with a nose injury. He was the top seed in the 150-pound division this year. "I feel about the best I've ever felt," he said later, "but I don't want to count anybody out."

Leaving the chapel after Mass, the boxers walked briskly back to their dorms, the snow squeaking underfoot like new shoes. Three of them headed across the lake to Moreau Seminary, the first seminarians within local memory to box in the Bouts. They had signed up together, and they had been training together—doing sit-ups and push-ups and leg raises in the triple digits every day, working on the speed bag and the heavy bag, tossing the medicine ball, even sparring against one another, though they were reluctant at first to throw any real punches.

"I hit him and knocked him back, and then I ran after him and grabbed him and said, 'Are you all right? Are you all right?' " Len Foley said. "The referee was saying 'Hit, hit.' It's a bad habit to go see if the other guy is all right. You don't do that when it's for real."

"Getting hit is a great way to figure out you need to hit back," said Scott Kenny, who did, quickly.

"Can you think of one piece of knowledge that you would be willing to say, 'That's a bad thing'?" Tom Morris asked the class, stepping rapidly up the tiered aisle like Phil Donahue without a mike.

"When you're gonna die," one student offered.

"OK, let's take a vote. How many of you would want to know the time and circumstances of your own death?"

Only two hands in the large lecture room went up, helping to prove his point that knowledge—like a hammer, capable of both driving a nail and smashing a skull—can be what he called "instrumentally bad."

"How many would not want to know?"

The room sprouted a thicket of upraised arms, Joe Carrigan's among them. Their reluctance was not surprising: They were, after all, college students, to whom life had no apparent end. Although he declined the chance to see clear to the finish of his future, Joe could already see further into it than most of his classmates. After graduation, he would be in the Navy for at least four years; he was waiting for his ship assignment now. Law school would probably follow. A senior government major, he had been lucky enough to get into Morris' class—Philosophy 265, "Philosophical Reflections on Christian Belief"—to fill his final philosophy requirement.

Morris had started with St. Anselm's definition of God ("that than which no greater can be conceived"), parsed the distinction between intrinsic and extrinsic goods, and was now exploring the importance of intuition—"naturally formed beliefs," according to the transparency he put on the overhead, "not deriving entirely from definition, evidence, testimony, inference or some experience."

"It seems like we couldn't survive in the world if we couldn't recognize certain things to be true," he said. "So many of the fundamental principles of human knowledge we can't prove to be true, yet we intuit them to be true." He reached for an example that was especially fitting at Notre Dame. "It's like the flow that athletes talk about. If you ask a defensive back who just made an interception, 'How did you know the ball was going in that direction?,' he'll say, 'I just did.' "

The students in Morris' class, mostly seniors, were required to read him as well as listen to him: The syllabus included two of his own books, *Our Idea of God*, an earlier academic work; and *Making Sense of It All*, a recent effort aimed at a more popular audience. Published by a theological press, *Making Sense of It All* was a popular parental gift among Morris' students; he had inscribed scores of copies in the weeks before Christmas. Working in his campus office now, in the mornings, before class, he was finishing a new book pitched at an even wider readership—a philosopher's guide to success, framed around the "Seven C's" lecture he had given the freshmen in Philo 101. It had already attracted the interest of several large publishers, who saw a market for it among the hordes of middle managers who devour self-improvement tomes of every stripe in search of useful, how-to-succeed-in-business wisdom. Morris was, they seemed to believe, Plato crossed with Tom Peters. In his restless efforts to stretch the boundaries of his profession, Morris was following the path of his father—a man whose great energies spilled over into careers as varied as radio-station owner, toy inventor, and real-estate salesman. But just as the younger Morris was rising, the elder Morris was fading, sick with lung cancer back home in North Carolina.

"Do we have enough information now?" Morris asked the class. They were puzzling over the problem of The Two Doors: Without knowing what's behind them, how do you choose which to destroy and which to preserve? On the overhead, he had labeled door number one "living," and door number two "not living."

"No," a student answered. "The thing that's living could be poison ivy, and it could be the *Mona Lisa* behind number two."

Morris relabeled the doors: "conscious" and "not conscious." "Now do we have enough?"

"No," Joe Carrigan volunteered. "Maybe we've got a conscious jerk behind one and a sleeping saint behind two."

Morris tried again: "conscious" and "not possibly conscious," the doors now read. "That rules out a person who is asleep or an embryo. Now, if you would pick door number one to preserve, raise your hand."

The room was again filled with upraised arms: They had, as was his intention, intuited their way straight into a naturally formed belief. "Most of you concur that consciousness is just an intrinsic good, and is worth preserving."

Joe concurred on a more practical level as well: Consciousness—his own, that is—was precisely what he wanted to preserve when he climbed into the ring for his first fight.

The ACC looked as if someone had dressed it up for an SYR and then forgotten to tell the grown-ups they weren't invited. The floor of the basketball arena had become a food court, ringed by booths dispensing hors d'oeuvres; the Sports Heritage Hall was home to a cash bar and a large cheese replica of the Main Building; and a campus band was playing "Sympathy for the Devil" beside the dance floor that had been cleared in the fieldhouse. The crowd that drifted densely through the loud, dim spaces was split between the generation to whom the Rolling Stones represented youth, and the generation to whom they represented age. The parents of three-quarters of the junior class had converged on campus for the forty-first annual installment of Junior Parents' Weekend—a ritual wherein, according to a senior who had participated last year, "your friends meet your parents and tell you, 'They're so cool,' and then you look at them and say, 'Wow, they're not the losers I thought they were.'" The juniors shepherded their parents around, introducing them to the life they had built for themselves in their time away from home.

"There's one friend I really want you to meet. I see his roommate, but I don't see him."

"So you live in Keenan, too."

"What are you majoring in?"

Monk Malloy stood in the middle of the reception, near the half-court circle on the arena floor, towering over a ring of students and parents who looked as if they expected him to jump for the tip-off. His own varsity days preceded the ACC—the defunct, drafty fieldhouse was home to the basketball team then—so he was more familiar with this court as a spectator than as a player: He often watched the games from the small courtside section reserved for Holy Cross priests, seated near his fellow seminary-gym rat, Joe Ross of Morrissey Hall. He passed the conversation deftly around the circle now, from student to parent and back to himself again. He had met the parents of many of his Sorin dormmates tonight, and also the children of some of his own classmates.

"This is where you perfect the pivot move," he said, turning to meet another new face. It was not an entirely natural move for him—he was a guard, after all, not a center—but he had all evening to practice. "You stand here for four hours and just keep pivoting."

The next morning, he was free to move up and down the court at will, having slipped back into the more comfortable position of guard. A special early session of Monk Hoops had convened in the gym of the Rockne Memorial—the juniors of Sorin Hall against their visiting fathers. Malloy pulled up at the top of the key and launched a jump shot.

"Ten–nine," he called after it swished, putting the fathers ahead again.

Malloy's teammates were able to summon up brief memories of old skills, but they mostly looked as if they hadn't played basketball since their own school days. They were especially fond of two-handed set shots, which their sons were sometimes generous enough not to block. Malloy did his best to keep all the fathers in the game, passing frequently, and often ineffectively; but whenever the sons threatened to pull too far ahead, he would square up for another jumper from three-point range.

"Twenty-one–eighteen," Malloy called after swishing another one; three-pointers counted for two in this game, two-pointers for one.

Chris Browning, Stephanie Gallo's running mate in the recent election, answered with his own long jumper: 21–20. He hit another soon after, putting the sons ahead 24–22.

"Youth is starting to win here," Malloy said, and youth then continued to win, scoring several unanswered points in succession. But Malloy kept playing as if the fathers were still ahead—passing the ball to his teammates, resisting the impulse to take the savior shots.

"Good game," he said to each of the other players, fathers and sons alike, after the sons had won, 30–25. At rest now, sweat drying in the chilly air, they could feet the small, hollow breeze that circled the cavernous gym. The gray winter light outlined the metal grates on the tall window like leafless trees. Malloy posed for a group photo, standing in the center of the fathers' row, with the sons kneeling before them. He collected the balls into his bag and headed back to Sorin.

"I probably could have made it so we would have won," he said. "I'm competitive, I don't like to lose, but the fathers won once and I saw it wasn't good. It's important for the sons to win. When they went ahead at the end, I kind of held back."

He was back on the court at the ACC later that afternoon, his sweats exchanged for vestments, celebrating Mass for the juniors and their parents in the basketball arena, and then, black suit and collar back in place, joining them for dinner in the banquet hall that had been set up in the adjacent fieldhouse. Junior Parents' Weekend was the halftime show between the two other big classwide gatherings, freshman orientation and graduation, and by the time it was Malloy's turn to speak, the crowd had worked itself into a state of high-Domer bliss, clapping and singing along with the Glee Club through the fight song and the alma mater. The junior-class president had delivered a witty, warm, and sentimental speech: You knew you were finally a true Domer, he said, "when your mother cries at the pep rally at the alma mater, and your father dresses like a *Rudy* extra." Then Malloy took the podium on the dais, speaking as if the Mass had never ended, or a late-night dorm conversation had just begun.

Malloy told the audience of parents and children a story about his own father. When he was spending a sabbatical year at a Holy Cross community house in California, his father, seventy-five at the time, had come out for a visit. "At the end of the ten days, I could feel a sense of completion in both our lives," he said after recounting the visit. "And we had reached a kind of dramatic reversal of roles, for I was now tending him, and looking after his needs. Two years later, he died, and I wasn't there. But I remember the feeling I had was that we had said it all and shared it all two years before."

It was the kind of heartfelt personal reflection more common to a homily than an after-dinner speech, and it showed that Malloy had been thinking deeply about the significance of this weekend—perhaps more deeply than many of the participants. "Junior Parents' Weekend isn't designed to be quite that dramatic," he continued. "But because it is the parents who are the guests now, there is a manifest recognition that a real change is happening in the relationship."

But, having revealed something of himself, Malloy then pulled back, switching from center to guard, shifting his rhetoric from the personal to the general. He has the professor's habit of assuming that, if you offer him a platform, you must want to hear his ideas, not his stories; and he has the private person's habit of assuming that he is the least interesting subject of all. No matter how large the forum, Malloy tends to speak as if he's in a small room—a strategy that produces moments both of real intimacy, like the story of his father, and of cool, detached distance. His address was light on humor and anecdote, and heavy on theme: how parents and children learn to stand beside one another as adults. He was at his most animated, sounding like a proud father himself, when he was talking about the students— their emerging minds and hearts and souls, their entry into what was often called the "Notre Dame family."

"Wherever you go in the world, you'll find Notre Dame people willing to open their households and their hearts to you," he said, his tone suggesting that he considered himself just another member of the clan, not its patriarch. "They will be ready to assist in the next stage in the evolution of your character." When Malloy finished, the crowd clapped respectfully but tentatively, as if they had come to think, sometime during the course of the speech, that they were listening not to a university president on a dais, but to a priest in a church, where such addresses are acknowledged by silence rather than applause.

At the farewell brunch the next morning, Father Hesburgh got a standing ovation just for stepping up to the microphone. Despite his emeritus status, and his low campus profile, Hesburgh still represented the franchise to many of these parents: Malloy was the one they could blame for tuition hikes, doctrinal transgressions, philosophical lapses, and whatever else they might find wrong with Notre Dame; Hesburgh was the one they could idealize, and venerate, for everything that was right about it.

"People say to me, 'What makes this place special?' " Hesburgh started off. "I certainly never did, I'm just an ordinary human being. If you really want to know, stand in the dark of night and look up at the golden figure on the Dome."

No matter how small the forum, Hesburgh, unlike Malloy, tends to speak as if he's in a large hall. His decades on the public stage have infused his rhetorical voice with a Mount Rushmore quality, a heavy weight of significance that is hard to shed. It is a voice that has counseled seven presidents and four popes, and it sounds every bit the part, however large or small the subject under discussion. He slipped easily now into the sentimental reminiscence that was the morning's dominant tone.

"I don't know how they get it, but they get it like three minutes after they get here—it's like a contagion for good in the air—and somehow they become bonded to this place immediately," Hesburgh said of the students. "One of the trustees used to say that this was the highest concentration of goodness of anyplace on earth. I won't make that boast—it's a little much. But today we do all stand in a special spot, and it's a special spot because it's guarded over by the Mother of God."

He charmed the crowd like the ultimate communion-breakfast raconteur, with a speech that was heavy on humor and anecdote and light on ideas. His chief mode of discourse is narration, not contemplation: He has traveled far and long enough to have a story for every occasion; roaming the world like an ecclesiastical anthropologist, he has collected droves of new parables and exemplary characters to add to the wide canon the Catholic church maintains. He is not shy about using the word "I"—some professors used to bet on how many times he would use it in his commencement speeches—and he is a habitual name-dropper; but the names he drops are as likely to be obscure as famous. Today he told the juniors and their parents about Tom Dooley—the late alumnus whose heroic work as a doctor among the refugees of Southeast Asia in the 1950s had earned him a statue in the Grotto and a high place in the uncanonized litany of Notre Dame saints—but he also told them about a young man none of them had ever heard of, a student who went on to work as a public-health specialist in Africa.

"Let me tell you about a fella named Mike," he said, his voice echoing back a second later from the rear of the fieldhouse, leaving the impression that even when he was finished he would still be heard, "a good name for a Notre Dame fella. . . ."

———

"Don't miss my thumb, Jack," Joe Carrigan said, perched on the edge of the trainer's table in the ACC locker room. He held his right hand out, getting it wrapped tightly in white tape for his fight. His face was set in a scowl of concentration—his brow knit, his eyes looking at a quiet fist but seeing a sharp jab. The small gold letters on his blue boxing trunks spelled out "Bengal Bouts."

"I'll get your thumb, don't worry," Jack Mooney assured him.

Joe tested his hands, punching the fist of one into the palm of the other, before bouncing out to the wide fluorescent corridor to shadow-box his way into a fighting mood. Another fighter took his place on the table, and Mooney started wrapping again. It was the first and busiest day of the Bouts—thirty-one fights, which would consume an entire Sunday afternoon; sixty-two fighters for Mooney to tape up and send out to the blue canvas ring on the arena floor (eleven other fighters had first-round byes), and sixty-two fighters to patch up after their return. The first bloody noses were already appearing back into the locker room. When Mooney finished with one fighter's hand, he turned his attention to another one's face, wiping it clean and plugging its leak.

"Nobody ever got hurt, but we've had some beautiful broken noses," Mooney said. "Hey, everybody got their cups on?"

Mooney had been part of the Bouts almost since the beginning—water boy, timekeeper, trainer, judge, referee—and he had aged now into the role of grandfatherly sage, a voluble repository of boxing wisdom and lore. He could tell his young charges all about the eight four-time champions in Bouts history, and he could show them what their jabs looked like. A Golden Gloves champion in South Bend back in the 1930s, he went on to a 14-and-2 record as a pro: He once fought on a Joe Louis card in Kalamazoo, Michigan, and on a Max Schmeling card here at home. When he worked at Studebaker—he had thirty-seven years in when it closed in 1963—he would race over to practice as soon as he punched out. Like everyone else connected with the Bouts, he was strictly a volunteer. He had no official connection to Notre Dame other than the roses he laid each week on Rockne's grave, and a devotion to boxing that, even at eighty, made him reluctant to retire.

"I teach 'em a good left jab," he said. "I don't believe in trying to teach 'em hooks. Hooks are for professionals. You gotta keep it out here, and work it like a piston."

Joe Carrigan's hands had been laced into the gloves now, and a blue robe was draped around his shoulder like a cape. He and his gold-robed opponent milled in the dim tunnel, waiting for the fight ahead of them to finish. Mooney had done what he could; now it was Father Bill Seetch's turn.

"The reason why you're here makes you both winners," Seetch told the two boxers when they stopped for a blessing on their way to the ring. They bowed together into a tight huddle, his hands resting on their padded headgear. "No matter what happens in the ring, you're both champs. May Almighty God bless and keep and protect both of you, in the name of the Father, the Son, and the Holy Spirit."

"Amen."

"I bat .500 no matter what," Seetch said as they climbed through the ropes. "Ted Williams never did that."

"In the blue corner," the ring announcer said, "a senior, representing Grace Hall, 'Joltin' Joe' Carrigan."

The two fighters tested each other with a cautious, jabbing dance in the first round, and what Joe found in his opponent—an eighth-seeded freshman who fought like a higher-seeded veteran—wasn't what he had expected. Joe's preferred strategy was to wait for an attack before launching a counterattack of his own, but his opponent forced him to go on the offensive in the second round. He met a surprising flurry of counterpunches that pushed him back against the ropes. Recovering quickly, he shifted from reverse to forward, and punched the freshman into the corner.

Joe's stamina—the product of his ROTC training on top of his Bouts conditioning—helped him in the third round, leaving him enough strength to land some convincing final punches. Standing in the center of the ring with the referee, awaiting the decision, he hoped his last barrage had been enough to impress the judges.

"And the winner, by split decision," the announcer said, "in the blue corner, 'Joltin' Joe' Carrigan."

"I was nervous about that decision," Joe said. "I didn't fight up to my level. I felt terrible out there. Everything I was doing in sparring practice I wasn't doing in there."

The crowd drifted in and out all through the afternoon, never more than a few hundred strong, mostly friends and dormmates of the fighters. The dorms that were well represented in the ring—especially Dillon and Grace, Joe's home—were well represented in the seats. Keenan had no boxers at all in the Bouts, but Patrick Lyons had come to watch anyway, accompanied by his father, Kevin, who was visiting for the weekend.

"He's got a nice jab," Kevin Lyons noted as a pair of fighters in the 160-pound division took the ring. He had seen plenty of bouts back when he was a student himself, but these were his first as the father of a student. "I'd give it to the guy in the gold."

After so many years of visiting Notre Dame as his father's guest, Patrick Lyons clearly relished the chance to serve as the host now. He was a vested member of the student establishment already, with an insider's insight into the campus present that well complemented his inherited, Domer-clan knowledge of its past. His campaign gamble had paid off: His alliance with Frank Flynn, and the distinctive diamond-shape posters he had designed for the winning ticket, made him a player within the new administration. He was angling for the top job at Adworks, the campus ad agency. He had now clearly crossed the threshold where a true believer becomes a proselytizer: He had just sent his brother—a high-school junior whose college-shopping list actually included Middlebury, Penn, and other schools that weren't Notre Dame—a pennant and a T-shirt for his birthday, and a letter.

"I told him there were two important questions to ask about where you were going to college: What color is the dome, and what bowl are they in?" he said. "He thinks he's too sophisticated for Notre Dame, but he'll get over that."

The semifinals moved into the ACC fieldhouse a few nights later, a smaller venue that made the crowd, which was larger, feel larger, too. The light on the canvas—from a stark array of ring lights hovering low overhead—was as bright and harsh as in an operating room, but it faded quickly beyond the ropes, leaving the bleachers in shadows as dusky and close as an old tank-town clubhouse. There was no smoke, but there were ashes—on the foreheads of some of the fighters. It was Ash Wednesday, the first day of Lent—the season when the dining halls stop serving meat on Fridays, and the food-sales concessions in the dorm basements wait until 11:45 p.m. to put the pepperoni pizzas in the ovens, timing it so they would be ready to eat when the ban lifted at midnight.

Joe Carrigan was unmarked when he went into the ring tonight—he planned to get his ashes at the dorm Mass later—and he was still unmarked when he came out. He went for his opponent's body with his left; his opponent went for his with both arms, grabbing. Pushed off after one clinch, Joe fell to the canvas, triggering a round of jeers directed at his opponent's tactics. Although he never found enough room to open up his full arsenal, he landed enough punches, and deflected enough more, to have his glove raised in victory. The decision was unanimous this time.

"Good job," Father Seetch said, congratulating him as he congratulated everybody, winner or loser.

"It was a little bit sloppy," Joe said, rendering his own verdict. "But it was better than last time."

Seetch stood in what he liked to call the Amen Corner, dispensing blessings to the entering fighters, his collar poking out of a Notre Dame Boxing sweatshirt. "How do you feel?" he asked Scott "The Moreau Mauler" Kenny, one of the pugilistic seminarians, who had lost his first-round bout on Sunday.

"The back of my head was sore the next day," said Scott, the front of whose head was smudged with ashes today, acquired at the 5:00 p.m. Mass at Moreau. He left Seetch to join the Amen Bleachers, the large contingent of priests, brothers, and seminarians from Moreau on hand to root for their two colleagues who had won on Sunday.

"C'mon, Len," they called as the bell rang to start Len "Holy Moly" Foley's match.

"That Len, he's got a good jab," noted Jack Mooney, who had come out from the locker room to watch. "But he's fighting one of the toughest kids we have."

When Len was backed into the corner, his jab was good enough to get him out, and when he was backed in again, it got him out again. But in the third round, neither the jab nor the ashes were sufficient protection against a huge right that caught him in the head. He took a standing eight-count before the referee stopped the fight.

"You remember anything?" Seetch asked when Len was dressed and cogent again.

"At first I didn't," Len answered. The blood had been wiped from his nose, but his eye was black, and ripening fast. "Now it's coming back."

The last seminarian was in the ring now, Jeff "The Boxing Bishop" Hurlbert, matched against a former varsity wrestler who had the kind of charging, ramming style that raised a blood-roar from the crowd. Leading with his left, Jeff deftly landed what jabs he could, but he spent more time dancing backward, dodging wild roundhouse rights. He lost a split decision.

"He hit me pretty hard, harder than anybody else had," Jeff told Jack Mooney. "I'm sure I'll have a headache, but he didn't ring my bell or anything."

He and Foley both embraced Mooney in turn—a gesture that borrowed equally from the rituals of athletic camaraderie and the sign of peace at Mass. "I'm so proud of you guys," Mooney said. "You've got a real good jab."

The Bouts moved back into the arena for the Friday-night finals, playing to a crowd that topped two thousand. Father Seetch was missing—gone off to Arizona to marry one of his old students from the Holy Cross high school where he had taught before returning to Notre Dame as a rector—one of four student weddings he had been asked to preside at this semester.

"The Amen Corner has been decimated tonight," said Father Terry Linton, the rector of the other tower, Grace Hall, and Seetch's partner in chaplaincy at the previous sessions.

"Remember, you're doing more than boxing—you're helping to give hope to people who can never thank you," Linton said, his hands on the shoulders of the two robed finalists in the 150-pound division. He gave his blessing to both fighters, but when they climbed into the ring he would give his cheers to the one who lived in his dorm, Joe Carrigan. "May God bless you and keep you from harm. In the name of the Father . . ."

Joe fought like the favorite he was in the first round, stepping nimbly out of reach of the punches of his opponent, Steve "Chocolate E" Clar, and then jabbing Clar back into the corner. A large contingent from Grace rooted loudly for him.

"Stick him, Joe, stick him!"

"Get after him, Joe!"

"Throw the jab, Joey!"

Joe threw the jab in the next two rounds, plenty of them, but Clar threw just as many, and maybe a few more. The momentum shifted back and forth, and when the two fighters embraced at the final bell, it was with the respect of equals. The decision was slow in coming. Standing in the center of the ring with the referee now, Carrigan and Clar had nothing left to do but await their final word.

"The winner, and 150-pound champ," the announcer finally said, "on a split decision, in the gold corner, Steve 'Chocolate E' Clar."

Joe accepted the news with the fixed aplomb of the Navy ensign he soon would be. "I won a bunch of split decisions, so I figured that maybe it wouldn't go my way somehow," he said after shedding his Bengals gloves for the last time. "What goes around comes around. I did my best boxing so far in the tournament tonight. I thought I'd feel more disappointed, but I really don't."

He was back at ringside a few fights later, working as a second in the corner of a friend. "Joltin' Joe" was retired now, having swapped his blue robe and trunks for a plain gray Notre Dame Boxing T-shirt with the name "Carrigan" stenciled military-style across the shoulders.

"In the blue corner," the announcer called, "a senior . . ."

14

As the line snaked through the cold night air toward the front door of the Linebacker Lounge, the students awaiting their turn inside stamped their feet and rubbed their arms for warmth. They were dressed the way college students convinced of their own indestructibility often dress—jacketless, hatless, some even sockless, a sartorial strategy that, as soon became apparent, was rooted tonight as much in practicality as bravado. As they crept inside, after showing their IDs and paying their two dollars, they traveled instantly from winter to summer, exchanging a frozen parking lot for a saunalike barroom. The temperature was at least sixty degrees higher inside, maybe more, a sudden blast of heat and humidity that was like a preview of spring break. The change in the decibel level was similarly explosive. The Four Seasons were trilling "December, 1963 (Oh, What a Night)" and the room was swaying more or less in rhythm to it. To move from one point to the next required the kind of intimate personal contact that was frowned upon on campus, and not often seen in public outside the snowball-fight tussles.

"Hey, you're fucking pissin' me off," spluttered a stocky malcontent trying to bull his way back to the bar for a refill he clearly didn't need. The precise identity of the offending party was hazy; his main problem seemed to be a lack of the proper Backertude—the understanding that, upon entering the Backer, as it was fondly known, you contracted to accept the smoke, the sweat, the spilled drinks, the noise, the claustrophobia, the general all-around discomfort, in exchange for a precious college experience. A circle of women stopped harmonizing with the Four Seasons and watched him fretfully, wondering if they'd soon be caught in a Bengal Bouts reprise. But his belligerence alone had opened enough space around him so that he moved on with no more than a dismissive grunt.

Because Notre Dame was originally a self-contained rural island—the students all but confined to a campus that was encircled by the farms the brothers tended—it never developed the kind of college-town ambience common to most schools its size. It is suburban now, like its students, and so is its off-campus infrastructure, a scattered, unfocused ring of pizza parlors, record stores, bookstores, liquor stores, restaurants, and ice-cream shops that are just barely accessible to students without cars. The bars are widely spaced, both geographically and conceptually. Bridget McGuire's catered to giddy underclassmen, Club 23 to what passed for the ponytail crowd, and The Commons to the unaffiliated middle. Corby's, refurbished for *Rudy*, was a picture-perfect student pub that felt like the movie set it was. Coach's was packed each Tuesday for its $2.50-a-pitcher special, but the rest of the week it was a sports bar just a touch too well appointed for a true student hangout. Senior Bar was clean and convenient, but it wasn't far enough outside the orbit of campus authority. It was left to the Backer to fill the indispensable role of beloved student swillhole.

"It's like a microcosm of Notre Dame," one senior observed. "People getting drunk, then making out because they're sexually frustrated, then getting tough with each other."

The Linebacker was a low, featureless concrete bunker just big enough and solid enough to contain a raucous Domer Saturday night without bursting. During the week it was another unremarkable local bar, but on weekends it was commandeered by the senior class as their unofficial clubhouse. Now that they were old enough to avoid the loud, hot, dense, quivering room parties in the dorms, they came to a loud, hot, dense, quivering bar where they had to pay cash for their drinks instead of reaching into a slushy trash can full of Meisterbräu. But here, of course, there was no rector hovering in the background, no parietals looming in the distance. The appeal of the Backer was that it offered the seniors a glimpse of the future—the rough and seedy edges of the real world they would soon enter—at the same time it offered them a haven from it: a closed society made up almost entirely of their peers.

"I gave up chocolate for Lent, not beer."

"I'm in total nonacademic senior mode."

"I have no social life. I see the same people over and over again."

"You have a crush on him? Oh-my-God, oh-my-God, oh-my-God!"

"You can say 'fuck,' but you can't say 'dick.' That's the worst word you can say in front of a girl—just the concept is worse."

"I'd go so far as to say I hate Wendy's. I'd never eat there by choice."

"The double with cheese is good, though."

The soundtrack they had to shout over was weighted heavily toward songs that had been hits when they were in grade school, or even earlier: "I Will Survive," "I Think I Love You," "Sweet Caroline," "Copacabana." Their conversation was weighted toward what they planned to do after graduation.

"I got a job with Andersen."

"She got into med school."

"I'm not ready to go yet."

"My parents don't want me to go to Detroit."

"You watch, it's amazing—you get a job and they won't mind at all."

"I got a job in Anaheim," Geoff Slevin told an acquaintance. "Come visit me."

The chemical engineers, like the accountants, had been mulling job offers lately, and Geoff's best one had come from ARCO, the California-based oil company. "They made me an offer I couldn't refuse, and I didn't," he said. He would be making more than $40,000 a year, an amount he found both "embarrassing and flattering," as a process-design engineer for a refinery. Several other job possibilities were still pending, and at least one offer had already been tendered—with a Chicago firm that would have sent him overseas for the best part of the next three years—but none were as attractive as ARCO. "The only thing that held me back a little was how far away it was from home." He was reluctant to leave the Midwest, and his large, close family in Illinois. "I really wanted them to say it's OK, and they did."

With a job secured, and a 3.65 grade-point average all but guaranteeing him a magna-cum-laude degree, he had the kind of time and freedom, finally, that engineers imagine as the perennial condition of liberal-arts majors. He was no longer leading the organic-chemistry review sessions. He was taking a couple of nonengineering electives that he counted among his best courses ever—philosophy of law, and Civil War history. He was also contemplating what to do about the last big unresolved question in his life—his relationship with his longtime girlfriend, Dana Ciacciarelli.

"I don't know, I may do it," he said about the prospect of proposing. He held a plastic cup with an Amaretto sour that had grown watery from inattention. "If I do it, it'll be totally spontaneous, like I'll buy the ring and give it to her the same day."

It was the season of diamonds for the seniors now, the first crop having appeared on newly affianced fingers upon the return from Christmas break, with more being added to the harvest almost weekly. Relations between men and women tend to have an all-or-nothing quality here—reaching precipitously from onetime SYR pairings to serious coupledom, with only a stunted casual-dating scene in between—and as graduation approached, the senior couples considered the possibility of a future together—or alone. Jobs were a key factor in the decision: Few seniors were willing to get engaged without the promise of a steady paycheck, or at least a secure spot in graduate school. Simply living together, without benefit of marriage, was not a widely discussed option.

"I know she didn't have that ring last semester."

"Everybody's getting engaged."

"I only went out with one girl here I would've married, and I fucked it up. It was my fault—she was a really cool girl. I'll be married someday and I'll think to myself, 'Wow, I could've been married to a cooler girl but I fucked up.' "

The on-campus witching hour of 2:00 a.m. passed unmarked, and the commotion continued until the lights went up at 2:45 for last call, a signal that lacked the ominous finality of the dorm deadlines. The crowd started breaking up, drifting toward the round of 2-to-7 parties under way at Campus View and Turtle Creek and Lafayette Square and several other off-campus locales beyond the reach of parietals. Nobody was telling them they had to go home yet, just that they couldn't stay here.

"So what are we doing now?" somebody asked nobody in particular.

"I don't know," came the answer. "What do you wanna do?"

Perched on a stool in the basement entomology lab, sharing bench space with ranks of impaled insect specimens, Dana Ciacciarelli busily took notes on the egg-laying habits of mosquitoes in the high Arctic. It was her last course with George Craig—Biology 562, "Aquatic Insects," the spring companion to the fall entomology class—and where she was going from here she still wasn't sure: To grad school or to work? With Geoff Slevin or without him?

"We've joked about it," she said about the idea of getting engaged. "But Geoff always kind of plays down our relationship. He can never even say the word 'girlfriend.' "

This morning, though, she was focused on smaller, colder things—the insects that breed in the snow-melt pools of the Far North, a habitat that sounded downright tropical when compared with South Bend about now. The snow here was still collecting, not melting, new powder topping the old like a bartender putting a fresh head on a mug of beer. One recent storm had dumped a foot and a half of snow on campus, closing school for the first time in fifteen years, and leaving the students a day free to sleep late, play snow football, and sled down the front steps of the Main Building on dining-hall trays.

"The high Arctic is something like the North Quad after the snow melts," Craig explained. "It doesn't drain, and you get a lot of standing water around."

Craig had been lucky enough to escape the snow occasionally this winter, heading south to various conferences to discuss the subject that had consumed most of his research energies lately—the Asian tiger mosquito, a potentially dangerous carrier of an encephalitis virus that can kill both horses and people. Native to northern Japan, the species had smuggled itself into the United States aboard a Texas-bound freighter in 1988, breeding in the small pools of stagnant water that had collected inside a load of old tires. Starting from a Houston tire dump, it spread quickly and aggressively, east to Florida and north as far as Chicago, forcing out the local mosquitoes and adapting its genetic code so efficiently to its new environment as to be a fast-forward illustration of natural selection. Craig's graduate students were even now haunting tire dumps in search of Asian tiger mosquitoes, and then bringing them back to the lab with the hope of finding some chinks in their formidable genetic armor. Craig's voice had been among the loudest in a scientific chorus that argued, in vain, for early control measures.

"It's too late now—they will be here forever," he said. "They were a temperate species in Japan, but they've already become a tropical species. They've started breeding year-round in Florida. They'll reach Miami this year, and then they'll go through the Caribbean like a dose of salts through a duck."

Craig's long years in the company of swarming masses of insects had helped shape in him a world-view that veered sharply from wonder to worry, from celebration to apocalypse. It was evident in his classes (the marvels of mosquito biology, the pestilence they wreak upon humanity), in his opinion of the campus community (great students, dismal officials), and, most recently, in his response to the ongoing discussion about the Catholic-

ity of Notre Dame. He had been largely a noncombatant until he read a
memo circulated among the faculty by Father Bill Miscamble—a well-
respected history professor, a rising star within the Holy Cross order, and
one of the leaders of the group that called itself the Conversation on the
Catholic Character. Miscamble had, on his own, taken the Conversation
one step further by drawing up a list of specific proposals for achieving its
goal of building a "great Catholic university": recruitment and hiring strategies, faculty orientation, resource allocation, "reflection" by each department on its "contribution to the Catholic identity and mission of Notre
Dame." The tone of the memo troubled some faculty members, and it recalled a debate that reached deep into Notre Dame's history.

"You and your associates propose that we give up top 25 [in the annual
U.S. News & World Report university rankings] as a goal and Princeton,
Stanford, Chicago as role models. Instead we should follow Liberty University, Oral Roberts U., Bob Jones U. and Brigham Young," Craig wrote in a
letter that he addressed to Miscamble and then circulated among his departmental colleagues. Imprinted on the stationery was a drawing of a giant
mosquito that looked ready to buzz off the page, a none-too-subtle reminder of the pesky role Craig often plays in university affairs. "How are
you going to accomplish this 'ethnic cleansing'? Who is to be the Grand In-
quisitor who will ensure that 'articulate, committed Catholics predominate
in every part of the university'?"

Craig's letter went on to recall an earlier era when, as he said, his rhetoric
maintaining its characteristic fever pitch, Notre Dame was "a battleground for
those who would turn the university into a parochial, catechism-dominated
backwater"—the decade around the turn of the century when Father Andrew
Morrissey was president and Father John Zahm was provincial of the Holy
Cross order. Now they are known mainly as a pair of men's dorms, but then
they represented two distinct ideas about what Notre Dame should be. Zahm
was a gifted scientist who argued that the theory of evolution was reconcilable
with Catholic doctrine; his book on the subject was subsequently condemned
by the Vatican and ordered withdrawn from circulation. He wanted Notre
Dame to attract a scholarly faculty, to build new laboratories and libraries, to
become "the intellectual center of the American West." Morrissey was a warm
and practical administrator, afraid of debt and content for Notre Dame to remain a small college. "The education of the head at the expense of the education of the heart is the crying evil of the day," he once wrote. "We can never
compete with those colleges that have such tremendous endowments. Our

very existence depends on giving Catholic boys a good preparatory foundation." Morrissey won, and Notre Dame moved only haltingly toward becoming what Sorin had ambitiously called it in his original charter: a university. Pockets of scientific excellence emerged sporadically—Father Nieuwland's synthetic-rubber formula, Jerome Green's early wireless messages, the germfree animal lab, the radiation lab, the wind tunnels in aeronautical engineering—but it really wasn't until the Hesburgh regime that Notre Dame achieved anything like the intellectual stature Zahm had envisioned.

"You can be sure," Craig's letter continued, "that there is not a first-class scientist in the country, Catholic or non-Catholic, who would ever consider coming to the kind of ghetto you and your associates want. In the end, you would have a seminary, not a university."

Craig, as is his habit, was firing ammunition of a larger caliber than the target probably required. Nobody was suggesting that he stop teaching evolution. Nobody now was as suspicious of scientific inquiry as some of the old clerics had been, like the devout brother who once sprinkled the whole science building with holy water after finding scuff marks high up on the walls of its museum and believing they were the footprints of the devil; in fact they were the shoeprints of a research assistant to Albert Zahm—John's younger brother, a prominent professor of mathematics and aeronautics—who had been swinging from an experimental glider suspended from the ceiling. But Craig's real concern—and it was shared by others whose language was much milder—was what he perceived as a move by the Holy Cross community to reassert its dominance over Notre Dame, and to inject religion into inappropriate places.

"They're destroying the house that Hesburgh built," he said. "There isn't a 'Catholic' biology, or a 'Catholic' physics. It's silly to talk about it."

Craig did not count himself as the kind of "committed Catholic" that the Miscamble memo, and the Colloquy report—and, for that matter, Hesburgh himself—argued should constitute the majority of the faculty. "I *was* a Catholic," was how he put it. "I'm like most scientists—I don't know anything about religion."

He drew his own strongest beliefs from biology, not theology. In class now he was rhapsodizing about niche partitions—how two different species can occupy the same territory without driving each other out, a lesson that seemed to have some wider implications for the Notre Dame faculty as well. He used as an example the case of two related species of mosquitoes in the high Arctic, both of which needed to lay their eggs in the mossy crevices of the slopes that got the most light from the never-setting sun. One species laid its eggs in one spot on a slope at noon, the other at another spot in the late afternoon.

"I think it's absolutely gorgeous," he said, "when two species can niche-partition without even a day-and-night difference."

"Are cultures static, nonchanging realities that are oblivious to outside judgments?" Father Malloy asked the freshmen arrayed around the long conference table in his Sunday-night seminar. He had his own answer, but he wanted to hear theirs.

"When one culture tries to impose its beliefs on another culture, that's not a good thing," one student suggested. "It's like 'Let's change what other people believe to what we believe.' "

The campus outside was as thoroughly glazed with ice as a Far Northern winter—Malloy himself had almost fallen twice on the short walk over here to the Main Building after dinner at Corby Hall—but the book on the table in front of each student was a ticket to the warmer side of the globe: *Heat and Dust*, by the Indian novelist Ruth Prawer Jhabvala.

"But a culture is always changing," Malloy said. "The question is: How do these kinds of changes happen?"

When he asked it of his students, here in his classroom, the question was theoretical, answerable by words alone; but when he asked it of himself, next door in his office—where he had been working lately on the final Colloquy report, a blueprint for a changing Notre Dame—it was practical, answerable instead by actions. The endless, often tedious round of Colloquy meetings in the library penthouse had ended; the committee reports had been published and circulated for comment. Now it was Malloy's job to synthesize it all into a set of specific recommendations. How many new faculty slots were needed? Should the enrollment grow? Which new buildings should be built first? Should the football stadium be expanded? What about financial aid? Minority recruiting? The whole "Catholic-character" issue?

"And what's Hinduism got to do with India?" he asked the students now, trying to draw out what they knew about the nation where this week's novel was set. "How many languages are spoken there? What else do we know?"

Some of what he knew he had learned a year earlier on his own visit to India, his first—a "seductive" land, as he described it to them, "off the charts as far as being unfamiliar to me." He told them about wild, nauseating cab rides, the Dalai Lama, the smell of yak-butter lamps in a monastery. Though he traveled widely, he had not yet acquired the casual, man-about-the-world air of Hesburgh; you could still hear in his tone some of the wide-eyed wonder of the civil servant's son from Washington, the first in his family to go to college. Having sketched the novel's background and setting for the class, he returned to a discussion of the characters.

"I think he probably feels she got the better experience of India than he did," one student said about one character.

"She's sitting there saying, 'This sucks.' "

"I'm sure it was a challenge on his part to withstand the temptations of the flesh, the belly dancing and the what have you."

"Was he gay?"

"I kinda disagreed with how they kept blaming all their carnal desires on the heat," Alex Montoya said. "They didn't see there were gonna be consequences for their actions. I don't think India should be blamed. I think it was their own lack of judgment."

It was a new crop of books for Malloy this semester, and a new crop of students—probably none of whom had traveled a harder road here than Alex. Back in the summer, when his freshman classmates were preparing for orientation, Alex was worried about deportation: A native of Medellín, Colombia, he had lived as an undocumented alien in California since the age of four; just before coming to Notre Dame, he applied for—and, after a hard fight, finally got—a green card. Earlier this evening, he had been late to class, slowed by the ice: With two artificial arms and an artificial leg—he was born with only one limb, his left leg—he sometimes found the South Bend winter difficult to negotiate.

"I had a hard time in the first semester—I stopped believing in myself," Alex said; but that was before the Penn State game. Standing on the bleacher seats in the freshman section that snowy day, straining to see the action at the far end of the field, rooting for an improbable, last-minute comeback, he felt a surge of Domerness—a new and powerful sense of belonging—wash over him when Notre Dame scored. "When Reggie Brooks caught that pass, I cried. It was a real emotional time for me, and when he caught it, it was like 'Dreams do come true.' "

He joined the rest of the crowd on the field after the game, collecting a small scrap of turf that he sealed in a Ziploc bag—a piece of Notre Dame that belonged to him now. He pulled out a 2.4 average for the fall, and was shooting for a higher spring. He was elected vice-president of LULAC, a Latin American student group. He lobbied for a golf cart to help him get around campus; when he got one, he named it "Scrappy" (it had been stolen

twice in the last week alone). He filled a scrapbook with mementos, including photos of himself with the leprechaun and with Rocket Ismail, who was
on campus this semester taking classes toward the degree he had left behind
when he turned pro. "Right when he saw my hook, it was like he lit up.
Something had obviously touched him. He said to enjoy these days, they're
the best of your life." His column had debuted in *The Observer*—"Hook
Shots," he called it. In his most recent column, he described his difficult
fifty-step climb up to this classroom each week, and he called for renovations that would make the Main Building—too old and unsteady to support
an elevator now—more accessible to the handicapped.

"Over Christmas vacation, everywhere I went it was like a hero's welcome—'Hey, he goes to Notre Dame, he goes to Notre Dame,' " he said.
"When I came back in January, I said to myself, 'Man, I'm going home
now—Notre Dame's my home.' "

At the short break in the middle of the long class, the students watched
part of the NBA All-Star Game on the television in the conference room.
Malloy returned to his office to watch while he did some paperwork. "I want
you to know that this is my favorite sporting event of the year, and I'm giving it up for class," he told them when they reconvened and resumed their
discussion of the book. "Now, tell me, what's a swami?"

"Don't they have that thing on their heads?"

"Like the thing Johnny Carson puts on his head?"

One student had a more serious answer. "About ten years ago in L.A., I
saw a swami for a while," Chandra Johnson said, and then laughed mod-
estly, knowing how such an admission might typecast her in the eyes of her
younger classmates. "My mother would die if she ever knew I went to a
swami. At the time I was married, and I asked him about my children and
my husband."

Chandra had been silent most of the class, not because she had too little
to say, but because she had too much. She had learned this semester that
when she started to speak the other students often stopped, out of deference
to her age and experience. They tended to see her less as a fellow student in
the classroom than as a second teacher—a role she had in fact taken last
week when she led the class in Malloy's absence. Now she usually waited until she was asked before speaking, or until she could illuminate a topic from
an angle no one else could—as she was doing now, lending insight into a
character who was, as she once was herself, a non-Hindu visitor to a Hindu
holy man.

"I think her willingness to even go there is her surrender to this new culture," she said of the character. "It's her way of saying, 'Yeah, I think I'm gonna be a part of this.' "

Chandra had made a similar surrender last summer, when she wrapped up the loose ends of her first thirty-eight years, sold everything but her clothes, which she packed, and her car, which she shipped ahead, and boarded a train for the two-day journey from her old home in South Central Los Angeles to her new home at Notre Dame. Her son and her daughter continued living with her ex-husband and his second wife; her freshman year here would end just a few weeks before her daughter graduated from high school there. Though she had worked as an executive secretary for a Big Six accounting firm, she had felt nearer her true vocation in her avocational role as a religious educator for the archdiocese. She planned to major in theology.

"My mother's convinced I'm here to join the convent," she said, but she wasn't. She came from a large and active family of black Catholics: Her late father had been a founding member of the Golden Gate Quintet, a famous gospel group; one of her brothers was a Paulist priest who worked at Ohio State's Newman Center. "I told him I wanted to get a degree in theology, and he told me, 'You're not getting any younger, so, when you get your paper, you need to get the right paper.' " A Notre Dame degree was—in his eyes, and hers, too—the best kind of paper to get.

On a campus with little tradition of nontraditional students, with no evening classes and few programs for adults who aren't full-time grad students, with an undergraduate population almost entirely under the age of twenty-two—the ex-Marine at the other end of the table in tonight's class, a Gulf War veteran, was another rare exception—Chandra hadn't found a natural community of peers waiting to embrace her. But on a campus with so few black women, she did soon find herself being sought out as a mentor. Once each week, she led a meeting of Just a Sister Away, a group for black women students that she had started upon her return from Christmas break. Every Friday afternoon, she drove to a South Bend housing project, often with several other students in tow, to work as a volunteer with Slice of Life, an after-school club for young black girls.

"I guess I'm just a romantic, but it takes a certain amount of vulnerability in order to become steeped in a culture that's not your own," Chandra said in class now, speaking about the character from the novel, not herself.

Malloy passed the discussion around the table for a while before finally taking it back, the clock ticking down, for the final shot. "Can you ever totally enter into the experience of another culture?" he asked, launching one deep from three-point range, its arc high enough, he hoped, to keep them thinking beyond the buzzer. "That's what we're trying to figure out in this class. Can you make judgments about a culture and its practices, and what does that say about your own culture? Can you find some common ground? Can you find some spirituality? Can you find some meaning?"

"I think what we're seeing in the administration is, hopefully, the death rattle of an old order that is benighted and befuddled, and the sooner we quit talking to them, the better."

"Once again, presumably straight people are telling us what we can and cannot be doing."

"We're obviously not getting anywhere with the Dome. What I think we should be doing instead is identifying faculty who are sympathetic."

Whenever they looked up from their rectangle of overstuffed lounge couches, out through the tall and serene Gothic windows on the third floor of the infirmary building, the ten people gathered here on a bright Sunday afternoon could see looming in the near distance the implicit subject of their discussion—the rear of the Main Building. Lodged therein was the administration with whom they had found so little common ground that they were forced to use their usual code language when placing an ad in *The Observer* to announce this meeting: "Call or write for location," the ad advised, and was signed, "That Gay and Lesbian Group—We're not allowed to publish our real name, but you know who we are." The name they used among themselves was Gays and Lesbians at Notre Dame and St. Mary's College (GLND/SMC, pronounced "gland smack"), a name the administration asked them not to use publicly, because it implied that the group had something they most assuredly did not have: official recognition. The empty corridor outside their meeting room was heavy with the kind of stark, white-enamel silence that only a student infirmary can produce—the same sound they believed the Main Building wanted to hear from them.

"They view this group as a political group with a political agenda."

"I'm against asking for recognition. I think the only people who need to recognize us are ourselves."

The voices at today's meeting, graduate students' mostly, were different from the voices at meetings in previous years, but they were still discussing the same central issue: how to get the university to take them seriously. Several times they had sought official recognition for the group, and several times they were firmly denied, despite support from the faculty senate and student opinion polls. They had decided not to bang their heads against the same wall this year. What they were considering now was a trial balloon being floated their way by the administration—a support group for gay undergraduates, run by the Campus Ministry office.

"It won't be what we really want," said Sharon Miller, the cochairman and a doctoral candidate in the sociology of religion. "But it is something."

What they really wanted—the open acceptance of their culture into the larger culture of Notre Dame—wasn't something they were likely to get any time soon. "The big question is official recognition and support," Father Malloy said, "and that's what I personally don't think is desirable, nor would the trustees at this point in our history be willing to approve if they had to. I think it puts us in a situation of conflict with the value system that we think we're representative of in a general way. There are plenty of other ways, academically and intellectually, that those matters can be discussed."

On a campus as squeamish as Notre Dame is about sexuality of any kind, the gay student group faced a set of barriers that didn't exist at most other schools. Parietals, single-sex dorms, ubiquitous rectors, the sexuality policy in *Du Lac,* the weight of a Catholic tradition that considered any sexual behavior outside of marriage a sin—all conspired to make sex here what it had been on other campuses decades ago: a furtive dance in the dim, rushed spaces between passion and apprehension. "Sex Kills," a popular T-shirt read, "So Come to Notre Dame and Live Forever." The nearest place to buy condoms was an all-night, off-campus drugstore. The nearest thing to pornography available on campus was the annual *Sports Illustrated* swimsuit issue; the wall hangings in even the raunchiest men's-dorm rooms were bikini-clad beer-babe posters, not *Playboy* centerfolds. The model for the life of the student community was in large measure derived from the Holy Cross community itself—individuals living closely together, bound by intellectual, emotional, and spiritual, but not sexual, intimacy.

"We call people to a way of life that is almost becoming countercultural, to an ideal that is very much rooted in our faith tradition," Patty O'Hara, the vice-president of student affairs, explained later. "We call all our students, heterosexual and homosexual, to the same standard. What we ask is hard, and it's hard for everybody."

It is a standard, of course, that the students frequently fall short of. Casual sex seems less prevalent than at other schools, but the campus is not entirely celibate. Parietals are sometimes broken, in the men's dorm far more often than in the women's. "The big problem is always that the girl has to go to the bathroom," one student lamented. A discreet final trip at a time

not too near the 2:00 a.m. deadline—1:15, say—was the best strategy; but
there were other options, too: "I make 'em go in a cup." Those less willing
to tempt fate sometimes sought shelter in the strip of motels along Highway 31. Inevitably, some women got pregnant. Some chose abortion, some
chose adoption—ads from childless couples were a regular feature in *The
Observer*'s classifieds—and some chose to keep their babies themselves. Two
undergraduate women were living in the graduate dorms with their young
children this year, quietly refuting the persistent misconception that pregnancy was tantamount to expulsion.

"We call people to chastity, but we're all human, and when someone fails
to meet expectations, we deal with them pastorally and compassionately,"
Patty O'Hara said.

The gay social scene was under even deeper cover, hidden not just from
the administration, but also from the other students. If they were old
enough, students could venture downtown to a gay bar. If they were not,
they had to rely instead on the uncertain possibility of somehow bumping
into another closeted colleague, or else chance an encounter in the basement
bathroom of the library, which had a reputation as a gay pickup spot. The
number of openly gay undergraduates was in the low single digits. National
Coming Out Day usually passed each fall without anybody's coming out.

The silence about homosexuality was usually so complete that, on the few
occasions when it was breached, the sound was, briefly at least, deafening.
"The Holy Cross Community is saddened by the events surrounding the
case of Father James Burtchaell, C.S.C.," the provincial superior of the order
had written in a public statement in the middle of the previous academic
year. "We acknowledge the serious nature of this matter and apologize to
those who may have been hurt." In the face of charges that he made improper sexual advances toward some male students he was counseling,
Burtchaell had been forced to resign from the faculty and was also, according to the provincial's statement, "asked to undergo psychological evaluation and treatment." The charges had apparently been circulating privately
for a long time, but had only become public after a story in the *National
Catholic Reporter*. Burtchaell's fall echoed especially loudly because it came
from such a high perch: He had emerged as a prominent campus figure in
his twenty-five years here—a widely respected theology professor, the origi-
nator of the late-night dorm Masses, the first provost in the university's history. At one time, he had been considered a prime candidate to succeed
Hesburgh. In his own statement, he acknowledged only that he "had be-

haved towards some former university students in ways that were wrong, and which I very much regretted." No criminal or civil charges were ever filed in court.

To the Notre Dame gay community, the Burtchaell case was an example of the cost of denial. To the administration, it was a regrettable incident that had now been resolved and was best not spoken of again. To the Congregation of Holy Cross, it was "an anomalous and painful event about which further public discussion is not possible without compromising confidentiality. We prayerfully seek closure and the healing we hope it will bring to all affected." Burtchaell remained in Princeton, where he had been on sabbatical when the charges broke—working under a Lilly Endowment grant on a book about the secularization of formerly religious colleges and universities. GLND/SMC remained unrecognized, meeting quietly to pursue alternative strategies.

"Our goal is to get it on campus, and there are compromises we made to get it on campus," Sharon Miller told the meeting now, referring to talks with Campus Ministry about a Mass for group members at the end of the semester. "At least the words 'gay and lesbian' will be said on this campus. I think you take bits and pieces. We take what we can get."

Later that day, the undergraduate support group—new this year, an off-shoot of the original group—met in the music building, in a room dominated by a large pipe organ. The agenda, as usual, was concerned less with strategy than with empathy. Night filled the windows, and the stray notes of a piano wandered through the hallway beyond the closed door.

"I really want to tell my mom—I was thinking of writing a letter. When it happens it'll happen."

"I wrote a ten-page letter to my parents."

"I was just so afraid of being found out. I was helped by the fact that one of my friends came out to me."

"I made seven calls asking about the meetings before I finally showed up for one."

"If you're not in the closet in one respect, you're in the closet in other respects."

The chief value of the undergraduate group was that, every other Sunday, it offered a rare patch of neutral territory on campus, where students who were gay could say they were gay, without fear of retribution. The membership hovered near twenty, seven of whom were here tonight. They mostly came singly to the meetings, not as couples. Many of them—less worldly, but also less bitter than their grad-student counterparts—were just getting used to the idea of being gay, and they were grateful for a forum to discuss what that meant.

"It's not a very friendly university if you're different, if you don't fit the Notre Dame mold, and we all know what that's like."

"I went to this old priest in the confessional, and he told me I needed psychiatric help."

"I thought for a while about becoming a priest. It was the only way to make sense of my life. I knew I didn't want to marry a woman."

"I found myself not wanting to go to the Linebacker and hear my friends talking about 'hooking up' with women. I would just cringe. It was intolerable."

"I went to SYRs until my senior year. You just put it away."

"Are you going to Washington?" somebody asked, turning the discussion toward a piece of practical politics, and away from the Notre Dame campus. A big gay-rights march would converge on Washington at the end of April, and a local contingent was planning to attend—traveling 600 miles to say in public there what they could only say in private here. "Lesbian and Gay Fighting Irish of Notre Dame/St. Mary's," announced the wide parade banner they planned to march behind.

"Are you going, too?"

15

All along the tall, shadowy corridor outside the president's office in the Main Building, under the stern gaze of the portraits of the previous occupants, the protesters sat quietly on the floor, cross-legged and patient, waiting to see the current occupant. Father Malloy was next door in his Sorin Hall room, reading the next novel for his Freshman Seminar: Graham Greene's *The Comedians.* His office was locked, occupied only by his secretary. It was lunchtime on a Friday afternoon, the hour when a college starts sliding toward the weekend, but the protesters weren't planning on leaving anytime soon. They had started their morning early, signing hymns and praying outside the nearby abortion clinic before marching single-file across South Bend Avenue and onto the Notre Dame campus, more than one hundred strong, aiming toward the Dome like Crusaders toward Jerusalem. They climbed to the third floor, faced Malloy's closed door, and knelt to pray the rosary. They sang more hymns, said more prayers, and settled in to wait.

"We're going to stay here until he agrees to talk to us," Claire Johnson said as she spread peanut butter on a saltine she had secured from the food-supply box. She leaned against the balustrade that encircled the central open shaft of the building's rotunda—the blue-sky mural of the inner dome soaring above her, its winged creatures riding on clouds; the hard-tile rotunda floor yawning below her. It was an angle from which the world appeared poised precipitously between heaven and earth. "We're not blocking anyone, and if anyone's disturbed by our praying, we're sorry."

Claire was one of just a few Notre Dame students among the protesters, most of whom were from other schools, some of whom weren't students at all. What had drawn them to South Bend was a two-week rally and conference organized by CALL, Collegians Activated to Liberate Life. It was originally slated to convene on the Notre Dame campus, but the administration had denied CALL's request, citing concerns about the size, length, and timing of the event, and the dominant role of people from outside the Notre Dame community. CALL members believed that official opposition had only crystallized after an ad announcing the rally appeared in *The Wanderer*, a conservative Catholic newspaper. "Help Restore Notre Dame to Its Catholic Heritage," the ad said. "A Bold New Project Combines Prayer and Action for Revival of Our Lady's University."

"I'm disappointed and humiliated that Notre Dame is unwilling to risk its precious reputation to stand up for God and for people who are dying," said Claire, whose role as the main local organizer for the event had caused some dissent within the campus Right to Life group. "All we want from Father Malloy is a commitment to pray publicly for the victims of abortion."

Without a forum on campus, the CALL event had fanned out to half a dozen sympathetic local churches—and to Bethel College, a small Christian college nearby—for its daily program of seminars, speeches, and rallies. The local prochoice forces had mobilized as well, aided by a small contingent of Domers. Although the week opened with a headline splash—a speech by prolife Congressman Henry Hyde, a prochoice demonstrator arrested for spitting on a priest—attendance was well below the five hundred students that organizers had originally projected. At the clinic this morning, the prolife side was outnumbered by both the prochoice crowd and the squadron of local police. Notre Dame had kept mostly to the sidelines so far, but CALL had kept trying to draw it onto the field. As the sit-in wore on through the afternoon, the taunts from the speakers grew harsher.

"Bill Clinton is allowed on this campus. Daniel Moynihan is allowed on this campus. But Catholic students for life are not allowed on this campus."

"It's a shame this university is more committed to its football program than it is to the dignity of human life."

"Yes, they are killing children here in this community, but the greater evil is that there are Christians three blocks away who do nothing about it."

"You're not just a university, you're a Catholic university. You are Catholic first, and a university second. You are challenged by the church to uphold Catholic teachings."

The plan for today's protest had been hatched the previous night, after Claire and two other students had made an 11:00 p.m. visit to Malloy's room in Sorin. Finding his "welcome" sign out, they knocked, were invited in, and presented their request. "We asked him to come and pray with us," Claire said. "He said that he couldn't be affiliated with CALL. We asked him to come and pray with Notre Dame students there, and he was noncommittal." It was the first time Claire had ever spoken to Malloy. "He was very cordial and very formal. He didn't invite us to sit down, though."

By inviting themselves to sit down outside his office today, they created a subtle, unusual dilemma for Notre Dame—an institution that sees itself as in disagreement with them only on tactics, not on beliefs. What had made the administration so wary of CALL from the beginning, and what made the decisions about how to handle the sit-in so difficult now, was the general belief that the prolife students, for all their good intentions, were being used as pawns by those who would reclaim Notre Dame as an outpost of the Vatican. CALL didn't want to hear any of the reasonable arguments today—that Notre Dame was demonstrably prolife in its policies and philosophy, but that it was also a university committed to the open exchange of ideas; that Pat Buchanan, Bob Casey, and plenty of other prolife speakers had been welcome on campus, too; that the university had offered to sponsor its own prolife student conference; that Malloy himself, like virtually every other member of the Holy Cross community, would unhesitatingly describe his own views as prolife. They wanted instead a confrontation that would highlight what they saw as Notre Dame's moral shortcomings.

The protesters stood to sing again, facing a large crucifix that one of them held solemnly in front of Malloy's door. They had the corridor to themselves, watched over only by a couple of hovering security officers. Various officials picked their way through the tumble of backpacks, jackets, and stretched-out legs as the hours passed, occasionally stopping to talk. But with no sign of Malloy, and with no indication of what the administration might be planning, the protesters were left to speculate among themselves. Arrests for trespassing seemed unlikely: The image was so unsettling—prolife students being hauled out in handcuffs, the Virgin Mary watching sorrowfully from atop the Dome—that they expected the university to avoid it at all costs. Would they be allowed to stay indefinitely? The building was scheduled to close at 7:00 p.m.—what would happen then? Would Malloy agree to a meeting? It seemed a simple enough request, but he was known for the distaste he felt at being backed into corners.

"Do we save more lives and impact South Bend and the nation more by staying here and praying, or do we impact more by going out to the killing center?"

"Our commitment is to stay here as long as we can to try to meet with Father Malloy. If that's two or three days, then it's two or three days."

At 3:30, Security stopped allowing nonstudents into the building, lending a vague sense of siege to the scene. Soon thereafter, a roar arose from outside, coming from the direction of the front steps and briefly raising in some protesters a vision of sympathetic reinforcements converging on the Dome like the cavalry. It turned out instead to be the men of Alumni Hall, posing on the steps for a dorm photo, smoking cigars and wearing knotted ties over their shirtless torsos. "Alumni Hall will wake her dead," the Alumni men chanted like monks, "we will sing their requiem." They had been wandering through campus that way, handing out flowers to women (roses to those they deemed the most attractive, carnations to the rest), in preparation for their annual Alumni Wake dance—a comic, surreal ritual that would culminate at midnight tomorrow, when one Elvis impersonator and several RAs dressed as priests, swinging incense-burning censers, would carry their rector in a coffin through the dorm's hallways.

Although today's sit-in had an odd, redundant, almost Scholastic quality about it—a hall-of-mirrors battle between adversaries who appeared from a distance more like allies—it followed in a long local tradition of protests that staked out a high moral ground. The 1960s had arrived later but reached deeper at Notre Dame than at other campuses. The debates here then had a thoughtful, spiritual dimension—long on philosophy and God, short on fire and blood—that was shaped both by the religious character of the institution, and the firm hand of the president. "[A]nyone or any group that substitutes force for rational persuasion, be it violent or nonviolent, will be given 15 minutes of meditation to cease and desist," Hesburgh wrote in a 1969 open letter that found a receptive audience far beyond the Notre Dame community it was originally addressed to. Hesburgh's fifteen-minute rule was invoked only once, when ten students were suspended after a sit-in at the Placement Bureau in the Main Building: Their protest was aimed at the recruiters from the CIA and Dow Chemical, the makers of napalm. Many of the protests and rallies of the era were solemnized by Masses—perhaps most memorably on Vietnam Moratorium Day in October 1969, when twenty-five hundred people filled the library mall, and four students and two professors burned their draft cards at the offertory.

At 5:30 p.m. on the day of this latest demonstration, seven hours after climbing up the Main Building steps, the protesters started climbing down. Malloy had agreed to meet with their representatives if the rest of them cleared the building. Claire Johnson was the only Notre Dame undergraduate among the four CALL members who filed into Father Dick Warner's office with four university officials—Malloy; Warner, the director of Campus Ministry and special counselor to Malloy; Denny Moore, director of public relations; and Matt Cullinan, Malloy's assistant. Malloy started the meeting with a prayer. Claire accepted the Diet Coke she was offered. "I was scared I'd spill it in the office," she said.

For Claire and her CALL colleagues, the mere fact of the meeting was a victory in itself: Whatever the outcome, they had gained an official forum to air their grievances. For Malloy, though, the meeting was a more perilous expedition, forcing him to seek a patch of ground that could be shared by the two main, and sometimes opposing, constituencies he had to answer to as Notre Dame's president—those who saw Notre Dame primarily as a flagship institution in the Catholic hierarchy (a group that included many large benefactors) and those who saw it primarily as a leading university in the secular American academy (a group that included his fellow presidents, few, if any, of whom would ever face a protest like CALL's). The meeting broke up after less than half an hour, each side having said what the situation required it to say, but neither having changed the other's mind.

"We asked him again to pray with us," Claire said.

"I gave them no commitment," Malloy said. "Their basic call is for me and for the university to be identified with a particular strategy with regard to abortion."

"We told him that we understood that he was praying privately, and that we appreciated his prayers, but that he was a leader, and his leadership was crucial," Claire said. "A lot of students would rethink their position on abortion if they knew Father Malloy was prolife."

"We will continue to do what we do now," Malloy said. "We pray. We teach. We do research. We have organizations that try to reach out into the community. We have people who are involved in antiabortion efforts. It's important that we have a noncoercive environment where people can seek for truth and speak freely. That's the role of a university. We don't force people to believe something or to take particular tactics just because they're here."

Before he returned to his room in Sorin Hall for the night, Malloy kept a date with the Sorin Society, the group of $1,000-a-year donors whose members were meeting on campus this weekend. Before she returned to her room in Farley Hall—the dorm that was the earliest and most active hive of antiwar activity on campus back in the 1960s—Claire went to a celebratory CALL rally in the Bethel College gym. Among the literature on sale at a table in the rear was a book whose title asked, accusingly, *Is Notre Dame Still Catholic?*

"I asked him three times if he would come for an hour and pray with us, and three times he gave a noncommittal answer," a CALL leader said in his speech, referring to Malloy and repeating the phrase "three times" at least two more times in case anyone missed the allusion to Peter's denial of Jesus. "I think it was a victorious day for us. We stood together, and we stood strong."

The sit-in had passed largely unnoticed by most of the students. It was the first week back from spring break—notable mostly for the giant blizzard that had stranded many of them back on the East Coast, and for the St. Patrick's Day celebrations that had decimated the classrooms and filled the bars all day long on Wednesday. The NCAA basketball tournament, proceeding on TVs all over campus, was attracting the most interest tonight. A light snow was falling, covering everything equally with a thin sheet of white.

"I currently believe that serious and potentially divisive problems exist with extremist interpretations of our Catholic character in some of the rhetoric that is originating from several of our colleagues," said Frank Castellino, dean of the College of Science, reading from his prepared remarks to a meeting of the Conversation on the Catholic Character. "These concerns legitimately arise in highly emotional areas surrounding the topic of tonight's discussion, such as implications of Catholic faculty quotas, of litmus tests of Catholicity during the interview process, and of indications that this is the only way of ensuring our Catholicity."

The Conversation had outgrown the smaller rooms that had accommodated its earlier meetings, and moved now, for its final session this semester, into the auditorium of the Center for Continuing Education, a hall large enough to require a microphone. As interest in its agenda had risen, so had attendance, voices, and tempers. It was no longer just a discussion among like-minded allies, but a debate that included wary adversaries. At the previous meeting, an angry contingent of scientists, taking the role of aggrieved Galileos, had challenged a conservative philosopher, casting him as the authoritarian pope.

The Catholic-character issue had inevitably triggered a larger, often contentious series of soul-searching questions about the shape of Notre Dame's future: Where was it going as a university? How would it get there? Who would be welcome on the journey? The debate moved through the faculty and administration with the insular urgency of a Political Correctness crisis at a secular school. In the battle lines that were drawn here, the Catholicity advocates were roughly analogous to the champions of the Western-Civ canon, defending a core of values and traditions; the wary secularists were the multiculturalists, eager to embrace other voices, other ideas.

Concern was mounting now that the theories about Catholicity might be evolving a bit too quickly into practice. Some professors were starting to worry about how the issue would affect them—their chances for tenure and promotion; what kind of research they did; how they practiced their faith, or didn't. The memo that spurred George Craig to such heights of rhetorical indignation in his entomology lab (Father Bill Miscamble's proposals for "Constructing a Great Catholic University") had raised hackles in other departments as well. Nervous jokes abounded about baptismal certificates and rosary-bead checks, and Craig's remark about "ethnic cleansing" was echoed in many quarters. Tonight Craig sat quietly near the front of the hall, leaving his letter, and his dean, to argue his position.

"We must not be viewed as are some of the other fundamentalist religious colleges and universities which we know so well, and which have limited impact outside of their own direct spheres of influence," Castellino concluded. "If we deny that it is important for Harvard, Princeton, Duke, and Northwestern to take us seriously, then I suggest that we are spending too much time together, reinforcing bad judgments. If we are not taken seriously, we will have no impact and our Catholic message will be lost."

For all the acrimony and suspicion the Catholicity debate had raised, nobody could really agree on precisely what they were all debating—which left them free to imagine the best, or the worst, and to argue accordingly. They were attacking phantoms more than one another. One side sketched a vague, unformed vision of a golden future—borrowing elements from before-the-Fall, presecular Yale, the thirteenth-century University of Paris, and today's Notre Dame to create some new species of institution they could describe in terms hardly more specific than I'll-know-it-when-I-see-it. The other side shrank from a hyperbolic memory of a darker past—suffocating authority, doctrinal orthodoxy, forbidding priests in black birettas, evolution as a matter for theology rather than biology. To one side, the debate was a bold journey into uncharted territory, Notre Dame's own version of Vatican II; to the other, it was the intellectual equivalent of the restoration of Sacred Heart, an attempt to return the rest of the university to the perfect image of its nineteenth-century self.

"What precisely is it that is to take place at Notre Dame in the intellectual or moral order that does not or could not transpire at some other university?" asked John Van Engen, a history professor and the director of Notre Dame's renowned Medieval Institute, in his remarks. "What intellectual ends are achieved, or could be achieved, only at a Catholic university? Until these are publicly laid out, does it make sense to argue who may or may not contribute to their achievement?"

The only tangible issue in the debate so far, and therefore the one that had drawn the most fire, was the question of faculty hiring. In the last twenty years, the number of Catholics on the faculty had dipped below the 60-percent threshold Hesburgh had once warned against—a decline that didn't seem to be slowing, and that was causing much concern under the Dome. The concern it caused among the faculty themselves was that theological correctness would substitute for academic ability when job offers and promotions were tendered. The Miscamble memo on the Catholicity issue had hit at a moment when the faculty felt most vulnerable: Not only was it the tense annual season of hiring and tenure decisions, but the final Colloquy report was due soon, a document that, with its likely call both for more professorships and more emphasis on Notre Dame's Catholic character, could significantly alter the shape and direction of the university's intellectual life.

"How do we mandate hiring Catholics if we do not agree among ourselves in public or in private about the meaning of the term?" Van Engen continued. "This is a university, not a parish, and there must be a level of scholarly accountability open and intelligible to all. How do we position ourselves to judge who fits the hiring profile of a Catholic university when we have no common intellectual understanding about what a Catholic university is for?"

When the floor was opened to questions and comments, far more hands shot up than could possibly be called upon, a sign that feelings ran deep enough to keep the debate alive long after the meeting was over.

"I read in one of the Colloquy reports a statement about 'the animation of Catholic intellectual life.' With all respect, I have no idea what that means."

"I don't think any of us know the answer to that. But I don't think it should be the people in the Golden Dome debating it—it should be the faculty."

"I don't think everybody in the Main Building understands what the Catholic intellectual tradition is."

"Why should I, in engineering, teach ethics and values? What, may I ask, are the philosophy and theology departments doing?"

"Harvard and Princeton and Duke—they lost it by choice, not by neglect. We're not making that choice."

"They didn't choose to do it—it happened bit by bit."

"This place does have a special attractiveness to Catholics, and I think this place will always have a special attractiveness to Catholics. I had offers from other universities, but if I didn't come here my father would've died."

"In another ten years, are there going to be enough Catholics here to raise these questions?"

"I'd rather have non-Catholics concerned with religious values than Catholics who are not."

"I'm *Rabbi* Michael Signer, and I *also* have a faith that gives me strength," said the newly installed Abrams Professor of Jewish Thought and Culture, providing the evening with its most electric moment. His presence here was evidence of how much Notre Dame had changed from the days when it was a bastion of the old Catholic ghetto; but his bristling tone questioned how deep and lasting that change was. "'There are two strains in the Catholic character—the one of openness and nurturing, and the one of exclusivity and intolerance. I'd be more comfortable if this were fifty or a hundred years after Vatican II—if sufficient time had passed so that the Catholic character we're discussing was understood to be the embracing and open strain. Right now I don't have a lot of trust in that."

Father Bill Miscamble, the implicit center of tonight's debate, listened quietly from his seat on the right side of the auditorium, as he had all evening, looking more like a casual spectator than one of the chief combatants. He didn't have to speak here to let his opinions be known; his memo had done that already, in great detail and at loud volume. When he finally did step to the podium, a small hush of anticipation opened around him: Academics usually do their fighting on paper, not in person, and they were wondering how he would respond.

"I'm glad you're here," Miscamble said, addressing Rabbi Signer, "and I want to apologize if something I've said has offended you."

His tone was soothing, meant to assure his faculty colleagues that he was not a fire-breathing Inquisitionist bent on purging their ranks. He did not apologize, however, for his ideas about what kind of university Notre Dame ought to be. "I reject the notion that my position is an extreme position. The extremists are those who say that Notre Dame is already too far down the path to secularization to be redeemed."

Miscamble spoke with a disarming Down Under accent that his years at Notre Dame had not bleached out of him: A fourth-generation native of Australia, he first came to Notre Dame in 1976 as a graduate student in history, and then came back in 1982 as a seminarian. He was a popular teacher (his introductory class, "The Development of Modern America," had achieved the same must-take status as Tom Morris' section of Philosophy 101) and a respected scholar (his book on George F. Kennan had just been published by Princeton University Press). He was genial and good-humored, with a taste for plain speaking that was not always well suited to an issue as subtle and contentious as Catholicity. He felt a deep, familial attachment to Notre Dame that lent his opinions about its future an extra dimension of passion: When he went home from tonight's meeting, it would be to a couple of small rooms in Zahm Hall, not a five-bedroom subdivision manse in one of the faculty suburbs, and when he died he would be buried under a small white cross in the community cemetery on the other side of the lakes.

Facing the dissent his memo had crystallized, Miscamble was invigorated, not intimidated. He made it plain that, if confronted by opposition, he would not shrink from his cause. He denied that he was "a Trojan horse for some authoritarian process," he decried "the absolutely scurrilous remarks about ethnic cleansing and so forth," and he applauded the candid turn the debate was taking. "I think it's better that people reveal what they think, rather than just edging on year after year." The issue had reached its rhetorical peak tonight, leaving each side clear on where the other side stood. The terms of engagement were now set for a battle that would likely drag on for many meetings more.

"I feel charged with a special responsibility as a member of the order to ensure that this place will be Catholic in a meaningful way in ten years' time," Miscamble said, speaking with a sense of belonging, ownership even, that few of his lay colleagues could match. "I intend to dedicate my life to this, what I think is a worthy cause."

After the meeting broke up, Miscamble sought out Signer and spoke with him privately—as he would, over the next few weeks, seek out many of his critics, George Craig included, stopping by their offices or joining them for lunch in the faculty club or coffee in the Huddle, explaining to them, outside the glare of a public forum, just what his thinking was on an issue that wasn't going away. This role was not unfamiliar to him: His scholarly interest, after all, was diplomatic history.

"I want to be sure that Notre Dame is something worth fighting over," Miscamble said later. "Ten or fifteen years from now, both the left and the right might be wondering what the hell went wrong, that Notre Dame isn't a place worth arguing over anymore."

"They speak the language of stalemate and gridlock," Professor Peri Arnold told his students, referring to Congress and the president in Washington, not the faculty and the administration at Notre Dame. "Their relationship is supposed to be productive, and it isn't. They don't seem to be able to solve any problems."

The steep lecture hall in DeBartolo where Arnold's class met reached down below ground level, and the small windows high on its walls peeked up onto a patch of earth that was, if you squinted and hoped hard enough, almost green. It was the same view a hibernating animal might see upon burrowing up from its winter den. The snow had receded, leaving a few diligent patches of slush and a quad-wide marshland of puddles big enough for ducks to colonize. Midterms had passed ("Why did Americans of the founding era fear executive strength?" was one of the essays on Arnold's test, a question that might also have been asked of the Notre Dame faculty in the current era), and the endgame had begun. Tom Morris's upper-level philosophy class had finished thinking about eternity—the South Bend winter had helped illustrate the concept for them—and moved on to one of his favorite figures, Blaise Pascal, the subject of his last book. The seniors in Carolyn Callahan's accounting class had learned how to handle consolidated statements, and were now working on intercompany profit transactions. In Teresa Ghilarducci's macroeconomics class, Kennedy had exited and Reagan had arrived. The government majors in Arnold's class were dissecting the complex, competitive relationship between the president and Congress.

"Eisenhower was able to carry on legislation with a bottle of good bourbon upstairs in the White House with Sam Rayburn and LBJ," Arnold said, drawing a contrast with the Washington of today, where the cast of power reached well beyond the familiar triumvirate of president, speaker of the House, and Senate majority leader. He traced the territorial grabs as each branch had tried to keep ahead of the other over the last half-century—the president expanding the White House bureaucracy, Congress expanding its committee structure, power dispersing through the scattered fiefdoms of a vast new permanent government. "Never shout 'Mr. Chairman' in the House cafeteria, because they'll all turn around and drop their trays. They're all chairman of *something*, as if it's a sin to be a member of the majority and not be chairman of something."

Arnold's knowledge of the ways of Congress was personal now, not just scholarly: Over spring break, while many of his students fled south to Florida, he had traveled east to Washington at the invitation of one of those many committee chairmen, John Glenn, chairman of the Senate Committee on Governmental Affairs. Some of Glenn's staffers had read his book, *Making the Managerial Presidency*, and asked him to testify at a hearing on "Improving Government Organization and Performance." The committee had before it four separate bills that would establish reform commissions, and wanted to sort through its options. Arnold's job was to draw some lessons from the many previous attempts at governmental reform.

"I never really thought of this in practical ways, although it is practical material," Arnold said. "It's not all that different from the way a physicist thinks about particles. It's a logic game—I want to crack some new ideas and get some new insights. But then I get asked, 'What would you do to make government work better?' I really put my mind to it intensely." If you work on esoteric enough stuff, it eventually becomes relevant to something. Every dog has its day.

He outlined for the committee the eleven bodies convened in this century for the purpose of reorganizing the national government—from Theodore Roosevelt's Keep Commission to Jimmy Carter's Reorganization Project. "History's main lesson is that past reorganization has been about adapting the executive branch to a growing government, and not at all about economy and constraining government," he testified. "There is no reason to think that reshaping organizations or streamlining bureaucracies will create more effective programs. . . . To make government work better and less expensively, the questions we must ask are about the justification, benefits, costs, and management of programs." He then offered some ideas about how to shape a new reform commission that might avoid the shortcomings of its ancestors: Be willing to make tough judgments about the value of specific programs; don't rely too heavily on business executives as commissioners, because history shows them to be "timid reformers"; concentrate not on the organizational shape of government agencies, but on how well they perform their functions; present the recommendations in a single, coherent package, not in piecemeal form, and then put it at the top of the congressional agenda.

"Much depends on what you do here," Arnold said as he concluded his testimony. "If we cannot make government work now, the next time we revisit the possibility of real reform it may be under much worse circumstances."

In class now, he discussed with his students the movement in Washington of which his own recent testimony was a modest example—the attempts, over the last dozen years or so, at reversing the decades of governmental expansion. "Congress is trying to grope for a structure that helps it constrain itself," he said. "Think of Gramm-Rudman," he continued, referring to the deficit-reduction law that limits congressional appropriations. "There's nothing like Gramm-Rudman in the history of Congress. Think of it as kind of a scream of the addicted, who says, 'Stop me, stop me—I can't help myself from drinking.' "

Arnold prodded them to cite more examples, but their attention was drifting up toward the small window of green. Spring was a tough rival for any course, especially one that had proved more demanding than some of its students expected. "A lot of us here have a sense that we're making too few demands of the students, that they're getting away with too much," Arnold said. "After the last time I taught it, a year and a half ago, I realized I was asking them to think about the presidency in a way that was below the way *I* was thinking about the presidency." A dozen students had formally dropped the class after less than two weeks of thinking about the presidency at his level; quite a few more were informally drifting away now, as the semester ticked down. So few showed up on St. Patrick's Day that the class looked more like a seminar than a lecture.

"Come on, you oughta know this," Arnold urged.

They coughed up a few answers before the clock released them into the afternoon sunshine. "It's a problem every spring," Arnold said. "The seniors have no stake in it any longer. They only need to pass, they don't need an A."

———

A week after their headline-grabbing sit-in under the Dome, two weeks after their arrival at Notre Dame, the members of CALL and their allies started the final day of their conference at the same place where they had started several other days recently—outside the abortion clinic near campus. About twenty-five of them were met there by ninety or so prochoice demonstrators, many of whom were from Notre Dame and St. Mary's. Blocked from the clinic property by a snow fence and a restraining order, the prolife demonstrators stayed on the street, an otherwise quiet cul-de-sac, where they shouted toward the few entering cars. The prochoice demonstrators stayed mostly on the clinic side of the fence, occasionally escorting a patient inside. The police had parked a rental truck nearby, in case mass arrests became necessary.

"Cheer, cheer for *Roe* versus *Wade*," some on the prochoice side sang, rendering the fight song unsuitable for the stadium.

Her jaw set tight, Claire Johnson walked outside the fence in a silent circle, directly behind a bearded young man who carried a crucifix as if he were an acolyte. She was already looking past Notre Dame toward the larger battle. The last two weeks had helped confirm for her the decision she had been leaning toward all year: She would take a two-semester leave of absence—unusual at a school that likes to move its students up and out in four straight years—and move to Wisconsin to work full-time for CALL, most likely as its communications director. She would live in a group house with other CALL members, drawing no salary, and would have to raise her $300 monthly expenses from family, friends, churches, and other supporters of the cause.

"This is a real leap of faith on my part," she said. "I don't know where the money's coming from. I hate to ask for money. But I can't stay in school when people are dying the way babies are dying now. It seems so selfish. In the time since I've been actively opposing abortion, probably ten million babies have died. I don't think many people have any concept of what it's like to *love* those babies, and I do *love* them."

As she walked, she carried on her back a pack heavy with books from the classes that the rush of CALL activities had caused her to neglect lately. At seven-fifteen the morning after the sit-in, she was in Merrillville, over near Gary, locking arms with fifty other CALL members to block the entrances to a Planned Parenthood clinic; three Notre Dame students and one from St. Mary's were arrested, but Claire was not among them. Catching up academically now would require some late nights in the botany lab, one of her favorite study spots, and some aggravation to her ulcers. Apart from an occasional chocolate bar, there was little sweetness in her life right now. "I have no social life," she said, and she had given up desserts in the dining hall for Lent. One thing she did have, though, was a fresh topic for a paper she had to write for "Issues of Justice," her philosophy class. "We have to imagine ourselves in the future, and think of what we would do to make the world more just." She planned to write about CALL.

"It's my body, and I'll breed if I want to," some of the prochoice voices sang now, borrowing a tune from Lesley Gore's "It's My Party."

On the other side of the fence from Claire, Beth Ann Fennelly stood near the clinic doors with two women from her "Feminist Theology" class and six other Notre Dame students. She had often expressed her politics in her poems, but she was new at expressing them through the louder medium of public protest. "It's the first time I've ever actually done anything like this," she said. A small ad in *The Observer* had caught her attention ("Stand Up for Choice!" it said. "Prove What We from ND/SMC Really Stand For"), and a short lesson in nonviolent-protest strategies from the local chapter of the National Organization for Women, which was leading the opposition to CALL, had put her on the front line.

"It's like a sin if you're prochoice here," Beth Ann said. "At the intercessions at Mass, there's always somebody who says, 'For the unborn.' I just grit my teeth. I can't say 'Lord be with you.'"

Like Claire, Beth Ann would be leaving Notre Dame soon—moving to Czechoslovakia after graduation to teach English for a year. After that, she hoped, would come graduate school, where there would be more poems to write. So far this semester, her poetry had already won her a $100 campus prize ("I really need the money," she said) and earned her a chance to stand in for Edward Albee: When the playwright's appearance at the Sophomore Literary Festival back in February was delayed by snow, she was among the students who read their work in his stead—a larger and wider crowd than she had faced at the Day of Women reading.

"I remember being a freshman and looking up to the seniors as if they were these mythical beings. It seems weird to be a senior myself now, and to think that the freshmen could be looking at me that way," she said. "When I walk around campus now, I feel as if I'm three stories up, looking down on everything—as if I've already started fading away."

By 10:00 a.m., the police trucks were still empty, the demonstrators were drifting away, and the clinic was left alone to listen to a sound it had heard little of lately: silence. Claire Johnson and Beth Ann Fennelly both headed back to campus. Before the end of the semester, though, Claire would return many times more, bringing her prayers when there were few others around to share them, or even to notice.

16

As the thin afternoon light was fading behind the Dome, as the students were winding toward the dining halls for the evening meal, a single, deep bell tolled slowly from the tower of Sacred Heart—a chill, discordant note of winter sadness on a campus that was edging into spring. The church was filled with women from Pasquerilla West, many of them dressed more formally than they normally would be on a weekday. In this green season of life, it was a death that drew them together here today—a special memorial Mass for a dormmate who hadn't returned from spring break. Some of them had known that Tara Deutsch's heart was enlarged, but nobody had expected her to die. Their rector, Laurie Brink, sat in the front pew in a navy blazer and a tan skirt, faced with the challenge of climbing into the pulpit later and trying to put words to the grief they all felt. They stood together as Father Malloy followed the entrance procession up the center aisle to the altar.

"We have lost one of our own," Malloy said in the greeting. "We entrust Tara to you, Lord. May she live radiant and young forever in your kingdom."

Brink was among the first people Tara's father called after his daughter died: He understood how important the dorm was in her life, and he wanted to make sure her friends there knew about her death. "What do you say to a man who has just lost his daughter?" Brink remembered wondering. "I just hoped God would give me something to say, because there are no words for that."

She flew to Oregon, at Notre Dame's expense, to join the family for the funeral. Back on campus, it was her unenviable job to tell those who hadn't

253

already heard about Tara, and comfort those who had. In the dorm the news triggered an unfamiliar, almost surreal emotion, equal parts disbelief and horror, the only response possible when a young life ends so suddenly. The loss of Tara made it brutally clear to the women of PW that death was not just a philosophical dilemma in Tom Morris' class, nor was it an affliction reserved only for their grandparents' generation. It had taken one of their own now, and left a hole too raw and gaping for anyone, even their rector, to fill. "This was something I couldn't fix," said Brink, though they turned to her anyway. "There was nothing I could do, and I'm a real doing person."

Despite all the Jell-O shots she had confiscated, the room parties she had reined in, the hours of community service she had imposed (that was why tulips would soon bloom at PW's entrance), Brink remained, like all good rectors, a sanctuary in times of both joy and sadness, the steady center of the brief, intense community that flourished in the dorm. She was where they came when love made them happy (six of her seniors had shown her their engagement rings already) and when love made them sad (the boyfriend of one junior had just decided to try the seminary for a year), when they had something to celebrate, and when they had something to mourn.

"All I could do was help them grieve, and grieve with them," she said.

Because of the way life proceeds on campus—the extended-family bonds of dorm life, the sacramental bonds of religious life—nobody dies alone at Notre Dame, and nobody grieves alone either. Prayers were offered for Tara and her family by people who had never known her. Candles were lit in her memory in the Grotto. The distinct spirit often thought to be present here—the "Notre Dame family" Malloy extolled in his speeches, the "Christian community" Brink spoke hopefully of in her homilies—achieves its fullest, finest form in the face of death. The lectors at today's Mass were two close friends of Tara's, fellow seniors from PW. "But the just man, though he die early, shall be at rest," read one in the first reading, from the Book of Wisdom.

"He will wipe every tear from their eyes, and there shall be no more death or mourning, wailing or pain, for the old order has passed away," read the second, from the Book of Revelation.

"It is to face, implicitly at least, our own mortality," Malloy said in his homily about the death of a peer. His remarks were warm and sincere, but also, since he hadn't known Tara, somewhat generic. "It's not the words that count now, it's the presence. It's being there."

Brink could only watch from the pew as Malloy spoke from the pulpit, the one place she wished she could go more often when she became a nun.

Her own reflections on Tara's death would have to wait until after communion. "I don't want to be a priest," said the woman who would start her novitiate year with a community of Dominican sisters at the end of the semester. "When I was younger, that was my whole desire, because priests were the only ministers I saw. Now I'd rather live in a community, with professional churchwomen who are out creating new models for being about the business of the church. The only thing priests do that I'd like to do is preach. The sacramental stuff doesn't really thrill me." She had been spending a lot of time in Chicago lately, doing what her students called "nun stuff" with her new community, the Sinsinawa Dominicans, among whose eleven hundred members were two other Notre Dame rectors. Her long-term plans included a Ph.D. in theology. Her short-term plans included a happier gathering of the PW clan soon after graduation—the New Orleans wedding of one of her RAs, Jen Avegno, and the leprechaun, Dan Wagner—and a fishing trip with her father. "He's a big Notre Dame fan. Back when I first told him I was interviewing here, he said to me, 'But, listen, did you meet Knute Rockne when you were there?' and I said, 'Well, gee, Dad, I met a lot of people, but I don't think so.' Then he told me who Knute Rockne was. When he was in high school, he always wanted to go to Notre Dame, so my being here has been just a pinnacle to him. He loves telling people that he has a daughter at Notre Dame."

At the "Our Father," the congregation held hands in a long chain that stretched taut where it crossed the wide center aisle. At the sign of peace that immediately followed, the chain went slack, collapsing into a heap of embraces. Under Brink's guiding eye, the women of PW had built a solid community together, and now, watching a crack open in its foundation sooner than anyone ever expected, they clung close together to try to shore it up, if only for a few more weeks. The seniors would be leaving soon, and when the rest of the dorm reassembled in the fall, it would be under a new rector.

"I've had whatever impact I'm going to have," Brink said about her decision to leave after three years. "Either you're a Domer or you're not—and if you're not, you'll never go far."

Despite her admitted, and conscious, lack of Domerness, she had in fact gone further than she might have guessed. Her dorm had been named "dorm of the year" the previous year. She had been involved in two alcohol interventions with PW women, both of whom were still sober. Back in the Year of Women, she had helped compile a magazine to showcase the literary work of campus women. Earlier this semester, she had helped organize and lead "Learning to Talk About Race," a weekend retreat designed to offer a group of sophomores a " 'plunge' experience in cultural diversity." And now, in Sacred Heart, communion finished, she was able to distill the emotions felt by those who had known Tara Deutsch into an address that raised the kind of grateful, cleansing tears the occasion required.

"And we are here today because we have all encountered Tara, been touched by her life in a tangible way," she said from the pulpit that she occupied with such ease. "What does that touch feel like? Is it a memory of a borrowed formal dress? Is it a confidential chat you shared? It is more than a single experience?"

In preparing her remarks for today's Mass, Brink had grafted the skills of the newspaper reporter she had once been onto the spirituality of the nun she would soon become. She collected the small stories that told fondly of Tara's life here, and she fit them into the larger story that told majestically of everyone's life elsewhere—"beyond the Dome," as she said, "beyond graduation, beyond the grave."

She sketched a portrait of a quiet, warmhearted young woman with an open mind and a large concern for the lives of other people, an accounting major who balanced her business focus with a second major in sociology and an active volunteer schedule. She told of small kindnesses Tara had performed for friends and roommates.

She spoke about Tara's semester in Greece, her work with the Overseas Development Network and the World Hunger Coalition. "Closer to home, when our own campus began to take more seriously the voices of the disenfranchised minorities, Tara and Elizabeth and Kim and Anita chose to live together in a quad—a German American, an Irish American, and two African Americans."

Her voice was steady and strong, seamless even in her sadness. The pulpit was far enough away from the pews so that she could pretend not to see the tears on the faces there. "Today Tara knows what we continue to hope for— that eternal life awaits us."

She gave the last words to Dostoevsky, quoting from the closing pages of *The Brothers Karamazov*. " 'And even if we are occupied with most important things,' " she read, " 'if we attain to honor or fall into great misfortune—still let us always remember how good it was once here, when we were all together, united by a good and kind feeling which made us, for a time, better perhaps than we are. . . .' "

The congregation lingered in the church for a long time after the Mass was ended, reluctant to leave one another's company.

———

"You guys are a Catholic school, right?" Jenny Tate asked her morning tour group, the sixth-graders from St. Joseph's School in Fort Wayne. "We're a Catholic school, too, and we're pretty proud of that."

Cramped from their two-hour bus ride, stoked by the doughnuts they had eaten for breakfast, the sixth-graders bounced around the main circle where they rendezvoused with Jenny. To their left was the Gothic fortress of the law school; Alumni Hall was to their right, the dorm that featured among its gargoyles and masonry ornaments carvings of both Knute Rockne (on its public side, facing the quad) and the similarly bald and round St. Thomas Aquinas (on its private side, facing the inner courtyard). The sixth-graders were interested in more familiar landmarks. Jenny led them toward the stadium.

"Please, please, please, do not go on the grass," she said as they emerged from the shadows of the entrance tunnel. Empty, veiled by a gray and chilly mist, the stadium was a pale skeleton of what they saw on Saturday-afternoon television. Working off their doughnuts, they clambered up and sprinted around the bowl of vacant bleachers.

Notre Dame is often said to be the second-most-popular tourist destination in Indiana—behind only the Indianapolis Speedway—attracting both organized groups and lone pilgrims, and keeping student tour guides like Jenny Tate busy all year. Her itinerary stuck mainly to the old postcard precincts of campus, avoiding the newer suburbs, where her own dorm, Pasquerilla West, was located. She had led the tour often enough to know what questions to expect from a group of schoolchildren: Are you a cheerleader? (No.) Do you date a football player? (No.) Can you introduce us to a football player? (Only if one happens to walk by.) Can you introduce us to Lou Holtz? (Only if he happens to walk by.)

"How're you all doing today?" Lou Holtz asked as he happened to walk by while they were going into the ACC—an encounter so serendipitous as to seem almost scripted.

"I shook Lou Holtz's hand. I was standing right here and I shook his hand."

"That was so awesome."

"I said, 'Is that Lou Holtz?,' and she said, 'No.'"

"That's his car, right there."

"I was this close to him."

"How lucky is that—to meet Lou Holtz!" Jenny said, almost as impressed as the kids were.

"Do you know Joe Montana?" one of them asked Jenny now, testing just how far her apparent sphere of influence extended. It didn't reach anywhere near Montana—or as far as Holtz either, as she pointed out to her young questioner—but it did include two football notables of a different stripe: the strong-armed quarterback of the PW Purple Weasels, and Rudy Ruettiger, the real-life model for the movie that had been filmed on campus last semester. PW's quarterback was Jenny's roommate; Ruettiger lived next door to the condominium where Jenny's brother had lived before graduating last year, and where she planned to live next year; and both were guests at the dinner Jenny's parents had hosted for her friends on Junior Parents' Weekend. (The dinner had allowed Jenny a glimpse of her father, the Kansas rancher, decked out in an uncharacteristic jacket and tie. "I only see him in a flannel shirt, Wranglers, and a ball cap.")

She guided the tour group under the gaze of Touchdown Jesus and into the heart of the school she loved so much that she planned to stay an extra year. After four years, she would be finished with all her courses in accounting, a subject that didn't especially move her, but that she believed would prove useful. The fifth year would allow her to finish majors in English and French, subjects that moved her more, but that she believed might prove less useful. Her brother's experience with a Big Six accounting firm in Dallas—she had stayed with him when she went to watch Notre Dame play in the Cotton Bowl—had convinced her that a similar job would not suit her temperament. Her own experience in her nonbusiness classes here—and in her work on *Scholastic*, where she had recently been bumped up the masthead to "departments editor"—had persuaded her that there might be other paths.

"Who's that guy on top of the Dome?" one of the young visitors asked as they neared the Main Building.

"Actually, it's a woman," she corrected him. "The Virgin Mary."

To the sixth-graders who trailed her respectfully across the God Quad, Jenny was unquestionably an adult, consigned to the same distant chronological category as their parents—a view she was beginning to share as her junior year neared its end. "I've had to be a lot older this year than I ever have before," said PW's copresident. "There's such a big division between freshman and sophomore years and junior and senior years, and I really crossed that gap this year. I became a more responsible person. I learned a lot about community living. I've never lived in a section like the section I live in." There was nothing special about the section itself—it was just the east wing of the third floor, down the hall from the section that had lost Tara Deutsch—but the women who lived there had achieved a personal bond that many other sections in many other dorms would find familiar. "It's like a family."

Later today, after classes were over, her section family would gather in her room, where the walls were hung with what she described as "cheesy beefcake calendars," for their regular week-ending, Friday-afternoon card game. Her closest neighbors in PW were also her closest friends, a situation she recognized as both a strength and a weakness of her Notre Dame experience. "My best friend in high school was a guy—I miss having guy friends. If you're hanging around with a guy here, they think there's something going on. If I have a guy in my room, I feel like I'm doing something wrong. There aren't any brother-sister kinds of relationships that can develop into real relationships."

Jenny led the sixth-graders down to the Grotto and then back up to Sacred Heart, leaving them plenty of time to make the eleven-thirty Mass. After Mass, they planned to visit another shrine—the bookstore—where they would spend their remaining trip money on T-shirts, pennants, miniature footballs, and other memories of their day at Notre Dame.

"Maybe we'll get to see Rick Mirer," one of them hoped.

"Wasn't Lou Holtz enough for you?" Jenny wondered.

"I swear to God, I'm like five years old," said Jimmy Zannino, who had turned the sixth-graders' transient enthusiasm into a permanent life-style when he moved from Pennsylvania to South Bend to be nearer the school, and the team, of his dreams. He was standing on the sidelines of the indoor practice field, watching the varsity scrimmage. The defense broke from its huddle with a collective grunt that was poetry to Zannino's ears. "I love the way they say 'Irish!' when they clap their hands."

Football at Notre Dame is an eternal condition, a sport that never goes out of season. It is—just as football is at the other big power schools—a multimillion-dollar, year-round enterprise, far larger, costlier, and more sophisticated than the scrawny operation that sent eighteen players but only fourteen pairs of cleats to the fateful Army game in 1913. To prepare for that 1913 season, two of the players—end Knute Rockne and quarterback Gus Dorais—practiced passing and receiving on the Lake Erie beach at Cedar Point, Ohio, where they were working as summer lifeguards; when they got to West Point and started using the forward pass, a relatively new and unorthodox strategy at the time, they startled Army into defeat, 35–13, and secured Notre Dame a lasting place in the national pantheon of sports mythology. Today's players have more cleats than they will ever need, and they prepare for the season by training all year in a lavish network of athletic facilities—and by suiting up for the fifteen spring practices permitted by the NCAA, which Jimmy Zannino attended as faithfully as he did the regular fall sessions.

"I'm predicting we're nine and two with a big bowl game," Zannino said, ruminating on the upcoming season with one of the team's student managers.

"I'm tired of those mediocre seasons with a big bowl game," the manager said. (Notre Dame is one of the few schools where a 9-and-2 season would be considered mediocre.) Their reverie was interrupted by a crash of pads, a heap of bodies, and the *woooo-hoooo!* rebel yell that follows a big hit.

"I can't believe how much this kid has grown in one year," Zannino said admiringly about the tackler. "When he's a senior, he's gonna be scary."

Zannino was still working nights in the Oak Room on the South Quad, serving up study-break snacks to the students, who knew him better as Jimmy Z, the ultimate fan. He had applied for a new job on campus, with the buildings-and-grounds department, hoping it would get him inside the stadium on game days. He got into the stadium himself on warm days now, climbing with his lunch and his newspaper up to the top row on the east side—a perch from which he could look out on the spire of Sacred Heart and the Dome of the Main Building, and down toward a vision of himself in the crowd come fall.

"If I get the job, I get to go on the field every game," he said. "That's all I've been praying for at the Grotto for two years."

In the absence of any actual games to sustain their habit now, Notre Dame football addicts fed instead on a mixed diet of information, speculation, rumor, gossip, and hope. They picked over the class of new recruits, familiarizing themselves with the blue-chip high-school seniors who had decided to come to Notre Dame next year. They pondered the possible successors to Rick Mirer at quarterback: Kevin McDougal, Paul Failla, or maybe even Ron Powlus, the recruit whose campus visit had been accorded the kind of attention usually reserved for heads of state. They counted the days to the Blue-Gold game, the intrasquad scrimmage in April that closes the spring-practice season and more than half fills the stadium with insatiable fans. They projected which Notre Dame players would be selected by which teams in which round in the upcoming NFL draft.

"We might have a record in the first round," Zannino said. "We're looking at five definites and three on the bubble."

Awaiting the draft even more eagerly than Zannino was one of his regular customers from the Oak Room—Tom Carter, the junior defensive back who had decided to leave school early to turn pro. Tom's stock had soared after his performance at the NFL combines in Indianapolis in February—a three-day session where the top college prospects display their wares, up close and personal, to their prospective employers. Competing against sixty other defensive backs, Tom ran the forty in 4.32 seconds, did a forty-three-and-a-half-inch vertical jump, and looked sharp in his position drills. He made such a commanding impression at the combines that he saw no need to embellish it, or perhaps detract from it, when several dozen coaches and scouts came to campus in March to watch an informal workout. He stood on the sidelines as fifteen of his teammates tried to play their way onto somebody's draft list.

"Some people say I could be a first-round pick," said Tom, who had previously been pegged as a second-rounder. "That's good news to me."

As his junior year wound down, Tom continued working out regularly in the varsity facilities, lifting weights and running through his mechanics drills ("After all, the NFL is my job now"), but he was only an occasional spectator at the spring practices. His gold helmet rested quietly atop the TV in his Dillon Hall room. "Our class is real tight, and it's kinda strange to look at them all out there, all the guys I came in with. This is Notre Dame, you know—I haven't even left and I'm still trying to cling to the place." Though his varsity career was over, his academic career was not. He was still going to classes, and he planned to return next spring, after his first pro season, to finish some of the twenty-seven hours he would have left on his degree. (In the various surveys that measure the academic success of college athletes, Notre Dame always ranks at or near the top, with graduation rates up above 90 percent.) "Coach Holtz told me that, if I don't get my education, it'll be like the worst recruiting mistake he ever made. I told him that the education was very important to me, and to my mother, too."

By the time he returned, he would be more than able to afford the car that he had so far done without. "I still use my two feet," he said. "I've seen other guys let it get to them—they go out and buy a car and stuff. Those things will come." The one big purchase he had made recently was an engagement ring for the woman who had been his girlfriend since sophomore year of high school; the wedding was scheduled for June. His fiancée was a senior at the University of Florida, and she hoped to attend graduate school in English—concentrating on African-American literature—in one NFL city or another.

"I consider myself ready to start my life," Tom said. "It seems like it was always going to school, school, school, and workout, workout, workout. Now it seems like, in the NFL, it'll all be different. I'll get married, I'll go to work, I'll get paid. It's like a coming-out party."

On the weekend of the Blue-Gold game, Tom planned to be back home in St. Petersburg, watching the draft on TV, and awaiting the lucrative phone call, in the company of family and friends. Jimmy Zannino planned to be on campus, in the company of visitors from his old home in Pennsylvania, squiring his brother and his girlfriend around his new home at Notre Dame.

"I'm absolutely driven with the idea that this is the only place in the world, that this is the Garden of Eden," Zannino said. "You walk around the lake and look up at the Dome and you tell me the Garden of Eden is that beautiful."

Out on the field now, Kevin McDougal, one of the quarterback contenders, was rushing toward his rival, Paul Failla, who had taken a hard hit while running the ball in for a score. "That's a beautiful picture," Zannino said, eyes widening at what he considered yet one more proof of the righteous nature of his chosen team. "Two guys in a heated battle for quarterback, one guy goes down, and the first guy to go over and check on him is the other quarterback. What a beautiful story."

"I believe there is a spirit at Notre Dame, and I tell our players this," Lou Holtz told the crowd—Dillon and Alumni residents mostly—who had gathered to hear him speak tonight under the high oak beams and the tall lancet windows of South Dining Hall. "It's like God. If you say, 'Is there a God?' Well, show me. I don't feel any God. 'Is there a Notre Dame spirit?' I don't feel any spirit. But if you say, 'There is a God, and I firmly believe there is a God,' you feel it. If you say, 'There is a spirit at Notre Dame, and I believe there's a spirit,' you feel it. Faith is believing when you have no proof."

Holtz wore a blue blazer and a blue tie with the khakis that he favored in practice, and he spoke at a lower volume and a slower pace than might have been expected by an audience more accustomed to his overheated pep-rally performances. The students, almost exclusively male, were quiet and respectful as he dished up his usual after-dinner fare of football anecdotes, toastmaster jokes, and coaching wisdom. He was deep into his off-season now, when he was as likely to be found on a dais as on a gridiron. A much-sought-after speaker, he tried to balance his paid appearances—earning five-figure fees from companies who hoped he could fire up their executives the way he fired up the varsity—with charity events and campus gatherings. (Moonlighting at the podium was an old tradition among Notre Dame coaches: Studebaker Motors once paid Rockne $10,000 for a series of speeches he gave to their dealers and salesmen.) His free appearances ranged from a fund-raising luncheon for the Center for the Homeless, to a conference on the Marian visions of Medugorje. ("Whether the Blessed Lady appeared or not is not for me to say—my beads didn't turn a certain color or anything," he said of his own visit to the Bosnian shrine. "But I believe that she must approve it, because so many lives have changed there.") He was making the rounds now of some of the dorms that had invited him in for visits.

"I don't believe that God is going to reach down, and the spirit of Notre Dame is going to make you faster or make the ball bounce your way. But what it does do is, it generates an attitude that usually enables you to rise up and meet most circumstances."

Notre Dame had learned during the Gerry Faust years that simply relying on God was an insufficient game plan for victory: The spirit may be willing, but the flesh must also be strong. In Holtz—previously a head coach at Minnesota, Arkansas, North Carolina State, William and Mary, and the New York Jets—Notre Dame had found someone who spoke about the school with the same childlike awe and devotion as Faust, and as fans like Jimmy Zannino, but who was also gifted as a strategist and motivator. He won a national title in his third season here, and the pressure to win another was crushing. "Perfection at Notre Dame is taken for granted," he had said after the tie with Michigan. "If you fail to live up to it, people feel cheated, and I can understand that."

Before he opened the floor to questions now, he offered the seniors in the audience a piece of advice that drew a round of laughter and scattered cheers. "Don't worry about how much money you're gonna make, because Clinton's going to take most of it anyway," said the man whose politics, like his offense, tended toward the conservative side: In the North Carolina Senate race one year, he had endorsed Jesse Helms.

"Why did you switch to the four-three defense?" the first questioner asked, beginning a string of knowing, deferential questions that made tonight's session sound like one of Holtz's Tuesday-afternoon teleconferences.

"Will Jeff Burris play any offense?"

"How will the kicking game be?"

"How did you feel about Jerome Bettis and Tom Carter coming out early for the draft?"

"I have no problem with it if you're making your decision based on family considerations," Holtz said, absolving Carter and Bettis on the basis of their stated reasons for turning pro early: Both were eager to help their financially strapped families. Neither Carter, a Dillon resident, nor Bettis, who lived in Alumni, had joined their dormmates here tonight. "I love Tom Carter and I love Jerome Bettis and I wish them the best. They're beautiful people. Both of them assured me that they were going to get their degrees. If they don't get their degrees, they're doing a tremendous disservice to themselves. You can't rely on your athletic ability for everything."

"Do you ever think about retiring or leaving?"

At fifty-six, Holtz was already the oldest man to hold the job, which ages young men quickly. Rockne looked, and felt, much older than forty-three, when a plane crash ended his driven and draining life. Parseghian, his blood pressure rising, retired at fifty-one. Leahy—who received last rites in the locker room from Father Ned Joyce after collapsing from pancreatitis at halftime of the 1953 Georgia Tech game—was eased out at forty-five, after he recovered and before he could coach himself into an early grave. It was Leahy more than Rockne whose career Holtz had studied closely, and whose well-thumbed biography he kept within easy reach of his desk in his ACC office. "He was the first one to follow a legend here," said Holtz, whose burden it was to follow several more. Though he didn't share Leahy's health troubles, or his habit of occasionally sleeping on a cot in the campus firehouse on the nights before games, he did share his obsessive drive: Holtz's workdays during football season started with 7:00 a.m. staff meetings, and ended near midnight in his home office, where he spent long hours poring over practice videos. Notre Dame had carved deep creases in his face, but it had not eroded his hyperkinetic personality. He showed no signs yet of succumbing to the easy temptations of the golf-and-lecture circuit, or of defecting to another job, whether college or pro, where he wouldn't be expected to make every season a championship season.

"I don't have plans to coach anywhere else but Notre Dame, as long as they want me here," he answered. What he didn't say, though, was that he had signed a five-year contract extension before the start of the previous season. "If they don't want me here, I'm going to a warmer climate."

The questions finished, Holtz stayed on to emcee a trivia contest between teams from Alumni and Dillon. When they took their seats at a long table—Holtz in the center, Alumni on his right, Dillon on his left—they formed a tableau that unconsciously echoed the *Last Supper* mural looming high on the dining-room wall. The questions were drawn alternately from Trivial Pursuit cards and from the minutiae of the campus's favorite TV show, *Cheers*.

"What is the name of Diane's mother's chauffeur?" Holtz asked.

"What New York Jets running back starred in the first Miller Lite commercial in 1972?"

"Why did Dick Cavett think Sam should write a book about his life?"

"What precious metal is the best conductor of electricity?"

"Who lit the fire that burned down Norm's favorite restaurant, The Happy Heifer?" Holtz asked. "You know, Norm went to Notre Dame," he reminded them in an aside. "According to him, he left to go to a party and never came back."

"Gus the busboy," somebody answered, correctly.

The contestants scored highest on the *Cheers* questions, which wasn't surprising, given the time they spent watching it—syndicated reruns every weeknight at seven and eleven, new episodes every Thursday in prime time. So many TVs in the men's dorms were tuned in at those times that you could walk through the corridors and not miss a line of dialogue. "Never call a guy during *Cheers*," one woman advised. "It's scary how much they bond with that show." Norm was a local hero of sorts—played by George Wendt, the Notre Dame dropout who had once returned in triumph to speak at the pep rally before a big Miami game—and the news that he and his barmates would soon be retired had occasioned a wave of lamentation on campus.

"How many baseball games did Sam win with his lucky charm in his pocket?"

"None," came the answer, quickly.

"Who was emperor of Rome when Christ was born?"

"Augustus," someone offered, after a too-long moment of contemplation.

"That was the correct answer," Holtz said, "but time ran out."

Up on the fourth floor of the Main Building, just under the mansard eaves, the Civil War was raging through an otherwise placid spring morning. The blackboard that ran the width of the room was covered with an elaborate chalk mural of maps and names. At Bull Run, the Confederates had just routed the largest army yet assembled in the Western Hemisphere. In Washington, General Winfield Scott, seventy-five now and too fat to mount a horse, was ensconced in the Willard Hotel on Pennsylvania Avenue, commanding the Union between courses of his four-hour lunches at the center table in the dining room. At the White House, Lincoln was looking for a new general. In the middle of the classroom, Geoff Slevin was examining an officer's dress saber.

"Weapons are designed to kill people, so be careful," warned the professor, Father Bob Kerby, from the front of the room. Also circulating among the students now were several other items Kerby had brought in to help illustrate the daily life of a Union soldier—a canteen, a ration of beans, hardtack. "Don't bite into it if you really want your teeth."

Geoff passed the sword to his neighbor and returned to his notes, trying to capture the booming cannon of Kerby's voice. History 454, "The Civil War Era"—unlike "Chemical Process Control," say, or "Polymer Engineering"—wouldn't help Geoff much when he started his job with ARCO in California, but he had waited long and eagerly for the chance to take it. Because Kerby's class was so popular—and, restricted though it was to seniors and history majors, so hard to get into—Geoff had resorted to guerrilla tactics to get himself registered: Using the DART line, the automated system that enables students to sign up for classes by telephone or computer, he snatched up the lone vacancy on Christmas morning; a friend who had gotten in but then had to drop it had held the slot for him, waiting until Christmas Eve before DARTing out.

"I knew nobody would be DARTing on Christmas morning," Geoff said. Chemical engineers have so few electives in their tight schedules that he wanted to spend his wisely. "Now that I'm done working for grades, I'm working for my education."

Although Geoff hadn't decided yet about whether to get engaged, his family was already treating his girlfriend, Dana Ciacciarelli, like one of their own. When his mother and four sisters, aged five to thirteen, came to campus for Sophomore Siblings' Weekend—his brother was a sophomore—they stayed in Dana's small room in Lewis Hall, sharing space with the specimen jars she used to collect insects for George Craig's class. They were also able to see Geoff's screen debut that weekend: He had a starring role in *Beelzeduck*, a horror-movie spoof some friends of his had made for the Morrissey Film Festival, an annual event that showcases student films and raises money for the St. Hedwig's Outreach Center. (It won in the best-actress category, but lost out for best picture to *Messiah II: He's Back*, wherein Jesus returned to earth as a Notre Dame student, and the miracle of the loaves and fish became instead the miracle of the beer cans.) "Run for your life, it's the duck from hell!" he had screamed while being chased through the Huddle by a six-foot duck. In class now, he listened closely as the Confederates were chasing General George McClellan and the Army of the Potomac away from Richmond to end the Peninsular Campaign.

"He gives you the inside scoop you don't know about," Geoff said of Kerby.

As was his habit in class, Kerby narrated the Civil War in the present tense, calling it so vividly to life that it seemed as if you could almost hear the roar of battle rising up over the trees and drifting in through the window from the direction of the distant stadium. He taught the war as Tolstoy might have written it—an epic drama of folly and glory, told through the stories of a wide cast of characters, set against the larger currents of history. "I'm not good at theory," he said. He was, however, very good at facts, consulting only a skeletal outline as he painted his grand and intricate mural. "I remember this stuff—that's what they pay me for." The maps and the timeline on the blackboard were his way of imprinting on his students' minds the essential matrix of geography and chronology that was so firmly embedded in his own. He had arrived, as usual, two hours early with his twelve-color box of Crayola chalks—he went through six boxes each semester—to start sketching. He resisted the multimedia lure of the new DeBartolo building, suspicious of an excessive reliance on technology and of chalkboards of dubious surface quality. He preferred sunlight through the tall windows, and his own low-tech, multimedia displays—the artifacts, the tapes of Civil War songs ("Johnny Is My Darling, My Union Volunteer" was today's selection), the thick scrapbooks. "It's the last gracious room on campus that can comfortably accommodate eighty people," he said of his Main Building refuge. "If the lights go out here, I just keep going."

Now, in the final weeks of the semester, Kerby had reached what he called the "slaughter, death, and devastation" portion of the class. He was marching the students toward Shiloh, Antietam, Gettysburg—battles big and fierce enough to kill thousands of men in a matter of hours. He had already put the Confederate Army on the field, introducing its leaders and analyzing its structure and strategy in a previous session. Today he was mobilizing the Union, an army that grew from 13,500 to 600,000 in a single year. The Union, he pointed out, started the war with two generals—the other four had defected to the Confederacy—and ended it with 2,091, two of whom were Notre Dame graduates.

"I can see you're proud of that," said Kerby, a graduate of Notre Dame himself, but also of Fordham Prep. "Well, my high school in New York, which was founded the same year as Notre Dame, produced four Union generals. But they're Jesuits."

It was as a boy in New York, even before the Jesuits got him, that Kerby—a descendant of Confederates who "were smart enough to move north when they knew they had lost"—became a student of the Civil War, hooked by a ten-volume pictorial history that sat on the first shelf of the bookcase in the family living room. It sits now on a shelf in his campus office. When he came to Notre Dame as a student, room selection was still determined by grade-point average. "I sailed through this place in the most glorious rooms on campus," he said. He came back after earning a Ph.D. at Columbia, and after being ordained a Melkite Catholic priest. He leads a small congregation in South Bend, and teaches a course in Byzantine history. "There's an appalling lack of knowledge of church history by undergraduates," said Kerby, who is a puzzle to many of them—a representative of a branch of Catholicism that is distinct from the Roman Catholic Church they are familiar with, and that permits its priests to marry. "It's my contribution to the Catholic character of Notre Dame."

Back in the Union Army, Lincoln had finally found his general—a man who, as Kerby told the class, graduated "dead center in his West Point class," who was asked to resign his commission because he drank too much, who failed at farming and at real estate and at selling firewood door-to-door, who was working as a storekeeper in Galena, Illinois, when he was asked to drill the local volunteer unit after the war broke out, and who went on to become the first four-star general since George Washington. " 'I cannot spare this man—he fights,' " Kerby said, quoting Lincoln's words upon choosing Ulysses S. Grant as the Union commander. On the horizon now were Spotsylvania, Cold Harbor, Petersburg, Appomattox.

"The Union began inventing the twentieth-century style of warfare," Kerby said: trench lines and artillery barrages; protracted battles of attrition; telegraph communications, Navy gunboats, pontoon bridges, and other technological advances. "The Confederate generals never did figure out that the war they were fighting was a new kind of war."

The map he drew on the board a few mornings later was of a war that similarly baffled one side's generals, and of a place he knew from experience as well as from books: Vietnam. "The first thing you must comprehend is that for the first time in our history we found ourselves fighting an Asian war the Asian way," he told the students in "American Military History," a class that was restricted—formally by the registrar, informally by the 8:00 a.m. start time, which was avoided at all costs by most civilians—to freshman ROTC cadets. Between Notre Dame and Columbia, Kerby had piloted military-transport planes in Southeast Asia, earning a Silver Star "for being exceptionally stupid," as he prefers to describe it. "It was Clausewitz's ideas that were played out in all the wars we've dealt with so far," he said, referring to the Prussian general whose *On War* had been a blueprint for generations of military strategists in the West. "In Indochina we find ourselves for the first time fighting people who had a different book. They hadn't read Clausewitz." They had read Suntzu instead, the Chinese general whose *The Art of War* was a blueprint for centuries of military strategists in the East.

In Kerby's class, Kevin Kuwik had read both Clausewitz and Suntzu, learning how wars were fought on either side of the globe. The two generals offered different lessons from Thomas Merton or Flannery O'Connor, the authors he had read for Brother Bonaventure Scully's Freshman Seminar back in the fall, but he absorbed them with equal facility, having earned A's on all of Kerby's tests so far, matching his A in Scully's class and the A's in all of his other fall classes. He was one of only seven freshmen to finish the fall semester with a perfect 4.0 average. "It's kinda dangerous to set that kind of precedent," he said. "People are too ready to stereotype you as a smart person."

Kerby turned to the Chinese yin-yang symbol he had earlier chalked on the board—a symbol that echoed the blue-and-gold design Kevin had painted on his face for the Michigan game, his debut as a Domer. "We think that a society is either at war or not," Kerby said, using "we" to stand for the West. "Now let's think in Chinese. The yin constantly flows into the yang, and it contains part of the yang. Either constantly flows into or, and contains part of or. Peace contains elements of war, war contains elements of peace."

Kevin's second semester was proving as successful as his first, with high marks in philosophy, physics, calculus, and materials science, the start of the long engineering grind that Geoff Slevin was just finishing. The ROTC grind would take even longer to complete, an eight-year Reserve commitment after graduation that he hoped would contain more elements of peace than war. He was still reporting at 6:45 a.m. twice each week for physical training, and he was packing his MRE packets for the once-a-semester Field Training Exercises at Fort Custer, Michigan. The buses were leaving at 5:00 a.m. on Saturday. He would head back home to Buffalo after finals to start his last Army-free summer for a decade.

"Why have I spent the bulk of this class talking about Chinese people who lived twenty-five hundred years ago? What the hell has that got to do with Vietnam?" Kerby asked the class rhetorically. The gruff edges and New York cadences of his rising voice made him sound like Walter Matthau. "Because Vietnam was part of China for a thousand years, and for a thousand years every time the Vietnamese fought a conventional military action against the Chinese they lost, and they lost, and they lost, and they lost, and they lost. They spent a thousand years learning the reality that a small state cannot defeat the overwhelming strength of a great aggressor by fighting a conventional war."

Kerby closed the class with the French defeat at Dien Bien Phu, leaving the stage set for America's early involvement in Vietnam—the same era as his own service there. He had been a captain when he left the Air Force; but "the highest rank," he likes to tell his students, "is 'civilian.' " He wears a gray crew cut that would pass muster at boot camp, but he confuses the effect by also wearing a trim gray beard, "so they can't really figure out what side I'm on." His summer would take him to more military installations than any of his ROTC freshmen: He planned to visit some War of 1812 forts on his annual historic-sites tour, and though he had already covered all the Civil War battlefields, he returned at least once each year to Gettysburg. "My wife calls it my shrine."

He started erasing the blackboard. "We have to do more in undergraduate teaching if we want to do what Thomas Jefferson thought a university should do—cultivate an educated citizenry. Somebody has to do the basics." His publications were sparser than many of his colleagues, but he had never—not even when he had a fever of 103—missed a class. He would be back here in room 411 early tomorrow morning, drawing new battle maps for his Civil War class. "I will die with a piece of chalk in my hand."

17

The ball caromed off the rim and sailed through the soft spring twilight in the general direction of Monk Malloy. Leaping as high as a fifty-one-year-old perennial guard could leap, Malloy met the ball at a height that was nearer low-air than midair. After the short return trip to earth, he secured the ball with two hands in front of his chest. A much younger defender was instantly on top of him, trying to swat the ball away. Caught in a spot where neither the collar of a priest nor the trappings of the presidency could help him exercise authority, he relied instead on his elbows. Swinging them wide, he cleared enough space to launch a pass to Lou Nanni, the director of the Center for the Homeless in South Bend and the point guard for All the President's Men, Malloy's annual entry in the Bookstore Basketball tournament. He trotted back upcourt, trailing the rest of his team, toward the men's tower dorms, which loomed behind the backboard of this outdoor court on the northern edge of campus. Apart from a green T-shirt, Malloy was gray all over, the color of a gym rat, blinking in the sun after a winter of hardwood courts and fluorescent lights. He rolled off a pick and took a pass on the foul line. His shot missed, but his team got the rebound. The ball eventually made its way back to him, farther out this time. His second shot hit, putting his team up, 5–3, over Woody and Four Other Stiffs.

"The only thing I can do well at this time in my life is basically shooting," Malloy said later. A finesse player and touch shooter like himself, though, is of limited utility in the rough-and-tumble, check-happy ethos of the Bookstore tournament. "Playing outdoors is like playing hockey—it's not the same sport as indoor basketball. So shooting is completely arbitrary, and all the things that I can contribute aren't very helpful. It becomes a game of foul after foul after foul, and it's just a matter of who gets tired of fouling, or misses."

The surest sound of spring at Notre Dame is the bouncing of basketballs on asphalt. Through the late afternoons and into the early evenings all through April—in sunshine, rain, and, this being South Bend after all, sometimes even snow—the outdoor courts on campus are busy hosting the grand exercise in playground Darwinism better known as Bookstore Basketball: 641 teams this year, five players apiece, games to 21, losers sit, winners advance to the next round. It started in 1972 as a casual sixty-four-team tourney on the two courts behind the bookstore, but it soon bloomed, in familiar Notre Dame fashion, into one of those huge, tradition-bound, local rituals that exude an aura of immutable inevitability. It tops seven hundred teams some years now, and it has spilled beyond the Bookstore courts, where savvy players know enough to dribble around the manhole cover, to the courts behind Lyons Hall, where one corner dips low enough to necessitate an extra foot or so of arc on a jump shot, and to the courts at the backside of campus, between the towers and Stepan Center, which are set so close together that a lay-up can land you in the game next door.

"I got it," said the guard for Woody and Four Other Stiffs, calling a foul on Malloy, who had broken up his attempt at a fast-break lay-up with an emphatic hack. Malloy's rank granted him no special dispensation in the tournament, other than a certain leeway in game scheduling: Today's game had been pushed back to accommodate his weekend trip to speak to alumni groups in Houston and Tucson. He came to the Stepan courts straight from the airport, stopping in his Sorin room only long enough to change into sweats.

"Lou!" shouted Malloy, wide open at the top of the key, to Lou Nanni. Their basketball partnership dated back to the early 1980s, when Nanni was a student living in Sorin Hall and playing in the Monk Hoops sessions that gave birth to the legendary Bookstore dynasty of Tequila White Lightning teams. Nanni occupied one of the young alumni seats on the board of trustees now, but during Bookstore season he was more prized for his sweet shooting and deft passing. Malloy caught his pass and in the same motion lofted a shot that swished through the net, tying the score at 7.

By the time they take the court to play their games, some Bookstore teams have already exhausted their creative energies in choosing their names. Like the Keenan Revue, the annual list of team names offers a raw glimpse inside the murkier recesses of the collective Domer subconscious—

a catalogue of campus satire, dorm in-jokes, pop-culture allusions, David Letterman absurdities, schoolyard taunts, and sexual innuendo. After the censors excised the crudest entries, this year's roster included such gems as Tom Carter, Jerome Bettis and Three Other Guys Who Pull Out Early; Moose, Krauss, and Three Other Guys Who Play Like They're Dead; The Vertically Challenged; Sexual Frustration Rechanneled; Monastic White Boys; You May Beat Us, but We're Drunk; Dicky and the Boys Take It to the Hole; Pontius Pilate and the Four Nail Drivers; Four Irishmen and a Fifth; and Five Guys Who Want to Know If You're Going to Be Anal About the Fouls.

"Whaat?!!" yelled one of the Four Other Stiffs, or maybe it was Woody himself, when Nanni called a foul. Bookstore games are self-refereed until the later rounds, and All the President's Men had not been shy about calling fouls; some hecklers at their last game had dubbed them "All the President's Jerks." In the jock culture that pervades Notre Dame, considerable bragging rights are conferred upon Bookstore champions, and, the nearer the tournament gets to the prize, the higher the temperatures rise on the courts. Voices sharpen, glares harden. Elbows, and sometimes fists, fly more frequently. Only 128 teams were left, and one of the two playing now would be exiting sooner than they had last year: Woody and Four Other Stiffs had made it to the Round of 64 then, whereas All the President's Men had lasted all the way to the Sweet 16.

At 17–14, it looked as if Malloy, who had played in more Bookstore games than anyone else now or ever, would be playing in at least one more. Woody's team had other ideas, reeling off several unanswered points. After Malloy missed from long, Woody came back to tie the game at 19. Down 20–19, Malloy missed again, a short jumper from the left side. The man he was guarding had better luck, launching a jumper that eluded Malloy's outstretched fingers and notched the victory point with an unmistakable swish.

"That was a pretty pathetic game," said Malloy, his Bookstore season over. His Monk Hoops season, played in the friendlier confines of the seminary gym, still had several sessions left before the semester ended. "I enjoy that—that's fun. Playing Bookstore, for me, is being part of a tradition, but it isn't fun. And our team wasn't as good as it was last year either."

On a neighboring court, one of Malloy's Sorin dormmates, a Monk Hoops regular, was also trying to shoot his team into the next round, with mixed results.

"Look at Corey hobbling around out there on his bad ankle," one member of the rooting section said to another.

The last play of his team's first game had put Corey Babington on crutches briefly, an air cast around his ankle, and it left him limping up and down the court now, a shooting guard rather than a point guard. His team, In It Ta' Win It, had won their first two games in a manner befitting their name, by scores of 21–9 and 21–5. But they were behind in their third game, trailing Fuzzy and the Carpet Baggers Head South by a score of 9–5. Corey squared up and hit a long jumper, his third in a row.

"All right, Bones!" another of his friends called, using the nickname that doubled as Corey's stage name when he was a rapper. He had eight original raps to his credit now, and he was working on more, but his last public performance was at Black Images back in the fall, when he closed the show with "You Want a Damn Degree?"

"I think of a story I've gone through," he said of his method of composing raps. "But not all your songs have to be about experiences you've had. They can be about experiences you hope to have, too."

Because he did in fact want his degree, just as his song said, he had been focusing on his classwork more than his rapping lately, trying to make up for the semester he had missed the previous year, when a cash crunch stranded him back home in Wisconsin, the victim of Notre Dame's tight, sometimes harsh financial-aid system. He worked in a machine shop then, and he worked in the lost-and-found office in the security building now, to stay solvent. He also worked as an unpaid volunteer at a local church each week, helping schoolkids with their English and math. He would graduate owing more than $20,000 in student loans.

"I lost some pride not being in school that semester, but I learned you can also learn for yourself outside of school," he said. "You do get depressed sometimes. School's hard. You try to get good grades, and there's a lot of pressure. I call home and they tell me, 'Just do the best you can,' but you've got a certain set of standards for excellence for going here. Everybody here plans on being the best—it's something about the character a school like this has. Everybody here was successful and the hotshot of their city."

Corey stole the ball in the backcourt from one of the Carpet Baggers, but his lay-up was stopped by a flagrant foul. "Hey, don't be grabbing on his shirt," one of his teammates advised the offender.

Corey tended to do best in classes that drew on the same writing skills that made him a good rapper. He had earned an A in his ethics class recently for an essay on abortion, an issue to which he felt a deep personal connection: His mother had been seventeen when she became pregnant with him, and she had heard many voices telling her not to have the baby. "I'm for life, unless it threatens the life of the mother," he said, and that was the position he took in his essay. "I'm basically a conservative-type person. I don't say I'm either a Democrat or a Republican, but I did vote for Bill Clinton."

He had hoped to cram enough into this spring and summer to graduate by December, but geology had blocked the way. His semester was top-heavy with science requirements for his major, the science-business sequence in the department of preprofessional studies, and though chemistry and biology had gone well, geology had proved enough of a struggle so that he finally dropped it. Since it was offered only in the spring, he would have to return for an unanticipated extra semester.

"At first I was disappointed," he said. But what helped ease the sting was the summer job he had landed—a research position in the university's Radiation Lab that would relieve some of his money headaches. "I've always been taught that things happen for a reason."

The extra semester would also mean an extra Bookstore season, which it looked as if he could use about now. "It ain't over yet," Corey said, trying to stoke his team when they were down, 19–14. But in fact it soon was over, 21–14.

"That was a poor effort," he said, heading back to Sorin Hall, a Bookstore spectator now. Like Malloy, he would have to wait until the next session of Monk Hoops to try to make the plays he had missed tonight. On the courts behind him, the balls kept bouncing, more wins and losses accumulating, as the evening slipped toward night.

Early on a bright Saturday morning, the streets of South Bend's near-southeast side were as packed with Domers as the South Quad on a sunny afternoon. They had arrived by the busload, eighteen hundred of them, wearing old jeans and sweatshirts, still rubbing the sleep from their eyes. Issued red-brimmed painter's caps that read "Christmas in April," they were armed with brushes, scrapers, rakes, brooms, caulk guns, and assorted other tools for the kinds of jobs for which youthful energy was a more important prerequisite than skill. They scattered through a five-square-block area—all up and down Broadway and Haney, Indiana and Dubail—to forty-seven houses and three churches that needed repairs and refurbishing. The shady, grassy, tree-lined neighborhood was by no means a slum, but some of the gracious old frame houses had fallen into decline in the years since the nearby Studebaker plant stopped issuing the paychecks that had once helped keep them in good trim.

"Everything changed tremendously when Studebaker closed," Mayor Joe Kernan said as he walked the streets in a blue Notre Dame baseball jacket, greeting and thanking the student volunteers from his old school. He had been a senior at St. Joseph's High School when Studebaker—the automaker that was the city's anchor industry for decades, with a payroll that peaked at twenty-two thousand during World War II—finally shut its doors a few weeks before Christmas in 1963, leaving its last eight thousand workers suddenly jobless. "When I was growing up, Studebaker affected every family in town."

Notre Dame is the largest employer in town now, a newly acquired role that carries with it certain civic duties the university sometimes shirked in the past. "The relationship a generation ago was much more adversarial," Kernan said. "The general population of the city did not appreciate the university, did not feel any affinity to Notre Dame. Today that's dramatically different." "Christmas in April," like the nearby Center for the Homeless, is the kind of community project that would have been unlikely in the Notre Dame of Kernan's era, when the cloister walls, invisible but formidable, that separated the school from the city were first starting to crumble.

Kernan held open a door for a student carrying several cans of basement waterproofing, then followed him into a house that was frantic with cleaning, scrubbing, scraping, and painting crews. Out at the curb, a front-end loader was scooping up an old water-heater that some volunteers had wrestled up the basement stairs. Professionals had already provided the skilled labor (roofs, electrical wiring, plumbing), leaving the students, joined by five hundred volunteers from the community, to tackle the basic weekend-chore projects that the residents—mostly poor or old or disabled—could neither do themselves nor pay someone else to do for them.

Kernan continued down the street, walking with the stiff, legs-apart gait of the catcher he had once been. "Good field, no hit," he said of his years on the Notre Dame varsity. A government major in the class of 1968, he had served in the Navy after graduation, flying on carrier-based reconnaissance planes in Vietnam. In 1972, on his twenty-sixth mission, his plane was hit by anti-aircraft fire, forcing him to eject. He was captured immediately, and spent eleven months as a prisoner of war. He was in the middle of his second term as mayor now. His fourteenth-floor office offered a panoramic vista of the steeple-studded city, but a tall bank building next door blocked his view of the Dome. He made up for the loss by living near campus, riding his bike there for exercise, worshiping at Sacred Heart, attending plenty of football, basketball, and baseball games. When Clinton spoke at Stepan Center, Kernan sat on the stage behind him.

"Thanks for coming out," he said for the hundredth time this morning, extending his hand to a volunteer.

Over on Broadway, three of Kernan's fellow Democrats had finished cleaning out a basement and were getting ready to tackle a garage. "We even took a pool table out of there," said Andrew Holmgren, president of the College Democrats, who was accompanied by the two vice-presidents, Chris Setti and Andrew Runkle. They had excavated a refrigerator, too, and built a wall along the curb with the bulging garbage bags they had filled. "God knows what's in the garage."

When they conducted a similar search-and-destroy mission on their own home recently—Andrew Runkle's room in Cavanaugh Hall, their *de facto* headquarters—they found a dead angelfish on the floor behind the aquarium. "The room smelled bad enough as it was," Andrew said. Bill and Tipper, two of the mollies they had named after their ticket, had survived the year, but Hillary and Al had joined the angelfish in eternity. They also found some leftover Clinton-Gore signs, a memory of their moment in the spotlight last fall.

"We did so much in the first two months that we felt burnt out after the election," Chris Setti said. "This semester, we've been lazier. We say, 'Let's have a meeting,' and then it never gets done. The campaign gave us something tangible to do. Now we have to refocus the club to intellectual awareness kinds of things, to broader issues, like labor issues or environmental issues."

Their first meeting in the fall had filled the auditorium in the Center for Social Concerns, but their last meeting in the spring fit into a booth at McDonald's—the usual triumvirate plus their faculty adviser, a philosophy graduate student, munching Big Macs under a copy of the famous photograph of Rockne's Four Horsemen backfield. The Club Coordination Council had denied their $500 funding request, allotting them only $100 for next year's budget.

"I loved being in the public eye," Chris said. "When I was a little kid, I was so scared of public speaking, but now I jump at the chance." After finals, he was bound for Cleveland, where he would live in a Catholic Worker House as part of his summer-service project. In preparation, he was reading a biography of Dorothy Day. And he had declared himself a government major. "Clinton made me want to be involved in politics in some way."

"I know I don't want to be in politics after this year," Andrew Runkle said. He was now a psychology major, and was taking all the requisite premed courses. "I'll take the MCATs next year and see what happens."

"I wish I knew what I wanted to do," said Andrew Holmgren, who had decided to become a history major. His brother had gone to law school after Notre Dame, a path he wasn't sure he wanted to follow. "I don't particularly want to go to law school. I don't particularly want to do anything. It's driving me crazy."

Exactly one block behind the Democrats, upstairs in a house on Haney Avenue, Rachel Stehle, having set aside her trumpet after football season ended, was wielding a paintbrush instead. "I got elected to paint the moldings," she said. Her sweatshirt was flecked with white, the new color of the moldings in the front bedroom, where she had spent all morning and would spend all afternoon. The house buzzed like a hive, swarming with students who were slapping a new face on the whole interior. "It's awesome. I never painted anything before."

Although the band was on hiatus until the fall, it was still a big part of her life: Her new boyfriend—the guy from Morrissey she had been seeing last semester was history—was a fellow trumpeter, a sophomore from Iowa who lived in Grace Hall. "Trumpet incest," she called it. "There are a couple of couples in trumpets. It's a good place to meet people." Their courtship had followed the classic Notre Dame script—long talks while walking around the lake, a movie at the theater in the campus art museum, dinner at The Olive Garden near the mall (he had a car), watching a movie together in her room. Her gave her a pair of rabbits, Jackson and Monroe, who were temporarily residing in his room, out of sight of the RA. "It's amazing just what a year can do."

Back in Ohio over spring break, she had bought a copy of the Four Seasons' greatest hits, thus ensuring that she could listen at will to the song she had heard at all the SYRs and formals and room parties she had attended: "December, 1963 (Oh, What a Night)" "I'm totally hooked on it," she said. She still planned to major in psychology, but she was thinking about adding anthropology as a second major. When she returned in the fall, she would join her three roommates in a "forced quad"—two regular double rooms facing each other across the hall, one crammed with lofts for sleeping, one left clear as a "social room."

Wearing a spot of white paint on her nose now, Stehle brushed carefully along the baseboard molding. "I want the actual schoolwork to end, but I don't want to leave," she said. "I'm gonna miss everybody so much."

"Gimme a P! . . . Gimme an A! . . . Gimme an N! . . ." they shouted from the middle of the lake, joined by their friends on the shore, spelling the name of their dorm, *"PANGBORN! Dorm of the year!"*

Pangborn Hall had in fact been named dorm of the year by the Hall Presidents Council recently, but Pasquerilla East was beating them in the race across St. Mary's Lake. Pangborn's entry in the annual Fisher Regatta—a soapbox derby of a boat race, pitting dorm against dorm in a contest that was as much about appearance as performance—consisted of a purple-painted door attached to four large inner tubes, powered by six kneeling women, the Violet Femmes, who were trying to make up in lung power and enthusiasm what they lacked in oarsmanship. Kathleen Bergin—a Pangborn resident, and a graduate of Brother Bonaventure Scully's Freshman Seminar in the fall—cheered them on as they straggled toward the finish line in second place.

"All right, Pangborn!" she called.

Kathleen had spent the previous day up on a scaffold outside a house on Fellows Street, scraping and painting the white clapboards as a "Christmas in April" volunteer. "It was the best day I've had since I've been here," she said, a spring flourish that helped mark her own emergence from winter's gloom. Her second semester had proved harder than her first. Her classes were more difficult, and less interesting. She encountered no books, no ideas, that moved her as much as Thomas Merton had in Scully's class. Her 3.4 average seemed certain to slip. She had studied until 4:30 a.m. on the night before her first economics midterm, but she still got a D. She grew homesick for Reno, and thought briefly about transferring. Her dining-hall job tried her patience. "I was working the dish belt one day," she said, meaning the conveyor where students deposit their dirty trays, "and somebody said, 'Ooooh, this is so gross.' I was in a bad mood, so I said, 'You know, I really choose to work here, it's really by choice.'" But her mood began to brighten as the weather did. She was buoyed by a visit from her sister, a high-school sophomore. She drove alone to Alabama over spring break for her grandmother's eightieth birthday party. She got an A− in her second economics midterm. She became one of the first of her friends to declare a major, choosing psychology. She was shedding the uncertain skin of a freshman, finding surer footing as an adult.

"I think a lot of it is that all of a sudden you're in this environment where you're around all these people who are more intellectual than any other people you've been around before, and you all challenge each other." She found her politics challenged. "I came here and I was very prolife. I was pretty conservative, but I considered myself a Democrat. I've become much more liberal. I consider myself prochoice now. That's a pretty big change, and it amazes my friends, since I was always the one who was adamant that you can't justify abortion." She found her religious beliefs challenged, too—a common experience at Notre Dame, where many students learn to stop accepting answers like children, and to start asking questions like adults. "I never thought too much about religion before. I'm kinda doubting my faith a little now. Of course, I might end up right back where I started from."

After hauling their boat out of the water, the Pangborn crew, sailors and shore support alike, gathered around it—and around Lou Holtz, who had spoken briefly as part of the festivities—for a photograph. Their smiles masked the tension that had arisen among some of them lately over the question of who would be living with whom, and where, next year. Room picks were under way—a spring ritual as regular as the Fisher Regatta, but more emotionally complex—and some feelings, inevitably, were being hurt. "People said room picks were bad, and they were right," said Kathleen, who was moving with a neighbor up to the second floor, the only two northward migrants from their close-knit basement crowd. "There were tears. People feel like we're ditching them. There was a big blowup; then we had a big talk. It's not like we don't want to be friends anymore, but I think we all kind of limited ourselves by just hanging out together. I still feel so guilty, though." The picture snapped, they headed back by land to the other side of the lake, where the Morrissey boat—an inner-tube catamaran with a Tiki torch attached to its mast—was poised at the starting line.

"Hey, Joe," a Morrissey rooter on the shore called to Father Joe Ross, the dorm rector, who was kneeling on the boat, "calm the waters!"

As near to God as Ross could sound when he was preaching, he was not endowed with the power of miracles, and the Morrissey boat was left to struggle through the same choppy, wind-whipped waters as its opponent from Zahm. The Morrissey crew had won an earlier heat, but they could only watch from behind now as the sleeker Zahm scull pulled ahead.

"Stroke! Stroke! Stroke!" they chanted as they paddled, trying to find a rhythm that would straighten their drifting course.

As the youngest of all the male rectors, Ross could enter the world of his students in ways some of his older colleagues could not. He joined some freshmen on a Bookstore Basketball team, losing in the first round. (In a previous year, with more seasoned teammates, he made it to the Round of 64.) He went to a U2 concert in Chicago. He spent an evening at an off-campus bar, and got a Sunday-night homily out of it. He cheered on the dorm's basketball team as it won the interhall championship, and he still kept the victory photo from *The Observer* posted on his door. On a subfreezing day back in February, he took off his shirt and ran through campus with scores of other Morrissey men in their second annual Polar Run, an event that raised $3,000 for scholarships in memory of the two members of the women's swim team who had died in the bus crash. "They love the idea of starting new traditions, and they love stuff that they can do together," Ross said. "Any time they get outside and don't end up in front of Dillon yelling 'Dillon sucks,' it's a triumph."

"Fight on for Morrissey," they sang from the middle of the lake now, clearly beaten but finding refuge in their own dorm fight song, "The black and gold for victory."

Rising behind them as they meandered toward the finish line was the slender spire of Sacred Heart, where Ross had attended the annual ordination of new Holy Cross priests yesterday, sitting in the pews with the congregation, rather than on the altar with the hundred other priests. He remained with the congregation when his fellow priests lined up for the laying on of hands, the solemn ritual in which they placed their hands upon the heads of each of the three kneeling candidates, passing along the power of the Holy Spirit. It was to him, like the other big concelebrated Masses he chose to forgo, an example of the kind of exclusive triumphalism he was uncomfortable with. After his own ordination four years earlier, he had invited the congregation at his first Mass—in the chapel of Fisher Hall, where he was assistant rector—to come to the altar and lay their nonclerical hands upon his head. He would return to Sacred Heart next weekend, to the altar this time, to preside at the marriage of one of his old Fisher RAs—the same one he had once enlisted for a practice ceremony when he was still a seminarian, rehearsing his sacraments.

The Morrissey crew dragged their boat up onto the shore, then stamped their feet and rubbed their arms for warmth. A chill wind blew through the gray sky, perhaps a reminder that spring on a college campus is not the season of beginnings it is in the rest of the world, but a season of endings. These closing weeks always drained Ross, and this year promised to leave him lower than ever: The Morrissey seniors were the first class that had truly been his own, having arrived in the dorm as freshmen the same year he arrived as rector. At the final Sunday-night Mass, he planned to yield the pulpit to two of the seniors for the farewell homily. Lifting together now, they carried their boat back toward home.

"When the hall empties out, there's a real sense of grief," Ross said. "You see them constantly, then not at all. It takes more energy to say goodbye to two hundred people than anybody should have to expend."

"We have a week and a half to go to the final and you're not panicked yet," Teresa Ghilarducci said to the students in her "Intermediate Macroeconomic Theory" class, as much a question as it was a statement. "So maybe the best way to go is to anticipate the panic and talk about your concerns now. Given that it's comprehensive, what kinds of materials worry you the most?"

Given that it was comprehensive, the material they had to master reached from before the gold standard to after Paul Volcker, a wide survey of the history and theory of macroeconomic policy that would serve as a foundation for their future studies as economics majors. They were sophomores mostly, and their economic focus had been widening through the year, from microeconomics in the fall to macroeconomics in the spring. When they picked up *The Wall Street Journal* now, they could read it—if they had been paying sufficient attention—with a more sophisticated understanding of the economic principles behind the day's big stories.

"All right, how do we know we're at a natural rate of unemployment?" Ghilarducci asked the class now.

"Doesn't a lot of it depend on who's in power?" one student ventured.

"I've created a class of cynics," Ghilarducci said, not unhappily. "You're right—it often is political. But I'm asking you a technical question—what do economists mean by that?

"The unemployment that exists at full employment."

"When everybody who's really ready for work has a job."

Though she had received no job offers from Washington yet, and the Labor Department had remained just a tantalizing possibility, some of her ideas were finding a welcome reception in the capital. The Clinton administration was well stocked with people she knew—including Labor Secretary Robert Reich, an acquaintance from her semester as a fellow at Radcliffe—people who knew people she knew, and people who knew her recent book, *Labor's Capital: The Economics and Politics of Private Pensions*, a prescription for reforming the American pension system. She had written memos for the administration on pet topics like "Economically Targeted Investments"—which would allow union pension funds to invest in projects (a new apartment complex, for instance) that would not only provide a good rate of financial return but would also create jobs for union members. Her work actually had the potential to influence policy now, a new sensation to a leftist economist who had come of professional age in a Republican era.

She had in fact been traveling frequently to Washington lately, but it was in pursuit of her own agenda, not the nation's: She was doing research at the headquarters of the operating engineers' union, working on her second book—an examination of a single pension fund, a micro complement to the macro perceptive of her first book. She had also traveled to several alumni clubs as one of the select few Hesburgh Series lecturers (Tom Morris was another). She had finally begun to say no occasionally to some of the campus service assignments and committees that were inevitably offered to the few available faculty women. "People don't realize how much of a tax women and minorities pay in an institution like this," she said. "But I also feel like I can't stay in a place without trying to do anything to make it better."

Ghilarducci erased the first chalkboard she had filled and started on the second, listing three different categories of unemployment: frictional ("There are jobs for all workers, but the workers are shifting jobs," one student offered when she asked for a definition), structural (workers' skills don't match the available jobs), cyclical. When she finished there, she started on her third board, outlining some common strategies for reducing inflation.

"Gradualism," she printed quickly with the chalk, explaining as she went: "A gradual slowing of the economy in order to reduce demand, prices, and wages."

"Cold Turkey," she wrote next. "That's what Volcker did," she said, referring to the Reagan era's Federal Reserve chairman. "Spike up interest rates and cause a recession. Now, what's the third way to reduce inflation? It's not American, but there is a third way." When nobody ventured a guess, she started writing again: "Wage and Price Controls." "That's where labor and business have made an agreement with each other about what their income will be, and prices and wages are set accordingly."

She pressed on into deeper, rougher waters—talking about rational expectations and adaptive expectations and trying to decipher just what factors determined how productive workers were in a given economy. Was their productivity strictly a function of how much training and skill they had, and how good the machinery and technology they used was? Or did it have something to do with how much they were paid?

"The case I will build rests on the assumption that wages and productivity are in fact connected," Ghilarducci said. She turned and started on yet another blackboard, the last of the morning but still a few away from the last of the semester, sketching a graph of the type that ranked high among the things that the students, according to the exam fears they had expressed earlier, would prefer to see little of on the final.

"Are you ready for the curves?" she asked, drawing sinuous, intersecting waves of supply and demand.

A few doors down the same second-floor corridor in DeBartolo Hall, the discussion focused on a smaller, more immediate issue of business economics. "Let's get back to the big question—are we going to give this guy an office?" one student asked, addressing his fellow seniors—and his professor, Carolyn Callahan, who was seated among them—in "Advanced Financial Accounting." Callahan had ceded the podium to a presentation by one of the groups the class was divided into. "He has only one client, but it's a big client. Can anybody else handle it? Is having one $6-million client OK, or is making two hundred calls a day better? These are the kinds of questions that we as public accountants are going to be facing in the next few years."

First, though, they had to face these questions as students. Accountancy 473 was designed to teach graduating majors the advanced corporate financial-reporting techniques they would soon need in their new jobs, but in Callahan's hands it also included a supplementary lesson in what she liked to call "character development and ethical training." It was her conviction that learning how to handle a difficult co-worker, the topic of the first half of today's class, was just as important as learning how to handle a difficult foreign-currency transaction, the topic of the second half. The group's presentation was based on a Harvard Business School case study of a branch office of a large brokerage firm—a practical, micro look at the daily grind of office life. The manager's dilemma was what to do with a broker who was responsible for a wealthy and important client but didn't play by the same rules as his fellow workers. Though he didn't seem to do much work besides talking to his single client, the broker had asked for a private office.

"There are guys who have been there twenty years who don't have their own offices," one group member said.

"But if he's bringing in that much money, shouldn't we try to keep him?"

"Six million is a lot of money—are you willing to risk losing it?"

"If he leaves, is he gonna take his client with him?"

"I don't think the problem was how he got his clients. It was when he demanded an office. He had only one client—he wasn't a consistent performer."

"If you're a manager and one employee is following a different strategy than the other employees, does it seem important to put parameters on that behavior?" Callahan asked. "The issue is, how did she manage the unstructured situation she had?"

She managed it by firing him. "It turned out the guy could speak English after all," the presenter said, referring to the big Taiwanese client. The broker, who spoke Chinese, had falsely staked a claim as the only person in the office who could communicate with him.

"You got it," Callahan said. "He had misrepresented the situation. He had acted as an individual contractor. You can't act as an individual contractor when you're in the firm."

Callahan's own professional life had followed a different arc from the lives of her CPA-bound students. "People think of a professor's job as a cushy job. It is not," she said later. "You have to invest fifteen to twenty years of your life"—from the Ph.D. novitiate through the frantic scramble to publish enough research to win tenure somewhere—"before you come to some level of stability." In her field, achievement is measured by articles published in the professional journals, each one representing maybe two years of number-crunching work. She had three to her credit so far, and she was awaiting decisions on three more. She had just submitted her most recent work, "Econometric Issues Associated with the Estimation of Abnormal Bid-Ask Spreads," to the *Journal of Financial Economics*, which had an acceptance rate of roughly 10 percent. "I've never taken a two-week vacation with my family, ever. I could never find that many days at a time."

Her students' lives were similarly busy right now. Most of them were studying for the grueling, three-day-long CPA exam, which fell right in the middle of finals week. Their evenings were spent at cram courses, sagging under the weight of heavy study guides. After a brief postgraduation respite, they would be flung into the white-collar boot camp of a first-year accounting job—facing high-powered audit assignments that didn't always conform to the accounting principles they had learned in their textbooks, starting the rigorous corporate climb Callahan was helping to prepare them for.

The case study finished, Callahan reclaimed the podium to review its lessons. "This turned out to be a win-lose situation—she won, he lost," she said about the manager and the broker. "How could it have turned out to be win-win?"

"You'd have to tell him," one student offered, "that the only way to achieve long-term success in the firm is the way that the other people who have offices did it."

"This is a case where a person has to be offered alternatives—'If we keep you, this is the kind of change in behavior we need to see,' " Callahan said. "Some people will adapt to a corporate structure in a month, and they'll be an Arthur Andersen man. Some people will take two years. I hope you've learned something that'll help you when you're supervising forty people." Though she could see how remote such a future seemed to them, she knew how near it really was. "In three to five years, most of you will be in supervisory positions. It happens sooner than you think."

"That was the Dirt Fishermen, with 'Cops,' " Steve Sabo said into the microphone in the small glassed-in studio of WVFI-AM, the campus alternative-rock station. "Before that was Lard, they're kind of a mixture of Jello Biafra and Ministry. It sounded a lot like the Butthole Surfers. Up next, the Loud Family."

The dense, discordant landscape of college music is crowded with bands whose names are often better than their songs, but Steve knew his way around it without a map. After starting at the station as a backup DJ in the fall, he had moved up to a regular lunchtime slot by the spring, roaming freely through a collection of discs and records larger than anything he could ever hope to accumulate in his room in Keenan Hall. He was alone in the studio today, unaccompanied by his freshman floormate Patrick Lyons, who had occasionally sat silent beside him in the fall. Since he had stopped reflexively saying "all right" on the air, he no longer needed Patrick prodding him to break the habit.

"I'm more comfortable on the air now," he said off the air as the Loud Family played on it. The next disc he cued up—so new that it had been heard by only a handful of Domers so far, and by almost nobody beyond campus—was evidence that the student music scene was, like him, beginning to find a comfortable place for itself at Notre Dame. "Here's Victoria's Real Secret with 'Fish,' " he announced, "from the new CD of campus bands."

Financed by the Student Union Board, recorded at a professional sound studio, produced by student producers, the disc—titled *Incubus,* after the sexual demon believed to descend upon sleeping women—was a compilation of sixteen original songs by sixteen bands from Notre Dame and St. Mary's who demonstrated a depth of musical talent and inventiveness that no one who had endured the endless SYR loop of Billy Joel and Meat Loaf would have ever dreamed existed. There were Indigo Girls harmonies, Pearl Jam power chords, R.E.M. minor-key melodies, horn-heavy white funk, even some piano jazz, but there was no rap. Some of the bands already had a wide campus following—Dissfunktion; XYZ Affair; The Sister Chain; Brian, Colin and Vince—but most were known mainly to the small flannel-shirt crowd that frequented Dalloway's Coffeehouse at St. Mary's, the Acoustic Cafe in the LaFortune basement, and the irregular circuit of house parties off-campus. Steve's own favorite band was playing now.

"A lot of people don't think V.R.S. are alternative enough," he explained. "They think that a band is a sellout because they start playing stuff that people like. I think that's absurd. If people like it, they can't help it. That's the goal of every band."

Since resigning his unofficial role as Steve's backseat editor, Patrick Lyons had established his own extracurricular home in the busy LaFortune Student Center, just a few doors down the third-floor corridor from the radio studio. All his backstage work for the denizens of student government, all the posters he had designed on his Apple Powerbook, had paid off with his appointment as head of Adworks, the campus advertising agency, a position usually reserved for a senior. The job paid $66 a week, put him in charge of forty people, and secured him access to blocks of scarce football tickets. During his nonwork hours, he planned to major in theology and government. "Even though everybody else does it, I'm still interested in it," he said of his choice of government, the most popular major on campus. What he had grown less interested in was the monotonous round of cramped room parties. "It was fun at the beginning of the year, but now—how many times can you get drunk with the guys?"

Though he and Steve did not share the same tastes in music, or the same passion for video games—one of the highlights of Steve's year was playing "Streets of Rage" with Rocket Ismail, who had come to Keenan to visit a friend—they had planned to room together before Steve was accepted into a sophomore-year-abroad program in France. Lyons would room instead with another floormate, Vishal Pahwa, the new executive assistant to the new student-body president, Frank Flynn. The Adworks office offered Lyons a welcome study refuge now, as exams approached and the library carrels filled up. He was working on a final paper for his introductory American-government class—seven pages on how Bill Clinton had bridged the gap between liberal Democrats and Reagan Democrats, and how the Republicans were now facing their own intraparty cultural divide. On the wall above his desk he had hung the treasured old Notre Dame pennant that had once graced his father's dorm room.

"I love hearing the alma mater," he said, secure and settled in his new office, as the Sacred Heart bells across the quad started one of their twice-daily renditions. "You need tickets for Florida State?"

18

The tall and heavy front doors of the Main Building were flung open wide, letting in enough of the spring afternoon, it seemed, to chase the last, lurking winter shadows from the far corners of the halls inside. Down the wide, sun-cleansed front steps, the tulips were blooming, the magnolias flowering. Several classes had migrated outside for cross-legged sessions on the lawns. From the distance behind Sorin Hall came the faint bouncing echo of Bookstore Basketball, which had dwindled down now to the Elite Eight. Clusters of prospective freshmen toured a campus that looked like all the best pictures of itself. As bright and golden as the day was, though, it couldn't completely mask a faint chill of sadness, the palpable sense of incompleteness and vague regret: Time was almost up, and there were many things, intellectual and emotional, that hadn't gotten done yet, and that might never get done.

"Somebody asked me, 'What would have happened if you had to play today?' " Monk Malloy said to his Freshman Seminar students, referring to the Bookstore tournament. His team's elimination meant that the games were proceeding without him today. "That was a good question, but, as Alex reminded me, that wasn't likely to happen."

"I told them you were getting a little old and tired," Alex Montoya said.

The class had switched times for its final meeting, from Sunday evening to Friday afternoon, but not location: It was still in the conference room next to Malloy's office, up the steep flights of stairs that had given Alex and his prosthetic leg such trouble all semester. The rest of campus was proving more hospitable to him now, free of treacherous snow and ice, and the weather had warmed enough to give him a preview of summer back home in San Diego. He had finally broken out his shorts again.

"I'm surprised that people are defending this character," Alex said. The novel under discussion was *The Moviegoer* by Walker Percy, who happened to be a past recipient of Notre Dame's Laetare Medal. "He got on my nerves from the beginning of the book. I couldn't find one good thing about him."

"I have to disagree," Chandra Johnson said about the same character, a spiritually adrift New Orleans stockbroker on the cusp of his thirtieth birthday. "I would like to think that some redeeming qualities were resurrected in this man who was such a jerk. There are a lot of people, including myself, who, when they reach the age of thirty, it's a real pivotal point in their lives."

"These people haven't even hit their twenties yet," Malloy reminded her.

"Sorry, I forgot," she said to much laughter, including her own.

"I didn't see any real scruples or morals in him," Alex said. "I didn't like his lack of backbone, his not standing up to his aunt. He always seemed to be thinking the world revolved around him."

The lives in the novels on Malloy's syllabus were of interest chiefly for what they said to the lives of the students who read them, and the students reading *The Moviegoer* found that it said something important about the mood that prevailed now in class, and on campus. To the freshmen, Notre Dame was no longer the special occasion it was to the high-school seniors wandering wide-eyed outside today, the people they had been a year earlier; it was instead the everyday routine of the people they had since become. After nearly nine months' gestation, they were emerging as genuine, true-born Domers—well versed in the local habits and rituals, both good and bad— but a larger transformation yet remained: What would they become next?

Malloy thumbed his book open to a page he had marked. " 'Where there is chance of gain, there is also chance of loss,' " he read. " 'Whenever one courts great happiness, one also risks malaise.' The question is, what in the world is this malaise? Is it simply something that applies only to older people? Or do you see people among your own peer group who are unwilling to take a risk and break out of the pattern?"

"I myself haven't experienced malaise yet," one student said, "but I haven't risked anything yet."

"Sometimes I'd rather have repetition than take a risk and go out on a limb and get shot down."

"There's always gonna be repetition and everydayness in everybody's life—you've gotta go to work, you've gotta go to school. It's not the position you're in, it's what you do with it."

"People have a hard time breaking the monotony because they're scared of what's out there."

"I think there's something to be said for everydayness and malaise—they keep people centered," Chandra Johnson said. "It takes a lot of courage to step out of the norm and what's comfortable." Since she left her previous life in Los Angeles, her own steps out of the norm had mostly proved sure and successful. The regular meetings of Just a Sister Away, the group for black women students she had started, culminated with a eucharistic service in a dorm chapel led by a female Episcopal priest. At her last visit to Slice of Life, the after-school girls' club where she volunteered each Friday, she used her essays from Malloy's class—she had earned an A on each one—to show the girls what they could achieve with hard work and persistence; she used her math grades, considerably lower, to show the frustrations they might encounter along the way.

"You don't know the stuff you're made of until you take that step," she said, an observation that applied as much to herself as to the character that had sparked the discussion.

The afternoon light was draining from the room's single corner window when Malloy, who had himself struggled with math back when he was a freshman, finally brought the discussion to rest at the head of the table, telling the class a story about one of the big steps in his own life. He took them with him to the Vatican for his first meeting with the pope. "Part of you steps back and thinks, 'I never thought I'd be here,' and then your mind's at the next step—'I'll tell him what I think if he asks me,' " he said. "Being there after you've been there doesn't mean that much. It's no bigger a deal than sitting down with anyone else." What was important, he told them, wasn't how near fame and fortune the steps of your life led you on the outside—however impressive it might seem to be received at the Vatican, or to be welcomed into the world as Domers—but how near wisdom they led you on the inside. "If you lived your life just to be there for the next thrill, you'd soon run out of thrills."

On the gray but dry Sunday afternoon of the Bookstore championship game, Monk Malloy—the steps of his life having led him out of the game and into the crowd—stood in the back row at the top of the grassy slope that rises like an amphitheater from the outdoor basketball courts at Stepan Center. His height afforded him a better view than many of the several thousand other fans packed shoulder to shoulder in the bleachers and on the lawns all around the homely patch of asphalt. He was alone, trying to look as inconspicuous as he could. He had come to watch, not preside. Mindful of the diplomatic demands of his position, he refrained from rooting openly for one team over another. Inside, however, he was cheering silently for the team in the dark shirts.

"I want Tequila to win," he said.

Tequila White Lightning—perhaps the final edition of the most storied team in Bookstore history, a family dynasty with roots deep in Sorin Hall and Monk Hoops—was playing Malicious Prosecution, a shorter-lived dynasty team from the law school. In eleven years of play, Tequila had made it to the Sweet 16 eleven times, to the Final Four seven times, and to the Final Two five times, but never won the championship. The twelfth year would probably be its last chance: Each edition had featured at least one brother from the Tequila Trinity of families—a Nanni, a Conlin, or a Cullinan— and the last brother, Shannon Cullinan, was a senior now. Last night—after Tequila beat Corby's II, 24–22, in overtime in the Final Four—Cullinan visited Malloy's room to discuss today's strategy.

"He knew that they were quicker and younger than the other team," Malloy said. "They need to have an uptempo game to win."

An uptempo game was exactly what Tequila was playing now, breaking a 3–3 tie with a run of fast-break lay-ups and quick jump shots that soon put them ahead 8–4. By halftime they were up 11–6, and threatening to walk away with the title. Lawyers, however, in basketball as in life, always try to get back up once you get them down, and Malicious started the second half with its own string of unanswered points, tying the score at 14.

The game unfolded with a steady flow of the kind of understated talent you might see at a small-college varsity match-up. Both teams played a style of basketball that placed a higher premium on team passing and careful shot selection than on individual acrobatics and both were more adept at jump shots than at slam dunks. And because both teams consisted of white players, the ugly racial divisions that had characterized some of the early-round contests—white fans rooting for white teams, black fans rooting for black teams—were missing today.

"For a vocal few on both sides, my calls were criticized solely on the basis of race," one of the Bookstore referees, a law student, wrote in a recent letter to *The Observer*, complaining publicly about an issue that was usually discussed in private. "The crowd also jeered the teams with racial stereotypes that went beyond the harmless generalizations of a basketball game and entered the venomous region of hate. . . . I saw both sides polarize into hostile camps. I saw blacks carry a distinctive chip on their shoulder, quite ready to blame me for perceived world injustices. I saw white bitterness and fear that I really had not seen before. I got the feeling that both sides wanted to be completely separate from the other. As long as this is the mentality, I fear that their wish will continue to be true."

In this year's tournament, the racial divide started widening even before the games began: A white team that called itself Ivory Side of the Dome, a none-too-subtle reference to the black team known as Ebony Side of the Dome, was asked to change its name. "The question that sticks in my mind," the captain of Ivory Side wrote in a letter to *The Observer*, "is why are the racial insinuations and innuendoes of Ebony Side glossed over and looked to as a positive expression of ancestral pride while Ivory Side is racist and motivated by bigotry? Is it not just as noble to to be proud of a European heritage as to find pride in an African one?" A white Ebony Side supporter wrote back in response. "On-campus black groups should not be looked at as some kind of exclusive society, but rather as people finding identity and support through others with similar backgrounds," her letter declared. "You cannot tell me that whites in our predominantly white society need support groups of other white people to reaffirm their identity as whites." A few rounds into the tournament, the great name debate was moot: Neither the ebony nor the ivory team made it as far as the Elite Eight.

Both of the teams that made it to the Final Two here today had relied on the services of players Lou Holtz had relied on, too—Eric Jones and Brian Ratigan for Tequila, Tom Gorman for Malicious. Part of the attraction of Bookstore is the opportunity it offers the laity to play with, or against, the varsity. Joe Montana played Bookstore, as did Bill Laimbeer, Tim Brown, John Paxson, Rocket Ismail, Bill Hanzlik, Rick Mirer, Adrian Dantley, Mark Bavaro, Orlando Woolridge, Tony Rice, and Kelly Tripucka, and many of them lost to teams led by anonymous five-foot-nine point guards whose careers in organized basketball had ended in high school. (Varsity basketball players are only permitted in Bookstore now when their NCAA eligibility has expired.) A bigger attraction, though, is the chance for a gym rat who usually plays to a soundtrack of empty echoes in the Rock to hear instead the kind of arena cheers Shannon Cullinan heard when he hit a jump shot. A four-point run by Tequila put them ahead now, 18–14.

As deep in the grip of spring as the campus seemed now, as far as it had traveled from the stadium weekends of football season—today was almost exactly halfway between the end of the last season and the start of the next— a persistent scent of autumn lingered in the air. The Blue-Gold game, the

varsity's spring scrimmage, had half filled the stadium yesterday, and the
campus had thrummed like a half-speed, practice version of a real football
weekend. Who played well and who didn't, and what it all meant for next
season, was the subject of much discussion today. Who would play where in
the pros come fall was another subject: The NFL draft was under way now.
Earlier this afternoon, more people had been watching ESPN in the dorm
lounges than were watching the Women's Bookstore championship game
here on this court. The Dillon Hall lounge had erupted in cheers when the
Washington Redskins, with the seventeenth pick in the first round, chose
dorm resident Tom Carter, who at this very moment was making his way
from his mother's small house in St. Petersburg, where he had watched the
draft in the close company of several dozen friends and family members, to
meet his new employers in the nation's capital. Three of his teammates were
also picked in the first round: quarterback Rick Mirer (second, by Seattle),
fullback Jerome Bettis (tenth, by the Los Angeles Rams), and tight end Irv
Smith (twentieth, by New Orleans).

"I'm glad it's over," Tom said when he returned to campus two days
later. "There's no more waiting. Now I can be the person I always wanted
to be."

The NFL draft didn't excuse Tom from the remaining days of the semester, but it did mean that his life would diverge sharply from his classmates'
once he finished his finals. He would report to the Redskins' minicamp,
where he hoped to room with his Notre Dame teammate Reggie Brooks,
Washington's second-round draft choice. He and his fiancée would be the
stars of a big Florida wedding; scheduled to serve among the ten grooms-
men were two other draft picks, Irv Smith and Demetrius DuBose (thirty-
fourth, by Tampa Bay); a fellow defensive back, junior John Covington; and
Carter's three-year roommate, Derrick Fluhme, whose athletic career was
confined to interhall teams and whose main preoccupation on draft day was
a fifteen-page virology paper due this week. Tom's new wife would weigh
her options among the graduate programs in English at universities in Redskins territory. He would sign a contract that would gain for him and his
mother a degree of financial security they had never experienced before.
"We have to wait for Rick Mirer and Bledsoe to sign first," the finance major
said, referring to the top two draft picks. "Supply and demand, baby." (The
contract he eventually signed was worth nearly $3 million over four years,
with a $1-million signing bonus.) He planned to return to Notre Dame next
spring, at the end of his first NFL season, to work toward finishing his degree, and to live off-campus with Fluhme.

No money, no careers, were at stake on the Stepan courts this afternoon, but the Bookstore final was proving to be a far more vivid athletic spectacle than the static NFL draft. Malicious whittled Tequila's ominous 18–14 lead to 18–17 before the teams resumed trading points. Tequila got the ball at 20–19, and the fans responded with a roar—some in hopes of staving off a defeat for Malicious, more in anticipation of celebrating a victory for Tequila, the tournament's sentimental favorites, and the vessels of under-graduate pride. Eric Jones missed from inside. Tequila got the ball again at 20–19, but Malicious stole it before they could take a shot. A Tequila foul al-lowed Malicious to make a successful free throw, forcing the game into win-by-two overtime. When Tequila scored its twenty-first point, a short turnaround jumper from Eric Jones in the lane, Malicious answered with its own. When Tequila scored its twenty-second point, a Brian Ratigan drive through a wall of defenders, Malicious answered again.

The crowd was on its feet now, roaring like a balmy, miniature reprise of the closing minutes of the snowy Penn State game, stoked by the dramatic climax of an otherwise lackluster An Tostal week. Bookstore Basketball had started as an offshoot of An Tostal (Gaelic for "The Festival"), a weeklong spring bash that featured keg tosses, mud pits, tug-of-war, and sundry other mildly masochistic varieties of college behavior. But the tighter alcohol pol-icy of recent years had removed the lubrication that made the festival run: "Who's gonna go into a mud pit sober?" one student asked rhetorically. More than one student watching here now was wearing the popular "Top 10 Lies Told at Notre Dame" T-shirt: "You don't need alcohol to have a good time at Notre Dame," was number one on the list. They looked excited enough now, though—and sober, too—as Tequila brought the ball upcourt, one point shy of victory.

Malicious had failed to answer Tequila's twenty-third point, a Brian Rati-gan free throw, leaving Tequila the chance to win the game—and the cham-pionship that had eluded all the other Tequila teams for twelve years—with a single, successful, sudden-death shot. In the back row, Malloy maintained his inscrutable demeanor. Tequila managed to get the ball inside to Eric Jones. The crowd surged expectantly. Jones moved toward the basket, but he was fouled before he got there. The crowd jeered: They didn't want to see such a dramatic game end from such an undramatic spot as the free-throw line. Jones obliged them, unwillingly, by missing. Tequila got the rebound, and the ball got back to Jones, way out at the top of the key, just beyond the three-point line. Undefended, he had the room to shoot, but, after just miss-ing a nearer free throw, did he have the touch? He did: The shot fell cleanly,

and the court filled with jubilant fans. The final score was 24–22, and the title was Tequila's. In the awards ceremony that followed, both Ratigan and
Jones were named to the All-Bookstore first team; Shannon Cullinan was
named Mr. Bookstore, the same honor his brother had received five years
earlier.

"The strategy worked," Malloy said, gratified. He slipped away quietly,
saving his congratulations for a less public forum, later—when Tequila, after twelve years of trying, finally brought the championship trophy home to
his dorm.

"How many people here have been to a funeral in the past five years?" Tom
Morris asked the students in the spring edition of his Philosophy 101 class.
Several dozen hands went up, and the low-pitched buzz that usually accom-
panied the start of each lecture began to fade. "My father died a week ago
Saturday, and it was the first funeral I've attended since seventh grade."

The steep lecture hall, filled though it was with freshmen, emptied of all
sound. They knew that Morris' father had died—the TAs told them when
class was canceled last week—but they hadn't heard him speak about it yet.
Notebooks stopped rustling, pens fell idle, and all eyes looked up to lock on
his: What he was telling them, they sensed, was something beyond the exam,
something that life alone could test them on. Set against the cathedral hush,
his voice had only the tiniest quaver in it.

"He died much too young, at the age of sixty-nine, after smoking three
packs of cigarettes a day for forty years," Morris, an only child, said of his father. The cancer was first detected in the lung, and the prognosis seemed
hopeful, but then it got into the brain, and the end came quickly. Not long
before his father died, Morris flew home to North Carolina with his wife
and their two children. His father could no longer speak by that point, but
he could still see and hear, and they were clearly the visitors he had been
waiting for. "There are things you already sort of know in your head, but it
takes living through them to give you existential knowledge. We're not just
talking theory here, we're talking reality."

Morris had originally planned to let his father's death pass unremarked
in class, but he soon realized that to do so would be to subvert what he perceived as his most important mission as a teacher, and as a philosopher—to
get people to think more deeply, more philosophically, about their lives. If
he could share the small stories of his life with his students—his loyalty to

Tarheels basketball, his Myrtle Beach rock-and-roll roots—then he should share the larger ones, too.

"I have to say, everything I believe as a Christian, everything I believe as a philosopher—nothing was contradicted by the texture of the experience," he said, sounding both gratified and comforted. "I learned so much last week, most of it confirming what I've spent decades learning and thinking about theoretically."

Trying to circle back toward the main topic of today's class—Blaise Pascal, the seventeenth-century French philosopher and scientist—Morris seemed to lose his way for a moment. As far off the point as he sometimes strayed, as many apparently unrelated stories and jokes as he told, his lectures usually flowed with a seamless narrative logic; but some cracks were showing now. His father's death was not in the lesson plan, and he strained for a suitable transition.

"We never know when people will be coming to our funerals," he said. "Will we have lived the kind of way we wanted to live?" A shaky bridge still lay between him and where he needed to be next. "Pascal was someone who grappled with life and death, with the question of what's important and what's not important."

Safely across now, Morris regained his bearings, telling the story of the mystical experience Pascal had at the age of thirty-one, his "night of fire," when the worldly young man became convinced that a person's relationship with God was the most important thing in life. The vision so transformed Pascal that, for the rest of his days, he carried a written account of that night on a parchment sewn into the lining of his coat. "He didn't want to be anybody's authority," Morris explained. "He wanted everybody to figure out for themselves what the ultimate truth was." Morris did, too, but he was willing to drop some hints. Turning to the overhead projector, he replaced his own crude drawing of Pascal's head with a more elegant rendering of one of Pascal's ideas.

"THERE ARE IMPORTANT MATTERS BEYOND THE SCOPE OF UNIVERSALLY CONVINCING, RATIONAL PROOF," he had printed in neat capital letters on the transparency, a declaration that echoed today with the oracular authority of chiseled granite.

Pascal was the subject of Morris' most recent book, *Making Sense of It All*, an attempt to find an audience beyond the fellow academics who constituted most of the readership for his previous nine books, and a precursor of sorts to the book he was writing now, *True Success: A New Philosophy of Ex-*

cellence. His dark days of personal loss had come amid an otherwise bright spring of professional gain. *True Success* had been bought by a big commercial publisher, Putnam's, earning him an advance of a size rarely seen by academic authors, and offering him a forum far larger than even the largest lecture hall could. He was at work on another book, too—*God and the Philosophers*, a collection of personal essays on religious belief by a variety of eminent philosophers that he was editing for Oxford University Press. He was in ever-greater demand as a speaker: Locally, he had addressed the Sorin Society members back on the weekend of the prolife sit-in; nationally, he had made a motivational video for a pharmaceutical company, aimed at nicotine-patch users who were having trouble quitting smoking. "Plato wrote lively dialogues, not abstract treatises," he often said, making no apologies for a career shift that drew sneers from some of his more staid colleagues. "If he were alive today, he'd be doing video and TV."

He placed a simple chart on the overhead now, with a sheet of paper covering all but the categories at the head of each column: "Bet," "Chance," "Payoff," "Cost," "Expectation." "Life is risk," he said by way of introducing the class to the subject of Pascal's Wager, the philosopher's memorable argument for belief in God. "Everything we do is a calculated bet. Everything we do is a wager. And how do rational gamblers bet?"

They bet by calculating their expectations against their risks: How good are the odds? How much is the bet? What is the potential payoff? "You can look at anything in life like this," Morris said. He then slid away the paper with the proud, expectant motion of a painter unveiling a portrait, revealing the chart that analyzed what happened when you looked at God through a gambler's eyes:

Bet	Chance	Payoff	Cost	Expectation
God	$^1/_2$	∞	Finite	∞
No God	$^1/_2$	Finite	0	Finite

"But it's the same no matter what numbers you use, even if the chance that God exists is only 1 percent," he said, pointing to the chance column.

If you bet that there is no God, your cost is nothing: You can lead a life without limits, heeding only the law of your own desires. You can lie, steal, cheat, even kill. You can indulge your every wish, and flout every rule of morality and custom. But what's the payoff if you're right? Only what you can consume and carry in this lifetime—after that lies nothing but a long, black eternity, and a moldering, worm-eaten grave.

"So what is the cost of believing in God?" Morris asked, outlining the alternative bet. "You have to do some things you might not want to do, like love your neighbor even if he's a jerk. You have to drag your half-dead carcass to church on Sunday morning. But it's still a finite cost. And what's the payoff if you're right? Eternal bliss, an infinite payoff."

A rational gambler, therefore—measuring the cost of each wager against the potential payoff—would bet on God. The argument, as Morris explained it, avoided the messy, theoretical question of whether God existed or not ("Reason cannot decide this question," Pascal wrote), and focused instead on the more practical question of whether, in the absence of proof one way or the other, it was cost-effective to believe in God anyway—a clear and simple exercise in rational deduction that broke like sunlight through the fuzzy clouds of logic in the average undergraduate mind. It was not a difficult point, but to grasp it made the freshmen feel like philosophers, just as Morris wanted.

"When it comes to putting your bets on, there's no middle ground," Morris told them. "Either you're living as if there is a God, or you're living as if there's no God. Which way are you betting?"

The band, having just finished the Marine Corps hymn, was tootling jauntily through "Anchors Aweigh" when Monk Malloy entered the building and walked quickly across the Astroturf, his long, athletic stride far out of step with the music. Massed at midfield, under the high Loftus Center roof, was close to 10 percent of the undergraduate population—all sharp edges, solemn faces, and silence, standing stiffly at attention for a ritual that was largely a mystery to the other 90 percent. The Army, Navy, Air Force, and Marines were joined together here today for the annual semester-ending exercise in military ecumenism known as the Joint ROTC Presidential Parade. A tiny handful of civilians watched from the sidelines. Malloy was wearing his own formal uniform, dress blacks, as he climbed the steps to the reviewing stand that had been erected at the fifty-yard line. The band struck up "Stars and Stripes Forever," and a color guard marched smartly past.

Standing amid the ranks of the Navy unit, the largest ROTC unit at Notre Dame, was the woman who had stood with the officers the previous semester, Allison McCurdy, the former battalion commander. "If you start to feel dizzy, you better flex your knees or you'll pass out," she reminded them. Today's was the fourth and final presidential parade for Allison and her sixty-nine fellow senior midshipmen. In less than three weeks, they would be commissioned, graduated, and dispatched to their first assignments. Twenty-four were headed to nuclear-power school to become submariners—a coveted and difficult path, and a testament to the strength of Notre Dame's unit—ten would train to be aviators, fifteen would serve on surface ships, and the rest would work either as supply officers or in various shore-duty jobs. Allison was bound for San Diego, her first choice, to become an industrial-hygiene officer, also her first choice. For the next two years, she would be visiting Navy workplaces in search of flaking asbestos, chemical pollutants, excessive noise, and other industrial hazards. "Some of my friends tell me to keep quiet if I even mention the number of days left to graduation," she said. "Me, I'm ready to go. I want to see new things and meet new people."

Her grade-point average was up around 3.6 again this semester, the same neighborhood she had first moved into last fall, but her senior surge wasn't enough to overcome her two D's in organic chemistry as a sophomore. Her original goal, medical school, was "definitely on the back burner now." After the last med-school rejection letter, she dropped biochemistry, a med-school requirement that was giving her more trouble than she needed, and replaced it with something more immediately useful, an independent study in industrial hygiene. "It took me until senior year to figure out how all this works," she said about academic life at Notre Dame.

She had figured out the Navy much earlier, and the Navy had shown its appreciation not only by making her battalion commander and granting her assignment request, but also by awarding her a ceremonial Navy sword—the same kind her father had—at an earlier gathering. The length of an officer's sword is determined by the officer's height, and since she was short, so was her sword. "There were two tall guys at the ceremony who got theirs first, and when I got up, somebody said, 'She's getting a dagger.' "

Joe Carrigan—her second-in-command last semester, back in the ranks with her today—received an honor of his own recently, too: He had lost the championship fight in the 150-pound division, but he was the winner when the sportsmanship award was announced at the Bengal Bouts banquet. His first stop in the Navy after commissioning would be Newport, Rhode Island—four months at Surface Warfare Officers' School, to prepare him for his first ship, the USS *Aubrey Fitch*, a frigate out of Jacksonville, Florida. Along the way, he hoped to get to some of the books his professors and commanders had recommended for the lifetime reading program he was compiling. "We were having a typical dorm conversation, and the idea for getting book lists came up," he said. Tom Morris, whose final class Joe would attend tomorrow, put together a list that included Plato, Kierkegaard, Wendell Berry, Freeman Dyson, J. R. R. Tolkien, and, inevitably, Pascal.

The midshipmen and cadets all stood at parade rest as their civilian commander took the podium. "Leadership is very simple descriptively, but complicated in the doing," said Malloy, who could have been talking as much about himself—trying to mediate the many competing interests at Notre Dame—as about his audience. "There are no simple answers for conflicts among groups and peoples."

The annual presidential parade was a chance for Malloy—who had neither served himself nor achieved the kind of honorary veteran status accorded Hesburgh, whose early career ambition was to be a Navy chaplain—to mark a close relationship between Notre Dame and the military that reaches back to the school's earliest years. During the Civil War, Sorin sent seven Holy Cross priests to serve as chaplains with the Union Army—most notably Father William Corby, later a president of Notre Dame, who accompanied the troops through such campaigns as Antietam, Fredericksburg, Chancellorsville, Spotsylvania, and The Wilderness. On the eve of battle at Gettysburg, Corby donned his purple stole, stood upon a rock, and offered absolution to all—a scene commemorated by the statue that stands now in front of Corby Hall, its right arm raised in a gesture of blessing that has earned it the familiar nickname of *Fair Catch Corby*. Later that century, some militia-minded students offered to join the Papal States in the fight against Garibaldi in Italy; the pope declined, asking them to send money instead. Tensions surfaced during the Vietnam era—at the 1968 parade, the ROTC students had to march around several hundred protesters who sat themselves down in front of the reviewing stand—and questions are still raised periodically about the apparent contradictions involved in maintaining such a large military presence at a Catholic university that also supports a Peace Institute; but the voices of dissent had been silent this year.

"The Vietnam Memorial moves me deeply," Malloy said, returning briefly to another place he had lived that was well stocked with military personnel, his hometown of Washington, D.C. "In its simplicity it reminds us that military service is not an individual enterprise, but the work of groups."

In addressing a ROTC audience like this, Malloy couldn't draw on the same body of experience as could Hesburgh, who still spoke with boyish enthusiasm about his aircraft-carrier visits and supersonic-jet rides. He focused instead on a theme he believed they all shared here—the surpassing value of community life, a lesson that he had learned as a member of both the Holy Cross and Notre Dame communities, and that he thought would prove useful to these future members of the military community. It was a sincere effort on his part to find some common ground, but his reflective tone didn't quite match the shiny, brassy atmosphere of the occasion. When he finished speaking, the band struck up another Sousa march, "The Washington Post," and the students started their parade. The blue and green units of cadets and midshipmen marched crisply by the review stand, turning smartly to salute their commanders as they passed. They continued upfield, advancing toward the goal line like some slow, giant backfield. When they crossed into the end zone, greeted by no fanfare, they turned a wide corner and marched right back to where they had started from.

In the dim, windowless entomology lab in the basement of the biology building, the screen on the TV monitor was bright with swarming images of mosquitoes at various stages of their life cycle. "While in the pupa stage, the mosquito is transforming into an adult," the video's narrator told the small morning audience—the students in George Craig's "Aquatic Insects" class, seniors mostly, who, on this final day of classes, were emerging from a pupa stage of their own. "The adult male feeds on plant juices. The adult female must also feed on animal blood in order to reproduce."

The material in this short video on mosquito control was barely past kindergarten level to Craig's students, who by now could tell one mosquito species from another, segment by segment. His purpose in screening it was to show them instead just how soon yesterday's control strategies became outdated, how quickly mosquitoes outsmarted humans, how fast evolution outran science, and how great a challenge awaited them as entomologists in the teeming world outside.

"OK, so everything's peachy keen," Craig said facetiously when the video ended. "I wish it were so. I'd like to end up with a few remarks about how none of it is working anymore. It's in a state of collapse."

His doom-struck rhetoric was familiar by now to his students, who knew it was his way of stressing to them the importance of entomological research. Far from throwing up his hands in the face of the pestilential swarms, he was instead eager to stay in the trenches, fighting. His research grant from the National Institutes of Health had just been renewed,

$2.5 million over the next five years. "That'll make forty years of continuous funding from NIH," he said, a record few scientists could match.

Craig outlined for the class the shortcomings of each of the existing methods of mosquito control. New wetlands-conservation laws mean that breeding-ground marshes can no longer be drained. Pesticides are suspect ("In the minds of the public, all pesticides are evil"), and chemical companies are reluctant to invest in efforts to develop new ones. Biological control—attacking the mosquitoes with special strains of bacteria, for instance—has failed to live up to its promises. Bug zappers, he said, are good "only if you like the smell of fried moth." The only real solution, in his view, is to close what he called the "terrible scientific talent gap"—to train more entomologists and send them into battle.

"The population assumes that everything's been done, but it's not true," he said, sounding like a recruiting poster.

Craig's pessimism about mosquitoes was balanced by his optimism about his students. Last month, he had taken five of them, undergraduates as well as graduates, to Fargo, North Dakota, to compete in the Linnaean Games, an insect-centric Trivial Pursuit match sponsored by the Entomological Society of America. The team had trained for weeks at special lunchtime study sessions: "There's an arsenical compound used in insect control that has a distinctive color—what is it?" someone would ask. "Paris green," somebody would quickly answer. They knew they were at a disadvantage going into the games—most of the other teams were exclusively grad students—but they had high hopes for their chances. Then they saw the match schedule.

"We got a bad draw," Craig said, understating his case for once. They faced Purdue, the defending national champions, in the first round. They lost, 65–60. "They were heroes," he said of his team's performance. "We're preparing for next year already. It's going to be high noon at Dodge City. They better come out with their guns blazing."

The day after exams ended, Craig would leave behind his lab—with its cages full of mosquitoes, forty species and two hundred strains in all—and return to the field, taking fifteen students with him on his annual trek up to Notre Dame's environmental-research center at Land O'Lakes, Wisconsin. "Aedes Boot Camp," he called it, after the virus-carrying genus of mosquitoes he studied most often. He would also leave behind, temporarily at least, the Catholic Character debate that had so thoroughly irritated him—and that had briefly faded now against the frantic scramble of semester's end.

"There are thirty species of mosquitoes there, lots of no-see-ums, black

flies, horseflies, deer flies, ticks with Lyme disease," he said, and there would
be little talk about Catholic hiring quotas. "What more could a medical entomologist want?"

Peri Arnold was headed north soon, too—after he graded the final exams
in his "American Presidency" class, to canoe and fish in the Canadian wilds
with a colleague from the physics department—but what a political scientist
wanted on such a trip was considerably different from what an entomologist
wanted: He would prefer to see as few, not as many, mosquitoes as possible.
"You do get a sense of the cycle of the year now, that you really are finished
with something," he said about the semester's end. First, though, he had to
teach one last class.

"What is success in the presidency?" he began, posing to the students the
rhetorical question that would occupy their final seventy-five minutes together. "What do we look for? What do we expect?"

What we expected from Bill Clinton or George Bush was, as Arnold had
pointed out all semester, much more than what our great-grandparents had
expected from Calvin Coolidge or Warren Harding. It was Franklin Roosevelt who did the most to change those expectations, fashioning the presidency into what Arnold called "the center of national planning" and
changing the standard by which all his successors would be measured.

"We have no ways of conceiving a presidential performance now other
than the ways we judge a rock star on a stage," Arnold said. "There is a logic
within the modern presidency that drives presidents to short-term considerations of goals and of the political consequences of goals."

But whereas a king might be what we long for now—a leader not beholden to politics, free to pursue long-term goals—a president is still what
the Constitution decrees that we shall have. "The institution simply doesn't
match the expectations," he said. "It's as if we expect Mick Jagger on that
stage and instead we're getting local beer-hall talent."

Next year Arnold would be doing his thinking about the presidency in a
library, not a classroom. He would be spending one week each month at a
University of Virginia's research center, where he had won a sabbatical-year
appointment, working on his second book—an examination of the pre-
FDR, Progressive-era seeds of institutional change in the presidency. Before
he left, though, he was due to pick up a special award at the Presidential
Dinner that follows graduation each year. "A colleague who consistently
represents the voice of reasoned argument, he is noted also for his open
mind and collegial goodwill," the citation read. "His scholarship on the

American presidency has earned him not only the appreciation of academic colleagues but also respect as an expert witness in Washington."

In sounding a final note for the class now, Arnold was almost as pessimistic about the state of politics as George Craig was about the state of entomology. "The script for the president is that you are the savior, you will change all bad things to good," he said in a tone that suggested the script needed rewriting. "I don't think the presidency at this point is a particularly healthy institution. American government is not in very good shape, and the presidency may be the key to the problem."

He left them with another, smaller warning, too—about the exam, which would consist of four essay questions. "And I want you to please try to keep it to twenty minutes apiece," he said. "The very thought of you all writing for a full two hours gives me a pain in my chest."

19

Monk Malloy's room in Sorin Hall is built along the same lines that he is, tall and thin, with eighteen-foot ceilings and a narrow girth, but tonight it made even him look small. He sat at his modest desk, finally tackling the *New York Times* that his cramped schedule had kept him from since morning, illuminated only by two small lamps that left the room's upper atmosphere clouded with shadows. A basketball game provided the low background music, the Trail Blazers playing the Spurs on the TV in the corner. He had changed out of his black priest's suit and into a red V-neck sweater and khakis. The "welcome" sign was up on the door outside, but he expected few visitors now. The campus all around him was sprinting toward the finish, busy and weary with the duties and rituals that had to be completed before the year could close. Monk Hoops had ended, and the final papers in his Freshman Seminar had been graded. The students would soon be leaving, bound for their homes, while he stayed here, bound to his.

"The mystique of Notre Dame, that seemingly incomprehensible measure of loyalty and devotion to the University that characterizes so many of our graduates and friends, is best-explained through the on-campus living experience of the students," Malloy had written in the final report of the Colloquy for the Year 2000, speaking both as a dorm resident and as the president. "The residence halls are places where values are clarified, friendships are formed, and faith is tested and professed. There is nothing to replace simply being there through the cycle of the seasons and the years."

After being here through most of the seasons of his adult life—after living for fourteen years on the same floor where a pair of undergraduates, brothers from Massachusetts, wrote the fight song in 1906—Malloy had emerged as the ur-Domer, a figure who encompassed the full range of the Notre Dame experience, from freshman to trustee; and his management style consisted largely in trying to get other people to see things through that same many-angled lens. As an associate provost, he had conducted a marathon string of individual interviews with almost every member of the faculty. As president, he had chosen more than a hundred people from every corner of Notre Dame to participate in the Colloquy, a year-long series of meetings that mulled over the questions, great and small, about the university's future, and that proved, like the late-night dorm bull sessions it echoed in form and ambition, both tedious and enlightening. The Colloquy so far had amply demonstrated what few people, even among his critics, had doubted about Malloy—his capacity to listen. Now that it was over, the question was whether it would also demonstrate what some remained unconvinced of—his capacity to lead. Like the post-FDR presidents under discussion in Peri Arnold's government class, Malloy had the burden of succeeding an outsized legend who had radically changed the shape and scope of the office. The Colloquy was his most ambitious attempt yet to remake the presidency in his own image. "There's a certain generational group for whom Ted was such a dominant personality in their exposure to Notre Dame—everything revolved around him," he said, referring to Hesburgh. "It doesn't revolve around me, nor do I want it to."

After all the Colloquy committee reports were in, Malloy took them with him to the NCAA Final Four in New Orleans. He shut the door to his hotel room, ordered room service, and—breaking only for the games and an NCAA Foundation board meeting—wrote "a big hunk, maybe two-thirds," of the final report. "Getting away was necessary for me to make real progress, because when I'm here there's too much stuff going on," he said.

The report was officially unveiled this morning, distributed through campus, and discussed at an all-day trustees' meeting—a thirty-eight-page essay that sketched a map of Notre Dame's future and offered an implicit spending plan for the money expected to be raised by the upcoming capital campaign. It was, as Malloy wrote in the preface, "my personal vision," and it included among its forty-three recommendations several that addressed issues of special personal concern to him—more financial aid, stepped-up efforts at achieving more "cultural diversity," a new bookstore that would actually be stocked with more books than T-shirts. It recognized areas of weakness—the library, the shortage of faculty, the uncertain place of women—and it called for more committees and studies to find ways to strengthen them. It plainly stated Notre Dame's ambitions for greater academic status: "The University should set the goal of becoming one of the premier private universities in the country, renowned for research as well as teaching," read recommendation 20. It compiled a list of planned and proposed building projects—a new home for the business school; a performing-arts facility; a new lab for George Craig's beloved research center at Land O'Lakes; a major overhaul of the Main Building; more twenty-four-hour social space in the dorms, where men and women could openly, legally, share one another's company after parietals.

To the wider world, the most newsworthy item was recommendation 33: "The University administration should move forward with concrete plans to expand the present football stadium," a prospect that would mortify traditionalists loath to change a single brick of the original Rockne shrine, but would mollify alumni frustrated by the ever-tighter ticket supply. To professors and administrators, though, the report's larger significance lay in its pervasive focus on the issue of Notre Dame's Catholic character.

"In recruiting new faculty, each department must make energetic efforts to hire faculty of the highest caliber who seek to participate in the intellectual life of a dynamic Catholic university," declared the very first recommendation. "All who participate in hiring faculty must be cognizant of and responsive to the need for dedicated and committed Catholics to predominate in number among the faculty."

There was a firebell echo in Malloy's recommendation, an undercurrent of alarm fed by the denominationally dismal results of the spring hiring season: Only 37 percent of the new faculty hired for next fall—and just one of the eight hired in the College of Science—were Catholic, the lowest percentage ever. "At the departmental level, we're not even seeing lip service being paid to the affirmative action for Catholics," Malloy said later. "If that's not addressed, you can just kiss Notre Dame goodbye over time as a Catholic university."

Even before its publication, the Colloquy report—particularly recommendation 1, which had already appeared in an earlier committee report—had set off some rumbling, most loudly in the faculty senate. The concern in the senate was that, despite the April Accords truce that had followed their threatened no-confidence vote last spring, the voices of the faculty still seemed to carry little weight under the Dome. Though he might appear to be listening to the professors, they feared that the only voices he really heard were the priests'—especially the two most prominent powers behind the throne: Father Dick Warner, the former Holy Cross provincial and the counselor to the president, and Father Bill Beauchamp, the executive vice president. Armed with polls showing faculty skepticism about the Colloquy, the senate had voted at their last meeting to ask that "no action be taken to implement" the recommendations until the final report had been more widely and thoroughly discussed.

"There are two possibilities," one member had speculated before the vote. "Either the president has grossly misread the sentiment of the faculty, or the president is willing to offer a vision of the university that goes against the sentiments of the majority of the faculty. Either one is a damnable offense."

"The president has backed himself into a political corner, and in a Gandhian sense we've got to give him a little room," another countered. "I don't think there's any possible way we can stop this train now. But I think it's important to let the trustees and the community know that we're not on this train."

"But he acts as if he received infallibility with ordination," fumed a third.

At today's meeting, the trustees—as they had planned all along, regardless of how the faculty senate voted—took no action on the Colloquy report beyond discussion, thus launching in private a debate that would continue for years in public, and that would reach beyond campus to the larger constituencies with a stake in Notre Dame: the alumni, the big donors, the Vatican, the entire American Catholic church, each with its own ideas about the theory and practice of Notre Dame's Catholicity. They all fight so hard for Notre Dame—conservatives and liberals alike, those who want to close abortion clinics and those who want to open the priesthood to women—because Notre Dame seems so tantalizingly close to their ideal vision of Catholicism, whatever it is. They tend to view Notre Dame's sins as what the old catechisms called sins of omission rather than sins of commission, and they are quick to forgive once they get within sight of the Dome.

"In the face of contemporary indifference to religion, only an institution like Notre Dame can provide credible evidence that academic freedom and denominational affiliation are compatible and mutually enriching values," Malloy wrote in the epilogue to the final Colloquy report, reaching his highest pitch of eloquence in its penultimate paragraph. "Only an institution like Notre Dame can expose both society and the Church to the kind of respectful but critical analysis that is conducive to structural renewal. Only an institution like Notre Dame can create an intellectual community and forum where every dimension of human experience is pondered, religious and secular, personal and social. The test of our Catholic character will be in the details. To this, let us devote our collective attention and good will."

In his room now, Malloy turned from his newspaper to the game on the TV, drawn by the crowd roar that followed a long-distance jump shot that touched nothing but net. It was exactly 10:00 p.m., and the bells next door at Sacred Heart started playing the alma mater. Theirs is a slow, tinny rendition, and through most of the year it calls to mind a child plinking on a toy piano. But tonight—the end looming, the Domers dispersing—it took on a different character, suggesting instead a lone mourner pecking at a parlor piano, haltingly and inexpertly, on the long afternoon of a wake. The lights in Malloy's room would stay on for several more hours yet, as the low, large yellow moon outside, just shy of full, rose higher through the sky over campus.

"There are fifty of us in the sanctuary," Father Hesburgh said from the altar of Sacred Heart, opening a special Mass marking the fiftieth anniversary of his ordination. "That seems to be an appropriate number for today."

The actual anniversary wasn't until next month, and the traditional jubilee Mass for his ordination class—for him and the eight other priests remaining from the sixteen young men ordained that day fifty years ago—wasn't until after graduation, but the trustees, visiting campus to discuss the future with Malloy, wanted also to honor the past with Hesburgh. The bells had pealed for fifteen minutes before the start of Mass, and the processional hymn, "Sing with All the Saints," had been sung to the tune of Beethoven's "Ode to Joy." The fifty concelebrating priests stood in close ranks behind the altar, the same number that had gathered here for the more solemn Mass that had closed the fall semester, Moose Krause's funeral. The front pews were dense with white-haired, dark-suited trustees. In attendance were all four of the men who had served as chairmen in the quarter-century since Hesburgh ceded control of Notre Dame to a lay board. Some seats were still available in the rear pews, though: To much of the campus, busy as it was now with the taking and grading of exams, Hesburgh had already passed into history.

After Malloy read the Gospel, Hesburgh took the pulpit to deliver a homily that barely mentioned his tenure as president, dwelling instead on his vocation as a priest. "I can think of fifty years of Masses, every day and all over the world," he said. Hesburgh tended toward the progressive in his politics—he had marched for civil rights with Martin Luther King, and spoken against the Vietnam War at campus protest rallies—but in his piety he was firmly traditional. He quietly blessed the campus whenever he flew over it in a plane, and he said Mass daily, whether he was in South Bend or at the South Pole, a streak that exceeded his obligations as a priest but fulfilled a pledge he had made to himself after his ordination. He had missed his daily Mass only once, when he was chaplain at Vetville, the married students' housing complex that sprang up after World War II, and he was standing vigil with an expectant father; the tiny premature boy he baptized that night went on to graduate from Notre Dame. "I think of Masses in very odd places, but always the same—always the offering of all we are and have, together, for the salvation of the world."

By this season of his life, Hesburgh had grown accustomed to hearing himself fêted at testimonials where his accomplishments were spoken of mostly in the past tense. He had already surpassed Herbert Hoover as the champion recipient of honorary doctorates, and he was slated to collect three more this spring—from Notre Dame College in New Hampshire, Mount Mercy College in Iowa, and Wake Forest University—bringing the total to 127. (Notre Dame's own commencement would mark a more personal milestone: His nephew was graduating, the fourteenth and last of his nieces and nephews to graduate from Notre Dame.) But as much as his public life was spent now in looking backward, in his private life, surrounded by books and mementos up in his library office, he was still looking ahead.

"One of the things I'm going to try to do this summer is to fiddle around with another paper on 'What is a Catholic university?' " he had said in his office recently. He had stayed on the sidelines through the debate about Notre Dame's Catholic character this year ("No one asked me," he said about his absence from the Conversation meetings; "I would have gone if I were asked"), but he had watched with great interest, and occasional frustration. "You get hackles up, because people don't put things in perspective. They say, 'Well, you can't be "predominantly Catholic," ' " he said, quoting the phrase from the Colloquy's mission statement that had sparked such consternation, "but the fact is we've been predominantly Catholic for the last 150 years." The issue struck a deep chord with Hesburgh—the president who was, after all, more instrumental than any of his predecessors in building a Notre Dame as noted for its scholarship as its faith ("First of all it's got to be a great university—that's the noun, 'university'; 'Catholic' is an adjective"); who knew what skepticism such ambitions could raise in secular academic circles ("Anti-Catholicism is the anti-Semitism of the intellectual"); who, one summer early in his presidency, had scouted Europe for Catholic intellectuals he hoped to lure to South Bend ("There's a longer tradition than the kind of facile, superficial intellectual tradition we have in many parts of America"); and who knew that doctrinal orthodoxy was not a substitute for academic excellence ("You don't honor God with mediocrity," he often said).

"I think I know what it means to be a great Catholic university. I think I can visualize doing it," he said. "I think that, rather than make this a big brawl, what we ought to do is simply say to anybody who wants to come here to teach, 'Look, we're a very special kind of institution. We pay well; we have greater freedom than most universities, including most state universities; we have great aspirations; and we have a great student body. But we are something definable, and here's what we are. Now, if that offends you, or you don't find it compatible with your own intellectual life, well, you'd be dumb to come here.' "

After Mass, Hesburgh heard more testimonials at a private dinner in his honor hosted by the trustees. Once the trustees were gone, he returned to his usual campus routine of saying his daily Mass in the tiny chapel up in his thirteenth-floor office suite, often alone or accompanied only by his long-time second-in-command, Father Ned Joyce. Featured prominently now in the sitting room adjacent to the chapel was his fiftieth-anniversary gift from the trustees—a small statue of the Madonna and Child, a copy of one that had been made for the pope. Also on display there was a small photo of a distant patch of night sky, an arrow pointing at a speck of white—the Hesburgh asteroid, 227 million miles away, in the constellation Coma Berenices. Named for him by an admiring astronomer, it has a diameter of eight miles, a circumference of twenty-five miles, and a magnitude of 15.6, and it makes him one of the few human beings who have become heavenly bodies while still on earth.

"Devote no more than *twenty* minutes to each question you choose," Peri Arnold's final exam reminded those students who might have forgotten his admonition at the last meeting of Government 404. Before they started writing, they scanned the eight questions, choosing the four they would answer. "Describe and explain the relationship between the emergence of the plebiscitary presidency and the state of American political parties," read one of them.

Rarely is the isolation of a college campus more apparent than during exam week, when the students all race toward their personal goal lines, deeply absorbed in a private saga of victory and defeat about which the wider world knows little and cares less. The computer rooms were backed up, the study lounges filled. Mountain Dew, with that extra jolt of caffeine, was as popular on cram nights as Meisterbräu on SYR nights, and Papa John's was delivering study-break pizzas by the carload. Who would make Dean's List and who wouldn't was being decided this week, who would pass and who would fail, who would be going to med school and who would be switching majors. The organic-chemistry final had left several students in tears.

"I'm supposed to start September 1—that's if they still let me go after they see my econ," Lou Blaum said about his own med-school plans. His orgo trials were long past, but there was still the matter of music, English, philosophy, a pair of psychology courses, and, unfortunately, economics. "I just can't get a grasp on it. I'm so science-minded, I need hard evidence— but in economics everything's so uncertain."

He sat on his bed in Stanford Hall, book open, jug of lemonade at his side. His room—disassembled already, like all the other rooms on campus, for the year-end damage inspections—had all the charm of a naked Army barracks. He had sold his loft to a freshman down the hall for $85. His desk held what few personal effects remained—a framed med-school acceptance letter from Thomas Jefferson University; a small yellow "Play Like a Champion Today" towel draped over the lamp; a perfumed teddy bear that his girlfriend in Mexico had sent as a birthday gift. He had met her when he went on a Caribbean cruise with his father last summer, stayed in touch through long-distance calls that sometimes pushed his monthly phone bill past $150, and hoped to visit her Mexico City home in August. "It keeps me from going out much," he said of his costly telephone habit.

The weather was warm enough now so that he had packed away the Irish Guard sweatshirt he had worn in the Bookstore Basketball tournament. "I didn't know until the day before the game," he said about his team's name: Four Social Drinkers and the Irish Guard. "Nobody wanted to tell me." They won in the first round, lost in the second. "It's kind of ironic, since they all drink much more than I do."

Lou set down one book and picked up another. "I'm one of those people who have to work for their grades," he said. His med-school acceptance had

finally eased the pressure some, though: For the first time in his undergraduate career, he expected to get through an exam week without a single all-
nighter. "All I do is associate this place with stress," he said about Notre
Dame. "But it actually paid off. It actually happened."

Kevin Kuwik, by contrast, had endured the longer nights of a freshman.
"I've had six hours of sleep in the last two nights," he said. "If it wasn't for
the rush of adrenaline, you'd be going, 'Oh my God, I haven't slept.' But
you're not sure you have the material grasped, that's what keeps you going."
His Army ROTC obligations were finished for the semester, his A's on all
the earlier tests had exempted him from the final in "American Military History," and his grade on the physics exam had already been posted: an A.
What remained were last-day finals in calculus and materials science.
"That's gonna be the hard one," he said of the latter. He often liked to study
on the tenth floor of the library, near a window with a view of the Dome,
but the eighty-degree sunshine this afternoon had lured him out to the wide
lawn beside DeBartolo Hall. He sat shirtless in the grass, working through
his materials-science text. "It's not enough in this class just to know the
facts."

On the other side of campus, in the sunny quad between the library and
her dorm, Siegfried Hall, Rachel Stehle sat cross-legged on a blanket, studying calculus. "Astronomy and anthropology weren't too bad," she said.
"Philosophy was pretty hard." Calculus would be, too, she expected. The
night exams finally ended, she and her boyfriend planned to have dinner at
The Olive Garden, a bittersweet occasion, both of farewell—they were parting for the summer, she to Sandusky, he to Des Moines—and of celebration.
They would be back on campus sooner than most of their classmates,
though, trumpets in hand, reporting for band practice. "It's just about
over," she sighed, mourning the end of her freshman year. "I don't want to
think about it."

As Rachel studied, the campus all around her was bustling with the machinery of departure—sophomores and juniors who, not tethered here until
the last day like the freshmen, had finished their work and were now packing up, loading up, and moving out. In Keenan Hall, old clothes and sneak-
ers were piling up outside Brother Bonaventure Scully's door, earmarked for
the St. Vincent de Paul Society. Scully himself was hurrying toward his car,
giving a Keenanite a ride to the bus. Even as the students were leaving, he
was still trying, gently but persistently, to recruit them for various volunteer
service positions. "There's a drug-rehab center in Louisiana that needs

somebody," he said. After graduation, he was headed to Europe for a two-week trip that would include a retreat in France and his first visit to Rome. He would be back at Keenan in the fall, teaching his Freshman Seminar again and facing a dorm populated by more seniors than he had expected, or thought wise. "I think they ought to move off-campus as seniors," said Scully, who believed the transition from adolescence to adulthood was protracted enough as it was. "They're twenty-one, they should know what a refrigerator is, they should know what a stove is. It's too easy for them here." His own retirement dream—to start a small community house in the inner city, perhaps in his hometown of Baltimore, that would be home to both brothers and lay people—would have to wait at least another year.

On the rector's door in Pasquerilla West, Laurie Brink—in Chicago briefly, on business with the Dominican community she was joining—had posted a simple message to those whose departures she would miss: "Have a good summer," it read, "I'll miss you." She had already said a more emotional goodbye at the dorm's final Sunday-night Mass—"definitely a three-tissue Mass," she said. The senior slide show before Mass had featured a section on Tara Deutsch, the PW resident who had died over spring break; a rose and a candle were set on a table before the altar in her memory. After communion, Brink gave the seniors the dream catchers she had made for each of them—small, round, weblike ornaments that, in the Ojibway Indian tradition, are meant to hang over a bed and catch the dreams drifting by. "The good dreams know the way and slip through the center hole and slide down off the soft feather so gently the sleeper below hardly knows they are dreaming," she explained. "The bad dreams, not knowing the way, get entangled in the webbing and perish with the first light of the new day."

In Flanner Hall, a student who feared he had blown a key exam turned to Father Bill Seetch for solace. "Is there anything you can do about it?" Seetch asked, knowing that the answer now, of course, was no. "Then let it go. Just let it go."

While the students cleared out the private spaces of Flanner this week, Seetch was busy in the public spaces, turning up several treasures for Brother Clarence—who worked on the other side of the lake, as director of maintenance for the Holy Cross community, and who cruised the Dumpsters at year's end in search of merchandise for the big annual garage sale he ran. One of the few remaining brothers from the huge corps that once constituted the bulk of the support staff on campus, Brother Clarence had filled a barn-sized garage behind the seminary with his finds, throwing it open for sale the week before each fall semester and earning as much as $15,000 for the community. He drove his familiar red pickup over to Flanner and carted off a refrigerator, a Ping-Pong table, and, best of all, an old Nehi cooler.

Seetch left the dorm and walked across the taut and nervous campus to Corby Hall for Mass in the chapel, dinner in the refectory, and a brief evening cigar in one of the high-backed cane rockers on the serene front porch. The Corby porch was a welcome refuge from dorm havoc for Seetch, and on those nights when he counted himself especially blessed, he was joined here by Father Charles Carey, the most articulate, courtly, and comprehensive source of local lore. Carey had been at Notre Dame for seventy-one years, all of them still intact in his memory now, unclouded by the fog of age. He had arrived as a freshman at the since-departed high-school seminary, a nephew of a Holy Cross priest who would later serve as president, Father Charles O'Donnell. The golf course had been a farm, and most of the South Quad wasn't even in the blueprint stage yet. He watched the Four Horsemen from the wooden stands at Cartier Field. He sang in the choir at Rockne's funeral, and marched in the procession nine years later, when the Pat O'Brien version was filmed. He still said Mass each morning at six at one of the private altars in the basement of Sacred Heart.

"That's who I want to be when I grow up," Seetch said.

Seetch rocked slowly with his cigar, waving occasionally at a passing student. He filled the chair more amply now than he had in the fall: Following its usual pattern, his weight had climbed through the course of the year, up toward 270 pounds. "I have three sizes of clothes," he said. "Large, extra-large, and Hindenburg." A summer stint at the Holy Cross camp in rural Maryland—chopping wood, clearing brush, cutting grass—would help put him back in fighting trim, and prepare him for another year as Flanner's rector. To prepare himself for another year as Flanner's interhall football coach, he had visited several varsity practices this spring, looking for ways to improve his own team. "You really see the importance of fundamentals at practice, the repetition of the basics," he said, finding some lessons there that had meaning beyond the gridiron. "The key thing is that you have to be able to be doing something in this moment while looking at the next."

As the evening faded into night, as the Corby porch emptied and the study lamps in the dorms flicked on, the bars off-campus started filling with unburdened upperclassmen who had taken their last exams. The Linebacker was doing an especially brisk trade with the seniors these days: It was slated to close soon, doomed by a new road project, and they saw in its imminent demise a fitting symbol for the demise of their own brief reign at Notre

Dame. Piled behind one of the North Quad dorms tonight was the stray lumber from several defunct lofts, raw studs and four-by-fours of the type that would catch Brother Clarence's eye. Scrawled on one wide beam was someone's parting message: "The Journey Has Ended."

"I'll see you later," Geoff Slevin said to Dana Ciacciarelli as she left Coach's and headed back to campus. He was heading on to the Linebacker with some friends.

"Call me," she said.

They had spent the evening celebrating an important milestone in their lives—the end of their academic careers at Notre Dame. Earlier today, Geoff had taken his Civil War history exam and turned in his final chemical-engineering assignment, a seventy-page group project that outlined a design for a propylene-oxide reactor. Dana had finished her specimen collection for George Craig's entomology class—110 insects, identified and labeled—and struggled through the final. "Everyone came out dumbfounded," she said of the exam, which asked the students to identify twenty-five insects and complete four "unbelievably hard" essays. "The collection took so much time, I didn't have time to study for the test."

In a few days, they would both graduate magna cum laude and head off to their first jobs—he to ARCO in California, she to an environmental-research firm in Virginia—but as of now, only Geoff knew what the chances were that they might have a future together beyond Notre Dame.

"I asked myself three things," Geoff said. "Could anybody love me better? Could I love anybody better? Is there a better possible mother on the face of the earth?" Answering no to each question, he went out and bought a half-carat diamond solitaire ring. He pulled the box out of his pocket and showed it to a friend. "Now I have to do it. I've burned my bridges."

He called her at 2:00 a.m., a reasonable hour in their world: Some of their best moments had been spent in quiet, small-hours conversation, over bags of vending-machine potato chips in the ghostly halls of the Nieuwland science building. Tonight, though, exhausted from her finals sprint, she was already asleep. She groggily pulled on plaid stretch pants and a sweatshirt and met him outside her dorm.

"How about the South Quad?" he asked, a hint that something was up, since their usual late-night route went past Zahm into the North Quad. They talked small at first, about all the work they had done these past few weeks, and then they talked large, about all the good times they had enjoyed together these past few years, and when they got to the walkway between St. Edward's and the Main Building, in the near and high shadow of the Dome, they stopped.

"It would really be a shame to end with graduation," he said, offering her the ring.

"Are you serious?" she said, momentarily stunned, before jumping in the air and saying, "Yes."

They continued down the Main Quad, floating under the elms, gliding past the dark and silent classrooms, until they reached the benches outside O'Shaughnessy Hall, where they sat talking for several more hours, finally free to discuss a subject that had largely been off-limits until tonight—what their life might look like next week, next month, next year. Detouring past the details (When would the wedding be? Who would be the one to give up a job and move when the time came?), they basked instead in the firm, warm embrace of commitment. The man who had barely been able to bring himself to say the word "girlfriend" now had to learn how to say what Dana called "the F word," "fiancée."

"It was perfect," she said of his proposal.

"It was simple and casual—not a one-knee-at-the-Grotto, syrupy Notre Dame thing," he said. "I would pay a million dollars to see that facial expression again."

20

Three nights before graduation, a long line of seniors streamed out the side door of Sacred Heart, passing under the chiseled portal that declared "God, Country, Notre Dame," and joining a slow, loose procession that wound through the cool spring darkness and around the back of the church down toward the Grotto. In their hands they each carried a small, unlighted candle. The Long Goodbye had finally arrived, kicking off with a misty-eyed tradition known as the Last Visit, a private, class-wide farewell that preceded the gala public celebrations of commencement weekend. The service they shared inside the church tonight was not a Mass, but a self-composed valedictory ceremony that was somewhere between a wake and a testimonial—a reflective series of prayers, songs, and readings that included a heartfelt account of their four-year journey together as Domers, narrated by four seniors from a script largely written by Geoff Slevin and Dana Ciacciarelli on the night after their engagement.

"Our time has come," the readers each repeated as a refrain, sounding a note of both triumph and loss.

The Glee Club sang hymns in Latin as the seniors filled the wide asphalt apron before the Grotto. Father Malloy stood in the shadows by the rocks, beneath the small niche where a statue of the Virgin Mary stood bathed in white light. Beside him was the large candle that would be placed among the other candles in the Grotto as a remembrance of the senior class. "Tonight we use the symbol of light as a way of leaving in this sacred place a memory of ourselves and our time together," he said. "Bless this candle, which represents the love and devotion of the class of 1993. May these graduates always be united in prayer with Notre Dame, Our Mother, and imitate her surpassing reverence and holiness."

From the candle Malloy lit, the flame was passed, person by person, to all the candles the seniors were holding. As the warm and subtle glow spread through the crowd, the Glee Club sang the "Ave Maria," and as their celestial voices rose, the Sacred Heart bells began their own tinny chorus—the nightly rendition of the alma mater.

"Nice touch," Geoff said to Dana, one of the Last Visit organizers, but they both knew that some things were beyond even the most careful planning, dependent instead on the kind of divine coincidence—intervention?—that seems to occur with greater frequency at Notre Dame than in the world at large. The two melodies, the voices and the bells, circled each other in a rich and complex round, musically dissonant but emotionally resonant—the universal hymn merging with the local hymn, the Old World entwined with the New, the soul soaring with the heart. When the voices had offered up the final amen, the air was left clear for the bells to chime their closing notes alone. At the end of the service, the seniors joined the Glee Club in their own reprise of the alma mater, arms around one another, swaying slowly back and forth like a breeze, but when they reached the final note they pushed up through it in a cheer, rather than swallowing it in a sob. The sign of peace that followed was a long, communal embrace. After they had wrestled with so many big ideas in their years here, it was only fitting that their emotions should be correspondingly large.

For most of the seniors, the six days since exams had ended had unfolded like the ultimate football weekend—without the football, of course, but also without any Monday classes beckoning. It was a green and sunny idyll, when they could finally enjoy all the pleasures of Notre Dame while bearing none of the responsibilities. They danced to loud music, they drained kegs of beer, they played cards late into the night, they took quiet walks around the lakes, they solved the world's problems in earnest bull sessions, they went on road trips—to baseball games, amusement parks, Lake Michigan beaches, anywhere that required a car ride long enough to qualify as a bonding experience. Their calendars were heavy with grand gestures of sentiment and nostalgia. But now the parents were arriving, and with them came the stark realization that the solemn mortarboard rituals of graduation—the inevitable collision between possibility and reality—could no longer be postponed.

"I, Allison McCurdy, having been appointed an ensign in the United States Navy, do solemnly swear that I will support and defend the Constitution of the United States against all enemies, foreign and domestic," the former battalion commander recited, repeating an oath of office in which she was joined this morning by her former executive officer, Joe Carrigan, and 129 other Army, Navy, Marine, and Air Force ROTC cadets, "that I will bear true faith and allegiance to the same; that I take this obligation freely, without any mental reservation or purpose of evasion; and that I will well and faithfully discharge the duties of the office upon which I am about to enter, so help me God." After they received their commissions, and before they sang the fight song, they threw their caps into the air with a cheer.

"Our challenge is to take the Notre Dame family and make it inclusive," Lou Nanni, Monk Malloy's basketball teammate, told a roughly equal number of seniors—all of them bound for a year of social service in various programs, here and abroad—at the Volunteer Send-Off Ceremony in Washington Hall. Brother Bonaventure Scully was in the crowd, still trying to fill that drug-rehab slot in Louisiana. "To take that love, and not keep it limited to campus, but to reach out to those who are the most outcast. If we make that love inclusive, that's what Notre Dame is about."

"You have as a model an institution that never thought small, and we must never think small either," said Blandina Cardenas-Ramirez—one of this year's honorary-degree recipients, a member of the U.S. Commission on Civil Rights and a leading advocate for minority students in higher education—to the Hispanic seniors and their families at the Hispanic Recognition Ceremony. " 'The Fighting Irish of Notre Dame'—that sent a message across this country at a time when the Irish were a community with little standing. Think about it—'The Fighting Latinos.' "

"You must remember time and time again—Don't quit and never give up," said Carolyn Callahan, sounding more like a preacher than an accounting professor as she spoke at the Celebration of African-American Excellence, more familiarly known as Black Graduation. She kept repeating the phrase like a refrain, and it was greeted by a rising swell of applause each time. "Many of you are going out to take your first position in a corporation. I'd love to be able to tell you there will be no struggles or hardship or pain. There will be. But what you have to do is, don't quit and never give up."

"We gather in prayer because we have discovered our need for God and one another," Father Malloy said in his greeting to the congregation at the Baccalaureate Mass. "Our strength is in a community that can surpass what we can achieve alone."

For their last Mass together as a class, and their final ordination as

Domers, the seniors had returned to the scene of their baptism—the ACC arena, where, four years earlier, as tentative and wary freshmen, they had gathered for their first class Mass during orientation. At many schools, the baccalaureate—a farewell sermon to the graduates—is little more than a vestigial academic ritual, an uncertain holdover from an era of open religious affiliation; but at Notre Dame, it is the solemn and joyous center of commencement weekend. The altar where Malloy stood was on a raised platform on the arena floor, draped with a cloth of blue and gold, the colors of both Notre Dame the university and Notre Dame the Mother of Jesus. The black-robed graduates filled the floor and the first tier of seats. The fifty white-robed priests stood behind Malloy like a hovering apparition. Among the priests today, participating in his first big concelebrated Mass, was Father Joe Ross: He had decided that the theological point he made by not joining these Masses, the style and structure of which he opposed on principle, was no longer worth the emotional gap it might create between himself and his community. His own liturgical farewell to his seniors in Morrissey had been a much smaller, simpler affair. At the last Sunday-night dorm Mass, he had called them up around the altar, asked the rest of the congregation to join him in a special senior blessing, then dispatched them with a final message. "Take what you've learned here," he said, "don't stray, and live the life of Jesus with vigor and courage in the world where God will lead you."

Malloy could not be as personal in his final blessing to the standing-room-only crowd at the Baccalaureate Mass, but he tried to be equally heartfelt. "May the days ahead be peaceful and life-giving," he said to the graduates from the altar. "May your gifts and your talents be a gift to the world that is so often fractured and divided. May God be with you in the days and years ahead. We will miss you deeply."

The altar was gone the next afternoon, the white-robed priests replaced by dark-robed academics. "It's very hard for me to address a president of Notre Dame as simply Monk, but I know that's what we do here," said Tom Brokaw, NBC News anchor and honorary-degree recipient, as he opened a commencement speech that included the requisite references to Lou Holtz, the football team, and the Irish Guard, and that lacked the political agenda of the previous year's speaker, George Bush. "You leave here with an education that your generational counterparts in Eastern Europe, the Soviet Union, China, South Africa would only envy. What do you think a young Czech, for example, would do with an education comparable to yours? Or a young South African? Or a young Chinese? Would they only trade on it for a new car, for a larger house, for a week in Aspen? Or would they use it as a national resource for the common welfare?"

After the honorary degrees had been dispensed—the loudest applause went to Alan Page, the former Notre Dame lineman and pro-football Hall of Famer who now sits on the Minnesota Supreme Court—and the graduates had stood, school by school, to hear their degrees conferred upon them en masse, Malloy asked the parents to stand, raise their hands over the sea of black gowns, and join him in a blessing—a graduation tradition here that never fails to raise tears in the eyes of both the blessers and the blessed. "Grant them truth that they may be set free," he said. "Grant them wisdom that they might know right from wrong. Give them courage in the face of moral challenge, and the sense of justice in our sometimes fractured world. May they be faithful in their life commitments and compassionate in response to human suffering and pain. And finally, dear God, in your love, keep them from harm. Amen."

The program officially concluded with another rendition of the alma mater, the voices of the assembly surging past the inevitable, collective lump in the throat raised by the final note. The students, however, had a different, unofficial ending in mind. "Cheer, cheer for old Notre Dame, wake up the echoes cheering her name," they sang, accompanied only by clapping hands and stamping feet, cheering today not for the varsity's triumphs, but their own. "While her loyal sons are marching onward to victory."

After marching together out of the arena, they fanned out individually across the campus to say their final goodbyes. Many of them posed for graduation portraits on the Main Quad, standing patiently in their gowns as their parents maneuvered for an angle that would include the Main Building looming in the background. The Dome was gleaming in the sharp spring sunlight this afternoon, exactly the kind of beacon Sorin had envisioned when, against the wishes of most of his fellow priests and administrators, he had insisted on having it gilded. It cost $860 to cover it with fine gold leaf in 1886, $70,000 to regild it for the eighth and most recent time in 1988; and whatever it costs to do it again—when the luster, as it must, begins to dim—there will be few arguments against it. The Dome glowed so brightly today—shining with a light that held the memory of the seniors' four years here, a light that had been gathering strength for 150 years now—that those who looked directly upon it soon found it necessary to wipe moisture from their eyes as they turned away.

ACKNOWLEDGMENTS
AND SOURCES

I incurred many debts in the year I spent at Notre Dame, and the subsequent year I spent back home writing about it—first and most obviously to the people whose names and stories grace the preceding pages. But many other people also offered their help and opened their lives up for inspection—394 in all, according to a survey of the 92 notebooks I accumulated. Their stories were equally interesting, and my gratitude to them is equally deep. Among them, thanks are due especially to:

Jeremy Akers, Kitty Arnold, Father Ernest Bartell, Father Bill Beauchamp, Christopher Beaudet, Chuck Beck, Sister Joris Binder, John Bingham, Brother Clarence Breitenbach, Father Richard Bullene, Greg Butrus, Father Charles Carey, Father Joseph Carey, Stephanie Carson, Dave Cathcart, Dave Certo, Angie Chamblee, Melanie Chapleau, Charles Colbert, Sister Regina Coll, Walt Collins, Father John Conley, Father Jim Connelly, Stacy Constantineau, Jeff Cosgrove, Alysia Courtot, Sue Cunningham, Bill Dailey, Christopher Daly, Tom D'Andrea, James Danehy, Rich Delevan, Patrick Delong, Bob Dilenschneider, John Donlan, Christopher Elmore, George Fischer, Father Mark Fitzgerald, Frank Flynn, Kate Foley, Lisa Fortier, Mitch Freehauf, Wil Freve, Vince Friedewald, April Gerber, Phil Gleason, Ben Gonring, Don Good, Kristin Greeley, Gerrie Griffin, Veronica Guzman, Ryan Hallford, Tom Halligan, Jahnelle Harrigan, Nathan Hatch, Tara Healy, John Heisler, Father Michael Himes, Emil Hofman, Mary Houck, Joe Incandela, Tom Isenbarger, Father John Jenkins, Father Dan Jenky, Nick Johns, Mae Lee Johnson, Terry Johnson, Carolyn Kelly, John Kelly, Tom Kelly, Paul Kimes, Doug Kinsey, Wes Kirkpatrick, Carleigh Landers, Chuck Lennon, Sister Jean Lenz, Cristiane Likely, Tom Looby, Steve Lundeen, David Lutz, Mike McCarthy, Pat McCarthy, Kevin McCracken, Father Tom McDermott, Dan McDevitt, Nicole McGrath, Linda McManus, Joe McNerney, Marylou McNerney, Brother Borromeo Malley, Jimmy Malloy, Mike Mathews, Marty Mennes, Mike Miller, Mark Mitchell, Bill Mohler, Frank Molchan, Jack Molchan, Art Monaghan, Carlo Monte-magno, Sister Marietta Murphy, Michelle Nasser, John Nickel, Laurie Nie-mann, Father Thomas O'Meara, Molly O'Neill, William O'Rourke, Annette Ortenstein, Ken Osgood, Iris Outlaw, Larry Patterson, Sam Pennington, Teresa Phelps, Bill Pifher, Al Plantinga, Mark Pogue, Father Mark Poorman, Brian Posnanski, Tom Poundstone, Joe Preza, Augie Pullo, Father Willie Purcell, Bob Raccuglia, Karen Riley, Sean Riley, Sister Josef Riordan, Kevin Rooney, Meg Rooney, Michelle Ryan, Ida Sandoval, Maria Santos, Ann Schlaffman, Father David Schlaver, Bob Schmuhl, Tim Schorn, Kevin Schroeder, Father Tim Scully, Christopher Shea, Shannon Shea, Eric Silk, Stephen Singular, Kelly Smith, Mike Smith, Thomas Gordon Smith, Steve Sostak, Sorin Spohn, Al Stashis, Kristin Stovall, Thomas Stritch, Tim Sulli-van, Mike Swanson, Anna Marie Tabor, George Tate, Judy Tate, Kerry Tem-ple, Father Bill Wack, Ira Wade, Father Dick Warner, Kathleen Weigert, Regina Weissert, Nikki Wellmann, Eddie Wetzel, John Whelan, Father Oliver Williams, Darcy Yaley, Bryant Young, Glenn Zubryd, Greg Zuschlag.

Special thanks are also due to Bill Sexton, Dick Conklin, and Denny Moore, who let me in to see it all without imposing any conditions or re-strictions, and to their colleagues, who helped open doors and gather infor-mation all along the way: Dennis Brown, Mike Garvey, Lyn Magliola, Maryanne Pfannerstill, and Cynthia Day.

And to the other faculty members who let me sit in on their classes: Fa-ther Dave Burrell, Jay Dolan, Father John Dunne, Mort Fuchs, Bill Gray, John Houck, Dave Leege, George Lopez, Stuart McComas, Father Richard McCormick, Marvin Miller, Father Steve Newton, Charles Rice, Tom Schlereth, Father Pat Sullivan, and Lee Tavis.

And to Jim Langford and the sophomores in his Arts-and-Letters core course, for the essays on life at Notre Dame.

And to Geoff Slevin and Dana Ciacciarelli and their parents, for inviting me to the wedding.

And to Monica Yant and Dave Kinney, editors of *The Observer*, and Patti Doyle and Margaret Kenny, editors of *Scholastic*, whose publications proved indispensable.

For information on Notre Dame and South Bend, I also relied upon *Notre Dame* magazine, the alumni quarterly (the sesquicentennial issue was especially valuable); *Notre Dame Report*, the administration's official news bulletin; *Dialogue*, the conservative campus magazine; *Common Sense*, its liberal companion; *The Dome*, the student yearbook; the *South Bend Tribune*; the *Chicago Tribune*; *Blue & Gold Illustrated*; and *Irish Sports Report*.

For information on wider issues, I consulted, among other publications, *America*, *The Chronicle of Higher Education*, *Commonweal*, *Crisis*, *First Things*, the *National Catholic Reporter*, *The New York Times*, and *The Wanderer*.

Among the books I used were:

Briggs, Kenneth A. *Holy Siege: The Year That Shook Catholic America*. San Francisco: Harper San Francisco, 1992.

Celizic, Mike. *The Biggest Game of Them All: Notre Dame, Michigan State and the Fall of '66*. New York: Simon & Schuster, 1992.

Connelly, Joel R., and Howard J. Dooley. *Hesburgh's Notre Dame: Triumph in Transition*. New York: Hawthorn Books, 1972.

Dolan, Jay P. *The American Catholic Experience: A History from Colonial Times to the Present*. Garden City, N.Y.: Doubleday, 1985.

Fischer, Edward. *Notre Dame Remembered: An Autobiography*. Notre Dame, Ind.: University of Notre Dame Press, 1987.

Gleason, Philip. *Keeping the Faith: American Catholicism Past and Present*. Notre Dame, Ind.: University of Notre Dame Press, 1987.

Greeley, Rev. Andrew M. *The Catholic Myth: The Behavior and Beliefs of American Catholics*. New York: Scribners, 1990.

————. *From Backwater to Mainstream: A Profile of Catholic Higher Education*. New York: McGraw-Hill, 1969.

Hesburgh, Rev. Theodore M., ed. *The Challenge and Promise of a Catholic University*. Notre Dame Ind.: University of Notre Dame Press, 1994.

Hesburgh, Rev. Theodore M., with Jerry Reedy. *God, Country, Notre Dame*. Garden City, N.Y.: Doubleday, 1990.

Holtz, Lou, with John Heisler. *The Fighting Spirit: A Championship Season at Notre Dame*. New York: Pocket Books, 1989.

Hope, Rev. Arthur J. *Notre Dame: One Hundred Years*. South Bend, Ind.: Icarus Press, 1978 (originally published in 1943).

Krause, Moose, and Stephen Singular. *Notre Dame's Greatest Coaches*. New York: Pocket Books, 1993.

Malloy, Rev. Edward A. *Culture and Commitment: The Challenges of Today's University*. Notre Dame, Ind.: University of Notre Dame Press, 1992.

Meaney, John W. *O'Malley of Notre Dame*. Notre Dame, Ind.: University of Notre Dame Press, 1991.

New Catholic Encyclopedia. New York: McGraw-Hill, 1967.

O'Rourke, James S. IV, ed. *Reflections in the Dome: Sixty Years of Life at Notre Dame*. Notre Dame, Ind.: Privately printed, 1988.

Phelps, Teresa G. *The Coach's Wife: A Notre Dame Memoir*. New York: Norton, 1994.

Rappoport, Ken. *Wake Up the Echoes*. Tomball, Tex.: Strode Publishers, 1988 (originally published in 1975).

Schlaver, Rev. David. *The Notre Dame Ethos: Student Life in a Catholic Residential University*. Ph.D. dissertation, University of Michigan, 1979.

Schlereth, Thomas. *A Dome of Learning: The University of Notre Dame's Main Building*. Notre Dame, Ind.: University of Notre Dame Alumni Association, 1991.

———. *A Spire of Faith: The University of Notre Dame's Sacred Heart Church*. Notre Dame, Ind.: University of Notre Dame Alumni Association, 1991.

———. *The University of Notre Dame: A Portrait of Its History and Campus*. Notre Dame, Ind.: University of Notre Dame Press, 1991 (originally published in 1976).

Schmuhl, Robert P. *The University of Notre Dame: A Contemporary Portrait*. Notre Dame, Ind.: University of Notre Dame Press, 1986.

Sorin, Rev. Edward. *The Chronicles of Notre Dame du Lac*. Edited and annotated by Rev. James T. Connelly. Notre Dame, Ind.: University of Notre Dame Press, 1992.

Sperber, Murray. *Shake Down the Thunder: The Creation of Notre Dame Football*. New York: Henry Holt, 1993.

Steele, Michael R. *The Fighting Irish Football Encyclopedia*. Champaign, Ill.: Sagamore Publishing, 1992.

Sterling, Mary Beth. *Look Out for the Manhole Cover: A History of Notre Dame's Bookstore Basketball Tournament*. Chicago: Wagner/Mark Publishing, 1993.

Stritch, Thomas. *My Notre Dame: Memories and Reflections of Sixty Years*. Notre Dame, Ind.: University of Notre Dame Press, 1991.

Sullivan, Richard. *Notre Dame*. New York: Henry Holt, 1951.

Wallace, Francis. *Notre Dame: Its People and Its Legends*. New York: David McKay, 1969.

For help at the other end of the book, I owe special thanks to Tom Benner, Jill Bilzi, Dan Breen, Theresa Burns, Ann and Budd Coyne, Brian Coyne, Doreen Coyne, Nancy Daley, Mike DiBenedetto, Joe and Jan Feldman, Reed Feuster, Kate Frank, Steve Giegerich, Michael Kennedy, Sally Kerans, Janet Koloski, Father Gerard McCarron, Heather McCreight, Shannon McCreight, Peter McDonnell, Andrew Miga, Tim Mulligan, Steve O'Connell, John and Yasmin Parr, Jeanne Perkins, Naznin Saifi, John Smothers, Stacey Tetto, Craig Tomashoff, Stuart Whalen, and Michael Whouley.

And to Sam Freedman and Greg Higgins, for their close readings of the manuscript and their wise and constant counsel.

And to my late grandfather Hank Coyne, a loyal subway alumnus, for first acquainting me with the stories of Notre Dame.

And to Reid Boates and Pam Dorman, who made it a book.

And to everyone at Viking who helped guide it along the way: Carolyn Carlson, Susan Elia, Barbara Grossman, Patti Kelly, Katy Riegel, Teddy Rosenbaum, Al Silverman, Paris Wald, and Terry Zaroff-Evans.

And finally, for all of the above and more, to Jane Kaye, and now Laura and Alice, too.